STATE OF THE UNION

By the same author

Beefsteak Raid

Ghost Ship of the Confederacy

Sea Devil of the Confederacy

The Wit and Wisdom of Congress

State of the Union

STATE

OF THE UNION

Highlights of American history, momentous events

and policies in the political, social, and

military life of the nation as revealed in the

State-of-the-Union and War Messages of the

Presidents: George Washington to John F. Kennedy.

Selected and Edited by EDWARD BOYKIN

FUNK & WAGNALLS COMPANY, INC.

NEW YORK

Library of Congress Catalogue Card Number 63–16337

Printed in the United States of America

To the thirty-four Presidents of the United States
who, with "strong hand and wary eye," have steered
the Ship of State for one hundred and seventy-four years

CONTENTS

CONTENTS   ix

PREFACE

*"He shall from time to time
give to the Congress information
on the state of the Union"*

It has been said that one can read the history and growth of the nation in the running story of the State-of-the-Union Messages of our thirty-four Presidents. For almost every significant event and policy in the country's history under the Constitution is told of or foreshadowed in these messages which, like steppingstones, run back to the founding of the government.

President Kennedy's State-of-the-Union Message, on January 14, 1963, was Number 177 of a distinguished line that reveals only two breaks in the one hundred and seventy-four years of presidential succession. Except for William Henry Harrison, who died one month after taking office, and the assassinated James A. Garfield, no Chief Executive has yet faltered in performing the duty imposed on him by the Constitution (Art. II, Sec. 3) of giving to the Congress, and the nation, "information on the state of the Union" and recommending "such measures as he shall judge necessary and expedient."

These messages, far more than the Inaugural Addresses, foretell, and frequently outline, momentous coming events and policies in our political, social, and military history. The Inaugurals are, to a considerable extent, showpieces splashed on a broad canvas. Far more history-in-the-making is wrapped up in the State-of-the-Union Messages, which, with their specific content, show the Presidents in action.

George Washington pioneered this important duty in New York City, then the nation's capital, on January 8, 1790. Anxious to live up to the letter of the Constitution which he helped frame, he climbed into his coach-and-four and clattered off to Federal Hall on Wall Street, where he read his First State-of-the-Union Message to an awed assemblage of Senators, Representatives, gentry, and commoners.

1

More than that, Washington named it State-of-the-Union Message, and set the yearly pace for it. In his initial precedent-making report, the first President uttered the most-quoted of all his words of wisdom, "To be prepared for war is one of the most effectual means of preserving peace."

The Constitution places no limit on what the President may say in his annual message. Most Presidents have interpreted this constitutional duty to suit themselves. Some have made strange requests. In his last State-of-the-Union Message, President Grant apologized for his inability as Chief Executive. He said, "failures have been errors of judgment, not of intent." President Arthur, in his December, 1881, annual message, used his constitutional license to ask Congress how to deal with fifty cowboys who were shooting up towns out in Arizona.

In December, 1823, James Monroe made his seventh annual message the vehicle for warning European powers to keep their hands off the Americas; thus, he announced the Monroe Doctrine. President Wilson, in his State-of-the-Union Message, December 2, 1918, set forth his famous Fourteen Points, outlining the indispensable conditions of peace with Germany and her allies.

Some of these messages are mighty state papers. The War Messages are all landmarks. Best known of all of President Woodrow Wilson's utterances are these words used in his War Message, April 2, 1917— "The world must be made safe for democracy"—when he asked Congress for a declaration of war against the Imperial German government. The average man in the street would likely be unable to quote four words from Wilson's two Inaugural Addresses, but it is a safe bet he would recall the statement above.

The first two Presidents—Washington and John Adams—delivered their annual messages with all the ceremony of a speech from the throne, but in December, 1801, Jefferson shocked Congress, and even his own party, by going to the other extreme and transmitting his message to be read to Congress by a clerk. This practice prevailed for over a century until December, 1913, when Wilson departed from the custom set by his party's founder. He, in turn, astonished Congress by personally appearing on Capitol Hill to read his State-of-the-Union Message. Since then, Presidents have varied the routine. Coolidge was the first President to have a national radio hookup for his State-of-the-Union Messages.

In George Washington's State-of-the-Union Messages you can almost see the wheels of the new government getting up speed for their long run. His last message, December 7, 1796, urged the establishment of a United States military academy at West Point and reiterated his warning to the nation to avoid war by keeping well armed.

John Adams' fourth annual message—November 22, 1800—is of special interest to Washingtonians. It was the first delivered in the new national capital on the Potomac. In it Adams congratulated Congress on having at last found a permanent home.

Jefferson used his First State-of-the-Union Message in December, 1801, to drive home his special ambitions for the nation: economy and simplicity in government. Seeking repeal of the harsh naturalization laws passed by the Adams administration, Jefferson, in this message, asked this often-echoed question, "Shall oppressed humanity find no asylum on this globe?"

James Madison's annual messages reflect his lack of leadership for a nation engaged in the War of 1812. Of all the Presidents, his messages were most unintelligible. His first annual message in November, 1809, was expressed in such cautious words that, as one commentator said, "every man puts what construction on it he pleases."

Jackson's annual messages breathed the turbulence of his eight-year reign. You can hear the thunder of his battle with the Bank of the United States and of his threats that forced France to settle the spoliation claims. His last annual message, December, 1836, glowed with pride in having extinguished the national debt for the first and only time in our history.

James K. Polk's last State-of-the-Union Message, December 5, 1848, started the gold rush to California. Polk simply confirmed the rumor that an "abundance of gold" had been discovered there—and the rush was on.

Facing the growing bitterness between the North and South on the slavery issue, Zachary Taylor closed his first and only State-of-the-Union Message with an appeal for union.

Millard Fillmore was the first President, in an annual message (1850), to ask representation for the District of Columbia in Congress. In this same message he hailed the new Capitol as "the emblem of our Union and the symbol of our greatness."

James Buchanan played both sides against the middle in his last annual message in December, 1860. He even accused the Founding Fathers of sowing in the Constitution itself the seeds of its destruction. Then he said amazingly, "How easy it would be for the American people to settle the slavery question forever and to restore peace and harmony to this distracted country." But he had no solution to offer other than to say, "Secession is neither more nor less than revolution."

Many of President Lincoln's finest utterances are contained in his State-of-the-Union Messages and his War Message that preceded them. Taken as a whole, his messages comprise the most remarkable treatise ever written on the moral aspects of the American Civil War.

In his War Message, July 4, 1861, Lincoln set the goal in these glowing words: "This is essentially a people's contest. On the side of the Union it is a struggle for maintaining in the world that form and substance of government, whose leading object is to elevate the condition of men; to lift artificial weights from all shoulders; to clear the paths of laudable pursuit for all; to afford all an unfettered start and a fair chance in the race of life."

His First State-of-the-Union Message, December 3, 1861, was a masterpiece. After reassuring the nation that the Union would ride out the storm of civil war, he announced his basic intention of saving the Union "whether or not." Another passage from this message has become legend: "Labor is prior to and independent of capital. Capital is only the fruit of labor, and could never have existed if labor had not first existed."

In his Second State-of-the-Union Message, emancipation was the theme. He closed with words both wondrous and historic—"Fellow-Citizens, We can not escape history. We of this Congress and this Administration will be remembered in spite of ourselves. No personal significance or insignificance can spare one or another of us. The fiery trial through which we pass will light us down in honor or dishonor to the latest generation."

Chester Arthur, lesser light among the Presidents, used his Third State-of-the-Union Message (1883) to insist on enlargement of the United States Navy, and thus created the fleet that won the Spanish-American War. This message also pioneered the first Presidential Succession Act.

Cleveland made the tariff a living issue in his message, December 6, 1887, when he used the famous words, "It is a condition which confronts us, not a theory." A year later, December 3, 1888, his State-of-the-Union Message contained this significant passage: "Communism is a hateful thing, and a menace to peace and organized government."

Theodore Roosevelt was the first President to send his message to Congress in typescript instead of script. He launched his "trust-busting" program in his first message, December, 1901. He used his December 7, 1903, annual message to justify the Panama "revolution" and seizure of the Canal Zone, saying the Isthmus had experienced fifty-three revolutions in fifty-seven years.

With Europe overrun by war, Woodrow Wilson's Second State-of-the-Union Message, December 8, 1914, promised, "We will not ask our young men to spend the best years of their lives making soldiers of themselves." A year later, December 7, 1915, he went all out for national defense and said it was "absolutely imperative" to raise a citizen army.

In his January, 1941, State-of-the-Union Message, Franklin D. Roosevelt made his historic report: "That the future and safety of our country and of our democracy are overwhelmingly involved in events far beyond our borders." In this message he summoned the nation to all-embracing national defense, full support to the nations resisting aggression, and no bargains with aggressors.

Only two of the presidential messages are reprinted in their entirety in this book—Lincoln's War Message of July 4, 1861, and Franklin Roosevelt's War Message of December 8, 1941.

A few of the messages are inordinately long. President Truman's, on January 21, 1946, for instance, runs over 25,000 words, the longest a President ever sent to Congress.

This book comprises careful selections from the entire, magnificent, and inspiring State-of-the-Union cavalcade, led off by the stately, felicitous sentences of George Washington setting the pace for the new nation in 1790 and closing with the lucid eloquence of John F. Kennedy bringing America face to face with the problems confronting her in this troubled nuclear age. Each of the thirty-four Presidents and the State-of-the-Union Messages are introduced by a vignette of the surging history and background of his administration.

These historic reports to the nation, some spoken, some written, partake of many things—eloquence, drama, politics, history, crisis upon crisis, the issues of the day, besetting problems, momentous decisions, trials and tribulations, defeats and victories, hoped-for goals and aspirations—all phrased in words that often glow like jewels. Here, too, one hears the call to arms, fighting words, that now and again have summoned the nation to battle.

The chief sources of the selections in this book are the *Congressional Record,* the *Congressional Globe,* the *Register of Debates,* and the *Annals of Congress.* Also, the *Messages and Papers of the Presidents* published pursuant to an act of the Fifty-second Congress. These several hundred volumes may be found in large libraries, including the magnificent Alderman Library at Jefferson's University of Virginia, to whose staff the Editor is indebted for many courtesies.

Perhaps the main source of material for the profiles of the Presidents preceding their respective messages is the Editor's very extensive dossier of political and personal facts about the Presidents.

The Editor has deleted many of the perfunctory salutations that opened the majority of the Presidents' messages, thus leaving more space for meatier subjects.

A word should be added about the symbols that indicate deletions and abrupt topical changes in the bodies of the messages. An effort was made to identify the Presidents and their administrations by such symbols. This was easy after the donkey and elephant came into political vogue. The same applied to the agrarian dynasty established by Jefferson, for which the deletion symbol is the crossed spade, hoe, and rake. For all major War Messages and wartime messages the symbol is a pair of crossed sabers. Several of the symbol identifications are arbitrary. Little flags were used in Washington's and John Adams' messages because they were both motivated by the purpose of solidifying the new Union, which the little flags seem to symbolize.

Clearly enough the Founding Fathers, in requiring the President, as captain of the Ship of State, to give Congress a "time to time" report of the course of his vessel, intended him to be the spokesman of the nation. Most of these messages have come from the hearts of the Presidents who wrote them—and, over the years, the evidence is strong that the American people have listened to their spokesmen and warmed to their words.

It is worth noting that Washington—ever seeking to fix the idea of UNION more firmly in the hearts of the people—datelined all but one of his State-of-the-Union Messages "United States" instead of New York, first capital of the nation, or its successor, Philadelphia. John Adams followed Washington's lead, even to his last State-of-the-Union Message, which was delivered in the nation's new permanent capital, Washington, D.C.

Ship of State

The year 1789 augured well for the destiny of the new American government that opened for business on March 4 of that year. The changeover from the unicameral Continental Congress under the Articles of Confederation to the three-pronged creation of the Founding Fathers was effected without a hitch.

To President Washington fell the delicate, intricate task of organizing a government from scratch. After all, the Constitution was only a framework. The President and Congress had to give it life. Forms, customs, and ceremonies must be originated. Every act of the first President literally set a precedent for posterity.

The new government had inherited an empty treasury from the old Confederation. Without money to run the government, the President and gentlemen of the Congress might as well pack their luggage and go home. Actually, the United States was without credit, burdened with debt, and in need of money to pay its day-to-day running expenses. Led by the "Great Little" James Madison, Washington's floor leader in the House, that body passed and sent on to the Senate the nation's first revenue legislation, a tariff bill that would help replenish the treasury. (Unknown at the time, it was the cleavage on the tariff that would divide the nation and provide legislative fireworks even unto this modern day.)

The First Congress began business without party lines, heavily Federalist in both the Senate and the House of Representatives. Washington himself was Federalist in spirit if not in name. Compromise was the order of the hour in the first session of 1789. The achievements of this Congress were, in fact, second in importance only to the framing of the Constitution itself. Around the blueprint drawn by the Founding Fathers, Congress constructed the actual machinery of government. Yet, inevitably, factional strife crept in. Differences of opinions brought bitter bickerings. The two-party system began with the Federalists and the anti-Federalists, later to style themselves Democratic-Republicans.

Before this first session of Congress ended in September, it had created the Treasury, War, and Foreign Affairs (later State) departments, the Supreme Court, and the offices of Attorney General and Postmaster General. In no phase of his administration did Washington display greater wisdom than in selecting the men to head these departments as well as choosing his other top advisers. To Alexander Hamilton went the Treasury portfolio; to Thomas Jefferson, that of Foreign Affairs. These two brilliant men stood at opposite political poles, but Washington, mindful of this fact, needed their unusual talents in working out the problems of the new United States. Indeed, at the time of Washington's First State-of-the-Union Message, Hamilton brought forward his masterly, all-embracing measures for solving the nation's financial woes.

At this session Congress also passed the first ten amendments to the Constitution—popularly known as the Bill of Rights—sending the document along to the states for ratification. The year closed on a high note. The twelfth state, North Carolina, joined the Union. Of the original thirteen colonies, only "Little Rhody" still stood aloof, outside the Union pale. But grave problems lurked ahead. Tension was rising overseas. A revolution that would metamorphose into a bloody Reign of Terror had exploded in France. The king who had espoused America's struggle for independence would be guillotined, and the Terrorists would seek to embroil all Europe, and even the newborn United States, in their bloody machinations.

GEORGE WASHINGTON
(1789–1797)

"My station is new . . .
I walk on
untrodden ground"

January 8, 1790, was a cold, bright day. Sunlight streamed into the ornate Senate chamber in Federal Hall on Wall Street, New York, falling in rich, red pools on the "Turkey" carpet on the floor. Promptly at 11:15 A.M., the doorkeepers of the Senate and House of Representatives shrilled in unison, "The President of the United States!"

Into the chamber strode *George Washington,* come to give the first accounting of his stewardship as Chief Magistrate and to recommend the measures and policies he deemed necessary to the future of the infant republic. The government under the Constitution was nine months and four days old.

Awaiting the President in the chamber was a buzzing assemblage of twenty-four Senators and about fifty Representatives, the Joint Congress of the United States, whose powdered wigs and colorful garb enlivened the scene. On the rostrum sat Vice President John Adams, twitchy and red as a beet; beside him, solemn-browed Speaker of the House Frederick Augustus Muhlenberg. Facing the rostrum were rows of red leather chairs reserved for the lawmakers, who were backstopped by a solid wall of spectators lured by the presence of the man who, at fifty-seven, was aging, but was still the dominant, magnetic figure of the nation.

As he made his way briskly up the center aisle, between Senators on the right and Representatives on the left, all eyes followed his tall form, elegantly clad in a suit of black velvet, with black silk stockings and silver shoe and knee buckles. His hair, fresh from the hands of the hairdresser, was gathered in a silken bag behind. At his side he wore a small dress sword, whose blade bore two inscriptions that seemed to personify the bearing of the man himself—*Recti fac etice* (Do what is right) and *Neminem timeas* (Fear no man). In his hand was the draft of his First State-of-the-Union Message penned in the bold, precise style of his mature years. Mounting the rostrum, he took the outstretched hands of the Vice President and Speaker in turn, then acknowledged the burst of applause that greeted him. Moving to the desk he unfolded his manuscript, adjusted his spectacles, and began reading. Formerly he had felt ill at ease speaking in public, but not today. There was no embarrassed halt between sentences as when he had delivered his Inaugural Address in this same chamber the previous April; the words and phrases fell clearly and distinctly from his lips.

What was the state of the Union? He summed it up in a characteristic paragraph. He then recommended legislation on eight matters he felt vital to the future welfare of the nation, two of which he stressed— national defense and "science and literature," the latter meaning general education. No one has ever urged the need of an adequately armed nation more succinctly than Washington urged on this occasion. Indeed his words have come ringing down to his compatriots of today with reverberating force.

Six minutes, and he was through. Eagerly his audience leaned forward to catch his closing words. One and all sensed once again this man's deep concern for the future of his country and his unswerving determination to make the Constitution the bulwark of the nation and its people.

GEORGE WASHINGTON
FIRST STATE-OF-THE-UNION MESSAGE
UNITED STATES, *January 8, 1790*

Fellow-Citizens of the Senate and House of Representatives:

I embrace with great satisfaction the opportunity which now presents itself of congratulating you on the present favorable prospects of our public affairs. The recent accession of the important State of North Carolina to the Constitution of the United

States, the rising credit and respectability of our country, the general and increasing good will toward the Government of the Union, and the concord, peace, and plenty with which we are blessed are circumstances auspicious in an eminent degree to our national prosperity.

In resuming your consultations for the general good, you can not but derive encouragement from the reflection that the measures of the last session have been as satisfactory to your constituents as the novelty and difficulty of the work allowed you to hope. Still further to realize their expectations and to secure the blessings which a gracious Providence has placed within our reach will in the course of the present important session call for the cool and deliberate exertion of your patriotism, firmness, and wisdom.

Among the many interesting objects which will engage your attention that of providing for the common defense will merit particular regard. To be prepared for war is one of the most effectual means of preserving peace.

A free people ought not only to be armed, but disciplined; to which end a uniform and well-digested plan is requisite; and their safety and interest require that they should promote such manufactories as tend to render them independent of others for essential, particularly military, supplies.

There was reason to hope that the pacific measures adopted with regard to certain hostile tribes of Indians would have relieved the inhabitants of our Southern and Western frontiers from their depredations, but you will perceive from the information contained in the papers which I shall direct to be laid before you that we ought to be prepared to afford protection to those parts of the Union, and, if necessary, to punish aggressors.

The interests of the United States require that our intercourse with other nations should be facilitated by such provisions as will enable me to fulfill my duty in that respect in the manner which circumstances may render most conducive to the public good, and to the end that the compensations to be made to the persons who may be employed should, according to the nature of their appointments, be defined by law, and a competent fund designated for defraying the expenses incident to the conduct of our foreign affairs.

Various considerations also render it expedient that the terms on which foreigners may be admitted to the rights of citizens should be speedily ascertained by a uniform rule of naturalization. Uniformity in the currency, weights, and measures of the United States is an object of great importance, and will, I am persuaded, be duly attended to.

The advancement of agriculture, commerce, and manufactures by all proper means will not, I trust, need recommendation; but I can not forbear intimating to you the expediency of giving effectual encouragement as well to the introduction of new and useful inventions from abroad as to the exertions of skill and genius in producing them at home, and of facilitating the intercourse between the distant parts of our country by a due attention to the post-office and post-roads.

Nor am I less persuaded that you will agree with me in opinion that there is nothing which can better deserve your patronage than the promotion of science and literature. Knowledge is in every country the surest basis of public happiness. In one in which the measures of government receive their impressions so immediately from the sense of the community as in ours it is proportionably essential. To the security of a free Constitution it contributes in various ways—by convincing those who are intrusted with the public administration that every valuable end of government is best answered by the enlightened confidence of the people, and by teaching the people themselves to know and to value their own rights; to discern and provide against invasions of them; to distinguish between oppression and the necessary exercise of lawful authority; between burthens proceeding from a disregard to their convenience and those resulting from the inevitable exigencies of society; to discriminate the spirit of liberty from that of licentiousness—cherishing the first, avoiding the last—and uniting a speedy but temperate vigilance against encroachments, with an inviolable respect to the laws.

Whether this desirable object will be best promoted by affording aids to seminaries of learning already established, by the institution of a national university, or by any other expedients will be well worthy of a place in the deliberations of the Legislature.

I saw with peculiar pleasure at the close of the last session the resolution entered into by you expressive of your opinion that an adequate provision for the support of the public credit is a matter of high importance to the national honor and prosperity.

I have directed the proper officers to lay before you, respectively, such papers and estimates as regard the affairs particularly recommended to your considerations, and necessary to convey to you that information of the state of the Union which it is my duty to afford.

The welfare of our country is the great object to which our cares and efforts ought to be directed, and I shall derive great satisfaction from a cooperation with you in the pleasing though arduous task of insuring to our fellow-citizens the blessings which they have a right to expect from a free, efficient, and equal government.

"There is a rank due the United States"

George Washington at the helm, the Ship of State sailed on. No first term in presidential history was ever more successful than his. One idea governed him: to promote the nation's welfare and progress under the Constitution he had helped to frame at Philadelphia in 1787.

Washington's eight State-of-the-Union Messages reveal the wise, methodical steps he suggested to set the nation on the "one straight course" toward its destiny. He stressed two essentials: "public credit," as he called it, and national defense. The infant nation was burdened with debt. The country must be set on a strong, financial foundation. Only by paying her debts could the United States take her proper station and acquire prestige among the nations of the world. Only by being properly armed, ready at all times for war, could she keep the peace she so urgently needed.

So "necessary and expedient" was protection of the frontiers against the Indians that the red man found a place in seven of Washington's eight messages. In his losing fight for his ancient hunting grounds, the Indian employed every atrocity known to the wilderness to halt the surge of white settlers westward over the mountains. The crowning Indian depredation of Washington's administrations occurred in 1791 when an army under General St. Clair was ambushed and cut to pieces in the backwoods of the Ohio Territory. The disaster shocked and sorrowed the nation. Washington acted at once. To his Revolutionary War compatriot, Anthony Wayne, he gave the task of training a new army that broke the power of the allied Indian tribes at Fallen Timbers in 1794 and crushed the Indian menace forever in that area. Wayne then exacted from the Indians the Treaty of Greenville, which pushed the Indian Boundary far to the northward. Washington disclosed this fact in his message of 1795.

In his messages, Washington hardly overlooked a facet of the nation's needs. A farmer himself, who understood the farmer's problems, he repeatedly urged Congress to give encouragement and practical aid to agriculture. He pleaded for aid to commerce, "manufactures," and navigation. His continued and urgent warnings on national defense led Congress to appropriate money to construct six super-modern frigates that later covered themselves with glory in the War of 1812. Three of these were the *Constitution, Constellation,* and *United States.* Thus he laid the foundation of the United States Navy.

With Europe in growing turmoil, foreign affairs went from bad to worse. In 1791, the French Revolutionists went berserk, guillotined the monarchy and declared war on Austria and Russia. In 1793, they declared a holy war on Great Britain and called on America to abide by her alliance of 1778. Insistent on keeping the nation out of Europe's broils, Washington immediately proclaimed neutrality, warning all Americans to refrain from hostile acts to either of the belligerents. In his fifth message, discussing his neutral stand, he spoke bluntly, "There is a rank due the United States among the nations which will be withheld, if not absolutely lost, by the reputation of weakness. If we wish to avoid insult, we must be able to repel it."

Determined to stabilize the nation's finances, Washington supported Alexander Hamilton's three-way plan to remedy the country's money woes. Hamilton proposed (1) to pay at once the interest on foreign loans, (2) to redeem at par the certificates of the Continental Congress by issuing new promissory notes, (3) to assume the debts the states had incurred in the common cause of winning the Revolution. Congress quickly passed the first two, but gagged on the assumption bill, which was finally approved but only after a masterly piece of log-rolling by Jefferson and Hamilton, in which the former traded Southern votes for assumption in return for Hamilton's delivery of Northern votes to fix the nation's permanent capital on the Potomac.

Hamilton next proposed that Congress establish the Bank of the United States, destined to become a political bone of contention. Jefferson said the Constitution did *not* authorize a bank and the bill, therefore, was illegal. Hamilton grounded his argument on Section 8 of the Constitution, the general-welfare clause. It was the first important recognition of the "implied powers" in the Constitution. Congress passed the bill after bitter arguments, and Washington signed it.

Hamilton now came up with the nation's first internal-revenue tax of twenty to thirty cents a gallon on whisky. This levy precipitated the first armed revolt against the national government, the so-called Whisky Rebellion in western Pennsylvania, where the frontier farmers had for years been making whisky and selling it to the East. Refusing to pay the tax, they tarred and feathered tax-collectors, shouldered their muzzle-loaders, and defied the authority of the government. Washington acted fast. Putting himself at the head of a force of militia, he marched to the scene of the "rebellion." The "Whisky Boys" melted away at the first show of federal force. Washington devoted almost his entire message of 1794 to this triumph of constitutional authority.

His 1795 message revealed the negotiation of a treaty with Great Britain by Chief Justice John Jay. The treaty was unpopular. Washington was attacked violently for accepting it but the Jay Treaty staved off a second war with England for nearly fifteen years.

In his Eighth, and last, State-of-the-Union Message, December, 1796, Washington urged the establishment of the United States Military Academy at West Point, at which officers could be trained in the art of war and prepared to lead the nation's armies in future wars, which, he felt, were as inevitable as sunrise at Mount Vernon.

GEORGE WASHINGTON
SECOND STATE-OF-THE-UNION MESSAGE
UNITED STATES, *December 8, 1790*

Fellow-Citizens of the Senate and House of Representatives:

In meeting you again I feel much satisfaction in being able to repeat my congratulations on the favorable prospects which continue to distinguish our public affairs. . . . The progress of public credit is witnessed by a considerable rise of American stock abroad as well as at home, and the revenues allotted for this and other national purposes have been productive beyond the calculations by which they were regulated. . . .

Since your last sessions I have received communications by which it appears that the district of Kentucky, at present a part of Virginia, has concurred in certain propositions contained in a law of that State, in consequence of which the district is to become a distinct member of the Union, in case the requisite sanction of Congress be added. For this sanction application is now made. . . .

It has been heretofore known to Congress that frequent incursions have been made on our frontier settlements by certain banditti of Indians from the northwest side of the Ohio. These, with some of the tribes dwelling on and near the Wabash, have of late been particularly active in their depredations, . . . they have, instead of listening to the humane invitations and overtures made on the part of the United States, renewed their violences with fresh alacrity and greater effect. The lives of a number of valuable citizens have thus been sacrificed, and some of them under circumstances peculiarly shocking, whilst others have been carried into a deplorable captivity.

These aggravated provocations rendered it essential to the safety of the Western settlements that the aggressors should be made sensible that the Government of the Union is not less capable of punishing their crimes than it is disposed to respect their rights and reward their attachments. As this object could not be effected by defensive measures, it became necessary to put in force the act which empowers the President to call out the militia for the protection of the frontiers, and I have accordingly authorized an expedition in which the regular troops in that quarter are combined with such drafts of militia as were deemed sufficient. . . .

The disturbed situation of Europe, and particularly the critical posture of the great maritime powers, whilst it ought to make us the more thankful for the general peace and security enjoyed by the United States, reminds us at the same time of the circumspection with which it becomes us to preserve these blessings. It requires also that we should not overlook the tendency of a war, and even of preparations for a war, among the nations most concerned in active commerce with this country. . . .

＊ ＊ ＊

The laws you have already passed for the establishment of a judiciary system have opened the doors of justice to all . . . persons. The patronage of our commerce, of our merchants and seamen, has called for the appointment of consuls in foreign countries. . . . The establishment of the militia, of a mint, of standards of weights and measures, of the post-office and post-roads are subjects which I presume you will resume of course, and which are abundantly urged by their own importance.

The sufficiency of the revenues you have established for the objects to which they are appropriated leaves no doubt that the residuary provisions will be commensurate to the other objects for which the public faith stands now pledged. Allow me, moreover, to hope that it will be a favorite policy with you, not merely to secure a payment of the interest of the debt funded, but as far and as fast as the growing resources of the country will permit to exonerate it of the principal itself. . . .

In pursuing the various and weighty business of the present session I indulge the fullest persuasion that your consultations will be equally marked with wisdom and animated by the love of your country. . . .

GEORGE WASHINGTON
THIRD STATE-OF-THE-UNION MESSAGE
UNITED STATES, *October 25, 1791*

Fellow-Citizens of the Senate and of the House of Representatives:
I meet you upon the present occasion with the feelings which are naturally inspired by a strong impression of the prosperous situation of our common country. . . .

Your own observations in your respective situations will have satisfied you of the progressive state of agriculture, manufactures, commerce, and navigation. In tracing their causes you will have remarked with particular pleasure the happy effects of that revival of confidence, public as well as private, to which the Constitution and laws of the United States have so eminently contributed; and you will have observed with no less interest new and decisive proofs of the increasing reputation and credit of the nation. . . .

The rapid subscriptions to the Bank of the United States, which completed the sum allowed to be subscribed in a single day, is among the striking and pleasing evidences which present themselves, not only of confidence in the Government, but of resource in the community.

In the interval of your recess due attention has been paid to the execution of the different objects which were specially provided for by the laws and resolutions of the last session.

Among the most important of these is the defense and security of the Western frontiers. To accomplish it on the most humane principles was a primary wish.

Those measures having proved unsuccessful, it became necessary to convince the refractory of the power of the United States to punish their depredations. Offensive operations have therefore been directed, to be conducted, however, as consistently as possible with the dictates of humanity. . . .

The powers specially vested in me by the act laying certain duties on distilled spirits have likewise been carried into effect. . . .

Pursuant to the authority contained in the several acts on that subject, a district of ten miles square for the permanent seat of the Government of the United States has been fixed and announced by proclamation, which district will comprehend lands on both sides of the river Potomac and the towns of Alexandria and Georgetown. A city has also been laid out agreeably to a plan which will be placed before Congress. . . .

The completion of the census of the inhabitants . . . will give you the pleasing assurance that the present population of the United States borders on four million persons. . . . I shall content myself with a general reference to former communications for several objects upon which the urgency of other affairs has hitherto postponed any definitive resolution. . . . There are, however, some of them of which I can not forbear a more particular mention. These are the militia, the post-office and post-roads, the mint, weights and measures, a provision for the sale of the vacant lands of the United States.

The first is certainly an object of primary importance whether viewed in reference to the national security, to the satisfaction of the community or to the preservation of order. In connection with this the establishment of competent magazines and arsenals and the fortification of such places as are peculiarly important and vulnerable naturally present themselves to consideration. . . .

The importance of the post-office and post-roads on a plan sufficiently liberal and comprehensive, as they respect the expedition, safety, and facility of communication, is increased by their instrumentality in diffusing a knowledge of the laws and proceedings of the Government, which, while it contributes to the security of the people, serves also to guard them against the effects of misrepresentation and misconception. . . .

The disorders in the existing currency, and especially the scarcity of small change, a scarcity so peculiarly distressing to the poorer classes, strongly recommend the carrying into immediate effect the resolution already entered into concerning the establishment of a mint.

An uniformity in the weights and measures of the country is among the important objects submitted to you by the Constitution, and if it can be derived from a standard at once invariable and universal, must be no less honorable to the public councils than conducive to the public convenience.

A provision for the sale of the vacant lands of the United States is particularly urged, among other reasons, by the important considerations that they are pledged as a fund for reimbursing the public debt; that if timely and judiciously applied they may save the necessity of burthening our citizens with new taxes for the extinguishment of the principal. . . .

GEORGE WASHINGTON
FOURTH STATE-OF-THE-UNION MESSAGE
UNITED STATES, *November 6, 1792*

Fellow-Citizens of the Senate and of the House of Representatives:

It is some abatement of the satisfaction with which I meet you on the present occasion that, in felicitating you on a continuance of the national prosperity generally, I am not able to add to it information that the Indian hostilities which have for some time past distressed our Northwestern frontier have terminated.

You will, I am persuaded, learn with no less concern than I communicate it that reiterated endeavors toward effecting a pacification have hitherto issued only in new and outrageous proof of persevering hostility on the part of the tribes with whom we are in contest. An earnest desire to procure tranquillity to the frontier, to stop the further effusion of blood, to arrest the progress of expense, to forward the prevalent wish of the nation for peace has led to strenuous efforts . . . to accomplish these desirable purposes. . . .

In the course of the attempts which have been made some valuable citizens have fallen victims to their zeal for the public service. A sanction commonly respected even among savages has been found in this instance insufficient to protect from massacre the emissaries of peace. It will, I presume, be duly considered whether the occasion does not call for an exercise of liberality toward the families of the deceased.

I have reason to believe that every practicable exertion has been made to be prepared for the . . . prosecution of the war in the event of a failure of pacific overtures. A large proportion of the troops authorized to be raised have been recruited, . . . and pains have been taken to discipline and put them in condition for the particular kind of service to be performed. . . .

The prosperous state of our revenue has been intimated. This would be still more the case were it not for the impediments which in some places continue to embarrass the collection of the duties on spirits distilled within the United States. . . . Measures have also been taken for the prosecution of offenders, and Congress may be assured that nothing within constitutional and legal limits which may depend upon me shall be wanting to assert and maintain the just authority of the laws.

Observations on the value of peace with other nations are unnecessary. It would be wise, however, by timely provisions to guard against those acts of our own citizens which might tend to disturb it, and to put ourselves in a condition to give that satisfaction to foreign nations which we may sometimes have occasion to require from them.

※ ※ ※

It is represented that some provisions in the law which established the post-office operate, in experiment, against the transmission of newspapers to distant parts of the country. Should this, upon due inquiry, be found to be the fact, a full conviction of the importance of facilitating the circulation of political intelligence and information will, I doubt not, lead to the application of a remedy.

I entertain a strong hope that the state of the national finances is now sufficiently matured to enable you to enter upon a systematic and effectual arrangement for the regular redemption and discharge of the public debt, according to the right which has been reserved to the Government.

※ ※ ※

The results of your common deliberations hitherto will, I trust, be productive of solid and durable advantages to our constituents, such as, by conciliating more and more their ultimate suffrage, will tend to strengthen and confirm their attachment to that Constitution of Government upon which, under Divine Providence, materially depend their union, their safety, and their happiness. . . .

GEORGE WASHINGTON
FIFTH STATE-OF-THE-UNION MESSAGE
PHILADELPHIA, *December 3, 1793*

Fellow-Citizens of the Senate and of the House of Representatives:
Since the commencement of the term for which I have been again called into office no fit occasion has arisen for expressing to my fellow-citizens at large the deep and respectful sense which I feel of the renewed testimony of public approbation. While on the one hand it awakened my gratitude for all those instances of affectionate partiality with which I have been honored by my country, on the other it could not prevent an earnest wish for that

retirement from which no private consideration should ever have
torn me. . . .

As soon as the war in Europe had embraced those powers [Eng-
land and France] with whom the United States have the most
extensive relations there was reason to apprehend that our intercourse with them might be interrupted and our disposition for
peace drawn into question by the suspicions too often entertained
by belligerent nations. It seemed, therefore, to be my duty to admonish our citizens of the consequences of a contraband trade and
of hostile acts to any of the parties, and to obtain by a declaration
of the existing legal state of things an easier admission of our right
to the immunities belonging to our situation. Under these impressions the proclamation which will be laid before you was issued.

. . . I can not recommend to your notice measures for the fulfillment of our duties to the rest of the world without again pressing
upon you the necessity of placing ourselves in a condition of complete defense and of exacting from them the fulfillment of their duties toward us. The United States ought not to indulge a persuasion
that, contrary to the order of human events, they will forever keep
at a distance those painful appeals to arms with which the history
of every other nation abounds. There is a rank due to the United
States among nations which will be withheld, if not absolutely lost,
by the reputation of weakness. If we desire to avoid insult, we
must be able to repel it; if we desire to secure peace . . . it must
be known that we are at all times ready for war. . . .

🏳 🏳 🏳

When we contemplate the war on our frontiers, it may be truly
affirmed that every reasonable effort has been made to adjust the
causes of dissension with the Indians north of the Ohio. . . . The
attempt, however, of an amicable negotiation having been frustrated, the troops have marched to act offensively. . . .

🏳 🏳 🏳

But here I can not forbear to recommend a repeal of the tax on
the transportation of public prints. There is no resource so firm
for the Government of the United States as the affections of the
people, guided by an enlightened policy; and to this primary
good nothing can conduce more than a faithful representation of

public proceedings, diffused without restraint throughout the United States.

The several subjects to which I have now referred open a wide range to your deliberations and involve some of the choicest interests of our common country. Permit me to bring to your remembrance the magnitude of your task. Without an unprejudiced coolness the welfare of the Government may be hazarded; without harmony as far as consists with freedom of sentiment its dignity may be lost.

GEORGE WASHINGTON
SIXTH STATE-OF-THE-UNION MESSAGE
UNITED STATES, *November 19, 1794*

Fellow-Citizens of the Senate and of the House of Representatives:

When we call to mind the gracious indulgence of Heaven by which the American people became a nation; when we survey the general prosperity of our country, and look forward to the riches, power, and happiness to which it seems destined, with the deepest regret do I announce to you that during your recess some of the citizens of the United States have been found capable of an insurrection. It is due, however, to the character of our Government and to its stability, which can not be shaken by the enemies of order, freely to unfold the course of this event.

During the session of the year 1790 it was expedient to exercise the legislative power granted by the Constitution of the United States "to lay and collect excises." In a majority of the States scarcely an objection was heard to this mode of taxation. . . . In the four western counties of Pennsylvania a prejudice, fostered and embittered by the artifice of men who labored for an ascendency over the will of others by the guidance of their passions, produced symptoms of riot and violence. . . . The very forbearance to press prosecution was misinterpreted into a fear of urging the execution of the laws, and associations of men began to denounce threats against the officers employed. . . . Hence, while the greater part of Pennsylvania itself were conforming themselves to the acts of excise, a few counties were resolved to frustrate them. It was now perceived that . . . further delay could only create an opinion of impotency or irresolution in the Government. Legal process was therefore delivered to the marshal against the rioters and delinquent distillers.

No sooner was he understood to be engaged in this duty than the vengeance of armed men was aimed at his person and the person and property of the inspector of the revenue. They fired upon the marshal, arrested him, and detained him for some time as a prisoner. He was obliged, by the jeopardy of his life, to renounce the service of other process on the west side of the Allegheny Mountain, and a deputation was afterwards sent to him to demand a surrender of that which he had served. A numerous body repeatedly attacked the house of the inspector, seized his papers of office, and finally destroyed by fire his buildings and whatsoever they contained.

Upon the testimony of these facts an associate justice of the Supreme Court of the United States notified me that "in the counties of Washington and Allegheny, in Pennsylvania, laws of the United States were opposed, and the execution thereof obstructed, by combinations too powerful to be suppressed by the ordinary course of judicial proceedings or by the powers vested in the marshal of that district." On this call, momentous in the extreme, I sought and weighed what might best subdue the crisis. On the one hand the judiciary was pronounced to be stripped of its capacity to enforce the laws; crimes which reached the very existence of social order were perpetrated without control; the friends of Government were insulted, abused, and overawed into silence or an apparent acquiescence; and to yield to the treasonable fury of so small a portion of the United States would be to violate the fundamental principle of our Constitution, which enjoins that the will of the majority shall prevail. On the other, to array citizen against citizen, to publish the dishonor of such excesses, to encounter the expense and other embarrassments of so distant an expedition, were steps too delicate, too closely interwoven with many affecting considerations, to be lightly adopted. I postponed, therefore, the summoning of the militia immediately into the field, but I required them to be held in readiness.

My proclamation of the 7th of August last was accordingly issued, and accompanied by the appointment of commissioners, who were charged to repair to the scene of insurrection. They were authorized to confer with any bodies of men or individuals. They were instructed to be candid and explicit in stating the sensations which had been excited in the Executive, and his earnest wish to avoid a resort to coercion; to represent, however, that, without submission, coercion must be the resort. . . .

Although the report of the commissioners marks their firmness and abilities, and must unite all virtuous men, by shewing that the means of conciliation have been exhausted, all of those who had committed or abetted the tumults did not subscribe to the mild form which was proposed as the atonement, and the indications of a peaceable temper were neither sufficiently general nor conclusive to recommend or warrant the further suspension of the march of the militia.

Thus the painful alternative could not be discarded. I ordered the militia to march, after once more admonishing the insurgents in my proclamation of the 25th of September last.

. . . Therefore, I put into motion fifteen thousand men, as being an army which, according to all human calculation, would be prompt and adequate in every view, and might, perhaps, by rendering resistance desperate, prevent the effusion of blood. . . .

As commander in chief of the militia when called into the actual service of the United States, I have visited the places of general rendezvous to obtain more exact information and to direct a plan for ulterior movements. Had there been room for a persuasion that the laws were secure from obstruction; that the civil magistrate was able to bring to justice such of the most culpable as have not embraced the proffered terms of amnesty, and may be deemed fit objects of example; that the friends to peace and good government were not in need of that aid and countenance which they ought always to receive, and, I trust, ever will receive, against the vicious and turbulent, I should have caught with avidity the opportunity of restoring the militia to their families and homes. But succeeding intelligence has tended to manifest the necessity of what has been done, it being now confessed by those who were not inclined to exaggerate the ill conduct of the insurgents that their malevolence was not pointed merely to a particular law, but that a spirit inimical to all order has actuated many of the offenders. . . .

■ ■ ■

While there is cause to lament that occurrences of this nature should have disgraced the name or interrupted the tranquillity of any part of our community, . . . it has demonstrated that our prosperity rests on solid foundations, by furnishing an additional proof that my fellow-citizens understand the true principles of government and liberty; that they feel their inseparable union; that notwithstanding all the devices which have been used to sway them from their interest and duty, they are now as ready to maintain the authority of the laws against licentious invasions as they were to defend their rights against usurpation. It has been a spectacle displaying to the highest advantage the value of republican government to behold the most and the least wealthy of our citizens standing in the same ranks as private soldiers, preeminently distinguished by being the army of the Constitution—undeterred by a march of three hundred miles over rugged mountains, by the approach of an inclement season, or by any other discouragement. . . .

■ ■ ■

To every description of citizens, indeed, let praise be given. But let them persevere in their affectionate vigilance over that precious depository of American happiness, the Constitution of the United States. Let them cherish it, too, for the sake of those who, from every clime, are daily seeking a dwelling in our land. . . .

Having thus fulfilled the engagement which I took when I entered into office, "to the best of my ability to preserve, protect, and defend the Constitution of the United States," on you, gentlemen, and the people by whom you are deputed, I rely for support.

■ ■ ■

The devising and establishing of a well-regulated militia would be a genuine source of legislative honor and a perfect title to public gratitude. I therefore entertain a hope that the present session will not pass without carrying to its full energy the power of organizing, arming, and disciplining the militia, and thus providing, in the language of the Constitution, for calling them forth to execute the laws of the Union, suppress insurrections, and repel invasions.

The intelligence from the army under the command of General Wayne is a happy presage to our military operations against the hostile Indians north of the Ohio. . . .

The Mint of the United States has entered upon the coinage of the precious metals, and considerable sums of defective coins and bullion have been lodged with the Director by individuals. There is a pleasing prospect that the institution will at no remote day realize the expectation which was originally formed of its utility.

. . . It may not be unseasonable to announce that my policy in our foreign transactions has been to cultivate peace with all the world; to observe treaties with pure and absolute faith; to check every deviation from the line of impartiality; to explain what may have been misapprehended and correct what may have been injurious to any nation, and having thus acquired the right, to lose no time in acquiring the ability to insist upon justice being done to ourselves. . . .

GEORGE WASHINGTON
SEVENTH STATE-OF-THE-UNION MESSAGE
UNITED STATES, *December 8, 1795*

Fellow-Citizens of the Senate and of the House of Representatives:
     I trust I do not deceive myself when I indulge the persuasion that I have never met you at any period when more than at the present the situation of our public affairs has afforded just cause for mutual congratulation, and for inviting you to join with me in profound gratitude to the Author of all Good for the numerous and extraordinary blessings we enjoy.

The termination of the long, expensive, and distressing war in which we have been engaged with certain Indians northwest of the Ohio is placed in the option of the United States by a treaty which the commander of our army has concluded provisionally with the hostile tribes in that region.

Though not before officially disclosed to the House of Representatives, you, gentlemen, are all apprised that a treaty of amity, commerce, and navigation has been negotiated with Great Britain, and that the Senate have advised and consented to its ratification upon a condition which excepts part of one article. Agreeably thereto, and to the best judgment I was able to form of the public interest after full and mature deliberation, I have added my sanction. The result on the part of His Britannic Majesty is unknown. When received, the subject will without delay be placed before Congress.

Contemplating the internal situation as well as the external relations of the United States, we discover equal cause for contentment and satisfaction. While many of the nations of Europe, with their American dependencies, have been involved in a contest unusually bloody, exhausting, and calamitous, in which the evils of foreign war have been aggravated by domestic convulsion and insurrection; in which many of the arts most useful to society have been exposed to discouragement and decay; in which scarcity of subsistence has embittered other sufferings; while even the anticipations of a return of the blessings of peace and repose are alloyed by the sense of heavy and accumulating burthens, which press upon all the departments of industry and threaten to clog the future springs of government, our favored country, happy in a striking contrast, has enjoyed general tranquillity—a tranquillity the more satisfactory because maintained at the expense of no duty. Faithful to ourselves, we have violated no obligation to others. Our agriculture, commerce, and manufactures prosper beyond former example, the molestations of our trade (to prevent a continuance of which, however, very pointed remonstrances have been made) being overbalanced by the aggregate benefits which it derives from a neutral position. Our population proportionally augments our strength and resources, and guarantees our future security. . . .

It is a valuable ingredient in the general estimate of our welfare that the part of our country which was lately the scene of disorder and insurrection now enjoys the blessings of quiet and order. . . .

Among the objects which will claim your attention in the course of the session, a review of our military establishment is not the least important. In this review you will doubtless allow due weight to the considerations that the questions between us and certain foreign powers are not yet finally adjusted, that the war in Europe is not yet terminated, and that our Western posts, when recovered, will demand provision for garrisoning and securing them. . . .

The progress in providing materials for the frigates and in building them, the state of the fortifications of our harbors, the measures which have been pursued for obtaining proper sites for arsenals and for replenishing our magazines with military stores, and the steps which have been taken toward the execution of the law for opening a trade with the Indians will likewise be presented for the information of Congress.

Temperate discussion of the important subjects which may arise in the course of the session and mutual forbearance where there is a difference of opinion are too obvious and necessary for the peace, happiness, and welfare of our country to need any recommendation of mine.

GEORGE WASHINGTON
EIGHTH STATE-OF-THE-UNION MESSAGE
UNITED STATES, *December 7, 1796*

Fellow-Citizens of the Senate and of the House of Representatives:
      In recurring to the internal situation of our country since I had last the pleasure to address you, I find ample reason for a

renewed expression of that gratitude to the Ruler of the Universe which a continued series of prosperity has so often and so justly called forth.

🏴 🏴 🏴

Measures calculated to insure a continuance of the friendship of the Indians and to preserve peace along the extent of our interior frontier have been digested and adopted.

🏴 🏴 🏴

The period during the late session at which the appropriation was passed for carrying into effect the treaty of amity, commerce, and navigation between the United States and His Britannic Majesty necessarily procrastinated the reception of the posts stipulated to be delivered beyond the date assigned for that event. . . .

🏴 🏴 🏴

To an active external commerce the protection of a naval force is indispensable. This is manifest with regard to wars in which a State is itself a party. But besides this, it is in our own experience that the most sincere neutrality is not a sufficient guard against the depredations of nations at war. To secure respect to a neutral flag requires a naval force organized and ready to vindicate it from insult or aggression. . . .

These considerations invite the United States to look to the means, and to set about the gradual creation of a navy. The increasing progress of their navigation promises them at no distant period the requisite supply of seamen, and their means in other respects favor the undertaking. . . . Will it not, then, be advisable to begin without delay to provide and lay up the materials for the building and equipping of ships of war, and to proceed in the work by degrees, in proportion as our resources shall render it practicable without inconvenience, so that a future war of Europe may not find our commerce in the same unprotected state in which it was found by the present?

Congress have repeatedly, and not without success, directed their attention to the encouragement of manufactures. . . . As a general rule, manufactures on public account are inexpedient; but where the state of things in a country leaves little hope that certain branches of manufacture will for a great length of time obtain, when these are of a nature essential to the furnishing and equipping of the public force in time of war, are not establishments for procuring them on public account . . . recommended . . . as an exception to the general rule? Ought our country to remain in such cases dependent on foreign supply, precarious because liable to be interrupted? If the necessary article should in this mode cost more in time of peace, will not the security and independence thence arising form an ample compensation? . . .

It will not be doubted that with reference either to individual or national welfare agriculture is of primary importance. In proportion as nations advance in population and other circumstances of maturity this truth becomes more apparent. . . . Institutions for promoting it grow up, supported by the public purse; and to what object can it be dedicated with greater propriety? . . .

I have heretofore proposed to the consideration of Congress the expediency of establishing a national university and also a military academy. The desirableness of both these institutions has so constantly increased with every new view I have taken of the subject that I can not omit the opportunity of once for all recalling your attention to them.

The assembly to which I address myself is too enlightened not to be fully sensible how much a flourishing state of the arts and sciences contributes to national prosperity and reputation. . . . True it is that our country, much to its honor, contains many seminaries of learning highly respectable and useful; but the funds upon which they rest are too narrow to command the ablest professors in the different departments of liberal knowledge for the institution contemplated, though they would be excellent auxiliaries.

Amongst the motives to such an institution, the assimilation of the principles, opinions, and manners of our countrymen by the common education of a portion of our youth from every quarter well deserves attention. . . . A primary object of such a national institution should be the education of our youth in the science of government. In a republic what species of knowledge can be equally important and what duty more pressing on its legislature than to patronize a plan for communicating it to those who are to be the future guardians of the liberties of the country?

The institution of a military academy is also recommended by cogent reasons. However pacific the general policy of a nation may be, it ought never to be without an adequate stock of military knowledge for emergencies. The first would impair the energy of its character, and both would hazard its safety or expose it to greater evils when war could not be avoided; besides that, war might often not depend upon its own choice. In proportion as the observance of pacific maxims might exempt a nation from the necessity of practicing the rules of the military art ought to be its care in preserving and transmitting, by proper establishments, the knowledge of that art. . . .

While in our external relations some serious inconveniences and embarrassments have been overcome and others lessened, it is with much pain and deep regret I mention that circumstances of a very unwelcome nature have lately occurred. Our trade has suffered and is suffering extensive injuries in the West Indies from the cruisers and agents of the French Republic, and communications have been received from its minister here which indicate the danger of a further disturbance of our commerce by its authority, and which are in other respects far from agreeable.

It has been my constant, sincere, and earnest wish, in conformity with that of our nation, to maintain cordial harmony and a perfectly friendly understanding with that Republic. This wish remains unabated, and I shall persevere in the endeavor to fulfill it to the utmost extent of what shall be consistent with a just and indispensable regard to the rights and honor of our country. . . .

The situation in which I now stand for the last time, in the midst of the representatives of the people of the United States, naturally recalls the period when the administration of the present form of government commenced, and I can not omit the occasion to congratulate you and my country on the success of the experiment, nor to repeat my fervent supplications to the Supreme Ruler of the Universe and Sovereign Arbiter of Nations that His providential care may still be extended to the United States, that the virtue and happiness of the people may be preserved, and that the Government which they have instituted for the protection of their liberties may be perpetual.

JOHN ADAMS
(1797–1801)

*"I congratulate
the people of
the United States"*

In 1796, George Washington declined a third term. The Federalists promptly nominated his Vice President *John Adams* as the logical candidate to succeed him. Adams' running mate was Thomas Pinckney of Maryland. To oppose Adams, the anti-Federalists (Democratic-Republicans) named a slate of Thomas Jefferson for President and Aaron Burr for Vice President.

In the ensuing November elections, Adams outpolled his friend Jefferson by three votes, 71 to 68. Under the provision of the Constitution at that time the two highest vote-catchers in the electoral college received the two highest offices. Thus, Adams became President, and the runner-up, Jefferson, Vice President.

Chubby, quick-tempered, somewhat vain, Adams was nonetheless as honest as daylight, as staunch a patriot as ever drew breath. In 1776, he had been the big gun in the wordy battle in the Continental Congress over the adoption of the Declaration of Independence. For fifty years his name was a household word for patriotism. He (like Jefferson) wrote his own epitaph—which was never used—"Here lies John Adams, who took upon himself the responsibility of the peace with France, in the year 1800."

Adams took office with a quasi-naval war on his hands, though not of his making. French cruisers were already preying on American shipping in the West Indies. France's smoldering resentment at America's neutrality while France was engaged in war with Britain and at the recent abrogation of the Treaty of 1778, had burst into flame.

How to keep America neutral and avoid actual war was the underlying theme of Adams' State-of-the-Union Messages. Hardly had he assumed the presidency when disturbing news arrived. France's Foreign Minister, Talleyrand, after insulting and expelling American Minister Charles Pinckney, had broken off diplomatic relations and stepped up French attacks on American commerce. Adams promptly summoned Congress into Extraordinary Session. In a Special War Message (first in the nation's history) Adams recounted America's grievance, denounced France, and asked Congress to strengthen the national defenses, but he did not ask an actual declaration of war. Instead, he announced his determination to try again to patch up the differences by dispatching another mission to Paris.

Adams' own party, the Federalists, berated his stand and grimly determined to have war with France. The anti-Federalists united on a single theme: War with France was unnecessary. In an atmosphere of violent party bitterness, the Federalists rushed through Congress a series of war measures that created the Navy Department, appropriated funds to finish arming the frigates, *Constitution, Constellation,* and *United States,* and authorized a large volunteer army with George Washington in command.

To make things unpleasant for the anti-Federalists and the French saboteurs in America, as well as to muzzle the critics of their policies, particularly the Jefferson Democratic-Republicans, the Federalists enacted the unpopular Alien and Sedition Acts. These statutes would be promptly repealed by Adams' successor.

Adams' First State-of-the-Union Message, November 22, 1797, announced the arrival of his new envoys in Paris—John Marshall, Elbridge Gerry, and Charles Pinckney—to seek a settlement "compatible with the safety, honor and interest of the United States." His third message refers to the celebrated XYZ Correspondence. Thus, the nation learned that America's envoys were not only rebuffed, but informed by three of Talleyrand's agents (whom Adams identified as X, Y, and Z in the copies he submitted to Congress) that America could have peace if a "douceur" of $250,000 was provided for the pockets of the Directory along with a loan of $12,000,000. Such blatant blackmail brought Pinckney's angry retort, "No, no, not a sixpence!"—which patriotic orators transmuted into the rousing "Millions for defense, but not one cent for tribute!"

Congress raged. The nation was incensed. The picture changed instantly. Militant patriotism ran high. War fever mounted. America's frigates sailed off to shoot it out with French cruisers in a two-year undeclared war in the Caribbean sea that the Supreme Court defined as a "limited war." Today it might be called a "police action." Whatever it was, France seized nearly a thousand American vessels while the nation's new navy captured or destroyed over eighty-five French armed vessels.

Yet, in his third message, Adams was still hopeful of an accommodation. In this he was gratified a year later when Napoleon, after ousting the French Directory, took control of France. He had other ideas than a long war with America. Negotiations were reopened, and a treaty of peace signed in September, 1800.

Adams' last message, November 22, 1800, was a landmark. It was the first of this historic cavalcade to be delivered in the nation's new permanent capital on the Potomac. Adams' invocation for the new city is a worthy peer of his celebrated blessing on the future occupants of the White House.

JOHN ADAMS
SPECIAL WAR MESSAGE
UNITED STATES, *May 16, 1797*

Gentlemen of the Senate and Gentlemen of the House of Representatives:

It would have afforded me the highest satisfaction to have been able to congratulate you on a restoration of peace to the nations of Europe whose animosities have endangered our tranquillity. . . . It is with extreme regret that I shall be obliged to turn your thoughts to other circumstances. . . .

After the President of the United States received information that the French Government had expressed serious discontents at some proceedings of the Government of these States said to affect the interests of France, he thought it expedient to send to that country a new minister, . . .

. . . A few days before his arrival at Paris the French minister of foreign relations informed the American minister then resident at

Paris of the formalities to be observed by himself in taking leave, and by his successor preparatory to his reception. These formalities they observed, and on the 9th of December presented officially to the minister of foreign relations, the one a copy of his letters of recall, the other a copy of his letters of credence.

These were laid before the Executive Directory. Two days afterwards the minister of foreign relations informed the recalled American minister that the Executive Directory had determined not to receive another minister plenipotentiary from the United States until after the redress of grievances demanded of the American Government. . . .

. . . The right of embassy is well known and established by the law and usage of nations. The refusal on the part of France to receive our minister is, then, the denial of a right; but the refusal to receive him until we have acceded to their demands without discussion and without investigation is to treat us neither as allies nor as friends, nor as a sovereign state.

While we are endeavoring to adjust all our differences with France by amicable negotiation, the progress of the war in Europe, the depredations on our commerce, the personal injuries to our citizens, and the general complexion of affairs render it my indispensable duty to recommend to your consideration effectual measures of defense.

The commerce of the United States has become an interesting object of attention, whether we consider it in relation to the wealth and finances or the strength and resources of the nation. With a seacoast of near two thousand miles in extent, opening a wide field for fisheries, navigation, and commerce, a great portion of our citizens naturally apply their industry and enterprise to these objects. Any serious and permanent injury to commerce would not fail to produce the most embarrassing disorders. To prevent it from being undermined and destroyed it is essential that it receive an adequate protection.

A naval power, next to the militia, is the natural defense of the United States. Our seacoasts, from their great extent, are more easily annoyed and more easily defended by a naval force than any other. . . .

🏴 🏴 🏴

With the same view, and as a measure which, even in a time of universal peace, ought not to be neglected, I recommend to your consideration a revision of the laws for organizing, arming, and disciplining the militia, to render that natural and safe defense of the country efficacious.

Although it is very true that we ought not to involve ourselves in the political system of Europe, but to keep ourselves always distinct and separate from it if we can, yet to effect this separation, early, punctual, and continual information of the current chain of events and of the political projects in contemplation is no less necessary than if we were directly concerned in them. . . .

🏴 🏴 🏴

JOHN ADAMS
FIRST STATE-OF-THE-UNION MESSAGE
UNITED STATES, *November 22, 1797*

Gentlemen of the Senate and Gentlemen of the House of Representatives:

Although I can not yet congratulate you on the reestablishment of peace in Europe and the restoration of security to the persons and properties of our citizens from injustice and violence at sea, we have, nevertheless, abundant cause of gratitude to the source of benevolence and influence for interior tranquillity and personal security, for propitious seasons, prosperous agriculture, productive fisheries, and general improvements, and, above all, for a rational spirit of civil and religious liberty and a calm but steady determination to support our sovereignty, as well as our moral and our religious principles, against all open and secret attacks.

Our envoys extraordinary to the French Republic embarked— one in July, the other early in August—to join their colleague in Holland. I have received intelligence of the arrival of both of them in Holland, from whence they all proceeded on their journeys to Paris within a few days of the 19th of September. . . .

Indeed, whatever may be the issue of the negotiation with France, and whether the war in Europe is or is not to continue, I hold it most certain that permanent tranquillity and order will not soon be obtained. The state of society has so long been disturbed, the sense of moral and religious obligations so much weakened, public faith and national honor have been so impaired, respect to treaties has been so diminished, and the law of nations has lost so much of its force, while pride, ambition, avarice, and violence have been so long unrestrained, there remains no reasonable ground on which to raise an expectation that a commerce without protection or defense will not be plundered.

The commerce of the United States is essential, if not to their existence, at least to their comfort, their growth, prosperity, and happiness. The genius, character, and habits of the people are highly commercial. Their cities have been formed and exist upon commerce. Our agriculture, fisheries, arts, and manufactures are connected with and depend upon it. In short, commerce has made this country what it is, and it can not be destroyed or neglected without involving the people in poverty and distress. Great numbers are directly and solely supported by navigation. The faith of society is pledged for the preservation of the rights of commercial and seafaring no less than of the other citizens. Under this view of our affairs, I should hold myself guilty of a neglect of duty if I forbore to recommend that we should make every exertion to protect our commerce and to place our country in a suitable posture of defense as the only sure means of preserving both.

It is my duty to recommend to your serious consideration those objects which by the Constitution are placed particularly within your [House of Representatives] sphere—the national debts and taxes.

Since the decay of the feudal system, by which the public defense was provided for chiefly at the expense of individuals, the system of loans has been introduced, and as no nation can raise within the year by taxes sufficient sums for its defense and military operations in time of war, the sums loaned and debts contracted have necessarily become the subjects of what have been called funding systems. The consequences arising from the continual accumulation of public debts in other countries ought to admonish us to be careful to prevent their growth in our own. The national defense must be provided for as well as the support of Government; but both should be accomplished as much as possible by immediate taxes, and as little as possible by loans.

We are met together at a most interesting period. The situations of the principal powers of Europe are singular and portentous. Connected with some by treaties and with all by commerce, no important event there can be indifferent to us. Such circumstances call with peculiar importunity not less for a disposition to unite in all those measures on which the honor, safety, and prosperity of our country depend than for all the exertions of wisdom and firmness.

JOHN ADAMS
SECOND STATE-OF-THE-UNION MESSAGE
UNITED STATES, *December 8, 1798*

Gentlemen of the Senate and Gentlemen of the House of Representatives:

The course of the transactions in relation to the United States and France which have come to my knowledge during your recess will be made the subject of a future communication. That communication will confirm the ultimate failure of the measures which have been taken by the Government of the United States toward an amicable adjustment of differences with that power. . . .

Hitherto, therefore, nothing is discoverable in the conduct of France which ought to change or relax our measures of defense. On the contrary, to extend and invigorate them is our true policy. . . .

But in demonstrating by our conduct that we do not fear war

in the necessary protection of our rights and honor we shall give no room to infer that we abandon the desire of peace. An efficient preparation for war can alone insure peace. It is peace that we have uniformly and perseveringly cultivated, and harmony between us and France may be restored at her option. But to send another minister without more determinate assurances that he would be received would be an act of humiliation to which the United States ought not to submit. It must therefore be left with France (if she is indeed desirous of accommodation) to take the requisite steps. The United States will steadily observe the maxims by which they have hitherto been governed. They will respect the sacred rights of embassy; and with a sincere disposition on the part of France to desist from hostility, to make reparation for the injuries heretofore inflicted on our commerce, and to do justice in future, there will be no obstacle to the restoration of a friendly intercourse. . . . But considering the late manifestations of her policy toward foreign nations, I deem it a duty deliberately and solemnly to declare my opinion that whether we negotiate with her or not, vigorous preparations for war will be alike indispensable. These alone will give to us an equal treaty and insure its observance.

Among the measures of preparation which appear expedient, I take the liberty to recall your attention to the naval establishment. . . . We ought without loss of time to lay the foundation for an increase of our Navy to a size sufficient to guard our coast and protect our trade. . . .

I have directed an estimate of the appropriations which will be necessary for the service of the ensuing year to be laid before you, accompanied with a view of the public receipts and expenditures to a recent period. It will afford you satisfaction to infer the great extent and solidity of the public resources from the prosperous state of the finances, notwithstanding the unexampled embarrassments which have attended commerce. . . .

I can not close this address without once more adverting to our political situation and inculcating the essential importance of uniting in the maintenance of our dearest interests; and I trust that by the temper and wisdom of your proceedings and by a harmony of measures we shall secure to our country that weight and respect to which it is so justly entitled.

JOHN ADAMS
THIRD STATE-OF-THE-UNION MESSAGE
UNITED STATES, *December 3, 1799*

Gentlemen of the Senate and Gentlemen of the House of Representatives:

It is with peculiar satisfaction that I meet the Sixth Congress of the United States of America. Coming from all parts of the Union at this critical and interesting period, the members must be fully possessed of the sentiments and wishes of our constituents.

Persevering in the pacific and humane policy which had been invariably professed and sincerely pursued by the Executive authority of the United States, when indications were made on the part of the French Republic of a disposition to accommodate the existing differences between the two countries, I felt it to be my duty to prepare for meeting their advances by a nomination of ministers upon certain conditions which the honor of our country dictated, and . . . I have directed them to proceed on their mission to Paris. They have full power to conclude a treaty, subject to the constitutional advice and consent of the Senate. . . .

The act of Congress relative to the seat of the Government of the United States requiring that on the first Monday of December next it should be transferred from Philadelphia to the District chosen for its permanent seat, it is proper for me to inform you that the commissioners appointed to provide suitable buildings for the accommodation of Congress and of the President and of the public offices of the Government have made a report of the state of the buildings designed for those purposes in the city of Washington, from which they conclude that the removal of the seat of Government to that place at the time required will be practicable and the accommodation satisfactory. . . .

🏴 🏴 🏴

I shall direct the estimates of the appropriations necessary for the service of the ensuing year, together with an account of the revenue and expenditure, to be laid before you. During a period in which a great portion of the civilized world has been involved in a war unusually calamitous and destructive, it was not to be expected that the United States could be exempted from extraordinary burthens.

. . . The result of the mission to France is uncertain; but however it may terminate, a steady perseverance in a system of national defense commensurate with our resources and the situation of our country is an obvious dictate of wisdom; for, remotely as we are placed from the belligerent nations, and desirous as we are, by doing justice to all, to avoid offense to any, nothing short of the power of repelling aggressions will secure to our country a rational prospect of escaping the calamities of war or national degradation. . . .

JOHN ADAMS
FOURTH STATE-OF-THE-UNION MESSAGE
UNITED STATES, *November 22, 1800*

Gentlemen of the Senate and Gentlemen of the House of Representatives:

Immediately after the adjournment of Congress at their last session in Philadelphia I gave directions, in compliance with the laws, for the removal of the public offices, records, and property. These directions have been executed, and the public officers have since resided and conducted the ordinary business of the Government in this place [Washington].

I congratulate the people of the United States on the assembling of Congress at the permanent seat of their Government, and I congratulate you, gentlemen, on the prospect of a residence not to be changed. Although there is cause to apprehend that accommodations are not now so complete as might be wished, yet there is great reason to believe that this inconvenience will cease with the present session.

May this territory be the residence of virtue and happiness! In this city may that piety and virtue, that wisdom and magnanimity, that constancy and self-government, which adorned the great character whose name it bears be forever held in veneration! Here and throughout our country may simple manners, pure morals, and true religion flourish forever!

It is with you, gentlemen, to consider whether the local powers over the District of Columbia vested by the Constitution in the Congress of the United States shall be immediately exercised. If in your opinion this important trust ought now to be executed, you can not fail while performing it to take into view the future probable situation of the territory for the happiness of which you are about to provide. You will consider it as the capital of a great nation advancing with unexampled rapidity in arts, in commerce, in wealth, and in population, and possessing within itself those energies and resources which, if not thrown away or lamentably misdirected, will secure to it a long course of prosperity and self-government.

THOMAS JEFFERSON

(1801–1809)

*"Consider
the state of
our beloved country"*

Thomas Jefferson, first of the Virginia Dynasty, came to the presidency
in 1801 after an election he called the Second American Revolution.
This blood-curdling campaign of 1800 produced the nation's first and
only tie vote for the presidency, with Jefferson and Aaron Burr, members of the same party, deadlocked at 73 electoral votes apiece.

Thus, for the first time, was election of a Chief Executive thrown into
the House of Representatives. Balloting began on February 11, 1801,
behind closed doors, in the cold, blasty House chamber in the unfinished Capitol in the embryonic city of Washington. Outside, a raging
snowstorm blocked all avenues to Capitol Hill. The sixteen states voted
as units. It took seven days and thirty-six ballots for Jefferson's floor
managers to round up the necessary votes of ten states to Burr's four.
Two states refrained from voting on the last ballot.

Jefferson's First State-of-the-Union Message—December 8, 1801—
cast him in his favorite role—tradition-breaker. Instead of riding in
state in a coach-and-six with military escort to deliver his message to
Congress in person, after the custom of his predecessors, Jefferson
simply sent his message to Capitol Hill by his private secretary to be
read to Congress by a clerk. Thus did "Republican simplicity" defy
what Jefferson termed "aristocratic foppery." The other method was
too reminiscent of the King's Speech from the throne. Many stood

aghast at such "undignified treatment of Congress," but Jefferson set a precedent that would endure until Woodrow Wilson broke with it in 1913.

This first message told much and prophesied much: The 1800 census showed America's population growing at a prodigious rate. (The actual figure was 5,308,483, greater by 1,379,269 than that of 1790.) Peace prevailed in the nation, even with the Indians. Europe's wars were subsiding. The sole exception were the pirates of Tripoli, but four of America's new frigates had sailed to the Mediterranean to chastise them. Said Jefferson of the expedition, "The measure was seasonable and salutary." The nation's finances were prospering, internal taxes should be eliminated, the government was running on a strict economy, spend-less, pay-as-you-go policy.

This message forecast repeal of the harsh naturalization laws passed by the Federalists which had increased to fourteen years the term of residence, and prompted Jefferson's historic query, "Shall oppressed humanity find no asylum on this globe?" The Judiciary Act, bundled through Congress in the dying hours of Adams' administration, must also be revoked. This act had created twenty-one new judgeships, all of which were feverishly filled with Federalist appointees, whose commissions were barely signed before midnight, March 3, 1801, thus earning for them the epithet Midnight Judges.

Jefferson's second message struck an ominous note, yet one prophetic with destiny. He intimated that "The cession of the Spanish Province of Louisiana to France" boded ill for the United States. Napoleon Bonaparte, intent on rebuilding France's new-world empire had, by secret treaty, forced Spain to re-cede to France the immense Louisiana domain stretching from the Mississippi to the Rockies. It meant a dictator lodged at the mouth of the Mississippi, the nation's back door, but it culminated in purchase of nearly half a continent. Jefferson succinctly summarized this achievement in his Third State-of-the-Union Message as "an ample provision for our posterity."

On the heels of this message came news that, pending cession of Louisiana to France, Spain had revoked the right of deposit at New Orleans, thus closing the Mississippi to American traffic. Jefferson immediately instructed Foreign Minister Robert Livingston at Paris to buy New Orleans and dispatched James Monroe to Paris to help get the deal through. Livingston and Monroe found themselves confronted with Napoleon's offer to sell the entire Louisiana territory for $15,000,000. They accepted the deal and Jefferson confirmed it. He had perhaps violated—as was so charged by his political foes—the strict constitutional observance set by Washington, but, after all, Jefferson was a tradition-breaker. One need only speculate what our history would have been had France remained the owner of everything west of the Mississippi.

Highlighting Jefferson's fifth message were the ravages of America's neutral shipping by the navies of France and England, again at war. This message foreshadowed the War of 1812. Britain was mistress of the seas; Napoleon's legions ruled Continental Europe. Caught between these fires, American rights were violated on all waters; her merchantmen were overhauled and thousands of her seamen impressed into the British navy.

To climax these indignities, the British *Leopard* fired on the American *Chesapeake* off the Virginia coast, killing and wounding twenty-one American seamen. The nation was outraged. Said Jefferson: "The affair of the *Chesapeake* put war in my hand. I had only to open it and let havoc loose."

Had he asked for war, the American people would have sanctioned it. But Jefferson, lover of peace, offered a substitute that he called "peaceable coercion." His new weapon was the Embargo Act, which, he said, would bring the offenders to terms without shedding blood. At his behest, Congress passed the ruinous embargo, forbidding American commerce with the belligerents. Lampooned as the "O-Grab-Me" (*embargo* spelled backward) Act, it stagnated American business and threw the nation into depression. Jefferson was forced to ask its repeal. In his final State-of-the-Union Message, he admitted failure of this "candid and liberal experiment."

In two of his State-of-the-Union Messages, Jefferson raised a question that bore staggering implications for the future. He suggested amending the Constitution so as to give the federal government power to spend money for the construction of roads and canals and for the advancement of education. His suggestions were too radical for Congress, but the seed he had sown was to bear stupendous harvests in the coming years. Even during Jefferson's administration, the nation began the first national road. In admitting Ohio to the Union in 1803, Congress agreed to build a road connecting that state with the East. Thus the old National, or Cumberland, Road, the first national highway, was begun in 1811.

The years 1801–1809 were ones of growth. Fifty thousand settlers moved into the Ohio and Tennessee valleys. Public land was being sold at $1.25 an acre. Flatboats plied the Ohio, and frontiers were beckoning. The lure of the West was on. New states and territories were shaping up. The Northwest Ordinance was paying off. Ohio reached statehood in 1802. Territory status came for Indiana in 1800; for Michigan, in 1805; for Illinois, in 1809.

THOMAS JEFFERSON
FIRST STATE-OF-THE-UNION MESSAGE
December 8, 1801

Fellow-Citizens of the Senate and House of Representatives:

It is a circumstance of sincere gratification to me that . . . I am able to announce . . . that the wars and troubles which have for so many years afflicted our sister nations have at length come to an end, and that the communications of peace and commerce are once more opening among them. . . .

Among our Indian neighbors also a spirit of peace and friendship generally prevails, and I am happy to inform you that the continued efforts to introduce among them the implements and the practice of husbandry and of the household arts have not been without success.

To this state of general peace with which we have been blessed, one only exception exists. Tripoli . . . had come forward with demands unfounded either in right or in compact, and had permitted itself to denounce war on our failure to comply before a given day. The style of the demand admitted but one answer. I sent a small squadron of frigates into the Mediterranean. . . . The arrival of our squadron dispelled the danger.

※　※　※

I lay before you the result of the census lately taken of our inhabitants, to a conformity with which we are now to reduce the ensuing ratio of representation and taxation. . . .

Other circumstances, combined with the increase of numbers, have produced an augmentation of revenue. . . . There is reasonable ground of confidence that we may now safely dispense with all the internal taxes . . . and that the remaining sources of revenue will be sufficient to provide for the support of Government, to pay the interest of the public debts, and to discharge the principals within shorter periods than the laws or the general expectation had contemplated. . . . Sound principles will not justify our taxing the industry of our fellow-citizens to accumulate treasure for wars to happen we know not when, and which might not, perhaps, happen but from the temptations offered by that treasure.

Agriculture, manufactures, commerce, and navigation, the four pillars of our prosperity, are then most thriving when left most free to individual enterprise. Protection from casual embarrassments, however, may sometimes be seasonably interposed. . . .

The judiciary system of the United States . . . will, of course, present itself to the contemplation of Congress, and, that they may be able to judge of the proportion which the institution bears to the business it has to perform, I have caused to be procured from the several States and now lay before Congress an exact statement of all the causes decided since the first establishment of the courts, and of those which were depending when additional courts and judges were brought in to their aid.

I can not omit recommending a revisal of the laws on the subject of naturalization. Considering the ordinary chances of human life, a denial of citizenship under a residence of fourteen years is a denial to a great proportion of those who ask it, and controls a policy pursued from their first settlement by many of these States, and still believed of consequence to their prosperity; and shall we refuse to the unhappy fugitives from distress that hospitality which the savages of the wilderness extended to our fathers arriving in this land? Shall oppressed humanity find no asylum on this globe? . . .

THOMAS JEFFERSON
SECOND STATE-OF-THE-UNION MESSAGE
December 15, 1802

To the Senate and House of Representatives of the United States:
When we assemble together, fellow-citizens, to consider the state of our beloved country, our just attentions are first drawn to those pleasing circumstances which mark the goodness of that

Being from whose favor they flow and the large measure of thankfulness we owe for His bounty. Another year has come around, and finds us still blessed with peace and friendship abroad; law, order, and religion at home; good affection and harmony with our Indian neighbors; our burthens lightened, yet our income sufficient for the public wants, and the produce of the year great beyond example. . . .

On the restoration of peace in Europe that portion of the general carrying trade which had fallen to our share during the war was abridged by the returning competition of the belligerent powers. This was to be expected, and was just. But in addition we find in some parts of Europe monopolizing discriminations, which . . . tend effectually to prohibit the carrying thither our own produce in our own vessels. . . . It rests with the Legislature to decide whether they will meet inequalities abroad with countervailing inequalities at home, or provide for the evil in any other way.

⚔ ⚔ ⚔

The cession of the Spanish Province of Louisiana to France, which took place in the course of the late war, will, if carried into effect, make a change in the aspect of our foreign relations which will doubtless have just weight in any deliberations of the Legislature connected with that subject.

In the Department of Finance it is with pleasure I inform you that the receipts of external duties for the last twelve months have exceeded those of any former year. . . . This has enabled us to answer all the regular exigencies of Government, to pay from the Treasury within one year upward of $8,000,000, principal and interest, of the public debt. . . .

⚔ ⚔ ⚔

Presuming it will be deemed expedient to expend annually a convenient sum toward providing the naval defense, . . . I can not but recommend that the first appropriations for that purpose may go to the saving what we already possess. . . . To avoid . . . waste of our resources it is proposed to add to our navy-yard here a dock within which our present vessels may be laid up dry and under cover from the sun. Under these circumstances experience proves that works of wood will remain scarcely at all affected by time. . . .

To cultivate peace and maintain commerce and navigation in all their lawful enterprises; to foster our fisheries as nurseries of navigation and for the nurture of man, and protect the manufactures adapted to our circumstances; to preserve the faith of the nation by an exact discharge of its debts and contracts, expend the public money with the same care and economy we would practice with our own, and impose on our citizens no unnecessary burdens; to keep in all things within the pale of our constitutional powers, and cherish the federal union as the only rock of safety— these, fellow-citizens, are the landmarks by which we are to guide ourselves in all our proceedings. . . .

THOMAS JEFFERSON
THIRD STATE-OF-THE-UNION MESSAGE
October 17, 1803

To the Senate and House of Representatives of the United States:

In calling you together, fellow-citizens, at an earlier day than was contemplated by the act of the last session of Congress, I have not been insensible to the personal inconveniences necessarily resulting from an unexpected change in your arrangements. But matters of great public concernment have rendered this call necessary. . . .

Congress witnessed at their late session the extraordinary agitation produced in the public mind by the suspension of our right of deposit at the port of New Orleans, no assignment of another place having been made according to treaty.

Previous, however, to this period we had not been unaware of the danger to which our peace would be perpetually exposed whilst so important a key to the commerce of the Western country remained under foreign power. . . . Propositions had therefore been authorized for obtaining on fair conditions the sovereignty of New Orleans and the provisional appropriation of $2,000,000 to be applied and accounted for by the President of the United States, intended as part of the price, was considered as conveying the sanction of Congress to the requisition proposed. The enlightened government of France saw with just discernment the importance to both nations of such liberal arrangements as might best and permanently promote the peace, friendship, and interests of both, and the property and sovereignty of all Louisiana which had been restored to them have on certain conditions been transferred to the United States by instruments bearing date the 30th of April last.

Whilst the property and sovereignty of the Mississippi and its waters secure an independent outlet for the produce of the Western States and an uncontrolled navigation through their whole course, . . . the fertility of the country, its climate and extent, promise in due season important aids to our Treasury, an ample provision for our posterity, and a wide spread for the blessings of freedom and equal laws.

We have seen with sincere concern the flames of war lighted up again in Europe. . . . While we regret the miseries in which we see others involved, let us bow with gratitude to that kind Providence which . . . guarded us from hastily entering into the sanguinary contest and left us only to look on and to pity its ravages. . . . Separated by a wide ocean from the nations of Europe and from the political interests which entangle them together, with productions and wants which render our commerce and friendship useful to them and theirs to us, it can not be the interest of any to assail us, nor ours to disturb them. We should be most unwise, indeed, were we to cast away the singular blessings of the position in which nature has placed us, the opportunity she has endowed us with of pursuing, at a distance from foreign contentions, the paths of industry, peace, and happiness, of cultivating general friendship, and of bringing collisions of interest to the umpirage of reason rather than of force. . . .

THOMAS JEFFERSON
FOURTH STATE-OF-THE-UNION MESSAGE
November 8, 1804

To the Senate and House of Representatives of the United States:
      To a people, fellow-citizens, who sincerely desire the happiness and prosperity of other nations . . . it will be a satisfac-

tion to observe that the war which was lighted up in Europe a little before our last meeting has not yet extended its flames to other nations. . . .

I have the satisfaction to inform you that the objections which had been urged by that Government [Spain] against the validity of our title to the country of Louisiana have been withdrawn . . . and to this is to be added that, having prepared and delivered the stock created in execution of the convention of Paris of April 30, 1803, in consideration of the cession of that country, we have received from the Government of France an acknowledgment, in due form, of the fulfillment of that stipulation.

These, fellow-citizens, are the principal matters which I have thought it necessary at this time to communicate for your consideration and attention. . . . Whether the great interests of agriculture, manufactures, commerce, or navigation can within the pale of your constitutional powers be aided in any of their relations; whether laws are provided in all cases where they are wanting; whether those provided are exactly what they should be; whether any abuses take place in their administration, or in that of the public revenues; whether the organization of the public agents or of the public force is perfect in all its parts; in fine, whether anything can be done to advance the general good, are questions within the limits of your functions which will necessarily occupy your attention. . . .

THOMAS JEFFERSON
FIFTH STATE-OF-THE-UNION MESSAGE
December 3, 1805

To the Senate and House of Representatives of the United States:
        At a moment when the nations of Europe are in commotion and arming against each other . . . and when the countenance of some of them toward our peaceable country threatens that even they may not be unaffected by what is passing on the general

theater, a meeting of the representatives of the nation . . . has
become more than usually desirable. . . .

X   X   X

Since our last meeting the aspect of our foreign relations has
considerably changed. Our coasts have been infested and our harbors watched by private armed vessels . . . committing piratical
acts beyond the authority of their commissions. They have captured in the very entrance of our harbors, as well as on the high
seas, not only the vessels of our friends coming to trade with us,
but our own also. They have carried them off under pretense of
legal adjudication, but not daring to approach a court of justice,
they have plundered and sunk them by the way or in obscure
places. . . . These enormities appearing to be unreached by any
control of their sovereigns, I found it necessary to equip a force
to cruise within our own seas, to arrest all vessels of these descrip-
tions found hovering on our coasts within the limits of the Gulf
Stream and to bring the offenders in for trial as pirates.

X   X   X

In reviewing these injuries from some of the belligerent powers
the moderation, the firmness, and the wisdom of the Legislature
will all be called into action. We ought still to hope that time and
a more correct estimate of interest as well as of character will produce the justice we are bound to expect. But should any nation
deceive itself by false calculations, and disappoint that expectation,
we must join in the unprofitable contest of trying which party can
do the other the most harm. Some of these injuries may perhaps
admit a peaceable remedy. Where that is competent it is always
the most desirable. But some of them are of a nature to be met
by force only, and all of them may lead to it. I can not, therefore,
but recommend such preparations as circumstances call for. . . .
In the meantime you will consider whether it would not be expedient for a state of peace as well as of war so to organize or class
the militia as would enable us on any sudden emergency to call
for the services of the younger portions, unencumbered with the
old and those having families. Upward of 300,000 able-bodied
men between the ages of eighteen and twenty-six years . . . will

furnish a competent number for offense or defense at any point where they may be wanted, and will give time for raising regular forces after the necessity of them shall become certain. . . .

Turning from these unpleasant views of violence and wrong, I congratulate you on the liberation of our fellow-citizens who were stranded on the coast of Tripoli and made prisoners of war. In the treaty, therefore, which has concluded our warfare with that State an article for the ransom of our citizens has been agreed to. . . .

On this first occasion of addressing Congress since . . . I have entered on a second term of administration, I embrace the opportunity to give this public assurance that I . . . exert my best endeavors to administer faithfully the executive department . . . will zealously cooperate with you in every measure which may tend to secure the liberty, property, and personal safety of our fellow-citizens, and to consolidate the republican forms and principles of our Government. . . .

THOMAS JEFFERSON
SIXTH STATE-OF-THE-UNION MESSAGE
December 2, 1806

To the Senate and House of Representatives of the United States:
It would have given me, fellow-citizens, great satisfaction to announce . . . that the difficulties in our foreign relations . . . had been amicably and justly terminated. I lost no time in taking those measures which were most likely to bring them to such a termination—by special missions charged with such powers and instructions as in the event of failure could leave no imputation on either our moderation or forbearance. . . .

Having received information that in another part of the United States a great number of private individuals were combining together . . . to carry on a military expedition against the territories of Spain, I thought it necessary . . . to take measures for preventing and suppressing this enterprise, for seizing the vessels, arms, and other means provided for it, and for arresting and bringing to justice its authors and abettors. [This was Aaron Burr's conspiracy.]

The expedition of Messrs. Lewis and Clark for exploring the river Missouri and the best communication from that to the Pacific Ocean has had all the success which could have been expected. They have traced the Missouri nearly to its source, descended the Columbia to the Pacific Ocean, ascertained with accuracy the geography of that interesting communication across our continent, learnt the character of the country, of its commerce and inhabitants; and it is but justice to say that Messrs. Lewis and Clark and their brave companions have by this arduous service deserved well of their country.

I congratulate you, fellow-citizens, on the approach of the period at which you may interpose your authority constitutionally to withdraw the citizens of the United States from all further participation in those violations of human rights which have been so long continued on the unoffending inhabitants of Africa, and which the morality, the reputation, and the best interests of our country have long been eager to proscribe. . . .

. . . There will still ere long be an accumulation of moneys in the Treasury beyond the installments of public debt which we are permitted by contract to pay. . . . The question therefore now comes forward: To what other objects shall these surpluses be appropriated, and the whole surplus of impost, after the entire discharge of the public debt and during those intervals when the purposes of war shall not call for them? Shall we suppress the impost and give that advantage to foreign over domestic manufactures? On a few articles of more general and necessary use the suppression in due season will doubtless be right, but the great mass of the articles on which impost is paid are foreign luxuries, purchased by those only who are rich enough to afford themselves the use of them. Their patriotism would certainly prefer its continuance and application to the great purposes of the public education, roads, rivers, canals, and such other objects of public improvement as it may be thought proper to add to the constitutional enumeration of Federal powers. . . . Education is here placed among the articles of public care, not that it would be proposed to take its ordinary branches out of the hands of private enterprise, which manages so much better all the concerns to which it is equal, but a public institution can alone supply those sciences which, though, rarely called for, are yet necessary to complete the circle, all the parts of which contribute to the improvement of the country and some of them to its preservation. The subject is now proposed for the consideration of Congress. . . . I suppose an amendment to the Constitution, by consent of the States, necessary, because the objects now recommended are not among those enumerated in the Constitution, to which it permits the public moneys to be applied.

This, fellow-citizens, is the state of the public interests at the present moment. . . . But such is the situation of the nations of Europe . . . that we can not rely with certainty on the present aspect of our affairs. . . . Our duty is, therefore, to act upon things as they are and to make a reasonable provision for whatever they may be. . . . A steady, perhaps a quickened, pace in preparations for the defense of our seaport towns and waters; an early settlement of the most exposed and vulnerable parts of our country; a militia so organized that its effective portions can be called to any point in the Union, or volunteers instead of them to serve a sufficient time, are means which may always be ready, yet never preying on our resources until actually called into use. . . . But much will depend on the promptitude with which these means can be brought into activity. If war be forced upon us, in spite of our long and vain appeals to the justice of nations, rapid and vigorous movements at its outset will go far toward securing us in its course and issue, and toward throwing its burthens on those who render necessary the resort from reason to force.

THOMAS JEFFERSON
SEVENTH STATE-OF-THE-UNION MESSAGE
October 27, 1807

To the Senate and House of Representatives of the United States:
Circumstances, fellow-citizens, which seriously threatened the peace of our country have made it a duty to convene you at an earlier period than usual. . . . The many injuries and depredations committed on our commerce and navigation upon the high seas for years past . . . and all the circumstances which induced the extraordinary mission to London are already known to you. . . . On this new reference to amicable discussion we were reposing in confidence, when on the 22nd day of June last by a formal order from a British admiral the frigate *Chesapeake,* leaving her port for a distant service, was attacked by one of those vessels which had been lying in our harbors under the indulgences of hospitality, was disabled from proceeding, had several of her crew killed and four taken away. On this outrage no commentaries are necessary. Its character has been pronounced by the indignant voice of our citizens with an emphasis and unanimity never exceeded. I immediately, by proclamation, interdicted our harbors and waters to all British armed vessels, forbade intercourse with them, and uncertain how far hostilities were intended, and the town of Norfolk, indeed, being threatened with immediate attack, a sufficient force was ordered for the protection of that place, and such other preparations commenced and pursued as the prospect rendered proper. . . .

The Government of that nation [England] has issued an order interdicting all trade by neutrals between ports not in amity with them. . . . Under this new law of the ocean our trade on the Mediterranean has been swept away by seizures and condemnations, and that in other seas is threatened with the same fate.

The appropriations of the last session for the defense of our seaport towns and harbors were made under expectation that a continuance of our peace would permit us to proceed in that work according to our convenience. It has been thought better to apply the sums then given toward the defense of New York, Charleston, and New Orleans chiefly, as most open and most likely first to need protection. . . .

The gunboats, too, already provided have on a like principle been chiefly assigned to New York, New Orleans, and the Chesapeake. Whether our movable force on the water, . . . should be augmented in this or any other form is left to the wisdom of the Legislature. . . .

⚔ ⚔ ⚔

Whether a regular army is to be raised, and to what extent, must depend on the information so shortly expected. In the meantime I have called on the States for quotas of militia, to be in readiness for present defense, and have, moreover, encouraged the acceptance of volunteers. . . .

I informed Congress at their last session of the enterprises against the public peace which were believed to be in preparation by Aaron Burr and his associates, of the measures taken to defeat them and to bring the offenders to justice. . . . I shall think it my duty to lay before you the proceedings and the evidence publicly exhibited on the arraignment of the principal offenders before the circuit court of Virginia. You will be enabled to judge whether the defect was in the testimony, in the law, or in the administration of the law; and wherever it shall be found, the Legislature alone can apply or originate the remedy. The framers of our Constitution certainly supposed they had guarded as well their Government against destruction by treason as their citizens against oppression under pretense of it, and if these ends are not attained it is of importance to inquire by what means more effectual they may be secured.

THOMAS JEFFERSON
EIGHTH STATE-OF-THE-UNION MESSAGE
November 8, 1808

To the Senate and House of Representatives of the United States:
It would have been a source, fellow-citizens, of much gratification if our last communications from Europe had enabled me

to inform you that the belligerent nations . . . had become awakened to the duty and true policy of revoking their unrighteous edicts. That no means might be omitted to produce this salutary effect, I lost no time in availing myself of the act authorizing a suspension, in whole or in part, of the several embargo laws. . . .

This candid and liberal experiment having thus failed, and no other event having occurred on which a suspension of the embargo by the Executive was authorized, it necessarily remains in the extent originally given to it. We have the satisfaction, however, to reflect that in return for the privations imposed by the measure, which our fellow-citizens in general have borne with patriotism, it has had the important effects of saving our mariners and our vast mercantile property, as well as of affording time for prosecuting the defensive and provisional measures called for by the occasion. It has demonstrated to foreign nations the moderation and firmness which govern our councils, and to our citizens the necessity of uniting in support of the laws and the rights of their country. . . .

Under a continuance of the belligerent measures which . . . overspread the ocean with danger, it will rest with the wisdom of Congress to decide on the course best adapted to such a state of things. . . .

Considering the extraordinary character of the times in which we live, our attention should unremittingly be fixed on the safety of our country. For a people who are free, and who mean to remain so, a well organized and armed militia is their best security. It is therefore incumbent on us at every meeting to revise the condition of the militia, and to ask ourselves if it is prepared to repel a powerful enemy at every point of our territories exposed to invasion. . . . Congress alone having the power to produce an uniform state of preparation in this great organ of defense, the interests which they so deeply feel in their own and their country's security will present this as among the most important objects of their deliberation.

. . . The probable accumulation of the surpluses of revenue beyond what can be applied to the payment of the public debt whenever the freedom and safety of our commerce shall be restored merits the consideration of Congress. Shall it lie unproductive in the public vaults? Shall the revenue be reduced? Or shall it not rather be appropriated to the improvements of roads, canals, rivers, education, and other great foundations of prosperity and union under the powers which Congress may already possess or such amendment of the Constitution as may be approved by the States? While uncertain of the course of things, the time may be advantageously employed in obtaining the powers necessary for a system of improvement, should that be thought best.

Availing myself of this the last occasion which will occur of addressing the two Houses of the Legislature at their meeting, I can not omit the expression of my sincere gratitude for the repeated proofs of confidence manifested to me by themselves and their predecessors since my call to the administration and the many indulgences experienced at their hands. The same grateful acknowledgments are due to my fellow-citizens generally, whose support has been my great encouragement under all embarrassments. In the transaction of their business I can not have escaped error. It is incident to our imperfect nature. But I may say with truth my errors have been of the understanding, not of intention, and that the advancement of their rights and interests has been the constant motive for every measure. . . .

JAMES MADISON
(1809–1817)

"British cruisers have wantonly spilt American blood"

In 1809, *James Madison,* second of the Virginia Dynasty, inherited two legacies from his predecessor—the presidency itself (Jefferson had hand-picked him over James Monroe) and a war with Great Britain. Madison's victory at the polls over Federalist Charles C. Pinckney was a mere formality. The Federalists were already on the way to political oblivion.

When Madison moved into the President's handsome mansion, he dreamed dreams that he, too, could keep the nation out of war by turning the other cheek. Quiet, scholarly, deeply imbued with Jefferson's policies and philosophy, "Little Jemmy" seems to have spent much of his time hoping for an "accommodation" with Great Britain that never came. Meanwhile American foreign policy bounced like a football from Embargo to Non-Intercourse to Non-Importation to Accommodation.

As Jefferson's Secretary of State, Madison had turned in a creditable job marked by much ability, but when victorious leadership was badly needed, Madison proved weak and indecisive. War with Britain would in the end be forced on him. Great of intellect, a scholar versed in law, history, and politics, he was "master of ideas, but not of men." Smallest of our Presidents, weighing less than one hundred pounds, he was barely five feet four. Tagged the Great Little Madison, he was chockful of dry Scotch wit. Washington hairdressers bemoaned the fact that the presidency was occupied by a little man whose queue was "no bigger than a pipestem."

He had achieved great honor as Father of the Constitution and author of the American Bill of Rights. It is not amiss to say that Madison's chief political asset as President was his luscious, buxom wife, Dolley, who remains a legendary figure in the first-lady cavalcade. As mistress of the President's mansion and the nation's official hostess, she set a pattern of hospitality and graciousness seldom if ever matched in White House history.

With two exceptions, an innocuous quality pervades Madison's eight State-of-the-Union Messages. They lack the force of the outstanding state papers of which he was capable. His message of September, 1814, contains the most amazing understatement in presidential history. It was delivered just a month after the British had captured and destroyed the nation's capital. Congress was assembled in temporary quarters, where they could gaze on the melancholy ruins of the Capitol and other government installations. Yet Madison characterized this crowning ignominy of the war as a "recent enterprise" by the British.

His first message was a rehash of America's grievances against Britain. After a noncommittal summation he said he would leave the solution of the country's problems to the "wisdom of the national legislature."

Into the Twelfth Congress that convened on November 4, 1811, surged a militant, fresh generation of youthful leaders, who shared, with Henry Clay, a passion for war and conquest. Dubbed "War Hawks" by John Randolph, they were eager and aggressive, hell-bent for hostilities. They longed to turn the undeclared war with England into a shooting affair. Wresting leadership, such as it was, from the hesitant Madison, they elected handsome, flag-waving Henry Clay of Kentucky Speaker of the House. Clay had, the year before in the Senate, boasted that the Kentucky militia alone could conquer Canada.

On November 5, Madison sent his pussyfooting Third State-of-the-Union Message to Congress. After reiterating England's insults, he tapped the war drum gently by asking Congress to put the nation "into an armor and attitude demanded by the crisis." That was enough for the War Hawks. They donned war panoply at once. Meanwhile, bad news came from the West. A horde of Indians, incited by the British, had inflicted grievous casualties on General Harrison's forces at Tippecanoe Creek in Indiana. The War Hawks clamored for war with England. Winter passed in gales of heated oratory. These fervid young Democratic-Republicans were in a minority; so were the Federalists, who wanted no war and were already scheming to separate New England from the Union. Control of Congress lay with the other Republicans, the moderates. One man alone could swing them because he was one of them. This was Madison, the hesitater.

A presidential nomination was in the offing, and Madison yearned to succeed himself. Accompanied by other topflight War Hawks, Henry Clay called on Madison and struck a bargain—they would drive his nomination through the party caucus if he would send his War Message to Congress before election. Madison accepted the deal, and the War Hawks forced his renomination.

On June 1, 1812, Madison sent his milksop War Message to Congress. Although he "abstained from recommending definitive measures," Henry Clay steamrollered a declaration of war through the House, and the Senate fell in line. The country was then plunged into a war for which it was ridiculously unprepared. The nation took the worst beating in its history and escaped only by the skin of its teeth and fancy footwork by American diplomats at Ghent, Belgium, in 1814.

"Mr. Madison's War" began in disaster, and the brunt of the blame fell on Jemmy Madison. Loss of Fort Detroit, which surrendered without firing a shot, all but crushed the nation's pride. The nation's capital was captured, burned, and pillaged. Save for the navy's thrilling victories on the high seas and Great Lakes, the performance was a sorry spectacle. General Andrew Jackson, thanks to the marksmanship of his frontier riflemen, gave a blaze-of-glory finish to the war by crushing the British invasion at New Orleans, but the treaty of peace had already been signed at Ghent, on Christmas Eve, 1814, before the battle was fought.

Madison's last two State-of-the-Union Messages had outstanding qualities. He asked for the reestablishment of the Bank of the United States (which Andrew Jackson would throttle to death in 1835), more adequate provision for national defense, and a protective tariff, and called attention to the need for roads and canals to be constructed by the government from surplus funds. In his next-to-last message he urged the desirability of a constitutional amendment that would permit Congress to spend money for internal improvements. In the last, however, he stressed "the expediency of exercising existing powers" for this purpose.

JAMES MADISON (1809–1817)
FIRST STATE-OF-THE-UNION MESSAGE
November 29, 1809

Fellow-Citizens of the Senate and of the House of Representatives:

At the period of our last meeting I had the satisfaction of communicating an adjustment with one of the principal belligerent nations. . . . It is with deep concern I am now to inform you that the favorable prospect has been overclouded by a refusal of the British Government to abide by the act of its minister plenipotentiary. . . .

With France, the other belligerent, . . . the posture of our relations does not correspond with the measures taken on the part of the United States to effect a favorable change.

Whatever may be the course of your deliberations on the subject of our military establishments, I should fail in my duty in not recommending to your serious attention the importance of giving to our militia . . . an organization the best adapted to eventual situations for which the United States ought to be prepared.

In the state which has been presented of our affairs with the great parties to a disastrous and protracted war carried on in a mode equally injurious and unjust to the United States as a neutral nation, the wisdom of the National Legislature will be again summoned to the important decision on the alternatives before them.

In the midst of the wrongs and vexations experienced from external causes there is much room for congratulation on the prosperity and happiness flowing from our situation at home. The blessing of health has never been more universal. The fruits of the seasons, though in particular articles and districts short of their usual redundancy, are more than sufficient for our wants and our comforts. The face of our country everywhere presents the evidence of laudable enterprise, of extensive capital, and of durable improvement. . . .

JAMES MADISON
SECOND STATE-OF-THE-UNION MESSAGE
WASHINGTON, *December 5, 1810*

Fellow-Citizens of the Senate and of the House of Representatives:
The embarrassments which have prevailed in our foreign relations . . . make it a primary duty in meeting you to communicate whatever may have occurred in that branch of our national affairs.

The act of the last session of Congress concerning the commercial intercourse between the United States and Great Britain and France having invited a termination of their edicts against our neutral commerce, copies of the act were immediately forwarded to our ministers at London and Paris. . . .

By the communication received through our minister at Paris it appeared that a knowledge of the act by the French Government was followed by a declaration that the Berlin and Milan decrees were revoked. . . .

From the British Government no communication on the subject of the act has been received. To a communication from our minister at London of a revocation by the French Government of its Berlin and Milan decrees it was answered that the British system would be relinquished as soon as the repeal of the French decrees should have actually taken effect.

Whilst it is universally admitted that a well-instructed people alone can be permanently a free people, and whilst it is evident that the means of diffusing and improving useful knowledge form so small a proportion of the expenditures for national purposes, I can not presume it to be unseasonable to invite your attention to the advantages of superadding to the means of education provided by the several States a seminary of learning instituted by the National Legislature within the limits of their exclusive jurisdiction. . . .

The fortifications for the defense of our maritime frontier have been prosecuted according to the plan laid down in 1808. . . . The improvements in quality and quantity made in the manufacture of cannon and small arms, both at the public armories and private factories, warrant additional confidence in the competency of these resources for supplying the public exigencies.

The Corps of Engineers, with the Military Academy, are entitled to the early attention of Congress. . . . The means by which war, as well for defense as for offense, are now carried on render these schools of the more scientific operations an indispensable part of every adequate system. . . . In no other way, probably, can a provision of equal efficacy for the public defense be made at so little expense or more consistently with the public liberty. . . .

JAMES MADISON
THIRD STATE-OF-THE-UNION MESSAGE
WASHINGTON, *November 5, 1811*

Fellow-Citizens of the Senate and of the House of Representatives:
. . . At the close of the last session of Congress it was hoped that the successive confirmations of the extinction of the French decrees . . . would have induced the Government of Great Britain to . . . authorize a removal of the existing obstructions to her commerce with the United States.

Instead of this reasonable step toward satisfaction and friendship between the two nations, the orders were . . . put into more rigorous execution. . . .

Among the occurrences produced by the conduct of British ships of war hovering on our coasts was an encounter between one of them and the American frigate commanded by Captain Rodgers, rendered unavoidable on the part of the latter by a fire commenced without cause by the former. . . .

. . . Notwithstanding the scrupulous justice, the protracted moderation, and the multiplied efforts on the part of the United States . . . , we have seen that the British cabinet perseveres not only in withholding a remedy for other wrongs, . . . but in the execution . . . of measures which . . . have the character as well as the effect of war on our lawful commerce.

With this evidence of hostile inflexibility in trampling on rights which no independent nation can relinquish, Congress will feel the duty of putting the United States into an armor and an attitude demanded by the crisis and corresponding with the national spirit and expectations.

I recommend, accordingly, that adequate provision be made for filling the ranks and prolonging the enlistments of the regular troops; for an auxiliary force to be engaged for a more limited term; for the acceptance of volunteer corps; . . . for detachments as they may be wanted of other portions of the militia, and for such a preparation of the great body as will proportion its usefulness to its intrinsic capacities. . . .

✕ ✕ ✕

In contemplating the scenes which distinguish this momentous epoch, . . . it is impossible to overlook those developing themselves among the great communities which occupy the southern portion of our own hemisphere. . . . An enlarged philanthropy and an enlightened forecast concur in imposing on the national councils an obligation to take a deep interest in their destinies, to cherish reciprocal sentiments of good will, to regard the progress of events, and not to be unprepared for whatever order of things may be ultimately established. . . .

JAMES MADISON
SPECIAL WAR MESSAGE
WASHINGTON, *June 1, 1812*

To the Senate and House of Representatives of the United States:
. . . Without going back beyond the renewal in 1803 of the war in which Great Britain is engaged, . . . the conduct of her

Government presents a series of acts hostile to the United States as an independent and neutral nation.

British cruisers have been in the continued practice of violating the American flag on the great highway of nations, and of seizing and carrying off persons sailing under it, not in the exercise of a belligerent right founded on the law of nations against an enemy, but of a municipal prerogative over British subjects. . . .

⚔ ⚔ ⚔

British cruisers . . . hover over and harass our entering and departing commerce . . . and have wantonly spilt American blood within the sanctuary of our territorial jurisdiction. . . .

⚔ ⚔ ⚔

. . . The cabinet of Britain resorted at length to the sweeping system of blockades, under the name of orders in council, which has been molded and managed as might best suit its political views, its commercial jealousies, or the avidity of British cruisers.

To our remonstrances . . . the first reply was that the orders were reluctantly adopted by Great Britain as a necessary retaliation on decrees of her enemy proclaiming a general blockade of the British Isles. . . .

⚔ ⚔ ⚔

It has become, indeed, sufficiently certain that the commerce of the United States is to be sacrificed, not as interfering with the belligerent rights of Great Britain; not as supplying the wants of her enemies, which she herself supplies; but as interfering with the monopoly which she covets for her own commerce and navigation. She carries on a war against the lawful commerce of a friend that she may the better carry on a commerce with an enemy. . . .

⚔ ⚔ ⚔

In reviewing the conduct of Great Britain toward the United States our attention is necessarily drawn to the warfare just renewed by the savages on one of our extensive frontiers—a warfare which is known to spare neither age nor sex and to be distinguished by features peculiarly shocking to humanity. It is difficult to account for the activity and combinations which have for some time been developing themselves among tribes in constant intercourse with British traders and garrisons without connecting their hostility with that influence. . . .

❉   ❉   ❉

. . . Our moderation and conciliation have had no other effect than to encourage perseverance and to enlarge pretensions. We behold our seafaring citizens still the daily victims of lawless violence. . . . We behold our vessels . . . confiscated . . . and their unfortunate crews dispersed and lost, or forced or inveigled in British ports into British fleets. . . .

We behold, in fine, on the side of Great Britain a state of war against the United States, and on the side of the United States a state of peace toward Great Britain.

Whether the United States shall continue passive under these progressive usurpations and these accumulating wrongs, or, opposing force to force in defense of their national rights, shall commit a just cause into the hands of the Almighty Disposer of Events . . . is a solemn question which the Constitution wisely confides to the legislative department of the Government. . . .

. . . I abstain at this time from recommending to the consideration of Congress definitive measures with respect to that nation [France] in the expectation that the result of unclosed discussions between our minister plenipotentiary at Paris and the French Government will speedily enable Congress to decide with greater advantage on the course due to the rights, the interests, and the honor of our country.

JAMES MADISON
FOURTH STATE-OF-THE-UNION MESSAGE
WASHINGTON, *November 4, 1812*

Fellow-Citizens of the Senate and of the House of Representatives:

On our present meeting it is my first duty to invite your attention to the providential favors which our country has experienced. . . .

With these blessings are necessarily mingled the pressures and vicissitudes incident to the state of war into which the United States have been forced by the perseverance of a foreign power in its system of injustice and aggression.

Previous to its declaration it was deemed proper . . . that a considerable force should be placed in the Michigan Territory with a general view to its security. . . .

Brigadier-General Hull was charged with this provisional service. . . . The expedition, nevertheless, terminated unfortunately, not only in a retreat to the town and fort of Detroit, but in the surrender of both and of the gallant corps commanded by that officer. . . .

The misfortune at Detroit was not, however, without a consoling effect. . . . The loss of an important post and of the brave men surrendered with it inspired everywhere new ardor and determination. . . .

✂ ✂ ✂

Our expectation of gaining the command of the Lakes by the invasion of Canada from Detroit having been disappointed, measures were instantly taken to provide on them a naval force superior to that of the enemy. . . .

✂ ✂ ✂

Among the incidents to the measures of the war I am constrained to advert to the refusal of the governors of Massachusetts and Connecticut to furnish the required detachments of militia toward the defense of the maritime frontier. The refusal was founded on a novel and unfortunate exposition of the provisions of the Constitution relating to the militia. It is obvious that if the authority of the United States to call into service and command the militia for the public defense can be thus frustrated, . . . the public safety may have no other resource than in those large and permanent military establishments which are forbidden by the principles of our free government. . . .

On the coasts and on the ocean the war has been as successful as circumstances inseparable from its early stages could promise.

. . . Our trade, with little exception, has safely reached our ports. . . . The frigate *Constitution,* commanded by Captain Hull, after a close and short engagement completely disabled and captured a British frigate, gaining for that officer and all on board a praise which can not be too liberally bestowed. . . .

The situation of our country, fellow-citizens, is not without its difficulties, though it abounds in animating considerations. . . . With more than one nation we have serious and unsettled controversies, and with one, powerful in the means and habits of war, we are at war. The spirit and strength of the nation are nevertheless equal to the support of all its rights. . . . Above all, we have the inestimable consolation of knowing that the war in which we are actually engaged is a war neither of ambition nor of vainglory; that it is waged not in violation of the rights of others, but in the maintenance of our own. . . .

JAMES MADISON
FIFTH STATE-OF-THE-UNION MESSAGE
WASHINGTON, *December 7, 1813*

Fellow-Citizens of the Senate and of the House of Representatives:
        In meeting you . . . it would have been highly satisfactory if I could have communicated a favorable result to the mission charged with negotiations for restoring peace. It was a just expectation, from the respect due to the distinguished Sovereign [Emperor of Russia] who had invited them by his offer of mediation, from the readiness with which the invitation was accepted on the part of the United States, and from the pledge to be found in an act of their Legislature for the liberality which their plenipotentiaries would carry into the negotiations, that no time would be . . . lost by the British Government in embracing the experiment for hastening a stop to the effusion of blood. . . .

The British cabinet, either mistaking our desire of peace for a dread of British power or misled by other fallacious calculations, has disappointed this reasonable anticipation. . . .

X   X   X

On Lake Erie, the squadron under command of Captain Perry having met the British squadron of superior force, a sanguinary conflict ended in the capture of the whole. The conduct of that officer, adroit as it was daring, and which was so well seconded by his comrades, justly entitles them to the admiration and gratitude of their country, and will fill an early page in its naval annals with a victory never surpassed in luster, however much it may have been in magnitude.

✗   ✗   ✗

. . . I recommend to Congress a revision of the militia laws for the purpose of securing more effectually the services of all detachments called into the employment and placed under the Government of the United States.

✗   ✗   ✗

If the war has increased the interruptions of our commerce, it has at the same time cherished and multiplied our manufactures so as to make us independent of all other countries. . . .

If much treasure has been expended, no inconsiderable portion of it has been applied to objects . . . necessary to our permanent safety.

If the war has exposed us to increased spoliations on the ocean and to predatory incursions on the land, it has developed the national means of retaliating the former and of providing protection against the latter. . . .

✗   ✗   ✗

The war has proved, moreover, that our free Government . . . acquires in its progress a force proportioned to its freedom, and that the union of these States . . . is strengthened by every occasion that puts it to the test.

✗   ✗   ✗

JAMES MADISON
SIXTH STATE-OF-THE-UNION MESSAGE
WASHINGTON, *September 20, 1814*

Fellow-Citizens of the Senate and of the House of Representatives:
. . . I was induced to call you together . . . that no delay
might happen in providing for the result of the negotiations on foot
with Great Britain, whether it should require arrangements adapted
to a return of peace or further and more effective provisions for
prosecuting the war.

✘   ✘   ✘

In the . . . present campaign the enemy . . . has little ground
for exultation, unless he can feel it in the success of his recent
enterprises against this metropolis and the neighboring town of
Alexandria, from both of which his retreats were as precipitate as
his attempts were bold and fortunate. . . .

✘   ✘   ✘

On our southern border victory has continued also to follow the
American standard. The bold and skillful operations of Major-
General Jackson . . . have subdued the principal tribes of hostile savages, and . . . guarded against the mischief of their cooperation with the British enterprises which may be planned
against that quarter of our country. . . .

In the recent attempt of the enemy on the city of Baltimore,
. . . he was received with a spirit which produced a rapid retreat
to his ships, whilst a concurrent attack by a large fleet was successfully resisted by the steady and well-directed fire of the fort
[Fort McHenry], and batteries opposed to it.

✘   ✘   ✘

. . . On Lake Champlain . . . the British squadron lately came
into action with the American, commanded by Captain Mac-
donough. It issued in the capture of the whole of the enemy's
ships. . . .

On the ocean the pride of our naval arms has been amply
supported. A second frigate has indeed fallen into the hands of the

enemy, but the loss is hidden in the blaze of heroism with which she was defended. . . .

In spite of the naval force of the enemy accumulated on our coasts, our private cruisers also have not ceased to annoy this commerce and to bring their rich prizes into our ports. . . .

✼   ✼   ✼

. . . It is not to be disguised that the situation of our country calls for its greatest efforts. Our enemy is powerful in men and in money, on the land and on the water. Availing himself of fortuitous advantages, he is aiming with his undivided force a deadly blow at our growing prosperity, perhaps at our national existence. . . . His barbarous policy has not even spared those monuments of the arts and models of taste with which our country had enriched and embellished its infant metropolis. From such an adversary hostility in its greatest force and in its worst forms may be looked for. The American people will face it with the undaunted spirit which in their revolutionary struggle defeated his unrighteous projects.

JAMES MADISON
SEVENTH STATE-OF-THE-UNION MESSAGE
WASHINGTON, *December 5, 1815*

Fellow-Citizens of the Senate and of the House of Representatives:

I have the satisfaction on our present meeting of being able to communicate to you the successful termination of the war which had been commenced against the United States by the Regency of Algiers. The squadron in advance on that service, under Commodore Decatur, lost not a moment after its arrival in the Mediterranean in seeking the naval force of the enemy . . . and succeeded in capturing two of his ships, one of them the principal ship, commanded by the Algerian admiral. The high character of the American commander was brilliantly sustained on the occasion which brought his own ship into close action with that of his adversary, as was the accustomed gallantry of all the officers and men actually engaged. Having prepared the way by this demonstration of American skill and prowess, he hastened to the port of Algiers, where peace was promptly yielded to his victorious force. . . .

※   ※   ※

. . . It is true that the improved condition of the public revenue will not only afford the means of maintaining the faith of the Government with its creditors inviolate, . . . but will also justify an immediate alleviation of the burdens imposed by the necessities of the war. It is, however, essential . . . that the benefits of an uniform national currency should be restored to the community. The absence of the precious metals will, it is believed, be a temporary evil, but until they can again be rendered the general medium of exchange it devolves on the wisdom of Congress to provide a substitute which shall equally engage the confidence and accommodate the wants of the citizens throughout the Union. If the operation of the State banks can not produce this result, the probable operation of a national bank will merit consideration; and if neither of these expedients be deemed effectual it may become necessary to ascertain the terms upon which the notes of the Government (no longer required as an instrument of credit) shall be issued upon motives of general policy as a common medium of circulation.

※   ※   ※

. . . I recommend also an enlargement of the Military Academy already established, and the establishment of others in other sections of the Union; and I can not press too much on the attention of Congress such a classification and organization of the militia as will most effectually render it the safeguard of a free state. . . .

※   ※   ※

In adjusting the duties on imports to the object of revenue the influence of the tariff on manufactures will necessarily present itself for consideration. However wise the theory may be which leaves to the sagacity and interest of individuals the application of their industry and resources, there are in this as in other cases exceptions to the general rule. Besides the condition which the theory itself implies of a reciprocal adoption by other nations, experience teaches that so many circumstances must concur in introducing and maturing manufacturing establishments . . . that a country may remain long without them, although sufficiently advanced and in some respects even peculiarly fitted for carrying them on with success. . . .

Among the means of advancing the public interest the occasion is a proper one for recalling the attention of Congress to the great importance of establishing throughout our country the roads and canals which can best be executed under the national authority. No objects within the circle of political economy so richly repay the expense bestowed on them . . . and it is a happy reflection that any defect of constitutional authority which may be encountered can be supplied in a mode which the Constitution itself has providently pointed out. . . .

JAMES MADISON
EIGHTH STATE-OF-THE-UNION MESSAGE
December 3, 1816

Fellow-Citizens of the Senate and of the House of Representatives:

In reviewing the present state of our country, our attention can not be withheld from the effect produced by peculiar seasons which have very generally impaired the annual gifts of the earth and threatened scarcity in particular districts. Such, however, is the variety . . . within our extensive limits that the aggregate resources for subsistence are more than sufficient for the aggregate wants. And as far as an economy of consumption . . . may be necessary, our thankfulness is due to Providence for what is far more than a compensation, in the remarkable health which has distinguished the present year.

Amidst the advantages which have succeeded the peace of Europe, and that of the United States with Great Britain, in a general invigoration of industry among us and in the extension of our commerce . . . it is to be regretted that a depression is experienced by particular branches of our manufactures and by a portion of our navigation. . . . The evil will not, however, be viewed by

Congress without a recollection that manufacturing establishments, if suffered to sink too low or languish too long, may not revive after the causes shall have ceased, and that in the vicissitudes of human affairs situations may recur in which a dependence on foreign sources for indispensable supplies may be among the most serious embarrassments.

As a subject of the highest importance to the national welfare, I must again earnestly recommend to the consideration of Congress a reorganization of the militia on a plan which will form it into classes according to the periods of life more or less adapted to military services. . . .

The importance which I have attached to the establishment of a university within this District . . . induces me to renew my recommendation of it to the favorable consideration of Congress. And I particularly invite again their attention to the expediency of exercising their existing powers, and, where necessary, of resorting to the prescribed mode of enlarging them, in order to effectuate a comprehensive system of roads and canals. . . .

The United States, having been the first to abolish within the extent of their authority the transportation of the natives of Africa into slavery . . . can not but be gratified at the progress made by concurrent efforts of other nations toward a general suppression of so great an evil. They must feel at the same time the greater solicitude to give the fullest efficacy to their own regulations. . . .

The period of my retiring from the public service being at little distance, I shall find no occasion more proper than the present for expressing to my fellow-citizens my deep sense of the continued confidence and kind support which I have received from them. . . .

. . . I can indulge the proud reflection that the American people have reached in safety and success their fortieth year as an independent nation; that for nearly an entire generation they have had experience of their present Constitution . . . ; that they have found it to bear the trials of adverse as well as prosperous circumstances; to contain in its combination of the federate and elective principles a reconcilement of public strength with individual liberty. . . . Nor is it less a peculiar felicity of this Constitution . . . that it is found to be capable . . . of expanding itself over a spacious territory with the increase and expansion of the community for whose benefit it was established.

JAMES MONROE
(1817–1825)

*"We should consider
any attempt . . . as dangerous
to our peace and safety"*

James Monroe, fifth President, is best known for his durable, now embattled foreign policy, which he promulgated in his Seventh State-of-the-Union Message on December 2, 1823.

Interlocked as it is with the future machinations of the Cuba-Moscow Axis, the Monroe Doctrine has currently assumed monumental significance in the face of its gravest challenge in 140 years.

Disparaged by some (even Americans) as out of date or a dead issue and by Premier Khrushchev as a "corpse," Monroe's pronouncement remains today the cornerstone of the nation's foreign policy. Monroe stated his proposition so simply as to defy misinterpretation: The independent American republics must be let alone by foreign powers—any attempt to interfere with or molest them by threats, invasion, colonization, or importation of foreign ideologies (Monroe's words were "extend their system") would be inimical to the interests and security of the United States. Monroe implied that the United States would by force uphold the doctrine against all comers, though at the time the nation's military power was woefully weak.

Monroe assumed the presidency in 1817, the year in which Spain's vast colonies in South and Central America were fighting for independence, a struggle toward which the United States was actively neutral—although most sympathetic. By 1822 the Latin-American peoples had broken their shackles and the United States recognized their new republics, the first nation to do so.

Meantime, other disturbances had bobbed up. Russia laid exclusive claim to fishing rights along the Pacific Coast and to all lands down as far as San Francisco. Bent on intervening in South America and restoring Spain's lost colonies, the Holy Alliance was formed by Russia, Prussia, and Austria. Monroe decided it was time to say "hands off," but before drafting his pronunciamento, he consulted Jefferson and Madison. His farsighted Secretary of State, John Quincy Adams, persuaded Monroe to go it alone and not make Britain a party to it, as Prime Minister George Canning had shrewdly suggested.

Monroe chose to incorporate his doctrine (though he never called it that) in his State-of-the-Union Message, 1823, because the annual messages of the Presidents were scanned eagerly in the courts of Europe. While his words displeased kings and emperors, they made a profound impact on their thinking.

Comparatively few Americans have ever read Monroe's actual words, and fewer still, until recently, have had the foggiest notion of what the doctrine means; yet it is probably closer to the American heart than any other facet of foreign policy. History books in American schools and colleges have given the Monroe Doctrine short shrift; yet it remains a living, enduring cornerstone of national policy. (Because of its significant, recent renaissance, Monroe's Seventh State-of-the-Union Message is cut to the doctrine itself and given first place in the sequence of his messages.) It should be noted that in his opening paragraphs, Monroe sought to impress on the American people the far-reaching nature of his pronouncement.

The doctrine was offered in two distinct parts, the first of which dealt with Russian claims on the Pacific Coast. The second part, so-called heart of the doctrine, dealt with the threat of European intervention in the Americas.

JAMES MONROE
SEVENTH [MONROE DOCTRINE] STATE-OF-THE-UNION MESSAGE
WASHINGTON, *December 2, 1823*

Fellow-Citizens of the Senate and House of Representatives:

Many important subjects will claim your attention during the present session, of which I shall endeavor to give, in aid of your deliberations, a just idea in this communication. I undertake this duty with diffidence, from the vast extent of the interests on which I have to treat and of their great importance to every portion of our Union. I enter on it with zeal from a thorough conviction that there never was a period since the establishment of our Revolution when, regarding the condition of the civilized world and its bearing on us, there was greater necessity for devotion in the public servants to their respective duties, or for virtue, patriotism, and union in our constituents.

Meeting in you a new Congress, I deem it proper to present this view of public affairs in greater detail than might otherwise be necessary. I do it, however, with peculiar satisfaction, from a knowledge that in this respect I shall comply more fully with the sound principles of our Government. The people being with us exclusively the sovereign, it is indispensable that full information be laid before them on all important subjects, to enable them to exercise that high power with complete effect. . . .

A precise knowledge of our relations with foreign powers as respects our negotiations and transactions with each is thought to be particularly necessary. Equally necessary is it that we should form a just estimate of our resources, revenue, and progress in every kind of improvement connected with the national prosperity and public defense. It is by rendering justice to other nations that we may expect it from them. It is by our ability to resent injuries and redress wrongs that we may avoid them.

At the proposal of the Russian Imperial Government, made through the Minister of the Emperor residing here, a full power and instructions have been transmitted to the Minister of the United States at St. Petersburg to arrange by amicable negotiation the respective rights and interests of the two nations on the northwest coast of this continent. A similar proposal has been made by his Imperial Majesty to the Government of Great Britain, which has likewise been acceded to. The Government of the United States has been desirous by this friendly proceeding of manifesting the great value which they have invariably attached to the friendship of the Emperor and their solicitude to cultivate the best understanding with his Government. In the discussions to which this interest has given rise and in the arrangements by which they may terminate, the occasion has been judged proper for asserting, as a principle in which the rights and interests of the United States are involved, that the American continents, by the free and independent condition which they have assumed and maintain, are henceforth not to be considered as subjects for future colonization by any European powers.

It was stated at the commencement of the last session that a great effort was then making in Spain and Portugal to improve the condition of the people of those countries, and that it appeared to be conducted with extraordinary moderation. It need scarcely be remarked that the result has been so far very different from what was then anticipated. Of events in that quarter of the globe, with which we have so much intercourse and from which we derive our origin, we have always been anxious and interested spectators. The citizens of the United States cherish sentiments the most friendly in favor of the liberty and happiness of their fellow-men on that side of the Atlantic. In the wars of the European powers in matters relating to themselves we have never taken any part, nor does it comport with our policy so to do. It is only when our rights are invaded or seriously menaced that we resent injuries or make preparation for our defense. With the movements in this hemisphere we are of necessity more immediately connected, and by causes which must be obvious to all enlightened and impartial observers. The political system of the allied powers is essentially different in this respect from that of America. This difference proceeds from that which exists in their respective Governments; and to the defense of our own, which has been achieved by the loss of so much blood and treasure, and matured by the wisdom of our most enlightened citizens, and under which we have enjoyed unexampled felicity, this whole nation is devoted. We owe it, therefore, to candor and to the amicable relations existing between the United States and those powers to declare that we should consider any attempt on their part to extend their system to any portion of this hemisphere as dangerous to our peace and safety. With the existing colonies or dependencies of any European power we have not interfered and shall not interfere. But with the Governments who have declared their independence and maintained it, and whose independence we have, on great consideration and on just principles, acknowledged, we could not view any interposition for the purpose of oppressing them, or controlling in any other manner their destiny, by any European power in any other light than as the manifestation of an unfriendly disposition toward the United States. In the war between those new Governments and Spain we declared our neutrality at the time of their recognition, and to this we have adhered, and shall continue to adhere, provided no change shall occur which, in the judgment of the competent authorities of this Government, shall make a corresponding change on the part of the United States indispensable to their security.

. . . Our policy in regard to Europe, which was adopted at an early stage of the wars which have so long agitated that quarter of the globe, nevertheless remains the same, which is, not to interfere in the internal concerns of any of its powers; to consider the government *de facto* as the legitimate government for us; to cultivate friendly relations with it, and to preserve those relations by a frank, firm and manly policy, meeting in all instances the just claims of every power, submitting to injuries from none. But in regard to those continents circumstances are eminently and conspicuously different. It is impossible that the allied powers should extend their political system to any portion of either continent without endangering our peace and happiness; nor can anyone believe that our southern brethren, if left to themselves, would adopt it of their own accord. It is equally impossible, therefore, that we should behold such interposition in any form with indifference. If we look to the comparative strength and resources of Spain and those new Governments, and their distance from each other, it must be obvious that she can never subdue them. It is still the true policy of the United States to leave the parties to themselves, in the hope that other powers will pursue the same course.

If we compare the present condition of our Union with its actual state at the close of our Revolution, the history of the world furnishes no example of a progress in improvement in all the important circumstances which constitute the happiness of a nation which bears any resemblance to it. At the first epoch our population did not exceed 3,000,000. By the last census it amounted to about 10,000,000, and, what is more extraordinary, it is almost altogether native, for the immigration from other countries has been inconsiderable. At the first epoch, half the territory within our acknowledged limits was uninhabited and a wilderness. Since then new territory has been acquired of vast extent, comprising within it many rivers, particularly the Mississippi, the navigation of which to the ocean was of the highest importance to the original States. Over this territory our population has expanded in every direction, and new States have been established almost equal in number to those which formed the first bond of our Union. This expansion of our population and accession of new States to our Union have had the happiest effect on all its highest interests. . . . It is unnecessary to treat here of the vast improvement made in the system itself by the adoption of this Constitution and of its happy effect in elevating the character and in protecting the rights of the nation as well as of individuals. To what, then, do we owe these blessings? It is known to all that we derive them from the excellence of our institutions. Ought we not, then, to adopt every measure which may be necessary to perpetuate them?

The Era of Good Feeling

James Monroe was the last of the Virginia Dynasty and last to be chosen by "King Caucus," the autocratic political boss composed of members of the majority party in Congress.

Jefferson sired King Caucus. Holding absolute control of his party, and thus of Congress, Jefferson manipulated the caucus so that the people really had no voice in the nomination or election of their Presidents. King Caucus dished out the presidency as he saw fit. Thus did King Caucus keep the Virginia Dynasty in the White House for twenty-four years.

In the 1816 election the Federalist party went out of existence and the nation embarked on an eight-year, one-party political utopia to which the Boston *Centinel* applied the felicitous appellation, "The Era of Good Feeling."

Known as the "Last Cocked Hat," Monroe was also the last veteran of the Revolutionary War to head the government. He still bore scars of the British bullet that had cut his jugular and almost taken his life at Trenton, Christmas Night, 1776.

Amid the disaster and incompetence of the War of 1812, Monroe had achieved the rare distinction of occupying two posts in Madison's Cabinet at the same time—Secretary of State and of War. His services as Minister to France in the 1790's, and as special envoy to help negotiate the Louisiana Purchase in 1803, had given him ample opportunity to observe foreign affairs at first hand.

In 1817, Monroe was inaugurated outside the temporary brick Capitol at Washington. The new Capitol was rising nearby on the burned-out ruins left by the British. In December, the magnificent Monroes moved into an even more splendid presidential mansion with a resounding social splash.

In this era the Supreme Court, under the aegis of John Marshall, was broadening its powers. Lured by cheap land, settlers were flocking westward. The tariff battles began in earnest. The slavery issue was rising, and the cold war between North and South opened with the bitter Missouri Compromise clash in Congress. The Cumberland Road was pushing toward the Ohio, and other roads and canals were fanning out across the land. The nation's flag was given its final basic design, thirteen horizontal stripes, alternate red and white, with a star on the blue field for every state—twenty-four by 1820. An American literature was emerging, with James Fenimore Cooper, Washington Irving, and William Cullen Bryant in the forefront.

In 1820, the Federalists nominated no candidate for the presidency. Monroe was reelected, unanimously except for a single vote cast by a New Hampshire elector. The census that year showed a population of 9,638,453.

Monroe's State-of-the-Union Messages were long but meaty. They touched on much history. His first message revealed the signing of the historic Rush-Bagot Treaty with Great Britain that limited armament on the Great Lakes to three small ships each carrying a single cannon to cope with smugglers. The treaty still stands, a model of peaceful coexistence.

He admitted the need of roads and canals, but insisted that Congress had no right to appropriate public moneys for internal improvements, unless, as pointed out by Jefferson and Madison, it was authorized by an amendment to the Constitution.

He voiced the nation's sympathy with the struggles of the South-American colonies to break Spain's hold, but insisted the United States must remain neutral. His sixth message reiterated this interest and sympathy, foreshadowing the Monroe Doctrine a year later.

Monroe opened his second message with a justification of Major General Jackson's foray into Spanish-owned Florida in 1818. Monroe actually presaged the acquisition of Florida from Spain that closely followed that famous invasion. As commander of the Southern Department, Jackson, acting under orders, attacked the marauding Seminoles and their lawless allies, pursued them into Florida, seized two Spanish posts at St. Marks and Pensacola, and hanged two British subjects for stirring up the Indians. Protests from Spain poured in.

Monroe's Cabinet, except for Secretary of State John Quincy Adams, felt Jackson had exceeded his authority. In straightening out the delicate situation, Adams quietly negotiated a treaty with Spain transferring the Floridas to the United States for $5,000,000, approximately the amount of American citizens' claims for commercial damages from Spain.

Monroe's last message, December 7, 1824, takes a sanguine look at the future of America. He noted the prospective and historic visit of Lafayette to this country and urged Congress to meet him with a "generous spirit." (Congress complied by a donation of $200,000 to the high-minded Frenchman.) Monroe also called attention to the growing importance of the Supreme Court in the councils of the nation.

JAMES MONROE
FIRST STATE-OF-THE-UNION MESSAGE
December 2, 1817

Fellow-Citizens of the Senate and of the House of Representatives:

At no period of our political existence have we so much cause to felicitate ourselves at the prosperous and happy condition of our country. The abundant fruits of the earth have filled it with plenty. An extensive and profitable commerce has greatly augmented our revenue. The public credit has attained an extraordinary elevation. . . .

I have the satisfaction to inform you that an arrangement which had been commenced by my predecessor with the British Government for the reduction of the naval force by Great Britain and the United States on the Lakes has been concluded, by which it is provided that neither party shall keep in service on Lake Champlain more than one vessel, on Lake Ontario more than one, and on Lake Erie and the upper lakes more than two, to be armed each with one cannon only, and that all the other armed vessels of both parties shall be dismantled. . . .

It was anticipated at an early stage that the contest between Spain and its colonies would become highly interesting to the United States. Should the colonies establish their independence, it is proper now to state that this Government neither seeks nor would accept from them any advantage in commerce or otherwise which will not be equally open to all other nations. . . .

※ ※ ※

In calling your attention to the internal concerns of our country the view which they exhibit is peculiarly gratifying. The payments which have been made into the Treasury show the very productive state of the public revenue. . . .

In the present state of the Treasury the whole of the Louisiana debt may be redeemed in the year 1819.

※ ※ ※

When we consider the vast extent of territory within the United States, the great amount and value of its productions, the connection of its parts, and other circumstances on which their prosperity and happiness depend, we can not fail to entertain a high sense of the advantage to be derived from the facility which may be afforded in the intercourse between them by means of good roads and canals. . . . A difference of opinion has existed . . . among our most enlightened and virtuous citizens respecting the right of Congress to establish such a system of improvement. . . . Disregarding early impressions I have bestowed on the subject all the deliberation which its great importance and a just sense of my duty required, and the result is a settled conviction in my mind that Congress does not possess the right. . . .

※ ※ ※

It appearing in a satisfactory manner that the revenue arising from imposts and tonnage and from the sale of the public lands will be fully adequate to the support of the civil Government, of the present military and naval establishments, including the annual augmentation of the latter to the extent provided for, to the payment of the interest of the public debt, and to the extinguishment of it at the times authorized, without the aid of the internal taxes, I consider it my duty to recommend to Congress their repeal. To impose taxes when the public exigencies require them is an obligation of the most sacred character, especially with a free people. . . . To dispense with taxes when it may be done with perfect safety is equally the duty of their representatives. . . .

JAMES MONROE
SECOND STATE-OF-THE-UNION MESSAGE
November 16, 1818

Fellow-Citizens of the Senate and of the House of Representatives:
. . . A state of things has existed in the Floridas, the tendency of which has been obvious to all who have paid the slightest attention to the progress of affairs in that quarter. Throughout the whole of those Provinces to which the Spanish title extends the Government of Spain has scarcely been felt. . . . Adventurers from every country, fugitives from justice, and absconding slaves have found an asylum there. . . .

This country had, in fact, become the theater of every species of lawless adventure . . . the Indian tribes have constituted the effective force in Florida. With these tribes these adventurers had formed at an early period a connection with a view to avail themselves of that force to promote their own projects of accumulation and aggrandizement. It is to the interference of some of these adventurers, in misrepresenting the claims and titles of the Indians to land, and in practicing on their savage propensities, that the Seminole War is principally to be traced. . . .

It was thought incumbent on the United States to suppress the establishment, and it was accordingly done. In pursuing these savages to an imaginary line in the woods it would have been the height of folly to have suffered that line to protect them. Had that been done the war could never cease. . . .

In suppressing the establishment at Amelia Island no unfriendliness was manifested towards Spain because the post was taken from a force which had wrested it from her. In authorizing Major General Jackson to enter Florida in pursuit of the Seminoles care was taken not to encroach on the rights of Spain. . . . The commanding general was convinced that he should fail in his object, that he should, in effect, accomplish nothing, if he did not deprive these savages of the resource on which they had calculated and of the protection on which they had relied in making war. . . .

Although the reasons which induced Major General Jackson to take these posts were duly appreciated, there was nevertheless no hesitation in deciding on the course which it became the government to pursue. By ordering the restitution of the posts those [amicable] relations were preserved. By this measure, so promptly taken, due respect was shown to the Government of Spain.

I communicate with great satisfaction the accession of another State [Illinois] to our Union. . . . By extending our Government on the principles of our Constitution over the vast territory within our limits, on the Lakes and the Mississippi and its numerous streams, new life and vigor are infused into every part of our system. . . .

JAMES MONROE
THIRD STATE-OF-THE-UNION MESSAGE
WASHINGTON, *December 7, 1819*

Fellow-Citizens of the Senate and of the House of Representatives:
    In the civil war existing between Spain and the Spanish Provinces in this hemisphere the greatest care has been taken to enforce the laws intended to preserve an impartial neutrality. . . .

The distance of the colonies from the parent country and the great extent of their population and resources gave them advantages which it was anticipated at a very early period would be difficult for Spain to surmount. . . . Should it become manifest to the world that the efforts of Spain to subdue these Provinces will be fruitless, it may be presumed that the Spanish Government itself will give up the contest. . . .

⚔ ⚔ ⚔

The great reduction of the currency which the banks have been constrained to make in order to continue specie payments, and the vitiated character of it where such reductions have not been attempted, instead of placing within the reach of these establishments the pecuniary aid necessary to avail themselves of the advantages resulting from the reduction in the prices of the raw materials and of labor, have compelled the banks to withdraw from them a portion of the capital heretofore advanced to them. That aid which has been refused by the banks has not been obtained from other sources, owing to the loss of individual confidence from the frequent failures which have recently occurred in some of our principal commercial cities.

An additional cause for the depression of these establishments may probably be found in the pecuniary embarrassments which have recently affected those countries with which our commerce has been principally prosecuted. Their manufactures, for the want of a ready or profitable market at home, have been shipped by the manufacturers to the United States, and in many instances sold at a price below their current value at the place of manufacture. . . .

⚔ ⚔ ⚔

For the protection of our commerce in the Mediterranean, along the southern Atlantic coast, in the Pacific and Indian oceans, it has been found necessary to maintain a strong naval force, which it seems proper for the present to continue. . . .

Due attention has likewise been paid to the suppression of the slave trade, in compliance with a law of the last session. Orders have been given to the commanders of all our public ships to seize all vessels navigated under our flag engaged in that trade, and to bring them in to be proceeded against in the manner prescribed by that law. It is hoped that these vigorous measures, supported by like acts by other nations, will soon terminate a commerce so disgraceful to the civilized world.

JAMES MONROE
FOURTH STATE-OF-THE-UNION MESSAGE
WASHINGTON, *November 14, 1820*

Fellow-Citizens of the Senate and of the House of Representatives:
　　Happy as our situation is, it does not exempt us from solicitude and care for the future. . . . The state of Europe is unsettled, and how long peace may be preserved is altogether uncertain; in addition to which we have interests of our own to adjust which will require particular attention. . . .

Considerable progress has been made during the present season in examining the coast and its various bays and other inlets, in the collection of materials, and in the construction of fortifications for the defense of the Union. . . . I am satisfied that every favorable anticipation which has been formed of this great undertaking will be verified, and that when completed it will afford very great if not complete protection to our Atlantic frontier in the event of another war. . . .

Our peace with the powers on the coast of Barbary has been preserved, but we owe it altogether to the presence of our squadron in the Mediterranean. It has been found equally necessary to employ some of our vessels for the protection of our commerce in the Indian Sea, the Pacific, and along the Atlantic coast. . . . In execution of the law of the last session for the suppression of the slave trade some of our public ships have also been employed on the coast of Africa, where several captures have already been made of vessels engaged in that disgraceful traffic.

JAMES MONROE
FIFTH STATE-OF-THE-UNION MESSAGE
WASHINGTON, *December 3, 1821*

Fellow-Citizens of the Senate and of the House of Representatives:

The progress of our affairs since the last session has been such as may justly be claimed and expected under a Government deriving all its powers from an enlightened people, and under laws formed by their representatives, on great consideration, for the sole purpose of promoting the welfare and happiness of their constituents. . . .

※ ※ ※

With Spain the treaty of February 22, 1819, has been partly carried into execution. Possession of East and West Florida has been given to the United States, but the officers charged with that service . . . have not only omitted . . . the performance of the express stipulation to deliver over the archives and documents relating to the property and sovereignty of those Provinces, . . . but defeated since every effort of the United States to obtain them, especially those of the greatest importance.

It is understood that the colonies in South America have had great success during the present year in the struggle for their independence. The new Government of Colombia has extended its territories and considerably augmented its strength, and at Buenos Aires, where civil dissensions had for some time before prevailed, greater harmony and better order appear to have been established. . . .

※ ※ ※

It may fairly be presumed that under the protection given to domestic manufactures by the existing laws we shall become at no distant period a manufacturing country on an extensive scale. Possessing as we do the raw materials in such vast amount, with a capacity to augment them to an indefinite extent; raising within the country aliment of every kind to an amount far exceeding the demand for home consumption, even in the most unfavorable years, and to be obtained always at a very moderate price; skilled also, as our people are, in the mechanic arts and in every improvement calculated to lessen the demand for and the price of labor, it is manifest that their success in every branch of domestic industry may and will be carried, under the encouragement given by the present duties, to an extent to meet any demand which under a fair competition may be made upon it.

JAMES MONROE
SIXTH STATE-OF-THE-UNION MESSAGE
WASHINGTON, *December 3, 1822*

Fellow-Citizens of the Senate and of the House of Representatives:
      Since your last session the prohibition which had been imposed on the commerce between the United States and the British colonies in the West Indies and on this continent has . . . been removed.

⚔ ⚔ ⚔

The organization of the several corps composing the Army is such as to admit its expansion to a great extent in case of emergency, the officers carrying with them all the light which they possess to the new corps to which they might be appointed.

With the organization of the staff there is equal cause to be satisfied. By the concentration of every branch with its chief in this city, in the presence of the Department, and with a grade in the chief military station to keep alive and cherish a military spirit, the greatest promptitude in the execution of orders, with the greatest economy and efficiency, are secured. The same view is taken of the Military Academy. Good order is preserved in it, and the youth are well instructed in every science connected with the great objects of the institution. . . .

⚔ ⚔ ⚔

It is understood that the Cumberland road, which was constructed at a great expense, has already suffered from the want of that regular superintendence and of those repairs which are indispensable to the preservation of such a work. This road is of incalculable advantage in facilitating the intercourse between the Western and the Atlantic States. . . . Believing that a competent power to adopt and execute a system of internal improvement has not been granted to Congress, but that such a power, confined to great national purposes and with proper limitations, would be productive of eminent advantage to our Union, I have thought it advisable that an amendment of the Constitution to that effect should be recommended to the several States.

It appears that our manufactures, though depressed immediately after the peace, have considerably increased, and are still increasing, under the encouragement given them by the tariff of 1816 and by subsequent laws. Satisfied I am, whatever may be the abstract doctrine in favor of unrestricted commerce . . . that there are other strong reasons applicable to our situation and relations with other countries which impose on us the obligation to cherish and sustain our manufactures. . . .

A strong hope was entertained that peace would ere this have been concluded between Spain and the independent governments south of the United States in this hemisphere. Long experience having evinced the competency of those governments to maintain the independence which they had declared, it was presumed that . . . Spain herself . . . would have terminated on that basis a controversy so unavailing and at the same time so destructive. . . .

Europe is still unsettled, and although the war long menaced between Russia and Turkey has not broken out, there is no certainty that the differences between those powers will be amicably adjusted. . . .

Whether we reason from the late wars or from those menacing symptoms which now appear in Europe, it is manifest that if a convulsion should take place in any of those countries it will proceed from causes which have no existence and are utterly unknown in these States, in which there is but one order, that of the people, to whom the sovereignty exclusively belongs. Should war break out in any of those countries, . . . we might reasonably presume that we should not be molested by them. This, however, ought not to be calculated on as certain. . . . The history of the late wars in Europe furnishes a complete demonstration that no system of conduct, however correct in principle, can protect neutral powers from injury from any party; that a defenseless position and distinguished love of peace are the surest invitations to war, and that there is no way to avoid it other than by being always prepared and willing for just cause to meet it. . . .

JAMES MONROE
EIGHTH STATE-OF-THE-UNION MESSAGE
WASHINGTON, *December 7, 1824*

Fellow-Citizens of the Senate and of the House of Representatives:
        The view which I have now to present to you of our affairs, foreign and domestic, realizes the most sanguine anticipations which have been entertained of the public prosperity. . . . Our expansion over the vast territory within our limits has been great. . . . We have daily gained strength by a native population in every quarter—a population devoted to our happy system of government and cherishing the bond of union with fraternal affection. . . .

The whole amount of the public debt on the 1st of January next may be estimated at $86,000,000. . . . A well-founded hope may be entertained that, should no unexpected event occur, the whole of the public debt may be discharged in the course of ten years. . . .

In conformity with a resolution of Congress of the last session, an invitation was given to General Lafayette to visit the United

States, with an assurance that a ship of war should attend at any port of France which he might designate to receive and convey him across the Atlantic. . . . He declined the offer of the public ship from motives of delicacy, but assured me that he had long intended and would certainly visit our Union in the course of the present year. In August last he arrived at New York, where he was received with the warmth of affection and gratitude to which his very important and disinterested services and sacrifices in our Revolutionary struggle so eminently entitled him. A corresponding sentiment has since been manifested in his favor throughout every portion of our Union, and affectionate invitations have been given him to extend his visits to them. . . . His high claims on our Union are felt, and the sentiment universal that they should be met in a generous spirit. Under these impressions I invite your attention to the subject, with a view that, regarding his very important services, losses, and sacrifices, a provision may be made and tendered to him which shall correspond with the sentiments and be worthy the character of the American people.

In turning our attention to the condition of the civilized world, in which the United States have always taken a deep interest, it is gratifying to see how large a portion of it is blessed with peace. . . .

With respect to the contest to which our neighbors are a party, it is evident that Spain as a power is scarcely felt in it. These new States had completely achieved their independence before it was acknowledged by the United States, and they have since maintained it with little foreign pressure. . . . The deep interest which we take in their independence, which we have acknowledged, and in their enjoyment of all the rights incident thereto, especially in the very important one of instituting their own Governments, has been declared, and is known to the world. Separated as we are from Europe by the great Atlantic Ocean, we can have no concern in the wars of the European Governments nor in the causes which produce them. The balance of power between them, into whichever scale it may turn in its various vibrations, can not affect us. . . .

Against foreign danger the policy of the Government seems to be already settled. The events of the late war admonished us to make our maritime frontier impregnable by a well-digested chain of fortifications, and to give efficient protection to our commerce by augmenting our Navy to a certain extent. . . . In the event of war it is on the maritime frontier that we shall be assailed. It is in that quarter, therefore, that we should be prepared to meet the attack. . . .

I can not conclude this communication, the last of the kind which I shall have to make, without recollecting with great sensibility and heartfelt gratitude the many instances of the public confidence and the generous support which I have received from my fellow-citizens in the various trusts with which I have been honored. Having commenced my service in early youth, and continued it since with few and short intervals, I have witnessed the great difficulties to which our Union has been exposed, and admired the virtue and intelligence with which they have been surmounted. From the present prosperous and happy state I derive a gratification which I can not express. . . .

JOHN QUINCY ADAMS
(1825–1829)

*"The spirit of improvement
is abroad
upon the earth"*

In 1824 five candidates competed to succeed Monroe. King Caucus gave the nod to William H. Crawford of Georgia, to whom the nomination had been promised, but to Crawford's dismay four eager rivals promptly challenged the right of outmoded King Caucus to make the next President. They were Henry Clay, John C. Calhoun, *John Quincy Adams,* and Andrew Jackson. A wild, scurrilous scramble for votes ensued.

In the November elections, Jackson was the popular favorite, but in December, when the electoral votes were counted, no one of the contestants had a majority. Jackson ran first with 99, Adams second with 84, while Crawford and Clay trailed with 41 and 37, respectively. Calhoun, promised the vice-presidency, had taken himself out of the race. Lacking a majority (131 were necessary then), the decision was thrown into the House of Representatives.

As low man Clay quit, but as Speaker of the House, with 37 votes in hand, he held the balance of power and promptly assumed the role of kingmaker, tossing his votes to Adams, who was elected on the first ballot. The next day Adams offered the State portfolio to Clay, whose same-day acceptance brought suspicions of a deal. The Jackson men charged "Bargain and Corruption," that Clay had agreed to trade his votes for the office of State. Jackson himself joined in the protest, denouncing Clay as "The Judas of the West." There followed a four-year war in Congress with the Jackson men blocking every move President Adams made.

Son of the second President, and the only President's son ever to occupy the White House, Adams was perhaps the canniest, ablest diplomat in American history. As a Federalist he had been elected to the Senate in 1808, only to resign five years later. Now a man without a party, he leaned toward Jefferson's Democratic-Republican philosophy.

Although he was not a social lion, or even a good mixer, Adams had sampled the splendors of almost every court in Europe. A quarter-century of diplomatic missions abroad and eight years as Monroe's Secretary of State had given him wide experience in foreign affairs. As co-negotiator of the Treaty of Ghent that ended the War of 1812, Adams did a masterful job of blocking preposterous British demands. Plump, red-faced like his father, cold-mannered, he had few close friends but integrity was bred in him. He was one of the hardest-working Presidents, rising at five in the morning to read his Bible and make his own fires. He often bathed in the Potomac at sunrise. It is said that every night of his life Adams knelt and repeated the prayer his mother had taught him as a child, "Now I lay me down to sleep, I pray the Lord my soul to keep. . . ."

Yet, strangely, social grandeur reached a new high in Louisa Adams' White House "drawing rooms," surpassing even the magnificent Monroes' glittering affairs.

Adams' State-of-the-Union Messages have the stamp of a progressive mind. He keynoted his first message with the words, "The spirit of improvement is abroad upon the earth." Specifically, he stressed internal improvements—the construction of highways, establishment of a federal university and of a national observatory (he called it "lighthouse of the skies")—and reminded Congress that the monument to the Father of his Country voted by its predecessors at the death of Washington in 1799 was still unbuilt. Inventors, he said, should be protected by "even a limited term of exclusive right to their discoveries." The nation should establish a naval academy "corresponding to the Military Academy at West Point"; thus he forecast the United States Naval Academy, at Annapolis, Maryland.

In this first message, Adams revealed that he had, without the advice and consent of the Senate, accepted Simón Bolívar's invitation to send delegates to the First Congress of the American Republics at Panama in 1826. His action whipped up a storm in the Senate. In a violent outburst Senator John Randolph denounced the Adams-Clay entente as a "coalition of Blifil and Black George . . . the combination of the Puritan and the blackleg." Clay challenged at once. He and Randolph fought a fantastic, bloodless duel on the Virginia side of the Potomac.

Adams closed his second message with a "momentary retrospect" of a most amazing coincidence in American history: the death of Thomas Jefferson and John Adams (the President's father) on the same day, July 4, 1826, while the nation was celebrating the fiftieth anniversary of the Declaration of Independence.

Highlighting his last message, December 2, 1828, was his call for a "revisal" of the Tariff of Abominations, as it was castigated by the South. It was designed primarily to help the woolen manufacturers, raising the duty on wool from 33 per cent to 45 per cent.

JOHN QUINCY ADAMS
FIRST STATE-OF-THE-UNION MESSAGE
WASHINGTON, *December 6, 1825*

Fellow-Citizens of the Senate and of the House of Representatives:
    Europe, with a few partial and unhappy exceptions, has enjoyed ten years of peace, during which all her Governments, whatever the theory of their constitutions may have been, are successively taught to feel that the end of their institution is the happiness of the people, and that the exercise of power among men can be justified only by the blessings it confers upon those over whom it is extended.

🐌   🐌   🐌

    Among the measures which have been suggested to . . . [the Latin-American Republics] by the new relations with one another . . . is that of assembling at the Isthmus of Panama a congress, at which each of them should be represented, to deliberate upon objects important to the welfare of all. The Republics of Colombia, of Mexico, and of Central America have already deputed plenipotentiaries to such a meeting, and they have invited the United States to be also represented there by their ministers. The invitation has been accepted, and ministers on the part of the United States will be commissioned to attend at those deliberations, and to take part in them so far as may be compatible with that neutrality from which it is neither our intention nor the desire of the other American States that we should depart.

꙰ ꙰ ꙰

The objects of the West India Squadron have been to carry into execution the laws for the suppression of the African slave trade. . . . The African slave trade has long been excluded from the use of our flag, and if some few citizens of our country have continued to set the laws of the Union as well as those of nature and humanity at defiance by persevering in that abominable traffic, it has been only by sheltering themselves under the banners of other nations less earnest for the total extinction of the trade than ours. . . .

꙰ ꙰ ꙰

. . . Among the first, perhaps the very first, instrument for the improvement of the condition of men is knowledge, and to the acquisition of much of the knowledge adapted to the wants, the comforts, and enjoyments of human life public institutions and seminaries of learning are essential. So convinced of this was the first of my predecessors in this office . . . that once and again in his addresses to the Congresses with whom he cooperated in the public service he earnestly recommended the establishment of seminaries of learning, to prepare for all the emergencies of peace and war—a national university and a military academy. . . .

꙰ ꙰ ꙰

Connected with the establishment of an university, or separate from it, might be undertaken the erection of an astronomical observatory, with provision for the support of an astronomer, to be in constant attendance of observation upon the phenomena of the heavens, and for the periodical publication of his observations. It is with no feeling of pride as an American that the remark may be made that on the comparatively small territorial surface of Europe there are existing upward of 130 of these light-houses of the skies, while throughout the whole American hemisphere there is not one. If we reflect a moment upon the discoveries which in the last four centuries have been made in the physical constitution of the universe by the means of these buildings and of observers stationed in them, shall we doubt of their usefulness to every nation? . . . Are we not cutting ourselves off from the means of returning light for light while we have neither observatory nor observer upon our half of the globe and the earth revolves in perpetual darkness to our unsearching eyes?

🕮   🕮   🕮

The laws relating to the administration of the Patent Office are deserving of much consideration and perhaps susceptible of some improvement. . . . If an honest pride might be indulged in the reflection that on the records of that office are already found inventions the usefulness of which has scarcely been transcended in the annals of human ingenuity, would not its exultation be allayed by the inquiry whether the laws have effectively insured to the inventors the reward destined to them by the Constitution—even a limited term of exclusive right to their discoveries? . . .

🕮   🕮   🕮

On the 24th of December, 1799, it was resolved by Congress that a marble monument should be erected by the United States in the Capitol at the city of Washington; that the family of General Washington should be requested to permit his body to be deposited under it, and that the monument be so designed as to commemorate the great events of his military and political life. In reminding Congress of this resolution and that the monument contemplated by it remains yet without execution, I shall indulge only the remarks that the works at the Capitol are approaching completion; that the consent of the family, desired by the resolution, was requested and obtained; . . . that a spot has been reserved within the walls where you are deliberating . . . in which the mortal remains may be deposited of him whose spirit listens with delight to every act of the representatives of his nation which can tend to exalt and adorn his and their country.

🕮   🕮   🕮

The spirit of improvement is abroad upon the earth. It stimulates the hearts and sharpens the faculties not of our fellow-citizens alone, but of the nations of Europe and of their rulers. While dwelling with pleasing satisfaction upon the superior excellence of our political institutions, let us not be unmindful that liberty is power; that the nation blessed with the largest portion of liberty must in proportion to its numbers be the most powerful nation upon earth.

JOHN QUINCY ADAMS
SECOND STATE-OF-THE-UNION MESSAGE
WASHINGTON, *December 5, 1826*

Fellow-Citizens of the Senate and of the House of Representatives:
In our intercourse with the other nations of the earth we have still the happiness of enjoying peace and a general good understanding. . . .

By the decease of the Emperor Alexander of Russia . . . the United States have been deprived of a long-tried, steady, and faithful friend. . . . A candid and confidential interchange of sentiments between him and the Government of the United States upon the affairs of Southern America . . . left to the other Governments of Europe no alternative but that of sooner or later recognizing the independence of our southern neighbors. . . .

In adverting to the present condition of our fiscal concerns and to the prospects of our revenue the first remark that calls our attention is that they are less exuberantly prosperous than they were at the corresponding period of the last year. The severe shock so extensively sustained by the commercial and manufacturing interests in Great Britain has not been without a perceptible recoil upon ourselves. A reduced importation from abroad is necessarily succeeded by a reduced return to the Treasury at home. . . .

. . . It is well for us, however, to be admonished of the necessity of abiding by the maxims of the most vigilant economy, and of resorting to all honorable and useful expedients for pursuing with steady and inflexible perseverance the total discharge of the debt.

A report from the Postmaster-General is likewise communicated, presenting in a highly satisfactory manner the result of a vigorous, efficient, and economical administration of that Department. . . .

🐝 🐝 🐝

. . . Since your last meeting at this place the fiftieth anniversary of the day when our independence was declared has been celebrated throughout our land, and on that day . . . two of the principal actors in that solemn scene—the hand that penned the ever-memorable Declaration and the voice that sustained it in debate— were by one summons, at the distance of 700 miles from each other, called before the Judge of All to account for their deeds done upon earth. They departed cheered by the benedictions of their country, to which they left the inheritance of their fame and the memory of their bright example. . . .

JOHN QUINCY ADAMS
THIRD STATE-OF-THE-UNION MESSAGE
WASHINGTON, *December 4, 1827*

Fellow-Citizens of the Senate and of the House of Representatives:
    . . . It is no small addition to the sum of our national happiness at this time that peace and prosperity prevail to a degree seldom experienced over the whole habitable globe. . . .

🐝 🐝 🐝

In the execution of the treaties of peace of November, 1782, and September, 1783, between the United States and Great Britain, which terminated the war of our independence, a line of boundary was drawn as the demarcation of territory between the two countries, extending over near 20 degrees of latitude, and ranging over seas, lakes, and mountains, then very imperfectly explored and scarcely opened to the geographical knowledge of the age. In the progress of discovery and settlement by both parties since that time several questions of boundary between their respective territories have arisen, which have been found of exceedingly difficult adjustment. . . .
    . . . Incidents have occurred of conflicting pretensions and of

dangerous character upon the territory itself in dispute between the two nations. . . .

🐝 🐝 🐝

In the American hemisphere the cause of freedom and independence has continued to prevail. Our friendly wishes and cordial good will, which have constantly followed the southern nations of America in all the vicissitudes of their war of independence, are succeeded by a solicitude equally ardent and cordial that by the wisdom and purity of their institutions they may secure to themselves the choicest blessings of social order and the best rewards of virtuous liberty. . . .

🐝 🐝 🐝

The deep solicitude felt by our citizens of all classes throughout the Union for the total discharge of the public debt will apologize for the earnestness with which I deem it my duty to urge this topic upon the consideration of Congress—of recommending to them again the observance of the strictest economy in the application of the public funds. . . .

🐝 🐝 🐝

. . . The fortification of the coasts and the gradual increase and improvement of the Navy are parts of a great system of national defense which has been upward of ten years in progress, and which for a series of years to come will continue to claim the constant and persevering protection and superintendence of the legislative authority. The establishment of a naval academy, furnishing the means of theoretic instruction to the youths who devote their lives to the service of their country upon the ocean, still solicits the sanction of the Legislature. . . .

🐝 🐝 🐝

Among the subjects which have heretofore occupied the earnest solicitude and attention of Congress is the management and disposal of . . . the public lands. . . . Under the present Government of the United States a sum little short of $33,000,000 has been paid from the common Treasury for that portion of this property which has been purchased from France and Spain, and for the extinction of the aboriginal titles. The amount of lands acquired is near 260,000,000 acres, of which on the 1st of January, 1826, about 139,000,000 acres had been surveyed, and little more than 19,000,000 acres had been sold. . . .

JOHN QUINCY ADAMS
FOURTH STATE-OF-THE-UNION MESSAGE
WASHINGTON, *December 2, 1828*

Fellow-Citizens of the Senate and of the House of Representatives:
        In the relations of our Federal Union with our brethren of the human race the changes which have occurred since the close of your last session have generally tended to the preservation of peace and to the cultivation of harmony. . . .
        The last friendly expedient has been resorted to for the decision of the controversy with Great Britain relating to the northeastern boundary of the United States. By an agreement with the British Government, carrying into effect the provisions of the fifth article of the Treaty of Ghent, and the convention of 29th September, 1827, His Majesty the King of the Netherlands has by common consent been selected as the umpire between the parties.

⁂ ⁂ ⁂

        The tariff of the last session was in its details not acceptable to the great interests of any portion of the Union, not even to the interest which it was specially intended to subserve. Its object was to balance the burdens upon native industry imposed by the operation of foreign laws, but not to aggravate the burdens of one section of the Union by the relief afforded to another. . . . Let a careful revisal of its provisions be directed to retain those which impart protection to native industry and remove or supply the place of those which only alleviate one great national interest by the depression of another.

⁂ ⁂ ⁂

        The attention of Congress is particularly invited to that part of the report of the Secretary of War which concerns the existing system of our relations with the Indian tribes. At the establishment of the Federal Government under the present Constitution of the

United States the principle was adopted of considering them as foreign and independent powers and also as proprietors of lands. They were, moreover, considered as savages, whom it was our policy and our duty to use our influence in converting to Christianity and in bringing within the pale of civilization.

As independent powers, we negotiated with them by treaties; as proprietors, we purchased of them all the lands which we could prevail upon them to sell; as brethren of the human race, rude and ignorant, we endeavored to bring them to the knowledge of religion and of letters. . . . In the practice of European States, before our Revolution, they had been considered *as children* to be governed; as tenants at discretion, to be dispossessed as occasion might require; as hunters to be indemnified by trifling concessions for removal from the grounds from which their game was extirpated. But in appropriating to ourselves their hunting grounds we have brought upon ourselves the obligation of providing them with subsistence; and . . . we have unexpectedly found them forming in the midst of ourselves communities claiming to be independent of ours and rivals of sovereignty within the territories of the members of our Union. This state of things requires that a remedy should be provided. . . . As the outline of a project to that effect, the views presented in the report of the Secretary of War are recommended to the consideration of Congress.

๛ ๛ ๛

Of these great national undertakings [by the Engineering Department] the Academy at West Point is among the most important in itself and the most comprehensive in its consequences. In that institution a part of the revenue of the nation is applied to defray the expense of educating a competent portion of her youth chiefly to the knowledge and the duties of military life. It is the living armory of the nation. . . .

ANDREW JACKSON
(1829–1837)

*"I will be
President of the nation
and not of a party"*

So said *Andrew Jackson,* who, in 1828, was swept into the White House on a surge of protest votes. Jackson, "Old Hickory," carried sixteen of the twenty-four states, with 178 electoral votes and 647,286 popular votes. John Quincy Adams, running for reelection against the man he had defeated in 1824, came off with 83 electorals and 508,064 popular. Born in a log cabin in South Carolina, Jackson came from the stratum Lincoln later defined as "the common people."

Old Hickory's election was really a social revolution, accompanied by the most ferocious mud-slinging in presidential history. In this contest the Democrats (an old party with a new look) squared off with the National Republicans. Both were spin-offs of Jefferson's old Democratic-Republicans, both plumbed the depths of scurrility in the mad scramble for votes.

In 1828, the American people had their first chance to vote for President. Voting qualifications based on religion and property ownership, with restrictions on white male suffrage, were being discarded. For the first time elaborate party machinery was set up, with keen politicians at the wheel. Steering Jackson's bandwagon was the smoothest political operator in America, Martin (Matty) Van Buren, then United States Senator and erstwhile Governor of New York. Matty invented the spoils system so much associated with Jackson's administrations.

Jackson spoke the language of the frontier. In the election the eleven frontier States had played an impressive role, voting solidly for him. He had won his first renown as a frontier judge and learned his politics in the rough-and-tumble backwoods of Tennessee. Duelist, cockfighter, horse racer, slave owner, and hard swearer, he became spokesman for the transmontane settlers. The glory of his victories over the Creeks at Horseshoe Bend and over the British at New Orleans in 1815 never lost its luster. Nor did his popularity ever lag. Twice he served Tennessee in the United States Senate.

His inauguration at Washington on March 4, 1829, was hilarious. Groaned Judge Story, "King Mob seemed triumphant," while poet-lawyer Francis Scott Key murmured ecstatically, "It is beautiful, it is sublime." Jackson took office with majorities in both the Senate and House of Representatives.

Jackson's State-of-the-Union Messages had a like-it-or-not quality. Bluff, determined, he used plain talk. His words seldom needed explanation. Nor did he ever employ disguised, hidden meanings.

In his first message he fired the opening shot of his forthright attack on the Bank of the United States, whose charter would come up for renewal by Congress in 1836.

This same message brought dismay to hundreds of government workers by announcing a new patronage maxim that Jackson called "rotation in office," but was translated historically into "spoils system." During Jackson's eight years, more than twenty-five hundred government workers were "rotated" out of office, one-fifth of all Federal job-holders. The repercussions of this message struck fear throughout the government. Anguished outcries of the dismissed rose high as Jackson's headsmen invaded every department. Public office, he averred, could no longer be looked on as a "species of property."

With revolutionary ardor he advocated abolishing the electoral college and asked removal of "all intermediate agency" in the election of President and Vice President. He urged: Let the popular votes of the people elect their President and let him be limited to a single term of four to six years. He repeated this same proposal in each of his seven State-of-the-Union Messages to follow. It never got anywhere.

The 1829 message clearly foreshadowed Jackson's policy of removal of the Cherokees, Creeks, and other tribes to land west of the Mississippi. His Indian Removal Act was passed by Congress within three months. It was this policy that led to his celebrated defiance of the Supreme Court: "John Marshall has made his decision. Now let him enforce it." Jackson always insisted that the executive had as much right as the judiciary to decide constitutional questions, which, in this case, involved the right of the Cherokees to maintain a separate state within the borders of Georgia.

But Jackson said not a word about the "petticoat war" that raged in 1829 over the social status of luscious Peggy Eaton, former barmaid and now wife of John Eaton, Jackson's Secretary of War. When other Cabinet wives snubbed her, Jackson rushed to her rescue. The upshot of this imbroglio, in which Bellona's virginity or lack of it was involved, was the dissolution of Jackson's first Cabinet.

Jackson began his second message jubilantly. Peace and plenty prevailed. He gave the nation a lift by prophesying extinction of the national debt and proposed that the ensuing surplus be distributed back to the states.

He vindicated his veto of several hotly contested bills permitting the government to invest in stock of private companies engaged in internal improvements, notably the Lexington-Maysville Road and the Louisville-Portland Canal Company. He concluded his message with a louder warning against the Bank of the United States and the "dangers which many of our citizens apprehend from that institution."

Jackson announced bluntly in his fourth message his intention of collecting some twenty-five million francs from France for spoliation of American commerce during the Napoleonic Wars. France had promised to pay but had reneged. When Jackson threatened to use force, France paid up in a hurry.

This same message reveals a little of the fierce clashes on Capitol Hill on the tariff, states rights, slavery, and other issues. He said nothing of the great Webster-Hayne debate in the Senate on the nature of the Union. Nor did he refer to his battles, with the Clay-Calhoun-Webster combine working to defeat his policies at every turn. He dismissed the nullification crisis in South Carolina with the assurance that the federal Union and South Carolina would soon conciliate their differences. Yet at that moment he was drafting the flaming proclamation that would demolish nullification overnight.

Congress had that year passed the bill rechartering the Bank of the United States, and Jackson had killed it with a resounding veto. Now, in his fourth message (1832), he wondered if the deposits of the government were really safe in the bank, thus presaging their removal, which stirred up a hornet's nest on Capitol Hill.

He also offered his famous recommendation on public lands, suggesting that, instead of being a source of revenue, they be sold to settlers at a price sufficient to pay the cost of surveying and selling.

And he congratulated the nation on the "near approach" of the extinction of the public debt, which Jackson accomplished in 1835, for the first and only time in American history.

He was overwhelmingly reelected in November, 1832. In his Fifth State-of-the-Union Message he explained the removal of the government deposits from the Bank of the United States—on his own responsibility he had ordered the removal because of "misconduct" by the bank's officials and the bank's attempt by huge loans to influence public officials—but he said nothing of the resolution steam-rollered through the Senate by Clay, Webster, and Calhoun condemning him for the removals.

He referred again to attempts to appropriate national funds to private works. "I am not hostile to internal improvements," he declared.

The slavery issue emerged with vehemence in his seventh message. A slave owner himself, Jackson denounced the "incendiary publications" broadcast by the abolitionists, notably William Lloyd Garrison with his *Liberator* and other literature inciting slaves to insurrection. He asked for a law that would forbid the post office to circulate such literature in the Southern states.

His last message was the calm before the storm, though Jackson must have seen it coming. The economic structure began tumbling. "Jackson prosperity" was wavering. The orgy of speculation collapsed when Jackson issued his Specie Circular requiring gold and silver in payment for government land. "Hard money" was scarce, and the Specie Circular had discredited all bank paper. The Distribution Act, apportioning the $37,000,000 surplus among the states, had touched off a fresh speculative splurge, but hard times were near.

Jackson closed with his final appeal to abolish the electoral college. It was his eighth demand for this change.

ANDREW JACKSON
FIRST STATE-OF-THE-UNION MESSAGE
December 8, 1829

Fellow-Citizens of the Senate and House of Representatives:

It affords me pleasure to tender my friendly greetings to you. . . . The task devolves on me . . . to present to you . . . a view of our affairs, and to propose such measures as . . . have suggested themselves as necessary to promote the objects of our Union.

≡ ≡ ≡

Our foreign relations, although in their general character pacific and friendly, present subjects of difference between us and other powers of deep interest as well to the country at large as to many of our citizens. . . .

From France, our ancient ally, we have a right to expect that justice which becomes the sovereign of a powerful, intelligent, and magnanimous people. . . . The claims of our citizens for depredations upon their property . . . remain unsatisfied, and must therefore continue to furnish a subject of unpleasant discussion and possible collision between the two Governments. . . .

The southern Republics of our own hemisphere have not yet realized all the advantages for which they have been so long struggling. We trust, however, that the day is not distant when the restoration of peace and internal quiet . . . will crown with complete success their long and arduous efforts in the cause of self-government. . . .

≡ ≡ ≡

I consider it one of the most urgent of my duties to bring to your attention the propriety of amending that part of our Constitution which relates to the election of President and Vice-President. Our system of government was by its framers deemed an experiment, and they therefore consistently provided a mode of remedying its defects.

To the people belongs the right of electing their Chief Magistrate; it was never designed that their choice should in any case be defeated, either by the intervention of electoral colleges or by the agency confided, under certain contingencies, to the House of Representatives. . . .

. . . Under the present mode of election a minority may often elect a President, and when this happens it may reasonably be expected that efforts will be made on the part of the majority to rectify this injurious operation of their institutions. But although no evil of this character should result from such a perversion of the first principle of our system—*that the majority is to govern*—

it must be very certain that a President elected by a minority can not enjoy the confidence necessary to the successful discharge of his duties.

. . . I would therefore recommend such an amendment of the Constitution as may remove all intermediate agency in the election of the President and Vice-President. . . . In connection with such an amendment it would seem advisable to limit the service of the Chief Magistrate to a single term of either four or six years. . . .

There are perhaps few men who for any great length of time enjoy office and power without being more or less under the influence of feelings unfavorable to the faithful discharge of their public duties. They are apt to acquire a habit of looking with indifference upon the public interests and tolerating conduct from which an unpracticed man would revolt. Office is considered a species of property, and Government rather as a means of promoting individual interests than as an instrument created solely for the service of the people. . . .

The duties of all public officers are so plain and simple that men of intelligence may readily qualify themselves for their performance. . . . I submit, therefore, to your consideration whether the efficiency of the Government would not be promoted and official industry and integrity better secured by a general extension of the law which limits appointments to four years.

In a country where offices are created solely for the benefit of the people no one man has any more intrinsic right to official station than another. Offices were not established to give support to particular men at the public expense. No individual wrong is, therefore, done by removal since neither appointment to nor continuance in office is a matter of right. . . . The proposed limitation would destroy the idea of property now so generally connected with official station. It would, by promoting that rotation which constitutes a leading principle in the republican creed, give healthful action to the system.

After the extinction of the public debt it is not probable that any adjustment of the tariff upon principles satisfactory to the people of the Union will until a remote period, if ever, leave the Government without a considerable surplus in the Treasury beyond what may be required for its current service. As, then, the period approaches when the application of the revenue to the payment of debt will cease, the disposition of the surplus will present a subject for the serious deliberation of Congress; and it may be fortunate for the country that it is yet to be decided. . . .

I recommend to your fostering care, as one of our safest means of national defense, the Military Academy. This institution has already exercised the happiest influence upon the moral and intellectual character of our Army. . . .

I would also suggest a review of the pension law, for the purpose of extending its benefits to every Revolutionary soldier who aided in establishing our liberties, and who is unable to maintain himself in comfort. These relics of the War of Independence have strong claims upon their country's gratitude and bounty. . . .

The condition and ulterior destiny of the Indian tribes within the limits of some of our States have become objects of much interest and importance. It has long been the policy of Government to introduce among them the arts of civilization, in the hope of gradually reclaiming them from a wandering life. A portion, however, of the Southern tribes . . . have lately attempted to erect an independent government within the limits of Georgia and Alabama. These States, claiming to be the only sovereigns within their territories, extended their laws over the Indians, which induced the latter to call upon the United States for protection. . . .

Under these circumstances the question presented was whether the General Government had a right to sustain those people in their pretensions. The Constitution declares that "no new State shall be formed or erected within the jurisdiction of any other State" without the consent of its legislature. If the General Government is not permitted to tolerate the erection of a confederate State within the territory of one of the members of this Union against her consent, much less could it allow a foreign and inde-

pendent government to establish itself there. There is no constitutional, conventional, or legal provision which allows them less
power over the Indians within their borders than is possessed by
Maine or New York. . . .

Actuated by this view of the subject, I informed the Indians
inhabiting parts of Georgia and Alabama that their attempt to
establish an independent government would not be countenanced
by the Executive of the United States, and advised them to emigrate beyond the Mississippi or submit to the laws of those States.

This emigration should be voluntary, for it would be as cruel as
unjust to compel the aborigines to abandon the graves of their
fathers and seek a home in a distant land. But they should be distinctly informed that if they remain within the limits of the States
they must be subject to their laws. . . .

The charter of the Bank of the United States expires in 1836,
and its stockholders will most probably apply for a renewal of
their privileges. In order to avoid the evils resulting from pre-
cipitancy in a measure involving such important principles and
such deep pecuniary interests, I feel that I can not . . . too soon
present it to the deliberate consideration of the Legislature and
the people. Both the constitutionality and the expediency of the
law creating this bank are well questioned by a large portion of
our fellow-citizens, and it must be admitted by all that it has
failed in the great end of establishing a uniform and sound currency.

I can not close this communication without bringing to your
view the just claim of the representatives of Commodore Decatur,
his officers and crew, arising from the recapture of the frigate
Philadelphia under the heavy batteries of Tripoli. . . . Besides
the justice of this claim, . . . it is the fruit of a deed of patriotic
and chivalrous daring which infused life and confidence into our
infant Navy and contributed . . . to elevate our national character. . . .

ANDREW JACKSON
SECOND STATE-OF-THE-UNION MESSAGE
December 6, 1830

Fellow-Citizens of the Senate and House of Representatives:

The pleasure I have in congratulating you upon your return to your constitutional duties is much heightened by the satisfaction which the condition of our beloved country at this period justly inspires. . . .

▰ ▰ ▰

Almost at the moment of the adjournment of your last session two bills—the one entitled "An act for making appropriations for building light-houses, light-boats, beacons, and monuments, placing buoys, and for improving harbors and directing surveys," and the other "An act to authorize a subscription for stock in the Louisville and Portland Canal Company"—were submitted for my approval. . . . I now avail myself of this early opportunity to return them to the Houses in which they respectively originated with the reasons which, after mature deliberation, compel me to withhold my approval.

▰ ▰ ▰

From a bill making *direct* appropriations for such objects I should not have withheld my assent. The one now returned does so in several particulars, but it also contains appropriations for surveys of a local character, which I can not approve. . . .
. . . The practice of thus mingling the concerns of the Government with those of the States or of individuals is inconsistent with the object of its institution and highly impolitic. . . .

The power which the General Government would acquire within the several States by becoming the principal stockholder in corporations, controlling every canal and each 60 or 100 miles of every important road, and giving a proportionate vote in all their elections, is almost inconceivable, and in my view dangerous to the liberties of the people.

▰ ▰ ▰

Humanity has often wept over the fate of the aborigines of this country, and Philanthropy has been long busily employed in devising means to avert it, but its progress has never for a moment been arrested, and one by one have many powerful tribes disappeared from the earth. To follow to the tomb the last of this race and to tread on the graves of extinct nations excite melancholy reflections. . . . Philanthropy could not wish to see this continent restored to the condition in which it was found by our forefathers. What good man would prefer a country covered with forests and ranged by a few thousand savages to our extensive Republic, studded with cities, towns, and prosperous farms, embellished with all the improvements which art can devise or industry execute, occupied by more than 12,000,000 happy people, and filled with all the blessings of liberty, civilization, and religion? . . .

And is it supposed that the wandering savage has a stronger attachment to his home than the settled, civilized Christian? Is it more afflicting to him to leave the graves of his fathers than it is to our brothers and children? Rightly considered, the policy of the General Government toward the red man is not only liberal, but generous. He is unwilling to submit to the laws of the States and mingle with their population. To save him from this alternative, or perhaps utter annihilation, the General Government kindly offers him a new home, and proposes to pay the whole expense of his removal and settlement.

While the chief object of duties should be revenue, they may be so adjusted as to encourage manufactures. In this adjustment, however, it is the duty of the Government to be guided by the general good. Objects of national importance alone ought to be protected. Of these the productions of our soil, our mines, and our workshops, essential to national defense, occupy the first rank. . . .

The present tariff taxes some of the comforts of life unnecessarily high; it undertakes to protect interests too local and minute to justify a general exaction, and it also attempts to force some kinds of manufactures for which the country is not ripe. Much relief will be derived in some of these respects from the measures of your last session.

The importance of the principles involved in the inquiry whether it will be proper to recharter the Bank of the United States requires that I should again call the attention of Congress to the subject. . . . In the spirit of improvement and compromise which distinguishes our country and its institutions it becomes us to inquire whether it be not possible to secure the advantages afforded by the present bank through the agency of a Bank of the United States so modified in its principles and structure as to obviate constitutional and other objections. . . .

ANDREW JACKSON
THIRD STATE-OF-THE-UNION MESSAGE
December 6, 1831

Fellow-Citizens of the Senate and House of Representatives:

In my message at the opening of the last session of Congress I expressed a confident hope that the justice of our claims upon France . . . would finally be acknowledged. This hope has been realized. A treaty has been signed which . . . must have the concurrence of both Houses before it can be carried into effect. By it the French Government engage to pay a sum which . . . will . . . be deemed satisfactory by those interested. . . .

I have heretofore recommended amendments of the Federal Constitution giving the election of President and Vice-President to the people and limiting the service of the former to a single term. So important do I consider these changes in our fundamental law that I can not . . . omit to press them upon the consideration of a new Congress. . . .

The extension of the judiciary system of the United States is deemed to be one of the duties of Government. One-fourth of the States in the Union do not participate in the benefits of a circuit

ANDREW JACKSON
FIFTH STATE-OF-THE-UNION MESSAGE
December 3, 1833

Fellow-Citizens of the Senate and House of Representatives:
. . . It gives me pleasure to congratulate you upon the happy condition of our beloved country. . . .

Our condition abroad is no less honorable than it is prosperous at home. Seeking nothing that is not right and determined to submit to nothing that is wrong, . . . the United States have gained throughout the world the confidence and respect which are due to a policy so just and so congenial to the character of the American people and to the spirit of their institutions. . . .

From this view of the state of the finances and the public engagements yet to be fulfilled you will perceive that if Providence permits me to meet you at another session I shall have the high gratification of announcing to you that the national debt is extinguished. . . . We have waged two wars since we became a nation, with one of the most powerful kingdoms in the world, . . . both successfully prosecuted and honorably terminated; and many of those who partook in the first struggle as well as in the second will have lived to see the last item of the debt incurred in these necessary but expensive conflicts faithfully and honestly discharged. . . .

The flourishing state of the finances ought not, however, to encourage us to indulge in a lavish expenditure of the public treasure. . . . The changes made in our revenue system by the acts of Congress of 1832 and 1833, and more especially by the former, have swelled the receipts of the present year far beyond duties. . . . I can not, therefore, recommend to you any alteration in the present tariff of duties. The rate as now fixed by law on the various articles was adopted at the last session of Congress, . . . and unless it is found to produce more than the necessities of the Government call for there would seem to be no reason at this time to justify a change.

Since the last adjournment of Congress the Secretary of the Treasury has directed the money of the United States to be deposited in certain State banks designated by him. . . . I concur with him entirely in the view he has taken of the subject, and some months before the removal I urged upon the Department the propriety of taking that step. . . . It was not until late in the month of August that I received from the Government directors an official report establishing beyond question that this great and powerful institution had been actively engaged in attempting to influence the elections of the public officers by means of its money. . . .

It being thus established by unquestionable proof that the Bank of the United States was converted into a permanent electioneering engine, it appeared to me that the path of duty which the executive department of the Government ought to pursue was not doubtful. . . .

At this time the efforts of the bank to control public opinion, through the distresses of some and the fears of others, are equally apparent, and, if possible, more objectionable. By a curtailment of its accommodations more rapid than any emergency requires, and even while it retains specie to an almost unprecedented amount in its vaults, it is attempting to produce great embarrassment in one portion of the community, while through presses known to have been sustained by its money, it attempts by unfounded alarms to create a panic in all.

. . . In my own sphere of duty I should feel myself called on by the facts disclosed to order a *scire facias* against the bank, with a view to put an end to the chartered rights it has so palpably violated, were it not that the charter itself will expire as soon as a decision would probably be obtained from the court of last resort. . . .

ANDREW JACKSON
SIXTH STATE-OF-THE-UNION MESSAGE
December 1, 1834

Fellow-Citizens of the Senate and House of Representatives:
        In performing my duty at the opening of your present session it gives me pleasure to congratulate you again upon the prosperous condition of our beloved country. . . .

Our foreign relations continue, with but few exceptions, to maintain the favorable aspect which they bore in my last annual message. . . .

Not only has the French Government been wanting in the performance of the stipulations it has so solemnly entered into with the United States, but its omissions have been marked by circumstances which would seem to leave us without satisfactory evidences that such performance will certainly take place at a future period. . . .

It is my conviction that the United States ought to insist on a prompt execution of the treaty, and in case it be refused or longer delayed take redress into their own hands. . . .

. . . I recommend that a law be passed authorizing reprisals upon French property in case provision shall not be made for the payment of the debt at the approaching session of the French Chambers.

Collision with France is the more to be regretted on account of the position she occupies in Europe in relation to liberal institutions, but in maintaining our national rights and honor all governments are alike to us. . . .

Circumstances make it my duty to call the attention of Congress to the Bank of the United States. Created for the convenience of the Government, that institution has become the scourge of the people. Its interference to postpone the payment of a portion of the national debt that it might retain the public money appropriated for that purpose to strengthen it in a political contest, the extraordinary extension and contraction of its accommodations to the community, its corrupt and partisan loans, its exclusion of the public directors from a knowledge of its most important proceedings, the unlimited authority conferred on the president to expend its funds in hiring writers and procuring the execution of printing, and the use made of that authority, the retention of the pension money and books after the selection of new agents, the groundless claim to heavy damages in consequence of the protest of the bill drawn on the French Government, have through various channels been laid before Congress. . . .

.≈ .≈ .≈

It seems due to the safety of the public funds remaining in that bank and to the honor of the American people that measures be taken to separate the Government entirely from an institution so mischievous to the public prosperity and so regardless of the Constitution and laws. By transferring the public deposits, by appointing other pension agents as far as it had the power, by ordering the discontinuance of the receipt of bank checks in the payment of the public dues after the 1st day of January, the Executive has exerted all its lawful authority to sever the connection between the Government and this faithless corporation.

.≈ .≈ .≈

Regarding the bill authorizing a subscription to the stock of the Maysville and Lexington Turnpike Company as the entering wedge of a system which, however weak at first, might soon become strong enough to rive the bands of the Union asunder, and believing that if its passage was acquiesced in by the Executive and the people, there would no longer be any limitation upon the authority of the General Government in respect to the appropriation of money for such objects, I deemed it an imperative duty to withhold from it the Executive approval.

From attempts to appropriate the national funds to objects which are confessedly of a local character we can not, I trust, have anything further to apprehend. My views in regard to the expedience of making appropriations for works which are claimed to be of a national character and prosecuted under State authority—assuming that Congress have the right to do so—were stated in my annual message to Congress in 1830, and also in that containing my objections to the Maysville road bill.

I am not hostile to internal improvements, and wish to see them extended to every part of the country. But I am fully persuaded, if they are not commenced in a proper manner, confined to proper objects, and conducted under an authority generally conceded to be rightful, that a successful prosecution of them can not be reasonably expected. The attempt will meet with resistance where it might otherwise receive support, and instead of strengthening the bonds of our Confederacy it will only multiply and aggravate the causes of disunion. . . .

ANDREW JACKSON
SEVENTH STATE-OF-THE-UNION MESSAGE
WASHINGTON, *December 7, 1835*

Fellow-Citizens of the Senate and House of Representatives:

Since the last session of Congress the validity of our claims upon France, as liquidated by the treaty of 1831, has been acknowledged by both branches of her legislature, and the money has been appropriated for their discharge; but the payment is, I regret to inform you, still withheld.

The subject had already been an affair of twenty years' uninterrupted negotiation, except for a short time when France was overwhelmed by the military power of united Europe. During this period, whilst other nations were extorting from her payment of their claims at the point of the bayonet, the United States intermitted their demand for justice out of respect to the oppressed condition of a gallant people to whom they felt under obligations for fraternal assistance in their own days of suffering and of peril. . . .

Disappointed in our just expectations, it became my imperative duty to consult with Congress in regard to the expediency of a resort to retaliatory measures in case the stipulations of the treaty should not be speedily complied with, and to recommend such as in my judgment the occasion called for. To this end an unreserved communication of the case in all its aspects became indispensable. I went out of my way to preclude a construction of the message by which the recommendation that was made to Congress might be regarded as a menace to France in not only disavowing such a design, but in declaring that her pride and her power were too well known to expect anything from her fears. . . .

The [French] minister of finance as the organ of the ministry declared the message, so long as it had not received the sanction of Congress, a mere expression of the personal opinion of the President, for which neither the Government nor people of the United States were responsible, and that an engagement had been entered into for the fulfillment of which the honor of France was pledged. . . .

       ▱   ▱   ▱

This is not the first time that the Government of France has taken exception to the messages of American Presidents. President Washington and the first President Adams in the performance of their duties to the American people fell under the animadversions of the French Directory. . . .

       ▱   ▱   ▱

The honor of my country shall never be stained by an apology from me for the statement of truth and the performance of duty; nor can I give any explanation of my official acts except such as is due to integrity and justice and consistent with the principles on which our institutions have been framed. This determination will, I am confident, be approved by my constituents. I have, indeed, studied their character to but little purpose if the sum of 25,000,-000 francs will have the weight of a feather in the estimation of what appertains to their national independence, and if, unhappily, a different impression should at any time obtain in any quarter, they will, I am sure, rally round the Government of their choice with alacrity and unanimity, and silence forever the degrading imputation.

Since my last annual communication all the remains of the public debt have been redeemed, or money has been placed in deposit for this purpose whenever the creditors choose to receive it. . . .

       ▱   ▱   ▱

The plan of removing the aboriginal people who yet remain within the settled portions of the United States to the country west of the Mississippi River approaches its consummation. . . .

The plan for their removal and reestablishment is founded upon the knowledge we have gained of their character and habits, and has been dictated by a spirit of enlarged liberality. A territory ex-

ceeding in extent that relinquished has been granted to each tribe.
. . . To these districts the Indians are removed at the expense of
the United States, and with certain supplies of clothing, arms,
ammunition, and other indispensable articles; they are also furnished gratuitously with provisions for the period of a year after
their arrival at their new homes. . . .

. . . I must also invite your attention to the painful excitement
produced in the South by attempts to circulate through the mails
inflammatory appeals addressed to the passions of the slaves . . .
calculated to stimulate them to insurrection. . . . There is doubtless no respectable portion of our countrymen who can . . . feel
any other sentiment than that of indignant regret at conduct so
destructive of the harmony and peace of the country, and so repugnant to the principles of our national compact and to the dictates of humanity and religion. . . .

. . . I would therefore call the special attention of Congress to
the subject, and respectfully suggest the propriety of passing such
a law as will prohibit, under severe penalties, the circulation in
the Southern States, through the mail, of incendiary publications
intended to instigate the slaves to insurrection.

I felt it to be my duty in the first message which I communicated
to Congress to urge upon its attention the propriety of amending
that part of the Constitution which provides for the election of
the President and the Vice-President of the United States. The
leading object which I had in view was the adoption of some new
provisions which would secure to the people the performance of
this high duty without any intermediate agency. In my annual communications since I have enforced the same views, from a sincere
conviction that the best interests of the country would be promoted
by their adoption. . . .

ANDREW JACKSON
EIGHTH STATE-OF-THE-UNION MESSAGE
WASHINGTON, *December 5, 1836*

Fellow-Citizens of the Senate and House of Representatives:

Addressing to you the last annual message I shall ever present to the Congress of the United States, it is a source of the most heartfelt satisfaction to be able to congratulate you on the high state of prosperity which our beloved country has attained. . . .

With France our diplomatic relations have been resumed. . . .

With Brazil and all our neighbors of this continent we continue to maintain relations of amity and concord. . . .

. . . The known desire of the Texans to become a part of our system . . . is calculated to expose our conduct to misconstruction in the eyes of the world. There are already those who, indifferent to principle themselves and prone to suspect the want of it in others, charge us with ambitious designs and insidious policy. . . .

The experience of other nations admonished us to hasten the extinguishment of the public debt; but it will be in vain that we have congratulated each other upon the disappearance of this evil if we do not guard against the equally great one of promoting the unnecessary accumulation of public revenue. No political maxim is better established than that which tells us that an improvident expenditure of money is the parent of profligacy. . . .

Under our present revenue system there is every probability that there will continue to be a surplus beyond the wants of the Government, and it has become our duty to decide whether such a result be consistent with the true objects of our Government.

Should a surplus be permitted to accumulate beyond the appropriations, it must be retained in the Treasury, as it now is, or distributed among the people or the States.

To retain it in the Treasury unemployed in any way is impracticable; it is, besides, against the genius of our free institutions to lock up in vaults the treasure of the nation. To take from the people the right of bearing arms and put their weapons of defense in the hands of a standing army would be scarcely more dangerous to their liberties than to permit the Government to accumulate immense amounts of treasure beyond the supplies necessary to its legitimate wants. Such a treasure would doubtless be employed at some time, as it has been in other countries, when opportunity tempted ambition.

The effects of an extension of bank credits and overissues of bank paper have been strikingly illustrated in the sales of the public lands. From the returns made by the various registers and receivers in the early part of last summer it was perceived that the receipts arising from the sales of the public lands were increasing to an unprecedented amount. In effect, however, these receipts amounted to nothing more than credits in bank. . . . Those credits on the books of some of the Western banks, usually called deposits, were already greatly beyond their immediate means of payment, and were rapidly increasing. Indeed, each speculation furnished means for another. . . .

The safety of the public funds and the interest of the people generally required that these operations should be checked; and it became the duty of every branch of the General and State Governments to adopt all legitimate and proper means to produce that salutary effect. Under this view of my duty I directed the issuing of the order which will be laid before you by the Secretary of the Treasury, requiring payment for the public lands sold to be made in specie, with an exception until the 15th of the present month in favor of actual settlers. This measure has produced many salutary consequences. . . .

It remains for Congress if they approve the policy which dictated this order to follow it up in its various bearings. Much good, in my judgment, would be produced by prohibiting sales of the public lands except to actual settlers at a reasonable reduction of price, and to limit the quantity which shall be sold to them. . . .

The lessons taught by the Bank of the United States can not well be lost upon the American people. They will take care never again to place so tremendous a power in irresponsible hands, and it will be fortunate if they seriously consider the consequences which are likely to result on a smaller scale from the facility with which corporate powers are granted by their State governments.

All my experience and reflection confirm the conviction I have so often expressed to Congress in favor of an amendment of the Constitution which will prevent in any event the election of the President and Vice President of the United States devolving on the House of Representatives and the Senate, and I therefore beg leave again to solicit your attention to the subject. . . .

Having now finished the observations deemed proper on this the last occasion I shall have of communicating with the two Houses of Congress at their meeting, I can not omit an expression of the gratitude which is due to the great body of my fellow-citizens, in whose partiality and indulgence I have found encouragement and support in the many difficult and trying scenes through which it has been my lot to pass during my public career. Though deeply sensible that my exertions have not been crowned with a success corresponding to the degree of favor bestowed upon me, I am sure that they will be considered as having been directed by an earnest desire to promote the good of my country, and I am consoled by the persuasion that whatever errors have been committed will find a corrective in the intelligence and patriotism of those who will succeed us. . . .

MARTIN VAN BUREN

(1837–1841)

The Little Magician
fails to pick prosperity
out of the air

On his way up the political ladder *Martin Van Buren* once observed, "To be President has ever been my most earnest desire . . . the great goal . . . the Ultima Thule of political life." He attained his goal on sunny, cold March 4, 1837.

Just before noon he and outgoing Andrew Jackson stepped into an elegant phaeton, made from timbers taken from the frigate *Old Ironsides* and drawn by four dappled grays, and drove off to the Capitol where, on the east portico, King Andrew the First lifted the diadem from his own grizzled head and placed it on the bald pate of King Martin the First. The crowds went wild. Van Buren's political adroitness had wafted him from potboy in his father's taproom at Kinderhook-on-the-Hudson to Chief Magistrate of the nation.

Posterity has never given Van Buren his due. The cyclone of ridicule whipped up against him by the Whigs in the 1840 campaign so deflated him that, even today, after 123 years, his prestige still lags. But these are facts: he was the master politician of all the Presidents; he was the first President born under the Stars and Stripes; he had more nicknames than any other President; and he was the best-dressed President.

Jackson had hand-picked Van Buren as his successor. In 1836, the "Little Magician," with Jackson's blessing, had prestidigitated 170

132

rabbits out of the electoral hat, 46 more than the total polled by his four opponents, chief of whom was General William Henry Harrison, whose dubious stand at Tippecanoe still wreathed him with military glory and political glamour. Van Buren ran off with 762,678 popular votes, but at that he only skinned through. With no majority for Vice President the Senate elected Richard M. Johnson of Kentucky, for Van Buren's running mate. Johnson's qualification for office was apparently the slaying of Tecumseh, the Shawnee chief, at the Battle of the Thames in 1812.

During his rise to the presidency, Van Buren had occupied various public posts, among them, Attorney General and Governor of New York, United States Senator, Minister to England, Secretary of State in Jackson's first Cabinet, and Vice President during Jackson's second term.

Van Buren created the New York political empire known as the Albany Regency and topped it off as Grand Sachem of Tammany Hall. Pinkish whiskers relieved his bald head. Sartorially he ran to colored coats with lace cuffs, yellow gloves, white trousers, and silk cravats. To this he added a superb elegance of manner.

Within three months after the coronation scene on the Capitol portico, Jackson's blaze-of-glory exit was snuffed out like a light. Prosperity vanished. The nation's economic structure collapsed over the luckless Van Buren's head. The crisis was hastened by several measures enacted during Jackson's last years in office. The Distribution Act, apportioning the Treasury surplus among the states, sent the nation zooming off on a last wild speculative splurge and its concomitant inflation. Alarmed by the volume of questionable paper, Jackson, to check speculation in public lands, had issued his famous Specie Circular, requiring hard money (gold or silver) in payment for government land. And the fight to destroy the Bank of the United States had not helped confidence.

The Depression of 1837 was the first in the nation's periodic cycles of boom and bust. Credit fell, trade vanished, hard times beset rich and poor alike. Thousands of discharged workers were starving. Immense fortunes melted away and bread riots broke out. On May 10, 1837, every bank in New York City closed its doors, followed shortly by banks in a dozen leading cities. Paper money lost its value, and real estate shot up to fantastic prices.

Meanwhile, Van Buren tried to stem the deluge with predictions of better times and a prosperity that was just around the corner. Not until bottom was reached in September, 1837, did he summon Congress in extra session to devise remedies for the nation's woes.

Van Buren's four State-of-the-Union Messages are run-of-the-mill, but his Special Panic Message had merit. He offered no panaceas, he disapproved of direct government aid to suffering people and he urged Congress to let business alone to right itself. To safeguard public funds in the future, he proposed his celebrated Sub-Treasury, or "Divorce," Bill: this would separate "Bank and State" by establishing an independent treasury with sub-treasuries in certain of the large cities to take care of the federal moneys that were then being handled by state banks. The Whig-controlled Congress stifled the bill, but in his first message Van Buren resubmitted his sub-treasury proposal, insisting that the great mass of the constituents of those who killed the bill were in favor of it and admonishing Congress to yield to what he believed was the voice of the people. But the Whigs, led by Henry Clay and Daniel Webster, repeatedly turned thumbs down on Van Buren's idea until the last days of his administration. Van Buren's proposal is today an integral part of the nation's monetary system.

In his first message, Van Buren used a cryptic sentence that brought hoots and howls of derision from the Whigs. He said, "We are blessed with all the elements of national prosperity." Such elements might exist, snickered the Whigs, but where were they? Why didn't the Little Magician pick prosperity out of the air?

Other problems rose to harass Van Buren. The slavery question was rising in intensity. Abolitionist propaganda flooded the nation. In Florida, the Seminoles refused to be transplanted beyond the Mississippi and resisted it bloodily. Along the northeastern boundary, sabers rattled in the so-called Aroostook War, which flared as Maine and New Brunswick lumberjacks clashed over the boundary claims of Canada and the United States. Complications with Mexico loomed as Texas, having won her revolution, sought to enter the Union.

MARTIN VAN BUREN
FIRST STATE-OF-THE-UNION MESSAGE
WASHINGTON, *December 5, 1837*

Fellow-Citizens of the Senate and House of Representatives:

The condition of our foreign relations has not materially changed since the last annual message of my predecessor. Of pending questions the most important is that which exists with the

Government of Great Britain in respect to our northeastern boundary. It is with unfeigned regret that the people of the United States must look back upon the abortive efforts made by the Executive, for a period of more than half a century, to determine what no nation should suffer long to remain in dispute—the true line which divides its possessions from those of other powers. . . .

Your attention was at the last session invited to the necessity of additional legislative provisions in respect to the collection, safe-keeping, and transfer of the public money. . . .

On that occasion three modes of performing this branch of the public service were presented for consideration. These were, the creation of a national bank; the revival, with modifications, of the deposit system established by the act of the 23d of June, 1836, permitting the use of the public moneys by the banks; and the discontinuance of the use of such institutions for the purposes referred to, with suitable provisions for their accomplishment through the agency of public officers. Considering the opinions of both Houses of Congress on the first two propositions as expressed in the negative, in which I entirely concur, it is unnecessary for me again to recur to them. In respect to the last, you have had an opportunity since your adjournment not only to test still further the expediency of the measure by the continued practical operation of such parts of it as are now in force, but also to discover what should ever be sought for and regarded with the utmost deference—the opinions and wishes of the people.

. . . The disposition of the public lands is one of the most important trusts confided to Congress. . . .

. . . Upward of 70,000,000 acres have been sold, the greater part of which is believed to have been purchased for actual settlement. The population of the new States and Territories created out of the public domain increased between 1800 and 1830 from less than 60,000 to upward of 2,300,000 souls, constituting at the latter period about one-fifth of the whole people of the United States. . . .

A large portion of our citizens have seated themselves on the public lands without authority since the passage of the last preemption law, and now ask the enactment of another to enable them to retain the lands occupied upon payment of the minimum Government price. They ask that which has been repeatedly granted before. If the future may be judged of by the past, little harm can be done to the interests of the Treasury by yielding to their request. . . .

The Military Academy continues to answer all the purposes of its establishment, and not only furnishes well-educated officers to the Army, but serves to diffuse throughout the mass of our citizens individuals possessed of military knowledge and the scientific attainments of civil and military engineering. At present the cadet is bound, with consent of his parents or guardians, to remain in service five years from the period of his enlistment. . . . This does not appear to me sufficient. . . .

MARTIN VAN BUREN
SECOND STATE-OF-THE-UNION MESSAGE
WASHINGTON, *December 3, 1838*

Fellow-Citizens of the Senate and House of Representatives:

The present year closes the first half century of our Federal institutions, and our system . . . has now been fully tested by experience.

The Constitution devised by our forefathers as the framework and bond of that system, then untried, has become a settled form of government; not only preserving and protecting the great principles upon which it was founded, but wonderfully promoting individual happiness and private interests. . . .

A convention for marking that part of the boundary between the United States and the Republic of Texas which extends from the mouth of the Sabine to the Red River was concluded and signed at this city on the 25th of April last. It has since been ratified by both Governments, and reasonable measures will be taken to carry it into effect on the part of the United States.

The application of that Republic for admission into this Union, made in August, 1837, and which was declined for reasons already made known to you, has been formally withdrawn.

It affords me sincere pleasure to be able to apprise you of the entire removal of the Cherokee Nation of Indians to their new homes west of the Mississippi. The measures authorized by Congress at its last session, with a view to the long-standing controversy with them, have had the happiest effects. . . .

MARTIN VAN BUREN
THIRD STATE-OF-THE-UNION MESSAGE
WASHINGTON, *December 2, 1839*

Fellow-Citizens of the Senate and House of Representatives:

I regret that I can not on this occasion congratulate you that the past year has been one of unalloyed prosperity. . . . Serious embarrassments yet derange the trade of many of our cities. . . .

For the settlement of our northeastern boundary the proposition promised by Great Britain for a commission of exploration and survey has been received, and a counter project, including also a provision for the certain and final adjustment of the limits in dispute, is now before the British Government for its consideration. A just regard to the delicate state of this question and a proper respect for the natural impatience of the State of Maine . . . have led me to believe that the present favorable moment should on no account be suffered to pass without putting the question forever at rest. . . .

. . . The creation in time of peace of a debt likely to become permanent is an evil for which there is no equivalent. The rapidity with which many of the States are apparently approaching to this

condition admonishes us of our duties in a manner too impressive
to be disregarded. . . .

        ▦   ▦   ▦

But let it be indelibly engraved on our minds that relief is not
to be found in expedients. Indebtedness can not be lessened by
borrowing more money or by changing the form of the debt. . . .
Our currency can not be improved by the creation of new banks
or more issues from those which now exist. . . . It is only by retrenchment and reform . . . that we are to expect effectual relief,
security for the future, and an enduring prosperity. . . .

MARTIN VAN BUREN
FOURTH STATE-OF-THE-UNION MESSAGE
WASHINGTON, *December 5, 1840*

Fellow-Citizens of the Senate and House of Representatives:
With all the powers of the world our relations are those of
honorable peace. . . . The excitement which grew out of the territorial controversy between the United States and Great Britain
having in a great measure subsided, it is hoped that a favorable
period is approaching for its final settlement. . . .

        ▦   ▦   ▦

When I entered upon the discharge of my official duties in
March, 1837, the act for the distribution of the surplus revenue
was in a course of rapid execution. Nearly $28,000,000 of the
public moneys were, in pursuance of its provisions, deposited with
the States in the months of January, April, and July of that year.
In May there occurred a general suspension of specie payments by
the banks, including, with very few exceptions, those in which the
public moneys were deposited and upon whose fidelity the Government had unfortunately made itself dependent for the revenues
which had been collected from the people and were indispensable
to the public service.

This suspension and the excesses in banking and commerce
out of which it arose, and which were greatly aggravated by its oc-

currence, made to a great extent unavailable the principal part of the public money then on hand, suspended the collection of many millions accruing on merchants' bonds, and greatly reduced the revenue arising from customs and the public lands. . . .

It affords me, however, great pleasure to be able to say that from the commencement of this period to the present day every demand upon the Government, at home or abroad, has been promptly met. This has been done not only without creating a permanent debt or a resort to additional taxation in any form, but in the midst of a steadily progressive reduction of existing burdens upon the people, leaving still a considerable balance of available funds which will remain in the Treasury at the end of the year. . . .

The new system established by Congress for the safekeeping of the public money, prescribing the kind of currency to be received for the public revenue and providing additional guards and securities against losses, has now been several months in operation. . . . A few changes and improvements in the details of the system, without affecting any principles involved in it, will be submitted to you by the Secretary of the Treasury, and will, I am sure, receive at your hands that attention to which they may on examination be found to be entitled.

. . . I have been guided in reference to two contested points in our public policy which were earliest in their development and have arisen under our complicated and difficult, yet admirable, system of government. I allude to a national debt and a national bank. . . .

Coming into office the declared enemy of both, I have earnestly endeavored to prevent a resort to either. . . .

The suppression of the African slave trade has received the continued attention of the Government. . . . It is hoped that by continuing to maintain this force in that quarter and by the exertions of the officers in command much will be done to put a stop to whatever portion of this traffic may have been carried on under the American flag. . . .

. . . I submit to your judgments whether this Government, having been the first to prohibit by adequate penalties the slave trade, the first to declare it piracy, should not be the first also to forbid to its citizens all trade with the slave factories on the coast of Africa, giving an example to all nations in this respect. . . .

JOHN TYLER
(1841–1845)

*"I appeal
to the impartial pen
of history"*

In 1840, the Whigs elected their first President, General *William Henry Harrison*, thanks to an orgy of log cabins, hard cider, coonskins, war whoops, and a campaign yowl, "Tippecanoe and Tyler, Too!" This extravaganza of political hocus-pocus, unsurpassed up to now, projected Harrison into the White House on a landslide of electoral votes.

Out of 294 votes in the electoral college, 234 went to Harrison and 60 to Martin Van Buren, who, running for reelection, never had a chance, saddled as he was with blame for the depression that dogged the nation like a nightmare. Surprisingly, Harrison's popular vote was only 6 per cent larger than his opponent's, but the Whigs had made the campaign so entertaining that the total popular vote was double that of the last presidential election.

Teamed with Harrison was a renegade Democrat, *John Tyler,* former United States Senator and Governor of Virginia. Tyler, an old-fashioned, pro-slavery states'-righter, had resigned from the Senate because he disagreed with Jackson on rechartering the Bank of the United States and on the Tariff of Abominations. Later, he had lined up with John C. Calhoun on nullification and states' rights.

When the Whigs nominated sixty-eight-year-old Harrison, he was a country gentleman, living in a big white house at North Bend, Ohio, where he served his stream of visitors an unvarying diet of ham—365

141

hams a year. As a leader to show the nation the way out of the depression, Harrison evaded all expressions of political opinion. What his future policies might have been can be gauged by his sole contribution to the Whig hullabaloo, a pathetic, almost incredible admission, "Should I be elected, I will give my assent to all laws which may pass both Houses of Congress, however much those laws may be against my own opinions and judgment."

But the Whig rejoicings over his election were short-lived. On the night of April 4, 1841, Harrison died in the White House (exactly one month after taking office), crying out in his last delirium against the swarms of Whig office seekers who camped in the hallways, refusing even to let him die in peace.

Vice President John Tyler promptly moved up to the top government spot, first President to be elevated to the office through the death of his predecessor. Tyler's administration soon degenerated into a political roughhouse. He inherited Harrison's Cabinet, but let it be known that he was boss and would tolerate no back talk, no foolishness from any of them. In short order Tyler vetoed Henry Clay's pet bill to create a new Bank of the United States. For this the Whigs outlawed him, and at a New York convention he was read out of the party. His Cabinet resigned in a body with the sole exception of Secretary of State Daniel Webster, who was engaged in settling the northeastern-boundary dispute with Great Britain. In four years Tyler changed his entire Cabinet four times. Never was a President more vilified. The Whigs hanged and burned him in effigy in a score of Northern cities. A resolution of impeachment was tried, but failed. Repudiated by the party that had elected him, he was dubbed the "President without a party." He went out of office probably the most unpopular of the Presidents. It took half a century for his sterling qualities to be appreciated.

Tyler's State-of-the-Union Messages reveal nothing of the bitterness between himself and the Whigs. Nor of the attempted impeachment resolution that failed to carry through the House.

In his first message, he confronted the nation with the unwelcome news that the Treasury was empty and that the bankers had refused to open their pocketbooks to the government. Slavery was the overshadowing question in America at that time, but his messages say little or nothing about it. The vital issue between the United States and Britain of which he speaks was the northeastern-boundary dispute that was settled peaceably in 1842 by the Webster-Ashburton Treaty.

His third message presaged the settlement of the Oregon question that would come two years later when James K. Polk called for a show-down with Britain. Admission of Texas to the Union was the thing nearest to Tyler's heart. She had already twice knocked at the door. In his message of December, 1844, Tyler urged Congress to enact a resolution authorizing the "immediate annexation" of Texas. He was prompted to do this by the election of James K. Polk in November on an expansionist platform, two of whose planks were "re-annexation of Texas and re-occupation of the whole of Oregon." The prefix *re* was used to avoid the possible stigma of aggression and further to imply that Texas was really a part of the Louisiana Territory pur-chased from France in 1803. Regarding Polk's election as a mandate for annexation, Tyler moved fast to seize the glory of acquiring Texas. Congress, also swayed by Polk's election, complied at once.

On March 1, 1845, three days before going out of office, Tyler signed the resolution and sped it off by express rider to Sam Houston, president of the Lone Star Republic. Tyler's signature on this treaty literally proclaimed the war with Mexico soon to follow.

JOHN TYLER
FIRST STATE-OF-THE-UNION MESSAGE
WASHINGTON, *December 7, 1841*

To the Senate and House of Representatives of the United States:
. . . At the opening of the last annual session the Presi-dent informed Congress of the progress which had then been made in negotiating a convention between this Government and that of England with a view to the final settlement of the question of the boundary between the territorial limits of the two countries. . . .

The commission appointed by this Government for the explora-tion and survey of the line of boundary separating the States of Maine and New Hampshire from the conterminous British Prov-inces is, it is believed, about to close its field labors and is ex-pected soon to report the results of its examinations to the Depart-ment of State. The report, when received, will be laid before Congress.

✪ ✪ ✪

The United States can not but take a deep interest in whatever relates to this young but growing Republic [Texas]. Settled principally by emigrants from the United States, we have the happiness to know that the great principles of civil liberty are there destined to flourish under wise institutions and wholesome laws, and that through its example another evidence is to be afforded of the capacity of popular institutions to advance the prosperity, happiness, and permanent glory of the human race. . . .

✪ ✪ ✪

I feel it my duty to bring under your consideration a practice which has grown up in the administration of the Government, and which, I am deeply convinced, ought to be corrected. I allude to the exercise of the power which usage rather than reason has vested in the Presidents of removing incumbents from office in order to substitute others more in favor with the dominant party. . . .

. . . It is of high importance to restrain as far as possible the stimulus of personal interests in public elections. Considering the great increase which has been made in public offices in the last quarter of a century and the probability of further increase, we incur the hazard of witnessing violent political contests, directed too often to the single object of retaining office by those who are in or obtaining it by those who are out. Under the influence of these convictions I shall cordially concur in any constitutional measure for regulating and, by regulating, restraining the power of removal. . . .

JOHN TYLER
SECOND STATE-OF-THE-UNION MESSAGE
WASHINGTON, *December 6, 1842*

To the Senate and House of Representatives of the United States:
I congratulate you, fellow-citizens, on the happy change in the aspect of our foreign affairs since my last annual message. Causes of complaint at that time existed between the United States and Great Britain which, attended by irritating circumstances, threatened most seriously the public peace. . . . It would have furnished additional cause for congratulation if the treaty

[Webster-Ashburton] could have embraced all subjects calculated in future to lead to a misunderstanding between the two Governments. . . .

. . . The Territory of the United States commonly called the Oregon Territory, . . . to a portion of which Great Britain lays claim, begins to attract the attention of our fellow-citizens. . . . Although the difficulty referred to may not for several years to come involve the peace of the two countries, yet I shall not delay to urge on Great Britain the importance of its early settlement. . . .

In revising the existing tariff of duties I can only repeat the suggestions and recommendations which upon several occasions I have heretofore felt it to be my duty to offer to Congress. . . . Extravagant duties defeat their end and object, not only by exciting in the public mind an hostility to the manufacturing interests, but by inducing a system of smuggling on an extensive scale and the practice of every manner of fraud upon the revenue, which the utmost vigilance of Government can not effectually suppress. I therefore . . . recommend moderate duties . . . as being . . . most advantageous to every interest of society.

○ ○ ○

. . . I felt it to be my duty to cause to be submitted to you at the commencement of your last session the plan of an exchequer, the whole power and duty of maintaining which in purity and vigor was to be exercised by the representatives of the people and the States, and therefore virtually by the people themselves. It was proposed to place it under the control and direction of a Treasury board to consist of three commissioners, whose duty it should be to see that the law of its creation was faithfully executed and that the great end of supplying a paper medium of exchange at all times convertible into gold and silver should be attained. Entertaining this opinion, it becomes my duty to urge its adoption upon Congress by reference to the strongest considerations of the public interests. . . .

○ ○ ○

It was the anxious desire of the Executive that in the effort to negotiate the loan [to keep the government solvent] abroad the American negotiator might be able to point the money lender to the fund mortgaged for the redemption of the principal and interest of any loan he might contract, and thereby vindicate the Government from all suspicion of bad faith or inability to meet its engagements. Congress differed from the Executive in this view of the subject. It became, nevertheless, the duty of the Executive to resort to every expedient in its power to do so.

After a failure in the American market a citizen of high character and talent was sent to Europe, with no better success; and thus the mortifying spectacle has been presented of the inability of this Government to obtain a loan so small as not in the whole to amount to more than one-fourth of its ordinary annual income. . . .

★ ★ ★

I recommend to Congress to take into consideration the propriety of reimbursing a fine imposed on General Jackson at New Orleans at the time of the attack and defense of that city, and paid by him. . . . The remission at this day may be regarded as not unjust or inexpedient. . . .

JOHN TYLER
THIRD STATE-OF-THE-UNION MESSAGE
WASHINGTON, *December, 1834*

To the Senate and House of Representatives of the United States:
. . . The treaty lately concluded with Great Britain has tended greatly to increase the good understanding which a reciprocity of interests is calculated to encourage. . . . A question of much importance still remains to be adjusted between them. The territorial limits of the two countries in relation to what is commonly known as the Oregon Territory still remain in dispute. . . . After the most rigid and, as far as practicable, unbiased examination of the subject, the United States have always contended that

their rights appertain to the entire region of country lying on the Pacific and embraced within 42° and 54°40′ of north latitude. This claim being controverted by Great Britain, those who have preceded the present Executive . . . have caused to be submitted to the British Government propositions for settlement and final adjustment, which, however, have not proved heretofore acceptable to it. . . .

✪ ✪ ✪

I communicate herewith certain dispatches received from our minister at Mexico. . . . It must but be regarded as not a little extraordinary that the Government of Mexico, in anticipation of a public discussion . . . in Congress, relating to the annexation of Texas to the United States, should have so far anticipated the result of such discussion as to have announced its determination to visit any such anticipated decision by a formal declaration of war against the United States. . . .

. . . Eight years have now elapsed since Texas declared her independence of Mexico, and during that time she has been recognized as a sovereign power by several of the principal civilized states. Mexico, nevertheless, perseveres in plans of reconquest, and refuses to recognize her independence. . . . This Government is bound by every consideration of interest as well as of sympathy to see that she [Texas] shall be left free to act, especially in regard to her domestic affairs, unawed by force and unrestrained by the policy or views of other countries. . . .

✪ ✪ ✪

I refer you particularly to that part of the Secretary's report which has reference to recent experiments in the application of steam and in the construction of our war steamers, made under the superintendence of distinguished officers of the Navy. . . . In addition to other manifest improvements in the construction of the steam engine and application of the motive power which has rendered them [steamships] more appropriate to the uses of ships of war, one of those officers has brought into use a power which makes the steamship most formidable either for attack or defense. I can not too strongly recommend this subject to your considera-

tion and do not hesitate to express my entire conviction of its
great importance.

○ ○ ○

It is due to every consideration of public policy that the lakes
and rivers of the West should receive all such attention at the
hands of Congress as the Constitution will enable it to bestow.
Works in favorable and proper situations on the lakes would be
found to be as indispensably necessary, in case of war, to carry
on safe and successful naval operations as fortifications on the
Atlantic seaboard. . . .

○ ○ ○

In connection with its other interests, as well as those of the
whole country, I recommend that at your present session you
adopt such measures in order to carry into effect the Smith-
sonian bequest as in your judgment will be best calculated to
consummate the liberal intent of the testator. . . .

JOHN TYLER
FOURTH STATE-OF-THE-UNION MESSAGE
WASHINGTON, *December 3, 1844*

To the Senate and House of Representatives of the United States:
. . . Since the close of your last session a negotiation has
been formally entered upon between the Secretary of State and
Her Britannic Majesty's minister plenipotentiary and envoy extraordinary residing at Washington relative to the rights of their
respective nations in and over the Oregon Territory. That negotiation is still pending.

○ ○ ○

In my last annual message I felt it to be my duty to make
known to Congress . . . my opinion in regard to the war which
has so long existed between Mexico and Texas. I repeat now what
I then said, that after eight years of feeble and ineffectual efforts to
reconquer Texas it was time that the War should have ceased. . . .
Since your last session Mexico has threatened to renew the

war. . . . A war of desolation, such as is now threatened by Mexico, can not be waged without involving our peace and tranquillity. . . .

. . . A controlling majority of the people and a large majority of the States have declared in favor of immediate annexation. . . . It is the will of both the people and the States that Texas shall be annexed to the Union promptly and immediately.

✪ ✪ ✪

. . . My happiness in the retirement which shortly awaits me is the ardent hope which I experience that this state of prosperity is neither deceptive nor destined to be short lived, and that measures which have not yet received its sanction, but which I can not but regard as closely connected with the honor, the glory, and still more enlarged prosperity of the country, are destined at an early day to receive the approval of Congress. . . .

JAMES K. POLK
(1845–1849)

*"Our manifest destiny
to overspread and possess
the whole of the continent"*

James Knox Polk, eleventh President, was the most ambitious expansionist ever to occupy our highest office. He was inaugurated March 4, 1845, standing in a driving rain on the Capitol steps with a bystander holding an umbrella over him.

Shortly after his inauguration, Polk revealed to George Bancroft, his Secretary of the Navy, that the four pet objectives of his administration were: "one, a reduction of the tariff; another, the independent treasury; third, the settlement of the Oregon boundary question; and, fourth, the acquisition of California." To these he might have added a fifth, his offer to buy Cuba from Spain for $100,000,000, though Cuba was never one of his prime goals.

To implement his program, he courted two wars and got one. Blessed with inflexible determination and ingrained patriotism, he achieved his first three objectives during the first year in office. To get California, he had to take it away from Mexico and that meant war. As to the unofficial fifth objective, Spain turned down Polk's offer, saying she would rather see Cuba "sunk in the ocean."

In May, 1844, at the Democratic convention in Baltimore, Polk had emerged as the first dark horse in presidential history. Martin Van Buren, still up to his old tricks, with a majority of the delegates pledged, apparently had the nomination in the bag, but somehow he

150

was unable to rally the necessary two-thirds. At this point, dark horse Polk was trotted out. His name was not even mentioned until the eighth ballot, when he got 44 votes. On the ninth, he romped off with 233 votes and the nomination bacon. So obscure was Polk that many of those who had nominated him began asking, "Who the hell is James K. Polk?"

To oppose Polk, the Whigs picked the once-debonair Kentucky charmer, Henry Clay, whose presidential aspirations were in their last blooming. In the ensuing campaign, Polk came down the home stretch with a lead of 1,337,243 popular votes to Clay's 1,299,068. Electorally, Polk did even better, 170 to 101.

For years after his death Polk was misunderstood and belittled, but he has emerged as one of the most powerful Presidents. Never was he a warm personality, or a good mixer. He possessed little personal magnetism, yet he represented his Tennessee district in the House of Representatives for fourteen years. After two years as Speaker of the House of the Twenty-seventh Congress, the Whigs refused to accord him the traditional vote of thanks because of his "most partial and unjust rulings." He was the only Speaker ever to graduate to the White House.

His besetting sin, if sin it was, was a passionate love of his country; party came second. Renomination was to him unthinkable. His health was ruined by his excessive labors, and he died within three months after leaving the White House. Polk was no statesman in the accepted sense, but he left behind a massive memorial. Only one President besides Polk could boast of adding over a million square miles to the nation's domain, an empire in itself.

The years of Polk's administration—1845–1849—were momentous ones for the nation. Jefferson's farm empire was passing the scepter to the industrial era. America's age of invention was setting in. Out in Ohio was born a child, Thomas A. Edison, whose wizardry would light up the world. A man named Charles Goodyear invented a vulcanizing process on which today's vast rubber industry was founded. With the acquisition of California the nation's march westward would reach the Pacific. Lush steamboats were plying the Mississippi and other navigable rivers, while New York's water front was lined with clippers that brought trade from the far corners of the world.

In 1845, a man named Edgar Allan Poe wrote a poem, "The Raven," that immortalized him. That same year saw the founding of the United States Naval Academy at Annapolis. New York City replaced Philadelphia as the nation's greatest commercial emporium. Fluffy white bolls of cotton were pouring wealth into the pockets of Southern planters. The tide of immigration was steadily rising—it would reach 370,000 by 1850. On the trails westward gleamed campfires of thousands of emigrants seeking new homes. At the Hermitage, near Nashville, died Andrew Jackson, who first caught the vision of Texas joining the Union. To climax it all came the fabulous gold rush to California 1848–49.

But a dark cloud hovered over these years of progress: the slavery issue that relentlessly split the nation. The cold war between North and South that had begun with the Missouri Compromise in 1819 was hurtling on toward the armed clash of the sixties.

Polk's State-of-the-Union Messages need little comment. Mexico, California (his most coveted prize), and Oregon dominated them. They are clear and explicit. Never did he deviate from his announced goals.

His first message spelled out mighty events: imminence of war with Mexico and a showdown with Britain on the Oregon question. In this same message he implemented the Monroe Doctrine by what is today designated the "Polk Doctrine," the essence of which was that the United States "cannot in silence permit any European interference on the American continent, and should any such interference be attempted, will be ready to resist it at any and all hazards."

Polk's War Message, asking hostilities against Mexico—May 11, 1846—was hotly attacked by the Whigs, notably by a lanky Congressman from Illinois, Abraham Lincoln, whose Spot Resolutions challenged Polk to identify the exact spot at which the Mexicans had shed American blood as stated by Polk in his message. Within two years American troops had overrun Mexico, destroyed her armies, and dictated the Treaty of Guadalupe Hidalgo, whereby Polk's dream of manifest destiny—"to overspread and possess the whole of the continent which Providence has given us for the great experiment in liberty"—was almost realized.

Polk's last State-of-the-Union Message touched off the Gold Rush of 1849, which would transform California into a state within two years. His simple statement that an "abundance of gold" had been discovered there caught the imagination of thousands, who dropped their toils in the East and joined the fevered rush west to dig for the yellow metal—and create a new El Dorado.

JAMES K. POLK
FIRST STATE-OF-THE-UNION MESSAGE
WASHINGTON, *December 2, 1845*

Fellow-Citizens of the Senate and House of Representatives:
. . . I am happy that I can congratulate you on the continued prosperity of our country.

In pursuance of the joint resolution of Congress "for annexing Texas to the United States," my predecessor, on the 3rd day of March, 1845, elected to submit the first and second sections of that resolution to the Republic of Texas as an overture on the part of the United States for her admission as a State into our Union. . . . The terms of annexation which were offered by the United States having been accepted by Texas, the public faith of both parties is solemnly pledged to the compact of their union. Nothing remains to consummate the event but the passage of an act by Congress to admit the State of Texas into the Union. . . .

This accession to our territory has been a bloodless achievement. No arm of force has been raised to produce the result. The sword has had no part in the victory. We have not sought to extend our territorial possessions by conquest, or our republican institutions over a reluctant people. . . .

Toward Texas I do not doubt that a liberal and generous spirit will actuate Congress in all that concerns her interests and prosperity, and that she will never have cause to regret that she has united her "Lone Star" to our glorious constellation.

I regret to inform you that our relations with Mexico since your last session have not been of the amicable character which it is our desire to cultivate with all foreign nations. On the 6th day of March last the Mexican envoy extraordinary and minister plenipotentiary to the United States made a formal protest against the joint resolution passed by Congress "for the annexation of Texas to the United States," which he chose to regard as a violation of the rights of Mexico, and in consequence of it he demanded his passports. . . .

Since that time Mexico has until recently occupied an attitude of hostility toward the United States. . . . I therefore deemed it proper, as a precautionary measure, to order a strong squadron to the coasts of Mexico and to concentrate an efficient military force on the western frontier of Texas. Our Army was ordered to take position in the country between the Nueces and the Del Norte, and to repel any invasion of the Texan territory which might be attempted by the Mexican forces. . . .

My attention was early directed to the negotiation which on the 4th of March last I found pending at Washington between the United States and Great Britain on the subject of the Oregon Territory. Several attempts had been previously made to settle the questions in dispute. . . .

On the 26th of August, 1844, the British plenipotentiary offered to divide the Oregon Territory by the forty-ninth parallel of north latitude from the Rocky Mountains to the point of its intersection with the northeasternmost branch of the Columbia River, and thence down that river to the sea, leaving the free navigation of the river to be enjoyed in common by both parties, the country south of this line to belong to the United States and that north of it to Great Britain. . . . The right of any foreign power to the free navigation of any of our rivers through the heart of our country was one which I was unwilling to concede. With this conviction the proposition . . . was by my direction subsequently withdrawn and our title to the whole Oregon Territory asserted, and, as is believed, maintained by irrefragable facts and arguments. . . . We shall have reached a period when the national rights in Oregon must either be abandoned or firmly maintained. That they can not be abandoned without a sacrifice of both national honor and interest is too clear to admit of doubt.

Oregon is a part of the North American continent, to which, it is confidently affirmed, the title of the United States is the best now in existence. . . .

The rapid extension of our settlements over our territories heretofore unoccupied, the addition of new States to our Confederacy, the expansion of free principles, and our rising greatness as a nation are attracting the attention of the powers of Europe and lately the doctrine has been broached in some of them of a "balance of power" on this continent to check our advancement. The United States, sincerely desirous of preserving relations of good understanding with all nations, can not in silence permit any European interference on the North American continent and should any such interference be attempted will be ready to resist it at any and all hazards.

We must ever maintain the principle that the people of this continent alone have the right to decide their destiny. Should any portion of them, constituting an independent State, propose to unite with our Confederacy, this will be a question for them and us to determine without any foreign interposition. We can never consent that European powers shall interfere to prevent such a union because it might disturb the "balance of power" they desire to maintain on this continent.

The attention of Congress is invited to the importance of making suitable modifications and reductions of the rates of duty imposed by our present tariff laws. The object of imposing duties on imports should be to raise revenue to pay the necessary expenses of Government. . . .

I trust it may not be deemed inappropriate to the occasion for me to dwell for a moment on the memory of the most eminent citizen of our country who during the summer that is gone by has descended to the tomb. The enjoyment of contemplating, at the advanced age of near fourscore years, the happy condition of his country cheered the last hours of Andrew Jackson, who departed this life in the tranquil hope of a blessed immortality. His death was happy, as his life had been eminently useful. . . . He departed amidst the benedictions of millions of free men. Coming generations will learn from his example the love of country and the rights of man.

JAMES K. POLK
SPECIAL WAR MESSAGE
WASHINGTON, *May 11, 1846*

To the Senate and House of Representatives:

The existing state of the relations between the United States and Mexico renders it proper that I should bring the subject to the consideration of Congress. . . .

In my message at the commencement of the present session I informed you that upon the earnest appeal both of the Congress and convention of Texas I had ordered an efficient military force to take a position "between the Nueces and the Del Norte." This had become necessary to meet a threatened invasion of Texas by the Mexican forces, for which extensive military preparations had been made. The invasion was threatened solely because Texas had determined, in accordance with a solemn resolution of the Congress of the United States, to annex herself to our Union, and under these circumstances it was plainly our duty to extend our protection over her citizens and soil.

✗ ✗ ✗

The movement of the troops to the Del Norte was made by the commanding general under positive instructions to abstain from all aggressive acts toward Mexico or Mexican citizens and to regard the relations between that Republic and the United States as peaceful unless she should declare war or commit acts of hostility indicative of a state of war. . . .

The Army moved from Corpus Christi on the 11th of March, and on the 28th of that month arrived on the left bank of the Del Norte opposite to Matamoros, where it encamped on a commanding position, which has since been strengthened by the erection of fieldworks. . . .

The Mexican forces at Matamoros assumed a belligerent attitude, and on the 12th of April General Ampudia, then in command, notified General Taylor to break up his camp within twenty-four hours and to retire beyond the Nueces River, and in the event of his failure to comply with these demands announced that arms, and arms alone, must decide the question. But no open act of hostility was committed until the 24th of April. On that day General Arista, who had succeeded to the command of the Mexican forces, communicated to General Taylor that "he considered hostilities commenced and should prosecute them." A party of dragoons of 63 men and officers were on the same day dispatched from the American camp up the Rio del Norte, on its left bank, to ascertain whether the Mexican troops had crossed or were preparing to cross the river, "became engaged with a large body of these troops, and after a short affair, in which some 16 were killed and wounded, appear to have been surrounded and compelled to surrender."

✗   ✗   ✗

. . . Upon the pretext that Texas, a nation as independent as herself, thought proper to unite its destinies with our own, she [Mexico] has affected to believe that we have severed her rightful territory, and in official proclamations and manifestoes has repeatedly threatened to make war upon us for the purpose of reconquering Texas. In the meantime we have tried every effort at reconciliation. The cup of forbearance had been exhausted even before the recent information from the frontier of the Del Norte. But now, after reiterated menaces, Mexico has passed the boundary of the United States, has invaded our territory and shed American blood upon the American soil. She has proclaimed that hostilities have commenced, and that the two nations are now at war.

✗   ✗   ✗

As war exists, and, notwithstanding all our efforts to avoid it, exists by the act of Mexico herself, we are called upon by every consideration of duty and patriotism to vindicate with decision the honor, the rights, and the interests of our country.

✗   ✗   ✗

In further vindication of our rights and defense of our territory, I invoke the prompt action of Congress to recognize the existence of the war, and to place at the disposition of the Executive the means of prosecuting the war with vigor, and thus hastening the restoration of peace. . . .

The most energetic and prompt measures and the immediate appearance in arms of a large and overpowering force are recommended to Congress as the most certain and efficient means of bringing the existing collision with Mexico to a speedy and successful termination. . . .

JAMES K. POLK
SECOND STATE-OF-THE-UNION MESSAGE
WASHINGTON, *December 8, 1846*

Fellow-Citizens of the Senate and of the House of Representatives:
    The existing war with Mexico was neither desired nor provoked by the United States. On the contrary, all honorable means were resorted to avert it. . . .

✕   ✕   ✕

Being involved in a war thus commenced by Mexico, and for the justice of which on our part we may confidently appeal to the whole world, I resolved to prosecute it with the utmost vigor.
    The various columns of the Army have performed their duty under great disadvantages with the most distinguished skill and courage. The victories of Palo Alto and Resaca de la Palma and of Monterey, won against greatly superior numbers and against most decided advantages in other respects on the part of the enemy, were brilliant in their execution, and entitle our brave officers and soldiers to the grateful thanks of their country. . . .

✕   ✕   ✕

The war has not been waged with a view to conquest, but, having been commenced by Mexico, it has been carried into the enemy's country and will be vigorously prosecuted there with a view to obtain an honorable peace, and thereby secure ample indemnity for the expenses of the war. . . .

✕   ✕   ✕

It will be important during your present session to establish a Territorial government and to extend the jurisdiction and laws of the United States over the Territory of Oregon. . . . As our citizens who now reside in that distant region have been subjected to many hardships, privations, and sacrifices in their emigration, and by their improvements have enhanced the value of the public lands in the neighborhood of their settlements, it is recommended that liberal grants be made to them of such portions of these lands as they may occupy, and that similar grants or rights of preemption be made to all who may emigrate thither within a limited period, prescribed by law. . . .

JAMES K. POLK
THIRD STATE-OF-THE-UNION MESSAGE
WASHINGTON, *December 7, 1847*

Fellow-Citizens of the Senate and of the House of Representatives:
        After an existence of near three-fourths of a century as a free and independent Republic, the problem no longer remains to be solved whether man is capable of self-government. The success of our admirable system is a conclusive refutation of the theories of those in other countries who maintain that a "favored few" are born to rule and that the mass of mankind must be governed by force. Subject to no arbitrary or hereditary authority, the people are the only sovereigns recognized by our Constitution.

X   X   X

No change has taken place in our relations with Mexico since the adjournment of the last Congress. The war in which the United States were forced to engage with the Government of that country still continues.

X   X   X

The existence of the war having thus been declared by Congress, it became my duty under the Constitution and the laws to conduct and prosecute it. . . . I have manifested a willingness to terminate it by a just peace. Mexico has refused to accede to any terms which could be accepted by the United States consistently with the national honor and interest.

The rapid and brilliant successes of our arms and the vast extent of the enemy's territory which had been overrun and conquered before the close of the last session of Congress were fully

known to that body. . . . History presents no parallel of so
many glorious victories achieved by any nation within so short a
period. Our Army, regulars and volunteers, have covered themselves with imperishable honors. . . .

X X X

Shortly after the adjournment of the last session of Congress the
gratifying intelligence was received of the signal victory of Buena
Vista, and of the fall of the city of Vera Cruz, and with it the
strong castle of San Juan de Ulloa, by which it was defended.
Believing that after these and other successes so honorable to our
arms and so disastrous to Mexico the period was propitious to
afford her another opportunity, if she thought proper to embrace
it, to enter into negotiations for peace, a commissioner was appointed to proceed to the headquarters of our Army with full
powers to enter upon negotiations and to conclude a just and
honorable treaty of peace. . . .

Our Army pursued its march upon the capital, and as it approached it was met by formidable resistance. Our forces first
encountered the enemy, and achieved signal victories in the
severely contested battles of Contreras and Churubusco. It was not
until after these actions had resulted in decisive victories and the
capital of the enemy was within our power that the Mexican Government manifested any disposition to enter into negotiations for
peace. . . .

X X X

It is well known that the only indemnity which it is in the power
of Mexico to make in satisfaction of the just and long-deferred
claims of our citizens against her and the only means by which
she can reimburse the United States for the expenses of the war
is a cession to the United States of a portion of her territory.
Mexico has no money to pay. . . .

X X X

The doctrine of no territory is the doctrine of no indemnity,
and if sanctioned would be a public acknowledgment that our
country was wrong and that the war declared by Congress with
extraordinary unanimity was unjust and should be abandoned—

an admission unfounded in fact and degrading to the national character.

The commissioner of the United States was authorized to agree to the establishment of the Rio Grande as the boundary from its entrance into the Gulf to its intersection with the southern boundary of New Mexico, and to obtain a cession to the United States of the Provinces of New Mexico and the Californias and the privilege of the right of way across the Isthmus of Tehuantepec. The boundary of the Rio Grande and the cession to the United States of New Mexico and Upper California constituted an ultimatum which our commissioner was under no circumstances to yield.

✕   ✕   ✕

The Provinces of New Mexico and the Californias are contiguous to the Territories of the United States, and if brought under the government of our laws their resources—mineral, agricultural, manufacturing, and commercial—would soon be developed.

Upper California is bounded on the north by our Oregon possessions, and if held by the United States would soon be settled by a hardy, enterprising, and intelligent portion of our population. The Bay of San Francisco and other harbors along the Californian coast would afford shelter for our Navy, for our numerous whale ships, and other merchant vessels employed in the Pacific Ocean. . . .

✕   ✕   ✕

These Provinces are now in our undisputed occupation, and have been so for many months, all resistance on the part of Mexico having ceased within their limits. I am satisfied that they should never be surrendered to Mexico. . . .

✕   ✕   ✕

It has never been contemplated by me, as an object of the war, to make a permanent conquest of the Republic of Mexico or to annihilate her separate existence as an independent nation. . . . We demand an honorable peace, and that peace must bring with it indemnity for the past and security for the future. . . .

✕   ✕   ✕

The attention of Congress was invited at the preceding session to the importance of establishing a Territorial government over our possessions in Oregon, and it is to be regretted that there was no legislation on the subject. Our citizens who inhabit that distant region of country are still left without the protection of our laws, or any regularly organized government. . . . They should have the right of suffrage, be represented in a Territorial legislature and by a Delegate in Congress, and possess all the rights and privileges which citizens of other portions of the territories of the United States have heretofore enjoyed or may now enjoy. . . .

JAMES K. POLK
FOURTH STATE-OF-THE-UNION MESSAGE
WASHINGTON, *December 5, 1848*

Fellow-Citizens of the Senate and of the House of Representatives:
Peace, plenty, and contentment reign throughout our borders, and our beloved country presents a sublime moral spectacle to the world.

Since the exchange of ratifications of the treaty of peace with Mexico our intercourse with the Government of that Republic has been of the most friendly character. . . . The amicable relations between the two countries, which had been suspended, have been happily restored, and are destined, I trust, to be long preserved. . . .

One of the most important results of the war into which we were recently forced with a neighboring nation is the demonstration it has afforded of the military strength of our country. Before the late war with Mexico, European and other foreign powers entertained imperfect and erroneous views of our physical strength as a nation and of our ability to prosecute war. . . . They had not conceived that it was possible for a nation without such [a large standing] army, well disciplined and of long service, to wage war successfully. . . . Our citizen soldiers are unlike those drawn from the population of any other country. They are composed indiscriminately of all professions and pursuits—of farmers, lawyers, physicians, merchants, manufacturers, mechanics, and laborers—and this not only among the officers, but the private soldiers in the ranks. . . .

The war with Mexico has thus fully developed the capacity of republican governments to prosecute successfully a just and necessary foreign war with all the vigor usually attributed to more arbitrary forms of government. . . .

Within less than four years the annexation of Texas to the Union has been consummated; all conflicting title to the Oregon Territory south of the forty-ninth degree of north latitude, being all that was insisted on by any of my predecessors, has been adjusted, and New Mexico and Upper California have been acquired by treaty. The area of these several Territories, according to a report carefully prepared by the Commissioner of the General Land Office from the most authentic information in his possession, contains 1,193,061 square miles, or 763,559,040 acres; while the area of the remaining twenty-nine States and the territory not yet organized into States east of the Rocky Mountains contains 2,059,513 square miles, or 1,318,126,058 acres. These estimates show that the territories recently acquired, and over which our exclusive jurisdiction and dominion have been extended, constitute a country more than half as large as all that which was held by the United States before their acquisition. . . .

It was known that mines of the precious metals existed to a considerable extent in California at the time of its acquisition. These mines are more extensive and valuable than was anticipated. The accounts of the abundance of gold in that territory are of such an extraordinary character as would scarcely command belief were they not corroborated by the authentic reports of officers in the public service who have visited the mineral district and derived the facts which they detail from personal observation. . . .

The effects produced by the discovery of these rich mineral deposits and the success which has attended the labors of those who have resorted to them have produced a surprising change in the state of affairs in California. . . . Nearly the whole of the male population of the country have gone to the gold districts. Ships arriving on the coast are deserted by their crews and their voyages suspended for want of sailors. . . .

This abundance of gold and the all-engrossing pursuit of it have already caused in California an unprecedented rise in the price of all the necessaries of life.

The question is believed to be rather abstract than practical, whether slavery ever can or would exist in any portion of the acquired territory even if it were left to the option of the slave-holding States themselves. But however this may be, the question, involving, as it does, a principle of equality of rights of the separate and several States as equal copartners in the Confederacy, should not be disregarded.

. . . If Congress shall abstain from interfering with the question, the people of these territories will be left free to adjust it as they may think proper when they apply for admission as States into the Union. No enactment of Congress could restrain the people of any of the sovereign States of the Union, old or new, North or South, slaveholding or nonslaveholding, from determining the character of their own domestic institutions as they may deem wise and proper. Any and all the States possess this right, and Congress can not deprive them of it. . . .

. . . Upon a great emergency, however, and under menacing dangers to the Union, the Missouri compromise line in respect to slavery was adopted. The same line was extended farther west in the acquisition of Texas. . . . I heretofore expressed the opinion that that line of compromise should be extended on the parallel of 36°30' from the western boundary of Texas, where it now terminates, to the Pacific Ocean. . . .

. . . But if Congress shall now reverse the decision by which the Missouri compromise was effected, and shall propose to extend the restriction over the whole territory, south as well as north of the parallel of 36°30′, it will cease to be a compromise, and must be regarded as an original question.

▰ ▰ ▰

Congress is earnestly invoked, for the sake of the Union, its harmony, and our continued prosperity as a nation, to adjust at its present session this, the only dangerous question which lies in our path. . . .

▰ ▰ ▰

During the period I have administered the executive department of the Government great and important questions of public policy, foreign and domestic, have arisen, upon which it was my duty to act. It may, indeed, be truly said that my administration has fallen upon eventful times. I have felt most sensibly the weight of the high responsibilities devolved upon me. With no other object than the public good, the enduring fame, and permanent prosperity of my country, I have pursued the convictions of my own best judgment. . . .

ZACHARY TAYLOR
(1849–1850)

*"I have endeavored to fulfill
what I considered
my honest duty"*

Thirty states voted in the election of 1848 that landed General *Zachary Taylor* in the White House. The Whigs, who had violently opposed the Mexican War, about-faced and commandeered the most popular figure of the war, Old Rough and Ready, who at the battle of Buena Vista had thrilled the nation with his order to a battery, "Doubleshot your guns and give 'em hell!"

Taylor did not want the job. His wife didn't want him to take it. He had never voted in his life. On returning from the war he had settled down on his Louisiana plantation near Baton Rouge, content to sit on the porch, sip mint juleps, and watch Old Man River roll by. But the Whigs wouldn't let him.

The general owned three hundred slaves, a bitter pill for the Whigs, but they swallowed it—party came first, and generals were vote-getters. Witness: Washington, Jackson, Harrison. With Taylor, the Whigs felt they couldn't lose. He was so little interested in the outcome that he let the letter notifying him of his nomination go to the dead-letter office rather than pay ten cents postage due on it. Called on for a declaration of his political principles he said, "I am a Whig but not an ultra Whig," whatever that meant.

Old Zack's presidential boom soared like a rocket. Like Harrison in the campaign of 1840, he refused to discuss issues, took no part in the campaign, said nothing, did nothing, while the Whigs bedaubed the nation with pictures of Taylor on his horse, Old Whitey, wreathed in battle smoke. The Whigs adopted no platform—Taylor was all they needed.

To oppose Taylor, the Democrats rustled up a general, Lewis Cass of Michigan, who, despite Lincoln's ridicule, served the nation and state ably. A new party, the Free Soilers, a splinter of the anti-slavery Democrats, entered the race. Their nominee was Martin Van Buren, who drew off enough Democratic votes to elect Taylor and his running mate, Millard Fillmore.

Grave problems confronted President Taylor, whose experience in statecraft was nil. Sturdy, blunt, honest, he had political courage and weighed public questions by what was best for the Union. He soon infuriated his Southern supporters by advising settlement of the bitter slavery dispute without regard to sectional or partisan feeling and urged Congress to outlaw slave-pens in the shadow of the Capitol. Opposed to the extension of slavery, he recommended admission of California as a free state.

The Thirty-first Congress that assembled in December, 1849, brought frenzied scenes to Capitol Hill. Southern fire-eaters vented their wrath on Taylor, threats of secession and violence hurtled across the floors. But Taylor stood his ground, as he had at Buena Vista.

So evenly matched were the Democrats and Whigs in the House that five Free Soilers held the balance of power; so violent was the turmoil that it required seventeen days and sixty-three ballots to elect a Speaker, Howell Cobb of Georgia.

California's admission had touched off a national crisis. The Free Soilers demanded that Congress enact the oft-sidetracked Wilmot Proviso that would exclude slavery from all territory snatched from Mexico. It was the fiercest challenge to slavery since the Missouri Compromise in 1819. Fiercely blocking the proviso at every turn, Southern lawmakers said their troops would march if the bill passed. At the same time, Northern agitators flooded Congress with petitions for the abolition of slavery in the District of Columbia. The South demanded an ironclad fugitive-slave law to replace that of 1793.

Into the meleé moved the Great Compromiser, Henry Clay, who had returned to the Senate impelled by a single purpose—to reconcile the conflicting sectional interests and save the Union. On the floor of the Senate, to which this nation looked for leadership out of the crisis, the Great Triumvirate—Henry Clay, John C. Calhoun, and Daniel Webster—staged their last throbbing scene.

Bent on saving the Union at all costs, Henry Clay came forward
with his massive, middle-of-the-road package, the Omnibus Bill, that he
hoped would assuage the nation's "eight bleeding wounds." On February 5, 1850, he made the last great effort of his career when he rose
to plead eloquently for his "bundle of compromises" that would settle
and soothe all the burning, dividing questions. After him came the Old
Nullifier, John C. Calhoun, four weeks from death, to warn against
Clay's bill that, he charged, would destroy the Union. Last came
Daniel Webster, who, with majestic eloquence that matched his Reply
to Hayne, shocked his New England supporters by supporting Clay's
compromises. He, too, had a single purpose—to save the Union.

Clay's Omnibus Bill, fought bitterly at every turn, was grinding
toward its piecemeal passage when Zachary Taylor died in the White
House on July 9, 1850. He had returned quite exhausted from a Fourth
of July celebration at the Washington Monument, where he sat for
hours in the oppressive heat. To refresh himself, he ate a bowl of
cherries, washing them down with huge draughts of iced milk. Cholera
morbus ensued quickly. Five days later he died with anguish on his
lips: "God knows I have endeavored to fulfill what I considered my
honest duty. But I have been mistaken. My motives have been mis-
construed and my feelings grossly outraged."

Taylor's one-and-only State-of-the-Union Message introduced the
nightmarish Cuban problem to the American people. He revealed he
had quashed a filibuster before it could leave its Florida rendezvous
for Cuba. It was the first of many fitted out in the United States in
fruitless efforts to break Spain's grip on the island.

Taylor also forecast the "absolute necessity" of a canal to join the
waters of the Atlantic and Pacific. Lastly, he sought to ease the slavery
tension by urging acceptance of Clay's compromise bill then in the
making. For these words he would be crucified anew in Congress.

ZACHARY TAYLOR
FIRST (AND ONLY) STATE-OF-THE-UNION MESSAGE
WASHINGTON, *December 4, 1849*

Fellow-Citizens of the Senate and House of Representatives:

Sixty years have elapsed since the establishment of this
Government, and the Congress of the United States again assembles to legislate for an empire of freemen. . . . The United States

of America at this moment present to the world the most stable and permanent Government on earth.

✪ ✪ ✪

Having been apprised that a considerable number of adventurers were engaged in fitting out a military expedition within the United States against a foreign country, and believing from the best information I could obtain that it was destined to invade the island of Cuba, I deemed it due to the friendly relations existing between the United States and Spain to exert the lawful authority of this Government in suppressing the expedition and preventing the invasion. . . . The expedition has been suppressed.

A contract having been concluded with the State of Nicaragua by a company composed of American citizens for the purpose of constructing a ship canal through the territory of that State to connect the Atlantic and Pacific oceans, I have directed the negotiation of a treaty with Nicaragua pledging both Governments to protect those who shall engage in and perfect the work. . . .

✪ ✪ ✪

The position of the Sandwich [Hawaiian] Islands with reference to the territory of the United States on the Pacific, the success of our persevering and benevolent citizens who have repaired to that remote quarter in Christianizing the natives . . . , and the use made by our numerous whale ships of the harbors of the islands as places of resort for obtaining refreshments and repairs all combine to render their destiny peculiarly interesting to us. . . . We could in no event be indifferent to their passing under the dominion of any other power. . . .

✪ ✪ ✪

No civil government having been provided by Congress for California, the people of that Territory . . . recently met in convention for the purpose of forming a constitution and the State government. It is believed they will shortly apply for the admission of California into the Union as a sovereign State. Should such be the case . . . I recommend their application to the favorable consideration of Congress. The people of New Mexico will also, it is believed, at no very distant period present themselves for admission into the Union. . . .

. . . Preparatory to the admission of California and New Mexico the people of each will have instituted for themselves a republican form of government. . . . By awaiting their action all causes of uneasiness may be avoided and confidence and kind feeling preserved. With a view of maintaining the harmony and tranquillity so dear to all, we should abstain from the introduction of those exciting topics of a sectional character which have hitherto produced painful apprehensions in the public mind. . . .

✪ ✪ ✪

The great mineral wealth of California and the advantages which its ports and harbors and those of Oregon afford to commerce . . . make it certain that there will arise in a few years large and prosperous communities on our western coast. It therefore becomes important that a line of communication . . . should be opened within the territory of the United States from the navigable waters of the Atlantic or the Gulf of Mexico to the Pacific. . . .

✪ ✪ ✪

. . . Attachment to the Union of the States should be habitually fostered in every American heart. For more than half a century, during which kingdoms and empires have fallen, this Union has stood unshaken. . . . Whatever dangers may threaten it, I shall stand by it and maintain its integrity to the full extent of the obligations and powers conferred upon me by the Constitution.

MILLARD FILLMORE
(1850–1853)

*"The emblem of our Union
and the symbol
of our greatness"*

Millard Fillmore of Buffalo, New York, last of the Whig dynasty, was sworn in as President on July 10, the day after Zachary Taylor died. One of the most handsome Presidents the United States has elected, he came up the hard way in America's best tradition of rags-to-political-greatness.

A New York farm boy, Fillmore never owned a book until he was nineteen. Virtually self-educated, he was admitted to the bar at twenty-three. He learned his politics campaigning for the New York legislature and during his four years in the House of Representatives at Washington. His anti-slavery views influenced the Whigs to tab him for the vice-presidency to balance the ticket headed by slave owner Zachary Taylor.

On September 18, 1850, Fillmore signed the fugitive-slave law, fifth section of Henry Clay's Omnibus Bill. In so doing, he not only split his party, but pronounced its death sentence and bankrupted his own political future. It was said that during the debates on the bill in the Senate, over which he presided, Fillmore was so impressed by the necessity of propitiating the South that he gladly signed the fugitive-slave enactment.

The immediate effect of the passage of the huge Compromise of 1850 was jubilation. The nation exulted. The Union was saved. Henry

171

Clay had saved it. His name was on every tongue. The vexing slavery issue was silenced forever. The Ship of State could now sail on to greater glories untrammeled by sectional strife. Crowds jammed the Capitol corridors to felicitate Congress. The forts surrounding New York Harbor fired hundred-gun salutes in honor of the historic enactments, and Jenny Lind, the Swedish Nightingale, sailed up the bay just in time to add her golden voice to the crescendo of joy.

But to thousands of Northerners the fugitive-slave provision was anathema. It was denounced from platform, pulpit, and newspaper as a blot on the soul of the nation.

The Thirty-first Congress that enacted Clay's compromises saw a new breed of younger politicians crowding out the old. It was the twilight of aging political gods. The bell was already tolling for the two greatest Whig figures, Daniel Webster and Henry Clay, who would pass from the scene in 1852. To the Senate, New York sent her former governor, caustic, radical William H. Seward, with his powerful abolition doctrine. A different sort was Stephen Douglas, the idolized "Little Giant," from Illinois. Small of stature, large of voice, he was a ranter, but powerful in debate and destined to become a storm center with his squatter-sovereignty ideas. From Texas came the picturesque Sam Houston, still wreathed in the glamour of San Jacinto. Massachusetts sent Charles Sumner, as handsome as he was eloquent, a relentless foe of slavery and slaveholders. Ohio boasted of two who would figure large in the coming decade: a bald, ambitious Free Soiler, Salmon Portland Chase, future Chief Justice of the United States; and "Bluff" Ben Wade, ruthless and hard as nails, who kept a sawed-off shotgun in his Senate desk. Tall and courtly was Mississippi's Jefferson Davis, who would inherit Calhoun's mantle and one day lead the South on its ill-starred venture. Into the House limped a bitter abolitionist, Thaddeus Stevens of Pennsylvania. One day he would whiplash the House into impeaching a President.

Inspired by the injustices of the fugitive-slave ruling, a woman took up her pen in 1851 and "with God's help" wrote the overnight propaganda sensation, Uncle Tom's Cabin, with its melodramatic, sentimental picture of slave life in the South. It sold 300,000 copies the first year, and it whipped up popular indignation in the North against the whole institution of slavery as nothing else had up to then.

Meanwhile, the South accepted the compromise, but warned that it expected faithful execution of the fugitive-slave provision. Into his First State-of-the-Union Message, Fillmore injected words that sought to quiet the wrath hurled at Clay's compromise. But the caldron seethed on. Fervently Fillmore urged wholehearted acceptance of the "series of measures passed with the view of healing sectional differences." He expressed his belief that the turmoil over slavery would soon be quieted forever.

In this first message, Fillmore bestowed on the nation's Capitol the historic appellation "Emblem of our Union. . . ." He also informed the nation that the United States and Britain had signed a "convention" to construct a jointly owned canal across Central America connecting the Atlantic and Pacific. This was the unpopular Clayton-Bulwer Treaty abrogated eventually in the 1890's.

His second message heralded the extension of the Capitol, which added to this wonderful structure the two wings—today's home of the Senate and House of Representatives—and crowned the whole with the glorious Dome that is the trademark of the nation. With California's admittance to the Union, Congress—now 62 Senators and 237 Representatives—needed more room.

In this same message, Fillmore called for revision of navy regulations, and the substitution of an effectual means of discipline to replace flogging, previously abandoned.

Two of Fillmore's messages reveal the growing irritant of Cuba. In his last message he warned against annexation of Cuba, yet admitted it would be a desirable acquisition only "if voluntarily ceded by Spain." He feared annexation would revive sectional conflicts since Cuba was so heavily engaged in slave trading.

In this final message, Fillmore reached the nation's hands across the Pacific. He made the historic announcement that he had ordered a squadron of American warships, commanded by Commodore Matthew G. Perry, to pry open the hermit empire of Japan to commerce and intercourse with the rest of the world.

MILLARD FILLMORE
FIRST STATE-OF-THE-UNION MESSAGE
WASHINGTON, *December 2, 1850*

Fellow-Citizens of the Senate and of the House of Representatives:

Being suddenly called in the midst of the last session of Congress by a painful dispensation of Divine Providence to the responsible station which I now hold, I contented myself with such communications to the Legislature as the exigency of the moment seemed to require. The country was shrouded in mourning for the loss of its venerable Chief Magistrate and all hearts were penetrated with grief. . . .

✪   ✪   ✪

A convention was negotiated between the United States and Great Britain in April last for facilitating and protecting the construction of a ship canal between the Atlantic and Pacific oceans and for other purposes. . . .

All experience has demonstrated the wisdom and policy of raising a large portion of revenue for the support of Government from duties on goods imported. The power to lay these duties is unquestionable, and its chief object, of course, is to replenish the Treasury. But if in doing this, an incidental advantage may be gained by encouraging the industry of our own citizens, it is our duty to avail ourselves of that advantage.

✪   ✪   ✪

A high tariff can never be permanent. It will cause dissatisfaction, and will be changed. . . . What the manufacturer wants is uniformity and permanency, that he may feel a confidence that he is not to be ruined by sudden changes. . . . I therefore strongly recommend a modification of the present tariff, which has prostrated some of our most important and necessary manufactures, and that specific duties be imposed sufficient to raise the requisite revenue. . . .

✪   ✪   ✪

There being no mint in California, I am informed that the laborers in the mines are compelled to dispose of their gold dust at a large discount. This appears to me to be a heavy and unjust tax upon the labor of those employed in extracting this precious metal, and I doubt not you will be disposed at the earliest period possible to relieve them from it by the establishment of a mint. . . .

✪   ✪   ✪

I entertain no doubt of the authority of Congress to make appropriations . . . in that class of public works . . . called works of internal improvement. This authority I suppose to be derived

chiefly from the power of regulating commerce with foreign nations and among the States and the power of laying and collecting
imposts. Where commerce is to be carried on and imposts collected there must be ports and harbors as well as wharves and
customhouses. . . . Other facilities and securities for commerce
and navigation are hardly less important; and those clauses of the
Constitution, therefore, to which I have referred have received
from the origin of the Government a liberal and beneficial construction. . . .

✪ ✪ ✪

The District [of Columbia], which has neither voice nor vote
in your deliberations, looks to you for protection and aid, and I
commend all its wants to your favorable consideration, with a full
confidence that you will meet them not only with justice, but with
liberality. It should be borne in mind that in this city, laid out
by Washington and consecrated by his name, is located the Capitol
of our nation, the emblem of our Union and the symbol of our
greatness. Here also are situated all the public buildings necessary
for the use of the Government, and all these are exempt from
taxation. It should be the pride of Americans to render this place
attractive to the people of the whole Republic. The Government
should therefore bear a liberal proportion of the burdens of all
necessary and useful improvements. . . .

✪ ✪ ✪

It was hardly to have been expected that the series of measures
passed at your last session with the view of healing the sectional
differences which had sprung from the slavery and territorial questions should at once have realized their beneficent purpose. . . .
It would be strange if they had been received with immediate approbation by people and States prejudiced and heated by the exciting controversies of their representatives. I believe those measures to have been required by the circumstances and condition of
the country. . . .

The series of measures to which I have alluded are regarded by
me as a settlement in principle and substance—a final settlement
of the dangerous and exciting subjects which they embraced. Most

of these subjects, indeed, are beyond your reach, as the legislation which disposed of them was in its character final and irrevocable. . . . For this reason I recommend your adherence to the adjustment established by those measures until time and experience shall demonstrate the necessity of further legislation to guard against evasion or abuse. . . . By that adjustment we have been rescued from the wide and boundless agitation that surrounded us. . . .

MILLARD FILLMORE
SECOND STATE-OF-THE-UNION MESSAGE
WASHINGTON, *December 2, 1851*

Fellow-Citizens of the Senate and of the House of Representatives:
         I congratulate you and our common constituency upon the favorable auspices under which you meet for your first session. . . . The agitation which for a time threatened to disrupt the fraternal relations which make us one people is fast subsiding, and a year of general prosperity and health has crowned the nation with unusual blessings. . . .
    Since the close of the last Congress certain Cubans and other foreigners resident in the United States, who were more or less concerned in the previous invasion of Cuba, instead of being discouraged by its failure, have again abused the hospitality of this country by making it the scene of the equipment of another military expedition against that possession of Her Catholic Majesty, in which they were countenanced, aided, and joined by citizens of the United States. I lost no time in issuing such instructions to the proper officers of the United States as seemed to be called for by the occasion. . . . This expedition was set on foot in palpable violation of the laws of the United States. Its leader was a Spaniard. The persons composing it, however, were mostly citizens of the United States.

                              ✪   ✪   ✪

    The Naval Academy at Annapolis, under a revised and improved system of regulations, now affords opportunities of education and instruction to the pupils quite equal, it is believed, for professional improvement, to those enjoyed by the cadets in the Military Academy. . . .

The advantages of science in nautical affairs have rarely been more strikingly illustrated than in the fact, stated in the report of the Navy Department, that by means of the wind and current charts projected and prepared by Lieutenant Maury, the Superintendent of the Naval Observatory, the passage from the Atlantic to the Pacific ports of our country has been shortened by about forty days.

✪ ✪ ✪

An act of Congress approved 30th September, 1850, contained a provision for the extension of the Capitol according to such plan as might be approved by the President, and appropriated $100,000 to be expended under his direction by such architect as he should appoint to execute the same. . . .

The great object to be accomplished was to make such an addition as would afford ample and convenient halls for the deliberations of the two Houses of Congress, with sufficient accommodations for spectators and suitable apartments for the committees and officers of the two branches of the Legislature. It was also desirable not to mar the harmony and beauty of the present structure, which, as a specimen of architecture, is so universally admired. Keeping these objects in view, I concluded to make the addition by wings, detached from the present building, yet connected with it by corridors. . . .

✪ ✪ ✪

In my last annual message I stated that I considered the series of measures which had been adopted at the previous session in reference to the agitation growing out of the Territorial and slavery questions as a final settlement in principle and substance of the dangerous and exciting subjects which they embraced, and I recommended adherence to the adjustment established by those measures until time and experience should demonstrate the necessity of further legislation to guard against evasion or abuse. . . . A year has now elapsed since that recommendation was made. To that recommendation I still adhere, and I congratulate you and the country upon the general acquiescence in these measures of peace which has been exhibited in all parts of the Republic.

MILLARD FILLMORE
THIRD STATE-OF-THE-UNION MESSAGE
WASHINGTON, *December 6, 1852*

Fellow-Citizens of the Senate and of the House of Representatives:
    Within a few weeks the public mind has been deeply affected by the death of Daniel Webster, filling at his decease the office of Secretary of State. . . . His commanding talents, his great political and professional eminence, his well-tried patriotism, and his long and faithful services in the most important public trusts have caused his death to be lamented throughout the country and have earned for him a lasting place in our history.

✪ ✪ ✪

The affairs of Cuba formed a prominent topic in my last annual message. They remain in an uneasy condition, and a feeling of alarm and irritation on the part of the Cuban authorities appears to exist. . . .
    Were this island comparatively destitute of inhabitants or occupied by a kindred race, I should regard it, if voluntarily ceded by Spain, as a most desirable acquisition. But under existing circumstances I should look upon its incorporation into our Union as a very hazardous measure. It would bring into the Confederacy a population of a different national stock, speaking a different language, and not likely to harmonize with the other members. It would probably affect in a prejudicial manner the industrial interests of the South, and it might revive those conflicts of opinion between the different sections of the country which lately shook the Union to its center, and which have been so happily compromised.

✪ ✪ ✪

Our settlements on the shores of the Pacific have already given a great extension, and in some respects a new direction, to our

commerce in that ocean. A direct and rapidly increasing intercourse has sprung up with eastern Asia. . . . I have accordingly
been led to order an appropriate naval force to Japan, under the
command of a discreet and intelligent officer of the highest rank
known to our service. He is instructed to endeavor to obtain from
the Government of that country some relaxation of the inhospi-
table and antisocial system which it has pursued for about two
centuries. . . .

○ ✪ ○

It has been the uniform policy of this Government, from its
foundation to the present day, to abstain from all interference in
the domestic affairs of other nations. . . .

But it is now said by some that this policy must be changed.
. . . Although no one proposes that we should join the fraternity
of potentates who have for ages lavished the blood and treasure
of their subjects in maintaining "the balance of power," yet it is
said that we ought to interfere between contending sovereigns and
their subjects for the purpose of overthrowing the monarchies of
Europe and establishing in their place republican institutions. It
is alleged that we have heretofore pursued a different course from
a sense of our weakness, but that now our conscious strength dictates a change of policy, and that it is consequently our duty to
mingle in these contests and aid those who are struggling for
liberty.

This is a most seductive but dangerous appeal to the generous
sympathies of freemen. Enjoying, as we do, the blessings of a free
Government, there is no man who has an American heart that
would not rejoice to see these blessings extended to all other nations. Nevertheless, is it prudent or is it wise to involve ourselves
in these foreign wars? . . . For the honor of the patriots who
have gone before us, I can not admit it. . . .

○ ✪ ○

We live in an age of progress, and ours is emphatically a country of progress. . . . The whole country is full of enterprise. Our
common schools are diffusing intelligence among the people and
our industry is fast accumulating the comforts and luxuries of life.
But whatever may be the cause of this unparalleled growth in

to colonel, and was soon promoted to Brigadier General of Volunteers. He participated in the battles around Mexico City, but apparently won little glory usable for political aims. At the Battle of Contreras he was thrown from his horse, and on the next day he fainted while leading his brigade in action at Churubusco. Because of this episode, the Whigs lampooned his military abilities unmercifully in the campaign.

To oppose Pierce, the Whigs picked another war hero (under whom Pierce had served in Mexico)—General Winfield Scott, ablest soldier of his age, but no politician. Absurdly enough, the Whigs turned Scott's passion for terrapin soup into a ridiculous campaign issue. Pierce made no campaign at all, and Scott refused to be smoked out on anything. Senator Seward of New York masterminded Scott's campaign and ordered him to keep his mouth shut. Scott complied by fending all questions on issues with recipes for soup. His ambiguous anti-slavery views griped both Southern and Northern Whigs. The latter summed up their feelings in a not-nice way, "We accept the candidate but spit on the platform."

The so-called Free Soilers nominated John P. Hale of New Hampshire, who never had a chance. Pierce ran off with 254 electoral votes, carrying twenty-seven of the thirty-one states. The election made it obvious that the people had endorsed Clay's compromise with finality.

Pierce's State-of-the-Union Messages are characterized, particularly the last, by hysterical arraignment of the "slavery reformers" as he called the abolitionists. He accused them of invading Southern rights. He was referring to the fresh wave of antagonism aroused by the Kansas-Nebraska Act of 1854, which spread rapine and bloodshed across the plains of "Bleeding Kansas."

This act created two new territories, Kansas and Nebraska, whose inhabitants were privileged to decide for themselves the question of slavery, thus legalizing squatter sovereignty. It repealed the Missouri Compromise. All questions of title to slaves could be carried to the Supreme Court for adjudication. It was the chrysalis of the American Civil War. Out of the fight against this bill emerged a new party, the Republicans, composed of the Northern Whigs, Free Soilers, and Anti-Nebraska Democrats, that would soon make its first campaign on the moral issue of slavery.

The Kansas-Nebraska Act revived the hot animosities presumably interred forever by Clay's Compromise of 1850. The bill, fathered by Stephen Douglas, witnessed one of the most desperate fights ever waged in Congress. Pierce backed the bill with all the power and prestige of his office.

In his last two State-of-the-Union Messages he lashed out at the agitators who were making a shambles of Kansas (although in his first message—before passage of the Kansas-Nebraska bill—he had spoken soothingly of the easing of the nation's controversies and, wishfully, had prophesied a new era of good feeling in the offing).

Pierce was an apostle of Polk's doctrine of Manifest Destiny. First on his expansionist agenda was annexation of Cuba. Apparently—although he never admitted it—he instructed the American Ministers to Great Britain, France, and Spain to draw up a scheme to buy the island from Spain. Meeting in August, 1854, at Ostend, Belgium, this trio of diplomats drafted the so-called Ostend Manifesto, proposing that the United States offer Spain $120,000,000 for Cuba and that, if Spain refused to sell, the United States take it by force. This suggestion stirred up a brief hornet's nest in the free states, Cuba being a dedicated stronghold of slavery. Singularly, Pierce said nothing of this in his next State-of-the-Union Message.

Other interesting facts emerge in Pierce's messages. Commodore Perry's door-opening mission to Japan had succeeded—he and his squadron of Black Ships were headed home with a treaty of trade and friendship that would bring the world to Japan's doorstep. Six new frigates were being constructed by the navy. One of them, the *Merrimack* (by way of history) would later be captured by the Confederates and be converted into the ironclad *Merrimack,* or *Virginia,* that battled with the *Monitor* in Hampton Roads. The nation's population, growing at a prodigious rate, would reach a hundred million by the end of the century. America was crowding England as the first maritime power of the world. The United States must observe strict neutrality in the Crimean War between Russia and England. American private enterprise had constructed a railroad across the Isthmus of Panama, foretelling a day fifty years hence when the waters of the Atlantic and Pacific would be wedded by the Panama Canal. The first transcontinental railroad was projected.

FRANKLIN PIERCE
FIRST STATE-OF-THE-UNION MESSAGE
WASHINGTON, D.C., *December 5, 1853*

Fellow-Citizens of the Senate and of the House of Representatives:
        The interest with which the people of the Republic anticipate the assembling of Congress and the fulfillment on that occa-

sion of the duty imposed upon a new President is one of the best evidences of their capacity to realize the hopes of the founders of a political system at once complex and symmetrical. . . .

In 1852 an expedition was sent to Japan, under the command of Commodore Perry, for the purpose of opening commercial intercourse with that Empire. Intelligence has been received of his arrival there and of his having made known to the Emperor of Japan the object of his visit. But it is not yet ascertained how far the Emperor will be disposed to abandon his restrictive policy and open that populous country to a commercial intercourse with the United States.

The controversies which have agitated the country heretofore are passing away with the causes which produced them and the passions which they had awakened; or, if any trace of them remains, it may be reasonably hoped that it will only be perceived in the zealous rivalry of all good citizens to testify their respect for the rights of the States, their devotion to the Union, and their common determination that each one of the States, its institutions, its welfare, and its domestic peace, shall be held alike secure under the sacred aegis of the Constitution.

Numerous applications have been and no doubt will continue to be made for grants of land in aid of the construction of railways. It is not believed to be within the intent and meaning of the Constitution that the power to dispose of the public domain should be used otherwise than might be expected from a prudent proprietor and therefore that grants of land to aid in the construction of roads should be restricted to cases where it would be for the interest of a proprietor under like circumstances thus to contribute to the construction of these works.

The subject of internal improvements, claiming alike the interest and good-will of all, has, nevertheless, been the basis of much political discussion and has stood like a deep-graven line of division between statesmen of eminent ability and patriotism. The rule of strict construction of all powers delegated by the States to the General Government has arrayed itself from time to time against the rapid progress of expenditures from the national treasury on works of a local character within the States. . . .

There is one subject of a domestic nature which, from its intrinsic importance and the many interesting questions of future policy which it involves, can not fail to receive your early attention. I allude to the means of communication by which different parts of the wide expanse of our country are to be placed in closer connection for purposes both of defense and commercial intercourse. . . .

. . . But the general subject will now present itself under aspects more imposing and more purely national by reason of the surveys ordered by Congress, and now in the process of completion, for communication by railway across the continent, and wholly within the limits of the United States.

The growth of our population has now brought us, in the destined career of our national history, to a point at which it well behooves us to expand our vision over the vast prospective. . . . The successive decennial returns of the census since the adoption of the Constitution have revealed a law of steady, progressive development, which may be stated in general terms as a duplication every quarter century. . . . The increased average duration of human life known to have already resulted from the scientific and hygienic improvements of the past fifty years will tend to keep up through the next fifty, or perhaps hundred, the same ratio of growth which has been thus revealed in our past progress. . . .

These considerations seem fully to justify the presumption that the law of population above stated will continue to act with undiminished effect through at least the next half century, and that thousands of persons who have already arrived at maturity and are now exercising the rights of freemen will close their eyes on the spectacle of more than 100,000,000 of population embraced within the majestic proportions of the American Union. . . .

FRANKLIN PIERCE
SECOND STATE-OF-THE-UNION MESSAGE
WASHINGTON, *December 4, 1854*

Fellow-Citizens of the Senate and of the House of Representatives:
The past has been an eventful year, and will be hereafter referred to as a marked epoch in the history of the world. . . .
Our foreign commerce has reached a magnitude and extent nearly equal to that of the first maritime power of the earth, and exceeding that of any other. . . . It is the duty of the executive and legislative branches of the Government to exercise a careful supervision and adopt proper measures for its protection. . . . Long experience has shown that, in general, when the principal powers of Europe are engaged in war the rights of neutral nations are endangered. Accordingly, a proposition embracing not only the rule that free ships make free goods, except contraband articles, but also the less contested one that neutral property other than contraband, though on board enemy's ships, shall be exempt from confiscation, has been submitted by this Government to those of Europe and America.

The naval expedition dispatched about two years since for the purpose of establishing relations with the Empire of Japan has been ably and skillfully conducted to a successful termination by the officer to whom it was intrusted. A treaty opening certain of the ports of that populous country has been negotiated. . . .

The suggestions which I submitted in my annual message of last year in reference to grants of land in aid of the construction of railways were less full and explicit than the magnitude of the subject and subsequent developments would seem to render proper and desirable. Of the soundness of the principle then asserted with regard to the limitation of the power of Congress I entertain no doubt. . . . Is it not the better rule to leave all these works to private enterprise, regulated and, when expedient, aided by the cooperation of States? . . .

FRANKLIN PIERCE
THIRD STATE-OF-THE-UNION MESSAGE
WASHINGTON, *December 31, 1855*

Fellow-Citizens of the Senate and of the House of Representatives:
One other subject of discussion between the United States and Great Britain has grown out of the attempt, which the exigencies of the war in which she is engaged with Russia induced her to make, to draw recruits from the United States.

It is the traditional and settled policy of the United States to maintain impartial neutrality during the wars which from time to time occur among the great powers of the world. . . .

In pursuance of this policy, the laws of the United States do not forbid their citizens to sell to either of the belligerent powers articles contraband of war or take munitions of war or soldiers on board their private ships for transportation; and although in so doing the individual citizen exposes his property or person to some of the hazards of war, his acts do not involve any breach of national neutrality nor of themselves implicate the Government. . . .

The construction of the six steam frigates for which appropriations were made by the last Congress has proceeded in the most satisfactory manner. Important as this addition to our naval force is, it still remains inadequate to the contingent exigencies of the protection of the extensive seacoast and vast commercial interests of the United States. In view of this fact and of the acknowledged wisdom of the policy of a gradual and systematic increase of the Navy an appropriation is recommended for the construction of six steam sloops of war.

In the Territory of Kansas there have been acts prejudicial to good order, but as yet none have occurred under circumstances to justify the interposition of the Federal Executive. . . . I cherish the hope, however, that the occurrence of any such untoward event will be prevented by the sound sense of the people of the Territory. . . .

When . . . it became requisite to organize the Territories of

Nebraska and Kansas, it was the natural and legitimate, if not the inevitable, consequence of previous events and legislation that the same great and sound principle which had already been applied to Utah and New Mexico should be applied to them—that they should stand exempt from the restrictions proposed in the act relative to the State of Missouri. . . .

The measure . . . was attacked with violence on the false or delusive pretext that it constituted a breach of faith. When before was it imagined by sensible men that a regulative or declarative statute, whether enacted ten or forty years ago, is irrepealable; that an act of Congress is above the Constitution? . . .

It is necessary to speak thus plainly of projects, the offspring of that sectional agitation now prevailing in some of the States, which are as impracticable as they are unconstitutional, and which if persevered in must and will end calamitously. It is either disunion and civil war or it is mere angry, idle, aimless disturbance of public peace and tranquillity. Disunion for what? If the passionate rage of fanaticism and partisan spirit did not force the fact upon our attention, it would be difficult to believe that any considerable portion of the people of this enlightened country could have so surrendered themselves to a fanatical devotion to the supposed interests of the relatively few Africans in the United States as totally to abandon and disregard the interests of the 25,000,000 Americans; or trample under foot the injunctions of moral and constitutional obligation, and to engage in plans of vindictive hostility against those who are associated with them in the enjoyment of the common heritage of our national institutions.

Nor is it hostility against their fellow-citizens of one section of the Union alone. The interests, the honor, the duty, the peace, and the prosperity of the people of all sections are equally involved and imperiled in this question. . . . The storm of frenzy and faction must inevitably dash itself in vain against the unshaken rock of the Constitution. . . . I know that the Union is stronger a thousand times than all the wild and chimerical schemes of social change which are generated one after another in the unstable minds of visionary sophists and interested agitators. . . .

FRANKLIN PIERCE
FOURTH STATE-OF-THE-UNION MESSAGE
WASHINGTON, *December 2, 1856*

In the brief interval between the termination of the last and the commencement of the present session of Congress the public mind has been occupied with the care of selecting for another constitutional term the President and Vice President of the United States.

It is impossible to misapprehend the great principles which by their recent political action the people of the United States have sanctioned and announced. They have asserted the constitutional equality of each and all of the States of the Union as States; they have affirmed the constitutional equality of each and all of the citizens of the United States as citizens; they have maintained the inviolability of the constitutional rights of the different sections of the Union. . . .

In doing this they have emphatically condemned the idea of organizing in these United States mere geographical parties, of marshaling in hostile array toward each other the different parts of the country, North or South, East or West.

Perfect liberty of association for political objects and the widest scope of discussion are the received and ordinary conditions of government in our country. Our institutions . . . do not forbid citizens . . . to attack by writing, speech, or any other methods short of physical force the Constitution and the very existence of the Union. Under the shelter of this great liberty . . . associations have been formed in some of the States of individuals who, pretending to seek only to prevent the spread of the institution of slavery into the present or future inchoate States of the Union, are really inflamed with desire to change the domestic institutions of existing States. . . .

They are perfectly aware that the change in the relative condition of the white and black races in the slaveholding States which they would promote is beyond their lawful authority; . . . that for them and the States of which they are citizens the only path to its accomplishment is through burning cities, and ravaged fields, and slaughtered populations, and all there is most terrible in foreign complicated with civil and servile war. . . .

. . . Violent attack from the North finds its inevitable consequence in the growth of a spirit of angry defiance at the South. . . . We had reached that consummation . . . of the attempt of a portion of the States, by a sectional organization and movement, to usurp the control of the Government of the United States.

In the long series of acts of indirect aggression, the first was the strenuous agitation by citizens of the Northern States, in Congress and out of it, of the question of Negro emancipation in the Southern States.

The second step in this path of evil consisted of acts of the people of the Northern States, and in several instances of their governments, aimed to facilitate the escape of persons held to service in the Southern States and to prevent their extradition when reclaimed according to law and in virtue of express provisions of the Constitution. . . .

Of this last agitation, one lamentable feature was that it was carried on at the immediate expense of the peace and happiness of the people of the Territory of Kansas. That was made the battlefield, not so much of opposing factions or interests within itself as of the conflicting passions of the whole people of the United States. . . .

. . . The attempt of a part of the inhabitants of the Territory to erect a revolutionary government, though sedulously encouraged and supplied with pecuniary aid from active agents of disorder in some of the States, has completely failed. . . .

It affords me unmingled satisfaction thus to announce the peaceful condition of things in Kansas, especially considering the means to which it was necessary to have recourse for the attainment of the end, namely, the employment of a part of the military force of the United States. The withdrawal of that force from its proper duty of defending the country against foreign foes or the savages of the frontier to employ it for the suppression of domestic insurrection is, when the exigency occurs, a matter of the most earnest solicitude. . . .

The present condition of the Isthmus of Panama, in so far as regards the security of persons and property passing over it, requires serious consideration. . . . Under the guaranties of treaty, citizens of the United States have, by the outlay of several million dollars, constructed a railroad across the Isthmus, and it has become the main route between our Atlantic and Pacific possessions, over which multitudes of our citizens and a vast amount of property are constantly passing; to the security and protection of all which and the continuance of the public advantages involved it is impossible for the Government of the United States to be indifferent.

In addressing to you my last annual message the occasion seems to me an appropriate one to express my congratulations, in view of the peace, greatness, and felicity which the United States now possess and enjoy. . . . We have at length reached that stage of our country's career in which the dangers to be encountered and the exertions to be made are the incident, not of weakness, but of strength. . . . In domestic relations we have to guard against the shock of the discontents, the ambitions, the interest, and the exuberant, and therefore sometimes irregular, impulses of opinion or of action which are the natural product of the present political elevation, the self-reliance, and the restless spirit of enterprise of the people of the United States.

JAMES BUCHANAN
(1857–1861)

*"Cuba is a constant source
of injury and annoyance
to the American people"*

In 1856, the Democrats and Republicans squared off for the historic
first of twenty-eight quadrennial contests for the presidential chair—
and the first issue between them, indeed the sole issue of this initial
battle, was slavery.

The Democrats were historically the party of slavery. Only recently
had they forced through the Kansas-Nebraska Act, revoking the Missouri Compromise and deluging Kansas with terror and bloodshed.
But for all that, they were old hands with forty years' experience in
political free-for-alls.

Standard-bearer for the Democrats was *James Buchanan* of Pennsylvania, a statesman-politician of the old school, who had occupied
so many government posts that in his Third State-of-the-Union Message he was led to dub himself "Old Public Functionary." He was a
ruddy, silver-haired bachelor of sixty-five. Son of an Irish immigrant,
Buchanan had come up the ladder rung by rung, starting way back as
a Federalist in his state legislature. His services included years in the
Senate and the House and he had been Secretary of State under President Polk. As a career diplomat, he had served as Minister to Russia
and more recently to Great Britain. Buchanan was short on glamour,
but his party was long on cash. For every Republican campaign dollar,
the Democrats had ten.

To make their debut in a presidential race, the Republicans picked a dashing figure, John Charles Frémont, forty-three, "Pathfinder of the West," who had explored the Rockies and helped filch California from Mexico. Frémont's added attraction was his wife, Jessie Benton Frémont, thirty-two, who so far outglamoured her husband that much campaigning was done in her name.

For a party waging its first fight, the Republicans put on a terrific show. Like the Whigs in 1840, they deluged the nation with songs, slogans, rallies, knickknacks, torchlight parades, and speeches. They got themselves a song that ran, "Free Speech, Free Press, Free Soil, Free Men, Fré-mont." Spellbinders like Charles Sumner, Henry Ward Beecher, and Wendell Phillips cut loose. Abraham Lincoln, who joined up with the new party, made ninety speeches for Frémont. To thousands of voters swept along by the whirlwind, Frémont looked an easy winner. Southern orators countered with threats of secession if Frémont won.

Forgotten in the fervor was the American Party (pro-slavery segment of the dying Whigs) that had allied with the Native Americans and nominated Millard Fillmore as a third candidate.

In the final count Buchanan carried nineteen states with 174 electoral votes; Frémont got 114 electorals. Fillmore carried only one state with 8 electoral votes, but he siphoned off enough popular votes to elect Buchanan "a minority President by nearly a million votes," as Andrew Johnson once observed.

Conscientious but irresolute, Buchanan was desirous above all of preserving the status quo, glossing over the bitter dispute that was ripping the nation apart. He believed the federal government lacked the power to compel a state to remain in the Union against its will. His tolerance of slavery marked him as a "Doughface," a word coined by John Randolph of Roanoke to describe a Northern man with Southern views. Disunion was unthinkable to him, but he knew no way to prevent it, or so he said.

Two days after his inauguration the Supreme Court handed down the fateful Dred Scott Decision that not only split the Democratic party, but inducted into the agitated slavery picture a gangling Illinois lawyer, Abraham Lincoln. In accepting the Republican nomination for Senator to oppose incumbent Stephen Douglas, Lincoln struck the high note of his career thus far: "A house divided against itself cannot stand." His debates with Douglas set his course inevitably toward the White House.

In the late 1850's, Washington was a grim city. On Capitol Hill the crackling sectional debates had degenerated into scenes of deadly animosity. Statesmen walked the aisles of Senate and House armed with revolvers and knives. Spectators crowded the galleries to watch the angry clashes between Southern hotspurs and determined Northerners. Soon the lawmakers would transfer their battles to a new prize ring. Two shiny, marble wings of the Capitol, begun in 1851, were almost ready for occupancy.

Out on the plains of Kansas, blood flowed as free-staters and slave-staters fought for control. Squatter sovereignty arose with brutality. Into the murky picture moved arch-abolitionist John Brown and his sons to give a dress rehearsal for his Harpers Ferry massacre by murdering five pro-slavery settlers on Pottawatamie Creek in retaliation for the sacking and burning of the Free Staters' capital.

After trying to wangle Kansas into the Union as a slave state, Buchanan straddled the issue, but too late. The Kansans themselves refused a compromise, and Kansas had to wait until 1861 before joining the Union.

Meanwhile, Buchanan, wavering like a reed in the wind, did nothing but advise peace and conciliation. To use force against a state would involve wastage of too much blood and treasure.

On March 4, 1861, Buchanan handed the reins of a crumbling Union to Abraham Lincoln, whom he greeted at the White House door with these words: "If you are as happy, my dear sir, on entering this house as I am on leaving it, you are the happiest man on earth."

Buchanan's State-of-the-Union Messages apparently reveal his true feelings better than any other of his utterances. Many passages are wishful, noncommittal. Kansas, he said, was a passing incident. "Like volcanoes burnt out," it would soon be gone and forgotten. His last message, written shortly before the secession of South Carolina in December, 1860, contains his two most quoted pronouncements: "How easy it would be for the American people to settle the slavery question forever . . ." and "Our Union rests upon public opinion and can never be cemented by the blood of its citizens. . . ."

Of John Brown's Raid on Harpers Ferry he prophesied that it would be "the means of preventing further outbreaks of a similar character," a freakish commentary indeed.

Repeatedly, in three of his State-of-the-Union Messages, Buchanan urged the acquisition of Cuba because of its "vital importance" to the United States. But Cuba was bypassed in the brewing hurricane of civil war.

JAMES BUCHANAN
FIRST STATE-OF-THE-UNION MESSAGE
WASHINGTON, *December 8, 1857*

Fellow-Citizens of the Senate and House of Representatives:

In obedience to the command of the Constitution, it has now become my duty "to give to Congress information of the state of the Union and recommend to their consideration such measures" as I judge to be "necessary and expedient."

*   *   *

The isthmus of Central America, including that of Panama, is the great highway between the Atlantic and Pacific over which a large portion of the commerce of the world is destined to pass. The United States are more deeply interested than any other nation in preserving the freedom and security of all the communications across this isthmus. It is our duty, therefore, to take care that they shall not be interrupted either by invasions from our own country or by wars between the independent States of Central America. Under our treaty with New Granada of the 12th December, 1846, we are bound to guarantee the neutrality of the Isthmus of Panama, through which the Panama Railroad passes. . . .

Under these circumstances I recommend to Congress the passage of an act authorizing the President, in case of necessity, to employ the land and naval forces of the United States to carry into effect this guaranty of neutrality and protection. . . .

*   *   *

It is unnecessary to state in detail the alarming condition of the Territory of Kansas at the time of my inauguration. The opposing parties then stood in hostile array against each other, and any accident might have relighted the flames of civil war. . . .

*   *   *

The convention to frame a constitution for Kansas met on the first Monday of September last. They were called together by virtue of an act of the Territorial legislature, whose lawful existence had been recognized by Congress in different forms and by different enactments. . . .

⸱ ⸱ ⸱

The convention, after an angry and excited debate, finally determined, by a majority of only two, to submit the question of slavery to the people. . . .

⸱ ⸱ ⸱

Kansas has for some years occupied too much of the public attention. It is high time this should be directed to far more important objects. When once admitted into the Union, whether with or without slavery, the excitement beyond her own limits will speedily pass away, and she will then for the first time be left, as she ought to have been long since, to manage her own affairs in her own way. . . . Under these circumstances it may well be questioned whether the peace and quiet of the whole country are not of greater importance than the mere temporary triumph of either of the political parties in Kansas.

⸱ ⸱ ⸱

A Territorial government was established for Utah by act of Congress approved the 9th September, 1850, and the Constitution and laws of the United States were thereby extended over it "so far as the same or any provisions thereof may be applicable." . . . Brigham Young was appointed the first governor on the 20th September, 1850, and has held the office ever since. Whilst Governor Young has been both governor and superintendent of Indian affairs throughout this period, he has been at the same time the head of the church called the Latter-day Saints, and professes to govern its members and dispose of their property by direct inspiration and authority from the Almighty. His power has been, therefore, absolute over both church and state.

⸱ ⸱ ⸱

With the religious opinions of the Mormons, as long as they remained mere opinions, however deplorable in themselves and revolting to the moral and religious sentiments of all Christendom, I had no right to interfere. Actions alone, when in violation of the

Constitution and laws of the United States, become the legitimate subjects for the jurisdiction of the civil magistrate. . . .

* * *

. . . For several years, in order to maintain his independence [Governor Young] has been industriously employed in collecting and fabricating arms and munitions of war and in disciplining the Mormons for military service. . . . This is the first rebellion which has existed in our Territories, and humanity itself requires that we should put it down in such a manner that it shall be the last. . . . In order to accomplish this object it will be necessary, according to the estimate of the War Department, to raise four additional regiments; and this I earnestly recommend to Congress. . . .

. . . Now if a military road over our own Territories be indispensably necessary to enable us to meet and repel the invader, it follows as a necessary consequence not only that we possess the power, but it is our imperative duty to construct such a road. It would be an absurdity to invest a government with the unlimited power to make and conduct war and at the same time deny to it the only means of reaching and defeating the enemy at the frontier. Without such a road it is quite evident we can not "protect" California and our Pacific possessions "against invasion." We can not by any other means transport men and munitions of war from the Atlantic States in sufficient time successfully to defend these remote and distant portions of the Republic.

* * *

Our system for the disposal of the public lands, originating with the fathers of the Republic, has been improved as experience pointed the way, and gradually adapted to the growth and settlement of our Western States and Territories. It has worked well in practice. Already thirteen States and seven Territories have been carved out of these lands, and still more than a thousand millions of acres remain unsold. What a boundless prospect this presents to our country of future prosperity and power! . . .

JAMES BUCHANAN
SECOND STATE-OF-THE-UNION MESSAGE
WASHINGTON CITY, *December 6, 1858*

Fellow-Citizens of the Senate and House of Representatives:

It was the resistance to rightful authority and the persevering attempts to establish a revolutionary government under the Topeka constitution which caused the people of Kansas to commit the grave error of refusing to vote for delegates to the convention to frame a constitution under a law not denied to be fair and just in its provisions. . . .

The convention, notwithstanding, proceeded to adopt a constitution unexceptionable in its general features, and providing for the submission of the slavery question to a vote of the people, which, in my opinion, they were bound to do under the Kansas and Nebraska Act. This was the all-important question which had alone convulsed the Territory; and yet the opponents of the lawful government, persisting in their first error, refrained from exercising their right to vote, and preferred that slavery should continue rather than surrender their revolutionary Topeka organization.

Under these circumstances I submitted to Congress the constitution thus framed, with all the officers already elected necessary to put the State government into operation, accompanied by a strong recommendation in favor of the admission of Kansas as a State. In the course of my long public life I have never performed any official act which in the retrospect has afforded me more heartfelt satisfaction. . . .

It is to be lamented that a question so insignificant when viewed in its practical effects on the people of Kansas, whether decided one way or the other, should have kindled such a flame of excitement throughout the country. . . .

My recommendation, however, for the immediate admission of Kansas failed to meet the approbation of Congress. They deemed it wiser to adopt a different measure for the settlement of the question. . . . I therefore cordially acquiesced in what has been called the English compromise and approved the "act for the admission of the State of Kansas into the Union" upon the terms therein prescribed.

                                                      ■   ■   ■

The present condition of the Territory of Utah, when contrasted with what it was one year ago, is a subject for congratulation. It was then in a state of open rebellion, and, cost what it might, the character of the Government required that this rebellion should be suppressed and the Mormons compelled to yield obedience to the Constitution and the laws. . . .

                                                      ■   ■   ■

The truth is that Cuba, in its existing colonial condition, is a constant source of injury and annoyance to the American people. It is the only spot in the civilized world where the African slave trade is tolerated, and we are bound by treaty with Great Britain to maintain a naval force on the coast of Africa, at much expense both of life and treasure, solely for the purpose of arresting slavers bound to that island. . . .

It has been made known to the world by my predecessors that the United States have on several occasions endeavored to acquire Cuba from Spain by honorable negotiation. If this were accomplished, the last relic of the African slave trade would instantly disappear. We would not, if we could, acquire Cuba in any other manner. . . .

The island of Cuba, from its geographical position, commands the mouth of the Mississippi and the immense and annually increasing trade, foreign and coastwise, from the valley of that noble river, now embracing half the sovereign States of the Union. With that island under the dominion of a distant foreign power this trade, of vital importance to these States, is exposed to the danger of being destroyed in time of war, and it has hitherto been subjected to perpetual injury and annoyance in time of peace. . . .

Whilst the possession of the island would be of vast importance to the United States, its value to Spain is comparatively unim-

portant. . . . I refer the whole subject to Congress and commend
it to their careful consideration.

◾   ◾   ◾

The public debt on July 1, 1858, the commencement of the
present fiscal year, was $25,155,977.66. . . . The rapid increase
of the public debt and the necessity which exists for a modification
of the tariff to meet even the ordinary expenses of the Government
ought to admonish us all, in our respective spheres of duty, to the
practice of rigid economy.

◾   ◾   ◾

I would again call your attention to the construction of a Pacific
railroad. . . .

Whilst disclaiming all authority to appropriate money for the
construction of this road, except that derived from the war-making
power of the Constitution, there are important collateral considerations urging us to undertake the work as speedily as possible.
. . . The first and most momentous of these is that such a road
would be a powerful bond of union between the States east and
west of the Rocky Mountains. . . .

But again, in a commercial point of view, I consider this the
great question of the day. With the eastern front of our Republic
stretching along the Atlantic and its western front along the
Pacific, if all the parts should be united by a safe, easy, and rapid
intercommunication we must necessarily command a very large
proportion of the trade both of Europe and Asia. Our recent
treaties with China and Japan will open these rich and populous
Empires to our commerce; and the history of the world proves
that the nation which has gained possession of the trade with
eastern Asia has always become wealthy and powerful. . . . To
reap the rich harvest, however, it is an indispensable prerequisite
that we shall first have a railroad to convey and circulate its
products throughout every portion of the Union. . . .

JAMES BUCHANAN
THIRD STATE-OF-THE-UNION MESSAGE
WASHINGTON CITY, *December 19, 1859*

Fellow-Citizens of the Senate and House of Representatives:

Whilst it is the duty of the President "from time to time to give to Congress information of the state of the Union," I shall not refer in detail to the recent sad and bloody occurrences at Harpers Ferry. Still, it is proper to observe that these events, however bad and cruel in themselves, derive their chief importance from the apprehension that they are but symptoms of an incurable disease in the public mind, which may break out in still more dangerous outrages and terminate at last in an open war by the North to abolish slavery in the South.

Whilst for myself I entertain no such apprehension, they ought to afford a solemn warning to us all to beware of the approach of danger. . . . In this view, let me implore my countrymen, North and South, to cultivate the ancient feelings of mutual forbearance and good will toward each other and strive to allay the demon spirit of sectional hatred and strife now alive in the land. This advice proceeds from the heart of an old public functionary whose service commenced in the last generation, among the wise and conservative statesmen of that day, now nearly all passed away, and whose first and dearest earthly wish is to leave his country tranquil, prosperous, united, and powerful.

We ought to reflect that in this age, and especially in this country, there is an incessant flux and reflux of public opinion. Questions which in their day assumed a most threatening aspect have now nearly gone from the memory of men. They are "volcanoes burnt out, and on the lava and ashes and squalid scoria of old eruptions grow the peaceful olive, and cheering vine, and the sustaining corn." Such, in my opinion will prove to be the fate of the present sectional excitement should those who wisely seek to apply the remedy continue always to confine their efforts within the pale of the Constitution. . . . I firmly believe that the events at Harpers Ferry, by causing the people to pause and reflect upon the possible peril to their cherished institutions, will be the means under Providence of allaying the existing excitement and prevent-

ing further outbreaks of a similar character. They will resolve that
the Constitution and the Union shall not be endangered by rash
counsels, knowing that should "the silver cord be loosed or the
golden bowl be broken . . . at the fountain" human power could
never reunite the scattered and hostile fragments.

I cordially congratulate you upon the final settlement by the
Supreme Court of the United States of the question of slavery in
the Territories. . . . The right has been established of every citizen to take his property of any kind, including slaves, into the
common Territories belonging equally to all the States of the Confederacy, and to have it protected there under the Federal Constitution. . . .

Our history proves that the fathers of the Republic, in advance
of all other nations, condemned the African slave trade. It was,
notwithstanding, deemed expedient by the framers of the Constitution to deprive Congress of the power to prohibit "the migration
or importation of such persons as any of the States now existing
shall think proper to admit prior to the year 1808". . . .

But we are obliged as a Christian and moral nation to consider
what would be the effect upon unhappy Africa itself if we should
reopen the slave trade. . . . The numerous victims required to
supply it would convert the whole slave coast into a perfect pande-
monium, for which this country would be held responsible in the
eyes both of God and man. . . . All hopes of African civilization
would thus be ended.

I need not repeat the arguments which I urged in my last annual
message in favor of the acquisition of Cuba by fair purchase. My
opinions on that measure remain unchanged. I therefore again invite the serious attention of Congress to this important subject.
Without a recognition of this policy on their part it will be almost
impossible to institute negotiations with any reasonable prospect
of success.

JAMES BUCHANAN
FOURTH STATE-OF-THE-UNION MESSAGE
WASHINGTON CITY, *December 3, 1860*

Fellow-Citizens of the Senate and House of Representatives:

How easy would it be for the American people to settle the slavery question forever and to restore peace and harmony to this distracted country! They, and they alone, can do it. All that is necessary to accomplish the object, and all for which the slave States have ever contended, is to be let alone and permitted to manage their domestic institutions in their own way. As sovereign States, they, and they alone, are responsible before God and the world for the slavery existing among them. For this the people of the North are not more responsible and have no more right to interfere than with similar institutions in Russia or in Brazil.

And this brings me to observe that the election of any one of our fellow-citizens to the office of President does not of itself afford just cause for dissolving the Union. . . . The late Presidential election, however, has been held in strict conformity with its [the Constitution's] express provisions. How, then, can the result justify a revolution to destroy this very Constitution? Reason, justice, a regard for the Constitution, all require that we shall wait for some overt and dangerous act on the part of the President elect before resorting to such a remedy. . . .

After all, he is no more than the chief executive officer of the Government. His province is not to make but to execute the laws. . . .

It is alleged as one cause for immediate secession that the Southern States are denied equal rights with the other States in the common Territories. But by what authority are these denied? Not by Congress, which has never passed, and I believe never will pass, any act to exclude slavery from these Territories; and certainly not by the Supreme Court, which has solemnly decided that slaves are property, and, like all other property, their owners have a right to take them into the common Territories and hold them there under the protection of the Constitution.

Only three days after my inauguration the Supreme Court of the United States solemnly adjudged that this power did not exist in a Territorial legislature. Yet such has been the factious temper of the times that the correctness of this decision has been extensively impugned before the people, and the question has given rise to angry political conflicts throughout the country. . . .

The most palpable violations of constitutional duty which have yet been committed consist in the acts of different State legislatures to defeat the execution of the fugitive-slave law. It ought to be remembered, however, that for these acts neither Congress nor any President can justly be held responsible. Having been passed in violation of the Federal Constitution, they are therefore null and void. . . . It is founded upon an express provision of the Constitution, requiring that fugitive slaves who escape from service in one State to another shall be "delivered up" to their masters. Without this provision it is a well-known historical fact that the Constitution itself could never have been adopted by the Convention. . . . Here, then, a clear case is presented in which it will be the duty of the next President, as it has been my own, to act with vigor in executing this supreme law against the conflicting enactments of State legislatures. Should he fail in the performance of this high duty, he will then have manifested a disregard of the Constitution and laws, to the great injury of the people of nearly one-half of the States of the Union. But are we to presume in advance that he will thus violate his duty? . . .

What, in the meantime, is the responsibility and true position of the Executive? He is bound by solemn oath, before God and the country, "to take care that the laws be faithfully executed," and from this obligation he can not be absolved by any human power. But what if the performance of this duty, in whole or in part, has been rendered impracticable by events over which he could have exercised no control? Such at the present moment is the case throughout the State of South Carolina so far as the laws of the United States to secure the administration of justice by means of the Federal judiciary are concerned. . . .

The fact is that our Union rests upon public opinion, and can never be cemented by the blood of its citizens shed in civil war. If it can not live in the affections of the people, it must one day perish. Congress possesses many means of preserving it by conciliation, but the sword was not placed in their hand to preserve it by force.

But may I be permitted solemnly to invoke my countrymen to pause and deliberate before they determine to destroy this the grandest temple which has ever been dedicated to human freedom since the world began? It has been consecrated by the blood of our fathers, by the glories of the past, and by the hopes of the future. The Union has already made us the most prosperous, and ere long will, if preserved, render us the most powerful, nation on the face of the earth. . . . Surely when we reach the brink of the yawning abyss we shall recoil with horror from the last fatal plunge.

. . . The slavery question, like everything human, will have its day. I firmly believe that it has reached and passed the culminating point. But if in the midst of the existing excitement the Union shall perish, the evil may then become irreparable.

I reiterate the recommendation contained in my annual message of December, 1858, and repeated in that of December, 1859, in favor of the acquisition of Cuba from Spain by fair purchase. I firmly believe that such an acquisition would contribute essentially to the well-being and prosperity of both countries in all future time, as well as prove the certain means of immediately abolishing the African slave trade throughout the world. . . .

ABRAHAM LINCOLN
(1861–1865)

*"This issue embraces more
than the fate
of these United States"*

On the Fourth of July, 1861, the nation was grim but confident as the Thirty-seventh Congress, called into Extraordinary Session by President *Abraham Lincoln,* assembled to hear his War Message asking for men, arms, and money to meet the onslaught of civil war and bring it to a quick, victorious end.

Four months to the day had elapsed since Lincoln, in his Inaugural Address, tendered the olive branch to the seceding Southern states. It was disdained, and Confederate cannon had battered Fort Sumter into surrender. By now eleven states had seceded, and the structure of the Union was tottering. Southern armies were already marching. Twenty miles from the nation's capital, at Manassas, the Confederacy had massed thirty thousand graybacks, poised to strike at Washington in any unguarded moment. Commanding this threatening force was Pierre Gustave Toutant Beauregard, the little Creole whose fame had soared prodigiously since his reduction of Fort Sumter.

By July 4, the gloom that had hovered over Washington was momentarily lifted in a burst of confidence. Regiments of raw militia and volunteers had poured into the city. The tramp of marching feet and lumbering of cannon sounded night and day. People were shouting exuberantly, "On to Richmond!" but were giving no thought about how it could be done with untried, untrained troops. Even General

206

Irvin McDowell, appointed by Lincoln to command them, had little confidence in his recruits. He said so openly. To the man in the street, however, the outward trappings of war and armies had assembled around the city, and all seemed well.

Such was the picture on July 4, 1861, as the nation listened anxiously to hear what the President had to say, what he intended to do to save the Union.

Lincoln's War Message (quoted here in its entirety) ranks well up with the finest of all his utterances. Never did he make his position or his intentions more eloquently clear. Cost what it may, he was determined to throw the full war power of the government into the task of preserving the Union of the States, though it involved raising armies greater than the nation had ever dreamed of. He told the nation that the struggle in which the Union was involved was a struggle that involved the whole family of man. The fate of posterity itself was at stake.

In abridging Lincoln's four State-of-the-Union Messages, every effort has been made to keep the glowing essentials of what he said. One of the amazing features of these messages is that each one contains words and sentiments that rank with the most lustrous he ever uttered.

ABRAHAM LINCOLN
SPECIAL WAR MESSAGE
July 4, 1861

Fellow-Citizens of the Senate and House of Representatives:

Having been convened on an extraordinary occasion, as authorized by the Constitution, your attention is not called to any ordinary subject of legislation.

At the beginning of the present Presidential term, four months ago, the functions of the Federal Government were found to be generally suspended within the several States of South Carolina, Georgia, Alabama, Mississippi, Louisiana, and Florida, excepting only those of the Post Office Department.

Within these States all the forts, arsenals, dockyards, custom-houses, and the like, including the movable and stationary property in and about them, had been seized and were held in open hostility to this Government, excepting only Forts Pickens, Taylor, and Jefferson, on and near the Florida coast, and Fort Sumter, in Charleston Harbor, South Carolina. The forts thus seized had been put in improved condition, new ones had been built, and armed forces had been organized and were organizing, all avowedly with the same hostile purpose.

The forts remaining in the possession of the Federal Government in and near these States were either besieged or menaced by warlike preparations, and especially Fort Sumter was nearly surrounded by well-protected hostile batteries, with guns equal in quality to the best of its own and outnumbering the latter as perhaps ten to one. A disproportionate share of the Federal muskets and rifles had somehow found their way into these States, and had been seized to be used against the Government. Accumulations of the public revenue lying within them had been seized for the same object. The Navy was scattered in distant seas, leaving but a very small part of it within the immediate reach of the Government. Officers of the Federal Army and Navy had resigned in great numbers, and of those resigning a large proportion had taken up arms against the Government. Simultaneously and in connection with all this the purpose to sever the Federal Union was openly avowed. In accordance with this purpose, an ordinance had been adopted in each of these States declaring the States respectively to be separated from the National Union. A formula for instituting a combined government of these States had been promulgated, and this illegal organization, in the character of Confederate States, was already invoking recognition, aid, and intervention from foreign powers.

Finding this condition of things and believing it to be an imperative duty upon the incoming Executive to prevent, if possible, the consummation of such attempt to destroy the Federal Union, a choice of means to that end became indispensable. This choice was made, and was declared in the inaugural address. The policy chosen looked to the exhaustion of all peaceful measures before a resort to any stronger ones. It sought only to hold the public places and property not already wrested from the Government and to collect the revenue, relying for the rest on time, discussion, and the ballot box. It promised a continuance of the mails at Government expense to the very people who were resisting the Government, and it gave repeated pledges against any disturbance to any of the people or any of their rights. Of all that which a President might constitutionally and justifiably do in such a case, everything was forborne without which it was believed possible to keep the Government on foot.

On the 5th of March, the present incumbent's first full day in office, a letter of Major Anderson, commanding at Fort Sumter, written on the 28th of February and received at the War Department on the 4th of March, was by that Department placed in his hands. This letter expressed the professional opinion of the writer that reenforcements could not be thrown into that fort within the time for his relief rendered necessary by the limited supply of provisions, and with a view of holding possession of the same, with a force of less than 20,000 good and well-disciplined men. This opinion was concurred in by all the officers of his command, and their memoranda on the subject were made enclosures of Major Anderson's letter. The whole was immediately laid before Lieutenant-General Scott, who at once concurred with Major Anderson in opinion. On reflection, however, he took full time, consulting with other officers, both of the Army and the Navy, and at the end of four days came reluctantly, but decidedly, to the same conclusion as before. He also stated at the same time that no such sufficient force was then at the control of the Government or could be raised and brought to the ground within the time when the provisions in the fort would be exhausted. In a purely military point of view this reduced the duty of the Administration in the case to the mere matter of getting the garrison safely out of the fort.

It was believed, however, that to so abandon that position under the circumstances would be utterly ruinous; that the *necessity* under which it was to be done would not be fully understood; that by many it would be construed as a part of a *voluntary* policy; that at home it would discourage the friends of the Union, embolden its adversaries, and go far to insure to the latter a recognition abroad; that, in fact, it would be our national destruction consummated. This could not be allowed. Starvation was not yet upon the garrison, and ere it would be reached Fort Pickens might be reenforced. This last would be a clear indication of *policy,* and would better enable the country to accept the evacuation of Fort Sumter as a military *necessity.* An order was at once directed to be sent for the landing of the troops from the steamship *Brooklyn* into Fort Pickens. This order could not go by land but must take the longer and slower route by sea. The first return news from the order was received just one week before the fall of Fort Sumter. The news itself was that the officer commanding the *Sabine,* to which vessel the troops had been transferred from the *Brooklyn,* acting upon some *quasi* armistice of the late Administration (and of the existence of which the present Administration, up to the time the order was dispatched, had only too vague and uncertain rumors to fix attention) had refused to land the troops. To now reenforce Fort Pickens before a crisis would be reached at Fort Sumter was impossible, rendered so by the near exhaustion of provisions in the latter-named fort. In precaution against such a conjuncture the Government had a few days before commenced preparing an expedition, as well adapted as might be, to relieve Fort Sumter, which expedition was intended to be ultimately used or not, according to circumstances. The strongest anticipated case for using it was now presented, and it was resolved to send it forward. As had been intended in this contingency, it was also resolved to notify the governor of South Carolina that he might expect an attempt would be made to provision the fort, and that if the attempt should not be resisted there would be no effort to throw in men, arms, or ammunition without further notice, or in case of an attack upon the fort. This notice was accordingly given, whereupon the fort was attacked and bombarded to its fall, without even awaiting the arrival of the provisioning expedition.

It is thus seen that the assault upon and reduction of Fort Sumter was in no sense a matter of self-defense on the part of the assailants. They well knew that the garrison in the fort could by no possibility commit aggression upon them. They knew—they were expressly notified—that the giving of bread to the few brave and hungry men of the garrison was all which would on that occasion be attempted, unless themselves, by resisting so much, should provoke more. They knew that this Government desired to keep the garrison in the fort, not to assail them, but merely to maintain visible possession, and thus to preserve the Union from actual and immediate dissolution, trusting, as hereinbefore stated, to time, discussion, and the ballot box for final adjustment; and they assailed and reduced the fort for precisely the reverse object—to drive out the visible authority of the Federal Union, and thus force it to immediate dissolution. That this was their object the Executive well understood; and having said to them in the inaugural address, "You can have no conflict without being yourselves the aggressors," he took pains not only to keep this declaration good, but also to keep the case so free from the power of ingenious sophistry as that the world should not be able to misunderstand it. By the affair at Fort Sumter, with its surrounding circumstances, that point was reached. Then and thereby the assailants of the Government began the conflict of arms, without a gun in sight or in expectancy to return their fire, save only the few in the fort, sent to that harbor years before for their own protection, and still ready to give that protection in whatever was lawful. In this act, discarding all else, they have forced upon the country the distinct issue, "Immediate dissolution or blood."

And this issue embraces more than the fate of these United States. It presents to the whole family of man the question whether a constitutional republic, or democracy—a government of the people by the same people—can or can not maintain its territorial integrity against its own domestic foes. It presents the question whether discontented individuals, too few in numbers to control administration according to organic law in any case, can always, upon the pretenses made in this case, or on any other pretenses, or arbitrarily without any pretense, break up their government, and thus practically put an end to free government upon the earth. It forces us to ask, Is there in all republics this inherent and fatal weakness? Must a government of necessity be too *strong* for the liberties of its own people, or too *weak* to maintain its own existence?

So viewing the issue, no choice was left but to call out the war power of the Government and so to resist force employed for its destruction by force for its preservation.

The call was made, and the response of the country was most gratifying, surpassing in unanimity and spirit the most sanguine expectation. Yet none of the States commonly called slave States, except Delaware, gave a regiment through regular State organization. A few regiments have been organized within some others of those States by individual enterprise and received into the Government service. Of course the seceded States, so called (and to which Texas had been joined about the time of the inauguration), gave no troops to the cause of the Union. The border States, so called, were not uniform in their action, some of them being almost *for* the Union, while in others, as Virginia, North Carolina, Tennessee, and Arkansas, the Union sentiment was nearly repressed and silenced. The course taken in Virginia was the most remarkable, perhaps the most important. A convention elected by the people of that State to consider this very question of disrupting the Federal Union was in session at the capital of Virginia when Fort Sumter fell. To this body the people had chosen a large majority of *professed* Union men. Almost immediately after the fall of Sumter many members of that majority went over to the original disunion minority, and with them adopted an ordinance for withdrawing the State from the Union. Whether this change was wrought by their great approval of the assault upon Sumter or their great resentment at the Government's resistance to that assault is not definitely known. Although they submitted the ordinance for ratification to a vote of the people, to be taken on a day then somewhat more than a month distant, the convention and the legislature (which was also in session at the same time and place), with leading men of the State not members of either, immediately commenced acting as if the State were already out of the Union. They pushed military preparations vigorously forward all over the State. They seized the United States armory at Harpers Ferry and the navy-yard at Gosport, near Norfolk. They received—perhaps invited—into their State large bodies of troops, with their warlike appointments, from the so-called seceded States. They formally entered into a treaty of temporary alliance and cooperation with the so-called "Confederate States," and sent members to their congress at Montgomery; and, finally, they permitted the insurrectionary government to be transferred to their capital at Richmond.

The people of Virginia have thus allowed this giant insurrection to make its nest within her borders, and this Government has no choice left but to deal with it *where* it finds it; and it has the less regret, as the loyal citizens have in due form claimed its protection. Those loyal citizens this Government is bound to recognize and protect, as being Virginia.

In the border States, so called—in fact, the Middle States—there are those who favor a policy which they call "armed neutrality"; that is, an arming of those States to prevent the Union forces passing one way or the disunion the other over their soil. This would be disunion completed. Figuratively speaking, it would be the building of an impassable wall along the line of separation, and yet not quite an impassable one, for, under the guise of neutrality, it would tie the hands of the Union men and freely pass supplies from among them to the insurrectionists, which it could not do as an open enemy. At a stroke it would take all the trouble off the hands of secession, except only what proceeds from the external blockade. It would do for the disunionists that which of all things they most desire—feed them well and give them disunion without a struggle of their own. It recognizes no fidelity to the Constitution, no obligation to maintain the Union; and while very many who have favored it are doubtless loyal citizens, it is, nevertheless, very injurious in effect.

Recurring to the action of the Government, it may be stated that at first a call was made for 75,000 militia, and rapidly following this a proclamation was issued for closing the ports of the insurrectionary districts by proceedings in the nature of blockade. So far all was believed to be strictly legal. At this point the insurrectionists announced their purpose to enter upon the practice of privateering.

Other calls were made for volunteers to serve three years unless sooner discharged, and also for large additions to the Regular Army and Navy. These measures, whether strictly legal or not, were ventured upon under what appeared to be a popular demand and a public necessity, trusting then, as now, that Congress would readily ratify them. It is believed that nothing has been done beyond the constitutional competency of Congress.

Soon after the first call for militia it was considered a duty to authorize the Commanding General in proper cases, according to his discretion, to suspend the privilege of the writ of *habeas corpus,* or, in other words, to arrest and detain without resort to the ordinary processes and forms of law such individuals as he might deem dangerous to the public safety. This authority has purposely been exercised but very sparingly. Nevertheless, the legality and propriety of what has been done under it are questioned, and the attention of the country has been called to the proposition that one who is sworn to "take care that the laws be faithfully executed" should not himself violate them. Of course some consideration was given to the questions of power and propriety before this matter was acted upon. The whole of the laws which were required to be faithfully executed were being resisted and failing of execution in nearly one-third of the States. Must they be allowed to finally fail of execution, even had it been perfectly clear that by the use of the means necessary to their execution some single law, made in such extreme tenderness of the citizen's liberty that practically it relieves more of the guilty than of the innocent, should to a very limited extent be violated? To state the question more directly, Are all the laws *but one* to go unexecuted, and the Government itself go to pieces lest that one be violated? Even in such a case, would not the official oath be broken if the Government should be overthrown when it was believed that disregarding the single law would tend to preserve it? But it was not believed that this question was presented. It was not believed that any law was violated. The provision of the Constitution that "the privilege of the writ of *habeas corpus* shall not be suspended unless when, in cases of rebellion or invasion, the public safety may require it," is equivalent to a provision—is a provision—that such privilege may be suspended when, in cases of rebellion or invasion, the public safety *does* require it. It was decided that we have a case of rebellion and that the public safety does require the qualified suspension of the privilege of the writ which was authorized to be made. Now it is insisted that Congress, and not the Executive, is vested with this power; but the Constitution itself is silent as to which or who is to exercise the power; and as the provision was plainly made for a dangerous emergency, it can not be believed the framers of the instrument intended that in every case the danger should run its course until Congress could be called together, the very assembling of which might be prevented, as was intended in this case, by the rebellion.

No more extended argument is now offered, as an opinion at some length will probably be presented by the Attorney General. Whether there shall be any legislation upon the subject, and, if any, what, is submitted entirely to the better judgment of Congress.

The forbearance of this Government had been so extraordinary and so long continued as to lead some foreign nations to shape their action as if they supposed the early destruction of our National Union was probable. While this on discovery gave the Executive some concern, he is now happy to say that the sovereignty and rights of the United States are now everywhere practically respected by foreign powers, and a general sympathy with the country is manifested throughout the world.

The reports of the Secretaries of the Treasury, War, and the Navy will give the information in detail deemed necessary and convenient for your deliberation and action, while the Executive and all the Departments will stand ready to supply omissions or to communicate new facts considered important for you to know.

It is now recommended that you give the legal means for making this contest a short and a decisive one; that you place at the control of the Government for the work at least 400,000 men and $400,000,000. That number of men is about one-tenth of those of proper ages within the regions where apparently *all* are willing to engage, and the sum is less than a twenty-third part of the money value owned by the men who seem ready to devote the whole. A debt of $600,000,000 *now* is a less sum per head than was the debt of our Revolution when we came out of that struggle, and the money value in the country now bears even a greater proportion to what it was *then* than does the population. Surely each man has as strong a motive *now* to *preserve* our liberties as each had *then* to *establish* them.

A right result at this time will be worth more to the world than ten times the men and ten times the money. The evidence reaching us from the country leaves no doubt that the material for the work is abundant, and that it needs only the hand of legislation to give it legal sanction and the hand of the Executive to give it practical shape and efficiency. One of the greatest perplexities of the Government is to avoid receiving troops faster than it can provide for them. In a word, the people will save their Government if the Government itself will do its part only indifferently well.

It might seem at first thought to be of little difference whether the present movement at the South be called "secession" or "rebellion." The movers, however, well understand the difference. At the beginning they knew they could never raise their treason to any respectable magnitude by any name which implies *violation* of law. They knew their people possessed as much of moral sense, as much of devotion to law and order, and as much pride in and reverence for the history and Government of their common country as any other civilized and patriotic people. They knew they could make no advancement directly in the teeth of these strong and noble sentiments. Accordingly, they commenced by an insidious debauching of the public mind. They invented an ingenious sophism, which, if conceded, was followed by perfectly logical steps through all the incidents to the complete destruction of the Union. The sophism itself is that any State of the Union may *consistently* with the National Constitution, and therefore *lawfully* and *peacefully,* withdraw from the Union without the consent of the Union or of any other State. The little disguise that the supposed right is to be exercised only for just cause, themselves to be the sole judge of its justice, is too thin to merit any notice.

With rebellion thus sugar-coated they have been drugging the public mind of their section for more than thirty years, and until at length they have brought many good men to a willingness to take up arms against the Government the day *after* some assemblage of men have enacted the farcical pretense of taking their State out of the Union who could have been brought to no such thing the day *before.* This sophism derives much, perhaps the whole, of its currency from the assumption that there is some omnipotent and sacred supremacy pertaining to a *State*—to each State of our Federal Union. Our States have neither more nor less power than that reserved to them in the Union by the Constitution, no one of them ever having been a State *out* of the Union. The original ones passed into the Union even *before* they cast off their British colonial dependence, and the new ones each came into the Union directly from a condition of dependence, excepting Texas; and even Texas, in its temporary independence, was never designated a State. The new ones only took the designation of States on coming into the Union, while that name was first adopted for the old ones in and by the Declaration of Independence. Therein the "United Colonies" were declared to be "free and independent States"; but even then the object plainly was not to declare their independence of *one another* or of the *Union,* but directly the contrary, as their mutual pledge and their mutual action before, at the time, and afterwards abundantly show. The express plighting of faith by each and all of the original thirteen in the Articles of Confederation, two years later, that the Union shall be perpetual is most conclusive. Having never been States, either in substance or in name, *outside* of the Union, whence this magical omnipotence of "State rights," asserting a claim of power to lawfully destroy the Union itself? Much is said about the "sovereignty" of the States, but the word even is not in the National Constitution, nor, as is believed, in any of the State constitutions. What is a "sovereignty" in the political sense of the term? Would it be far wrong to define it "a political community without a political superior"? Tested by this, no one of our States, except Texas, ever was a sovereignty; and even Texas gave up the character on coming into the Union, by which act she acknowledged the Constitution of the United States and the laws and treaties of the United States made in pursuance of the Constitution to be for her the supreme law of the land. The States have their status in the Union, and they have no other lega! status. If they break from this, they can only do so against law and by revolution. The Union, and not themselves separately, procured their independence and their liberty. By conquest or purchase the Union gave each of them whatever of independence and liberty it has. The Union is older than any of the States, and, in fact, it created them as States. Originally some dependent colonies made the Union, and in turn the Union threw off their old dependence for them and made them States, such as they are. Not one of them ever had a State constitution independent of the Union. Of course it is not forgotten that all the new States framed their constitutions before they entered the

Union, nevertheless dependent upon and preparatory to coming into the Union.

Unquestionably the States have the powers and rights reserved to them in and by the National Constitution; but among these surely are not included all conceivable powers, however mischievous or destructive, but at most such only as were known in the world at the time as governmental powers; and certainly a power to destroy the Government itself had never been known as a governmental—as a merely administrative power. This relative matter of national power and State rights, as a principle, is no other than the principle of *generality* and *locality*. Whatever concerns the whole should be confided to the whole—to the General Government—while whatever concerns *only* the State should be left exclusively to the State. This is all there is of original principle about it. Whether the National Constitution in defining boundaries between the two has applied the principle with exact accuracy is not to be questioned. We are all bound by that defining without question.

What is now combated is the position that secession is *consistent* with the Constitution—is *lawful* and *peaceful*. It is not contended that there is any express law for it, and nothing should ever be implied as law which leads to unjust or absurd consequences. The nation purchased with money the countries out of which several of these States were formed. Is it just that they shall go off without leave and without refunding? The nation paid very large sums (in the aggregate, I believe, nearly a hundred millions) to relieve Florida of the aboriginal tribes. Is it just that she shall now be off without consent or without making any return? The nation is now in debt for money applied to the benefit of these so-called seceding States in common with the rest. Is it just either that creditors shall go unpaid or the remaining States pay the whole? A part of the present national debt was contracted to pay the old debts of Texas. Is it just that she shall leave and pay no part of this herself?

Again: If one State may secede, so may another; and when all shall have seceded none is left to pay the debts. Is this quite just to creditors? Did we notify them of this sage view of ours when we borrowed their money? If we now recognize this doctrine by allowing the seceders to go in peace, it is difficult to see what we can do if others choose to go or to extort terms upon which they will promise to remain.

The seceders insist that our Constitution admits of secession. They have assumed to make a national constitution of their own, in which of necessity they have either *discarded* or *retained* the right of secession, as they insist it exists in ours. If they have discarded it, they thereby admit that on principle it ought not to be in ours. If they have retained it, by their own construction of ours they show that to be consistent they must secede from one another whenever they shall find it the easiest way of settling their debts or effecting any other selfish or unjust object. The principle itself is one of disintegration, and upon which no government can possibly endure.

If all the States save one should assert the power to *drive* that one out of the Union, it is presumed the whole class of seceder politicians would at once deny the power and denounce the act as the greatest outrage upon State rights. But suppose that precisely the same act, instead of being called "driving the one out," should be called "the seceding of the others from that one," it would be exactly what the seceders claim to do, unless, indeed, they make the point that the one, because it is a minority, may rightfully do what the others, because they are a majority, may not rightfully do. These politicians are subtle and profound on the rights of minorities. They are not partial to that power which made the Constitution and speaks from the preamble, calling itself "we, the people."

It may well be questioned whether there is today a majority of the legally qualified voters of any State, except, perhaps, South Carolina, in favor of disunion. There is much reason to believe that the Union men are the majority in many, if not in every other one, of the so-called seceded States. The contrary has not been demonstrated in any one of them. It is ventured to affirm this even of Virginia and Tennessee; for the result of an election held in military camps, where the bayonets are all on one side of the question voted upon, can scarcely be considered as demonstrating popular sentiment. At such an election all that large class who are at once *for* the Union and *against* coercion would be coerced to vote against the Union.

It may be affirmed without extravagance that the free institutions we enjoy have developed the power and improved the condition of our whole people beyond any example in the world. Of this we now have a striking and an impressive illustration. So large an army as the Government has now on foot was never before known without a soldier in it but who had taken his place there of his own free choice. But more than this, there are many single regiments whose members, one and another, possess full practical knowledge of all the arts, sciences, professions, and whatever else, whether useful or elegant, is known in the world; and there is scarcely one from which there could not be selected a President, a Cabinet, a Congress, and perhaps a court, abundantly competent to administer the Government itself. Nor do I say this is not true also in the army of our late friends, now adversaries in this contest; but if it is, so much better the reason why the Government which has conferred such benefits on both them and us should not be broken up. Whoever in any section proposes to abandon such a government would do well to consider in deference to what principle it is that he does it; what better he is likely to get in its stead; whether the substitute will give, or be intended to give, so much of good to the people. There are some foreshadowings on this subject. Our adversaries have adopted some declarations of independence in which, unlike the good old one penned by Jefferson, they omit the words "all men are created equal." Why? They have adopted a temporary national constitution, in the preamble of which, unlike our good old one signed by Washington, they omit "We, the people," and substitute "We, the deputies of the sovereign and independent States." Why? Why this deliberate pressing out of view the rights of men and the authority of the people?

This is essentially a people's contest. On the side of the Union it is a struggle for maintaining in the world that form and substance of government whose leading object is to elevate the condition of men; to lift artificial weights from all shoulders; to clear the paths of laudable pursuit for all; to afford all an unfettered start and a fair chance in the race of life. Yielding to partial and temporary departures, from necessity, this is the leading object of the Government for whose existence we contend.

I am most happy to believe that the plain people understand and appreciate this. It is worthy of note that while in this the Government's hour of trial large numbers of those in the Army and Navy who have been favored with the offices have resigned and proved false to the hand which had pampered them, not one common soldier or common sailor is known to have deserted his flag.

Great honor is due to those officers who remained true despite the example of their treacherous associates; but the greatest honor and most important fact of all is the unanimous firmness of the common soldiers and common sailors. To the last man, so far as known, they have successfully resisted the traitorous efforts of those whose commands but an hour before they obeyed as absolute law. This is the patriotic instinct of plain people. They understand without an argument that the destroying the Government which was made by Washington means no good to them.

Our popular Government has often been called an experiment. Two points in it our people have already settled—the successful *establishing* and the successful *administering* of it. One still remains —its successful *maintenance* against a formidable internal attempt to overthrow it. It is now for them to demonstrate to the world that those who can fairly carry an election can also suppress a rebellion; that ballots are the rightful and peaceful successors of bullets, and that when ballots have fairly and constitutionally decided there can be no successful appeal back to bullets; that there can be no successful appeal except to ballots themselves at succeeding elections. Such will be a great lesson of peace, teaching men that what they can not take by an election neither can they take it by a war; teaching all the folly of being the beginners of a war.

Lest there be some uneasiness in the minds of candid men as to what is to be the course of the Government toward the Southern States *after* the rebellion shall have been suppressed, the Executive deems it proper to say it will be his purpose then, as ever, to be guided by the Constitution and the laws, and that he probably will have no different understanding of the powers and duties of the Federal Government relatively to the rights of the States and the people under the Constitution than that expressed in the inaugural address.

He desires to preserve the Government, that it may be administered for all as it was administered by the men who made it. Loyal citizens everywhere have the right to claim this of their government, and the government has no right to withhold or neglect it. It is not perceived that in giving it there is any coercion, any conquest, or any subjugation in any just sense of those terms.

The Constitution provides, and all the States have accepted the provision, that "The United States shall guarantee to every State in this Union a republican form of government." But if a State may lawfully go out of the Union, having done so it may also discard the republican form of government; so that to prevent its going out is an indispensable *means* to the *end* of maintaining the guaranty mentioned; and when an end is lawful and obligatory the indispensable means to it are also lawful and obligatory.

It was with the deepest regret that the Executive found the duty of employing the war power in defense of the Government forced upon him. He could but perform this duty or surrender the existence of the Government. No compromise by public servants could in this case be a cure; not that compromises are not often proper, but that no popular government can long survive a marked precedent that those who carry an election can only save the government from immediate destruction by giving up the main point upon which the people gave the election. The people themselves, and not their servants, can safely reverse their own deliberate decisions.

As a private citizen the Executive could not have consented that these institutions shall perish; much less could he in betrayal of so vast and so sacred a trust as these free people had confided to him. He felt that he had no moral right to shrink, nor even to count the chances of his own life, in what might follow. In full view of his great responsibility he has so far done what he has deemed his duty. You will now, according to your own judgment, perform yours. He sincerely hopes that your views and your action may so accord with his as to assure all faithful citizens who have been disturbed in their rights of a certain and speedy restoration to them under the Constitution and the laws.

And having thus chosen our course, without guile and with pure purpose, let us renew our trust in God and go forward without fear and with manly hearts.

ABRAHAM LINCOLN
FIRST STATE-OF-THE-UNION MESSAGE
WASHINGTON, *December 3, 1861*

Fellow-Citizens of the Senate and House of Representatives:
    The war continues. In considering the policy to be adopted for suppressing the insurrection I have been anxious and careful that the inevitable conflict for this purpose shall not degenerate into a violent and remorseless revolutionary struggle. I have therefore in every case thought it proper to keep the integrity of the Union prominent as the primary object of the contest on our part, leaving all questions which are not of vital military importance to the more deliberate action of the Legislature.

So also, obeying the dictates of prudence, as well as the obligations of law, instead of transcending I have adhered to the act of Congress to confiscate property used for insurrectionary purposes. The Union must be preserved, and hence all indispensable means must be employed. We should not be in haste to determine that radical and extreme measures, which may reach the loyal as well as the disloyal, are indispensable.

The last ray of hope for preserving the Union peaceably expired at the assault upon Fort Sumter, and a general review of what has occurred since may not be unprofitable. What was painfully uncertain then is much better defined and more distinct now, and the progress of events is plainly in the right direction. The insurgents confidently claimed a strong support from north of Mason and Dixon's line, and the friends of the Union were not free from apprehension on the point. This, however, was soon settled definitely, and on the right side. Maryland was made to seem against the Union. Kentucky, too, for some time in doubt, is now decidedly and, I think, unchangeably ranged on the side of the Union. Missouri is comparatively quiet, and, I believe, can not again be overrun by the insurrectionists. These three States of

Maryland, Kentucky, and Missouri, neither of which would promise a single soldier at first, have now an aggregate of not less than 40,000 in the field for the Union, while of their citizens certainly not more than a third of that number, and they of doubtful whereabouts and doubtful existence, are in arms against us. After a somewhat bloody struggle of months, winter closes on the Union people of western Virginia, leaving them masters of their own country.

✵ ✵ ✵

It continues to develop that the insurrection is largely, if not exclusively, a war upon the first principle of popular government—the rights of the people. Conclusive evidence of this is found in the most grave and maturely considered public documents, as well as in the general tone of the insurgents. Monarchy itself is sometimes hinted at as a possible refuge from the power of the people. In my present position I could scarcely be justified were I to omit raising a warning voice against this approach of returning despotism.

It is not needed nor fitting here that a general argument should be made in favor of popular institutions, but there is one point, with its connections, not so hackneyed as most others, to which I ask a brief attention. It is the effort to place capital on an equal footing with, if not above, labor in the structure of government. It is assumed that labor is available only in connection with capital; that nobody labors unless somebody else, owning capital, somehow by the use of it induces him to labor. This assumed, it is next considered whether it is best that capital shall hire laborers, and thus induce them to work by their own consent, or buy them and drive them to it without their consent. Having proceeded so far, it is naturally concluded that all laborers are either hired laborers or what we call slaves. And further, it is assumed that whoever is once a hired laborer is fixed in that condition for life.

Now there is no such relation between capital and labor as assumed, nor is there any such thing as a free man being fixed for life in the condition of a hired laborer. Both these assumptions are false, and all inferences from them are groundless.

Labor is prior to and independent of capital. Capital is only the fruit of labor, and could never have existed if labor had not first existed. Labor is the superior of capital, and deserves much the higher consideration. Capital has its rights, which are as worthy of protection as any other rights. Nor is it denied that there is, and probably always will be, a relation between labor and capital producing mutual benefits. The error is in assuming that the whole labor of community exists within that relation. A few men own capital, and that few avoid labor themselves, and with their capital hire or buy another few to labor for them. A large majority belong to neither class—neither work for others nor have others working for them. In most of the Southern States a majority of the whole people of all colors are neither slaves nor masters, while in the Northern a large majority are neither hirers nor hired. Men, with their families—wives, sons, and daughters—work for themselves on their farms, in their houses, and in their shops, taking the whole product to themselves, and asking no favors of capital on the one hand nor of hired laborers or slaves on the other.

✗   ✗   ✗

Again, as has already been said, there is not of necessity any such thing as the free hired laborer being fixed to that condition for life. Many independent men everywhere in these States a few years back in their lives were hired laborers. The prudent, penniless beginner in the world labors for wages awhile, saves a surplus with which to buy tools or land for himself, then labors on his own account another while, and at length hires another new beginner to help him. No men living are more worthy to be trusted than those who toil up from poverty; none less inclined to take or touch aught which they have not honestly earned. Let them beware of surrendering a political power which they already possess, and which if surrendered will surely be used to close the door of advancement against such as they and to fix new disabilities and burdens upon them till all of liberty shall be lost.

From the first taking of our national census to the last are seventy years, and we find our population at the end of the period eight times as great as it was at the beginning. The increase of those other things which men deem desirable has been even greater. We thus have at one view what the popular principle, applied to Government through the machinery of the States and the

Union, has produced in a given time, and also what if firmly maintained it promises for the future. There are already among us those who if the Union be preserved will live to see it contain 250,000,000. The struggle of to-day is not altogether for to-day; it is for a vast future also. With a reliance on Providence all the more firm and earnest, let us proceed in the great task which events have devolved upon us.

ABRAHAM LINCOLN
SECOND STATE-OF-THE-UNION MESSAGE
December 1, 1862

Fellow-Citizens of the Senate and House of Representatives:

Since your last annual assembling another year of health and bountiful harvests has passed, and while it has not pleased the Almighty to bless us with a return of peace, we can but press on, guided by the best light He gives us, trusting that in His own good time and wise way all will yet be well.

If the condition of our relations with other nations is less gratifying than it has usually been at former periods, it is certainly more satisfactory than a nation so unhappily distracted as we are might reasonably have apprehended.

The civil war, which has so radically changed for the moment the occupations and habits of the American people, has at the same time excited political ambitions and apprehensions which have produced a profound agitation throughout the civilized world. In this unusual agitation we have forborne from taking part in any controversy between foreign states and between parties or factions in such states. We have attempted no propagandism and acknowledged no revolution. But we have left to every nation the exclusive conduct and management of its own affairs. Our struggle has been, of course, contemplated by foreign nations with reference less to its own merits than to its supposed and often exaggerated effects and consequences resulting to those nations themselves. Nevertheless, complaint on the part of this Government, even if it were just, would certainly be unwise.

Applications have been made to me by many free Americans of

African descent to favor their emigration, with a view to such colonization as was contemplated in recent acts of Congress. Liberia and Haiti are as yet the only countries to which colonists of African descent from here could go with certainty of being received and adopted as citizens; and I regret to say such persons contemplating colonization do not seem so willing to migrate to those countries as to some others, nor so willing as I think their interest demands.

I have favored the project for connecting the United States with Europe by an Atlantic telegraph, and a similar project to extend the telegraph from San Francisco to connect by a Pacific telegraph with the line which is being extended across the Russian Empire.

The Territories of the United States, with unimportant exceptions, have remained undisturbed by the civil war; and they are exhibiting such evidence of prosperity as justifies an expectation that some of them will soon be in a condition to be organized as States and be constitutionally admitted into the Federal Union.

The Indian tribes upon our frontiers have during the past year manifested a spirit of insubordination. In the month of August last the Sioux Indians in Minnesota attacked the settlements in their vicinity with extreme ferocity, killing indiscriminately men, women, and children. This attack was wholly unexpected, and therefore no means of defense had been provided. It is estimated that not less than 800 persons were killed by the Indians, and a large amount of property was destroyed. How this outbreak was induced is not definitely known, and suspicions, which may be unjust, need not to be stated. The State of Minnesota has suffered great injury from this Indian War. A large portion of her territory has been depopulated, and a severe loss has been sustained by the destruction of property.

On the 22d day of September last a proclamation was issued by the Executive. In accordance with the purpose expressed in the second paragraph of that paper, I now respectfully recall your attention to what may be called "compensated emancipation."

The main points are, first the emancipation; secondly, the length of time for consummating it (thirty-seven years); and, thirdly, the compensation.

The emancipation will be unsatisfactory to the advocates of perpetual slavery, but the length of time should greatly mitigate their dissatisfaction. The time spares both races from the evils of sudden derangement—in fact, from the necessity of any derangement —while most of those whose habitual course of thought will be disturbed by the measure will have passed away before its consummation. They will never see it. Another class will hail the prospect of emancipation, but will deprecate the length of time. They will feel that it gives too little to the now living slaves. But it really gives them much.

The proposed emancipation would shorten the war, perpetuate peace, insure this increase of population, and proportionately the wealth of the country. With these we should pay all the emancipation would cost, together with our other debt, easier than we should pay our other debt without it. If we had allowed our old national debt to run at 6 per cent per annum, simple interest, from the end of our revolutionary struggle until to-day, without paying anything on either principal or interest, each man of us would owe less upon that debt now than each man owed upon it then; and this because our increase of men through the whole period has been greater than 6 per cent—has run faster than the interest upon the debt. Thus time alone relieves a debtor nation, so long as its population increases faster than unpaid interest accumulates on its debt.

As to the second article, I think it would be impracticable to return to bondage the class of persons therein contemplated. Some of them, doubtless, in the property sense belong to loyal owners, and hence provision is made in this article for compensating such.

The third article relates to the future of the freed people. It does not oblige but merely authorizes Congress to aid in colonizing such as may consent. I can not make it better known than it already is that I strongly favor colonization; and yet I wish to say that there is an objection urged against free colored persons remaining in this country which is largely imaginary, if not sometimes malicious.

But it is dreaded that the freed people will swarm forth and cover the whole land. Are they not already in the land? Will liberation make them any more numerous? Equally distributed among the whites of the whole country, there would be but one colored to seven whites. Could the one in any way greatly disturb the seven? There are many communities now having more than one free colored person to seven whites and this without any apparent consciousness of evil from it. But why should emancipation [in the] South send the free people North? People of any color seldom run unless there be something to run from. Heretofore colored people to some extent have fled North from bondage, and now, perhaps, from both bondage and destitution. But if gradual emancipation and deportation be adopted, they will have neither to flee from.

I do not forget the gravity which should characterize a paper addressed to the Congress of the nation by the Chief Magistrate of the nation nor do I forget that some of you are my seniors, nor that many of you have more experience than I in the conduct of public affairs. Yet I trust that in view of the great responsibility resting upon me you will perceive no want of respect to yourselves in any undue earnestness I may seem to display.

Is it doubted, then, that the plan I propose, if adopted, would shorten the war, and thus lessen its expenditure of money and of blood? Is it doubted that it would restore the national authority and national prosperity and perpetuate both indefinitely? Is it doubted that we here—Congress and executive—can secure its adoption? Will not the good people respond to a united and earnest appeal from us? Can we, can they, by any other means so certainly or so speedily assure these vital objects? We can succeed only by concert. It is not "Can any of us imagine better?" but "Can we all do better?" Object whatsoever is possible, still the question recurs, "Can we do better?" The dogmas of the quiet past are inadequate to the stormy present. The occasion is piled high with difficulty, and we must rise with the occasion. As our case is new, so we must think anew and act anew. We must disenthrall ourselves, and then we shall save our country.

Fellow-Citizens, we can not escape history. We of this Congress and this Administration will be remembered in spite of ourselves. No personal significance or insignificance can spare one or another of us. The fiery trial through which we pass will light us down in honor or dishonor to the latest generation. We say we are for the

Union. The world will not forget that we say this. We know how to save the Union. The world knows we do know how to save it. We, even we here, hold the power and bear the responsibility. In giving freedom to the slave we assure freedom to the free—honorable alike in what we give and what we preserve. We shall nobly save or meanly lose the last best hope of earth. Other means may succeed; this could not fail. The way is plain, peaceful, generous, just—a way which if followed the world will forever applaud and God must forever bless.

ABRAHAM LINCOLN
THIRD STATE-OF-THE-UNION MESSAGE
December 8, 1863

Fellow-Citizens of the Senate and House of Representatives:
        Another year of health and of sufficiently abundant harvests has passed. For these, and especially for the improved condition of our national affairs, our renewed and profoundest gratitude to God is due.
    We remain in peace and friendship with foreign powers.
    The efforts of disloyal citizens of the United States to involve us in foreign wars to aid an inexcusable insurrection have been unavailing. Her Britannic Majesty's Government, as was justly expected, have exercised their authority to prevent the departure of new hostile expeditions from British ports. The Emperor of France has by a like proceeding promptly vindicated the neutrality which he proclaimed at the beginning of the contest.
    Satisfactory arrangements have been made with the Emperor of Russia, which, it is believed, will result in effecting a continuous line of telegraph through that Empire from our Pacific coast.
    I recommend to your favorite consideration the subject of an international telegraph across the Atlantic Ocean, and also of a telegraph between this capital and the national forts along the Atlantic seaboard and the Gulf of Mexico. Such communications, established with any reasonable outlay, would be economical as well as effective aids to the diplomatic, military, and naval service.
    When Congress assembled a year ago, the war had already lasted

nearly twenty months, and there had been many conflicts on both land and sea, with varying results; the rebellion had been pressed back into reduced limits; yet the tone of public feeling and opinion, at home and abroad, was not satisfactory. With other signs, the popular elections then just past indicated uneasiness among ourselves, while, amid much that was cold and menacing, the kindest words coming from Europe were uttered in accents of pity that we were too blind to surrender a hopeless cause. Our commerce was suffering greatly by a few armed vessels built upon and furnished from foreign shores, and we were threatened with such additions from the same quarter as would sweep our trade from the sea and raise our blockade. We had failed to elicit from European Governments anything hopeful upon this subject. The preliminary emancipation proclamation, issued in September, was running its assigned period to the beginning of the new year. A month later the final proclamation came, including the announcement that colored men of suitable condition would be received into the war service. The policy of emancipation and of employing black soldiers gave to the future a new aspect, about which hope and fear and doubt contended in uncertain conflict. According to our political system, as a matter of civil administration, the General Government had no lawful power to effect emancipation in any State, and for a long time it had been hoped that the rebellion could be suppressed without resorting to it as a military measure. It was all the while deemed possible that the necessity for it might come, and that if it should the crisis of the contest would then be presented. It came, and, as was anticipated, it was followed by dark and doubtful days. Eleven months having now passed, we are permitted to take another review. The rebel borders are pressed still farther back, and by the complete opening of the Mississippi the country dominated by the rebellion is divided into distinct parts, with no practical communication between them.

Of those who were slaves at the beginning of the rebellion full 100,000 are now in the United States military service, about one-half of which number actually bear arms in the ranks, thus giving the double advantage of taking so much labor from the insurgent cause and supplying the places which otherwise must be filled with so many white men. So far as tested, it is difficult to say they are not as good soldiers as any.

Looking now to the present and future, and with reference to a resumption of the national authority within the States wherein that authority has been suspended, I have thought fit to issue a proclamation. On examination of this proclamation, it will appear, as is believed, that nothing will be attempted beyond what is amply justified by the Constitution. True, the form of an oath is given, but no man is coerced to take it. The man is only promised a pardon in case he voluntarily takes the oath. The Constitution authorizes the Executive to grant or withhold the pardon at his own absolute discretion, and this includes the power to grant on terms, as is fully established by judicial and other authorities. But if it be proper to require as a test of admission to the political body an oath of allegiance to the Constitution of the United States and to the Union under it, why also to the laws and proclamation in regard to slavery? Those laws and proclamations were enacted and put forth for the purpose of aiding in the suppression of the rebellion. To give them their fullest effect there had to be a pledge for their maintenance. In my judgment, they have aided and will further aid the cause for which they were intended. To now abandon them would be not only to relinquish a lever of power, but would also be a cruel and an astounding breach of faith. I may add at this point that while I remain in my present position I shall not attempt to retract or modify the emancipation proclamation, nor shall I return to slavery any person who is free by the terms of that proclamation or by any of the acts of Congress.

In the midst of other cares, however important, we must not lose sight of the fact that the war power is still our main reliance. To that power alone can we look yet for a time to give confidence to the people in the contested regions that the insurgent power will not again overrun them. Until that confidence shall be established little can be done anywhere for what is called reconstruction. Hence our chiefest care must still be directed to the Army and Navy, who have thus far borne their harder part so nobly and well; and it may be esteemed fortunate that in giving the greatest efficiency to these indispensable arms we do also honorably recognize the gallant men, from commander to sentinel, who compose them, and to whom more than to others the world must stand indebted for the home of freedom disenthralled, regenerated, enlarged, and perpetuated.

ABRAHAM LINCOLN
FOURTH STATE-OF-THE-UNION MESSAGE
December 6, 1864

Fellow-Citizens of the Senate and House of Representatives:
      Again the blessings of health and abundant harvests claim our profoundest gratitude to the Almighty God.
      The condition of our foreign affairs is reasonably satisfactory.
      Mexico continues to be a theater of civil war. While our political relations with that country have undergone no change, we have at the same time strictly maintained neutrality between the belligerents.
      Official correspondence has been freely opened with Liberia, and it gives us a pleasing view of social and political progress in that Republic. It may be expected to derive new vigor from American influence, improved by the rapid disappearance of slavery in the United States.
      I solicit your authority to furnish to the Republic a gunboat at moderate cost, to be reimbursed to the United States by installments. Such a vessel is needed for the safety of that State against the native African races, and in Liberian hands it would be more effective in arresting the African slave trade than a squadron in our own hands.
      The report of the Secretary of Navy presents a comprehensive and satisfactory exhibit of the affairs of that Department and of the naval service. It is a subject of congratulation and laudable pride to our countrymen that a Navy of such vast proportions has been organized in so brief a period and conducted with so much efficiency and success.
      The general exhibit of the Navy, including vessels under construction on the 1st of December, 1864, shows a total of 671 vessels, carrying 4,610 guns, and of 510,396 tons, being an actual

increase during the year, over and above all losses by shipwreck or in battle, of 83 vessels, 167 guns, and 42,427 tons.

The organization and admission of the State of Nevada has been completed in conformity with law, and thus our excellent system is firmly established in the mountains, which once seemed a barren and uninhabitable waste between the Atlantic States and those which have grown up on the coast of the Pacific Ocean.

The great enterprise of connecting the Atlantic with the Pacific States by railways and telegraph lines has been entered upon with a vigor that gives assurance of success. The route of the main line of the road has been definitely located for 100 miles westward from the initial point at Omaha City, Nebraska, and a preliminary location of the Pacific Railroad of California has been made from Sacramento eastward to the great bend of the Truckee River in Nevada.

The most remarkable feature in the military operations of the year is General Sherman's attempted march of 300 miles directly through the insurgent region. It tends to show a great increase of our relative strength that our General in Chief should feel able to confront and hold in check every active force of the enemy, and yet to detach a well-appointed large army to move on such an expedition. The result not yet being known, conjecture in regard to it is not here indulged.

At the last session of Congress a proposed amendment of the Constitution abolishing slavery throughout the United States passed the Senate, but failed for lack of the requisite two-thirds vote in the House of Representatives. Although the present is the same Congress and nearly the same members, and without questioning the wisdom or patriotism of those who stood in opposition, I venture to recommend the reconsideration and passage of the measure at the present session.

The election has exhibited another fact not less valuable to be known—the fact that we do not approach exhaustion in the most important branch of national resources, that of living men. While it is melancholy to reflect that the war has filled so many graves and carried mourning to so many hearts, it is some relief to know that, compared with the surviving, the fallen have been so few. While corps and divisions and brigades and regiments have formed and fought and dwindled and gone out of existence, a great majority of the men who composed them are still living. The important fact remains demonstrated that we have more men now than we had when the war began; that we are not exhausted nor in process of exhaustion; that we are gaining strength and may if need be maintain the contest indefinitely. This as to men. Material resources are now more complete and abundant than ever.

The national resources, then, are unexhausted, and, as we believe, inexhaustible. The public purpose to reestablish and maintain the national authority is unchanged, and, as we believe, unchangeable. The manner of continuing the effort remains to choose. On careful consideration of all the evidence accessible it seems to me that no attempt at negotiation with the insurgent leader could result in any good. He would accept nothing short of severance of the Union, precisely what we will not and can not give. His declarations to this effect are explicit and oft repeated. He does not attempt to deceive us. He affords us no excuse to deceive ourselves. He can not voluntarily reaccept the Union; we can not voluntarily yield it. Between him and us the issue is distinct, simple, and inflexible. It is an issue which can only be tried by war and decided by victory. If we yield, we are beaten; if the Southern people fail him, he is beaten. Either way it would be the victory and defeat following war. What is true, however, of him who heads the insurgent cause is not necessarily true of those who follow. Although he can not re-accept the Union, they can. Some of them, we know, already desire peace and reunion. The number of such may increase. They can at any moment have peace simply by laying down their arms and submitting to the national authority under the Constitution.

In presenting the abandonment of armed resistance to the national authority on the part of the insurgents as the only indispensable condition to ending the war on the part of the Government, I retract nothing heretofore said as to slavery. I repeat the declaration made a year ago, that "While I remain in my present position I shall not attempt to retract or modify the emancipation proclamation, nor shall I return to slavery any person who is free by the terms of that proclamation or by any of the acts of Congress." If the people should, by whatever mode or means, make it an Executive duty to reenslave such persons, another, and not I, must be their instrument to perform it.

In stating a single condition of peace I mean simply to say that the war will cease on the part of the Government whenever it shall have ceased on the part of those who began it.

ANDREW JOHNSON
(1865–1869)

*"My winding sheet
the brave
old flag"*

At 10:00 A.M. April 15, 1865, Vice President *Andrew Johnson,* who never went to school a day in his life, took the oath as seventeenth President of the United States. The assassinated Abraham Lincoln was barely three hours dead when Johnson repeated the oath of office after Chief Justice Salmon P. Chase and affirmed it by kissing the Bible.

What now for Abraham Lincoln's policies? In the first wave of hysterical grief and rage over Lincoln's assassination, Johnson had vowed to hang Jefferson Davis and his entire "diabolical crew." Yet, in his First State-of-the-Union Message seven months later, Johnson outlined his intended policy of reconciliation toward the beaten, bled-white South, a policy based on Lincoln's proposed, humane, no-revenge policy of moderation. Johnson proposed—as had Lincoln—to treat the Southern states as if they were truant children who had never left the Union.

This State-of-the-Union Message infuriated the coterie of vindictive Radicals now in control of Congress and foreshadowed fetters for the South and impeachment of a President. They had expected Johnson to make good his vengeful threat to hang Jefferson Davis and other leaders of the Confederacy. But Johnson hanged nobody. Instead, three months later, he proclaimed a general amnesty for the rank and file of the Confederate armies and, on personal application, for all but a few of the Confederate military and political leaders.

237

The Radicals wanted vengeance. The South must pay for its misdeeds. White supremacy must go. So must all of Lincoln's saner, milder ideas for reconstruction of the devastated States. The South must be treated as conquered territory. The plantations of slavocracy must be cut up in small pieces and distributed to their former slaves. A new democratic South must rise from the ashes and confiscation of the old.

Andrew Johnson was born a "poor white" in a Tennessee mountain village. At ten he was a tailor's apprentice. A fellow workman taught him to read, but he was twenty-one before he learned to write, taught by his wife. Johnson scaled the political ladder so fast that in 1857, at the age of forty-nine, he took his seat in the United States Senate. He had his faults, but lack of courage was not one of them. Utterly devoted to the Constitution and Union, he stood rockfast when his state hovered between secession and Union. In those hectic days of 1861, he stumped Tennessee, pleading with his countrymen not to cut themselves off from the Union. Fearlessly he faced rebuff, hostility, and threats of violence. Retracting not a word, he closed his final plea with "I am a citizen of the South and of the State of Tennessee. I am also a citizen of the United States and I shall forever be."

Courageous as ever, in 1867, when the Radicals in Congress began passing the shackling Reconstruction Acts, Johnson vetoed them *seriatim,* only to have his vetoes overridden. He was the first President ever to have a law passed over his veto. On Capitol Hill, Senate and House rang with denunciation of him. Nothing was left unsaid. Intent on crippling his authority, the Radicals enacted the Tenure of Office Act that virtually stripped him of power of appointment and removal without the advice and consent of the Senate. It was a trap into which Johnson walked with his eyes open. Five months later, in sheer disregard of the act, he fired holdover Secretary of War Stanton for double-dealing with the Radicals. This was the "great transgression"— the high crimes and misdemeanors—for which Johnson was impeached and brought (*in absentia*) to the bar of the Senate and acquitted by one vote.

In 1869, Johnson returned home to Greenville, Tennessee. Five years later he ran for the Senate, won, and took his seat in March, 1875. Within three months he was dead.

Now this echo: In 1861, when the Senate resounded with threats of overthrow of the Union, Constitution, and downfall of the flag, Senator Andrew Johnson rose in his place to say, "When this Union is interred, I want no more honorable winding sheet than that brave old flag, and no more glorious grave than to be interred in the tomb of the Union."

And thus was he buried on August 2, 1875—under his head the worn, thumbed copy of the Constitution he had carried for fifty years, wrapped about his body a silken flag with thirty-seven stars.

Be it said to Johnson's credit that despite the hate and venom spat at him by the Radicals on Capitol Hill, not a vindictive word to his enemies crept into his State-of-the-Union Messages. Nor did these messages contain a hint of gloating over the discomfiture of the enemies who had, with cold injustice, sought to drive him, disgraced and perhaps imprisoned, from the presidency. He did say, in his last message, that, influenced by party passions and sectional prejudice, Congress had passed the Tenure of Office Act, and he called for its repeal, but Congress laughed it off.

One question he asked repeatedly in his State-of-the-Union Messages: Why are the ten Southern states not represented in Congress? Why do the seats of fifty members of the House and twenty members of the Senate remain vacant? Why the continued "disorganization" of the Union?

In his last message, he, like other Presidents before and after him, predicted that one day in the future the United States would have to resolve the festering Cuban problem. His words preceded the Spanish-American War by exactly thirty years, a war that the politicians said would dissipate the Cuban enigma, but which apparently made it worse.

ANDREW JOHNSON
FIRST STATE-OF-THE-UNION MESSAGE
WASHINGTON, *December 4, 1865*

Fellow-Citizens of the Senate and House of Representatives:

To express gratitude to God in the name of the people for the preservation of the United States is my first duty in addressing you. Our thoughts next revert to the death of the late President by an act of parricidal treason. The grief of the nation is still fresh. It finds some solace in the consideration that he lived to enjoy the highest proof of its confidence by entering on the renewed term of the Chief Magistrate to which he had been elected; that he brought the civil war substantially to a close. . . .

I found the States suffering from the effects of a civil war. Resistance to the General Government appeared to have exhausted itself. Whether the territory within the limits of those

States should be held as conquered territory, under military authority emanating from the President as the head of the Army, was the first question that presented itself for decision.

The policy of military rule over a conquered territory would have implied that the States whose inhabitants may have taken part in the rebellion had by the act of those inhabitants ceased to exist. But the true theory is that all pretended acts of secession were from the beginning null and void. . . . The States attempting to secede placed themselves in a condition where their vitality was impaired, but not extinguished; their functions suspended, but not destroyed.

On this principle I have acted, and have gradually and quietly, and by almost imperceptible steps, sought to restore the rightful energy of the General Government and of the States. . . .

I know very well that this policy is attended with some risk; but it is a risk that must be taken. In the choice of difficulties it is the smallest risk; and to diminish and if possible to remove all danger, I have felt it incumbent on me to assert one other power of the General Government—the power of pardon. . . .

The relations of the General Government toward the 4,000,000 inhabitants whom the war has called into freedom have engaged my most serious consideration. On the propriety of attempting to make the freedmen electors by the proclamation of the Executive I took for my counsel the Constitution itself, the interpretations of that instrument by its authors and their contemporaries, and recent legislation by Congress. . . . Such an act would have created a new class of voters, and would have been an assumption of power by the President which nothing in the Constitution or laws of the United States would have warranted.

On the other hand, every danger of conflict is avoided when the settlement of the question is referred to the several States. . . . In my judgment the freedmen, if they show patience and manly virtues, will sooner obtain a participation in the elective franchise through the States than through the General Government, even if it had power to intervene. . . .

. . . I can not too strongly urge a dispassionate treatment of this subject, which should be carefully kept aloof from all party strife. We must equally avoid hasty assumptions of any natural impossibility for the two races to live side by side in a state of mutual benefit and good will.

🇺🇸 🇺🇸 🇺🇸

. . . I meet you at a time when the nation has voluntarily burdened itself with a debt unprecedented in our annals. Vast as is its amount, it fades away into nothing when compared with the countless blessings that will be conferred upon our country and upon man by the preservation of the nation's life. We must aim at nothing less than the complete effacement of the financial evils that necessarily followed a state of civil war. . . .

🇺🇸 🇺🇸 🇺🇸

The throngs of emigrants that crowd to our shores are witnesses of the confidence of all peoples in our permanence. Here is the great land of free labor, where industry is blessed with unexampled rewards and the bread of the workingman is sweetened by the consciousness that the cause of the country "is his own cause, his own safety, his own dignity. . . ." Here exists the democratic form of government; and that form of government, by the confession of European statesmen, "gives a power of which no other form is capable, because it incorporates every man with the state and arouses everything that belongs to the soul."

Where in past history does a parallel exist to the public happiness which is within the reach of the people of the United States?

ANDREW JOHNSON
SECOND STATE-OF-THE-UNION MESSAGE
WASHINGTON, *December 3, 1866*

Fellow-Citizens of the Senate and House of Representatives:

I deem it a subject of profound regret that Congress has thus far failed to admit to seats loyal Senators and Representatives from the other States whose inhabitants, with those of Tennessee, had engaged in the rebellion. Ten States—more than one-fourth of the whole number—remain without representation; the seats of fifty members in the House of Representatives and of twenty members in the Senate are yet vacant, not by their own consent, not by a failure of election, but by the refusal of Congress to accept their credentials. . . .

The Constitution of the United States makes it the duty of the President to recommend to the consideration of Congress "such measures as he shall judge necessary and expedient." I know of no measure more imperatively demanded by every consideration of national interest, sound policy, and equal justice than the admission of loyal members from the now unrepresented States. This would consummate the work of restoration and exert a most salutary influence in the reestablishment of peace, harmony, and fraternal feeling. . . .

The entire success of the Atlantic telegraph between the coast of Ireland and the Province of Newfoundland is an achievement which has been justly celebrated in both hemispheres as the opening of an era in the progress of civilization. . . .

. . . Our Government is now undergoing its most trying ordeal, and my earnest prayer is that the peril may be successfully and finally passed without impairing its original strength and symmetry. The interests of the nation are best to be promoted by the revival of fraternal relations, the complete obliteration of our past differences, and the reinauguration of all the pursuits of peace.

ANDREW JOHNSON
THIRD STATE-OF-THE-UNION MESSAGE
WASHINGTON, *December 3, 1867*

Fellow-Citizens of the Senate and House of Representatives:
    The continued disorganization of the Union, to which the President has so often called the attention of Congress, is yet a subject of profound and patriotic concern. . . .

When a civil war has been brought to a close, it is manifestly the first interest and duty of the state to repair the injuries which the war has inflicted. . . . This duty was, upon the termination of the rebellion, promptly accepted, not only by the executive department, but by the insurrectionary States themselves, and restoration in the first moment of peace was believed to be as easy and certain as it was indispensable. The expectations, however, then so reasonably and confidently entertained were disappointed by legislation from which I felt constrained by my obligations to the Constitution to withhold my assent.

It is therefore a source of profound regret that in complying with the obligation imposed upon the President by the Constitution to give to Congress from time to time information of the state of the Union I am unable to communicate any definitive adjustment, satisfactory to the American people, of the questions which since the close of the rebellion have agitated the public mind. On the contrary, candor compels me to declare that at this time there is no Union as our fathers understood the term, and as they meant it to be understood by us. The Union which they established can exist only where all the States are represented in both Houses of Congress; where one State is as free as another to regulate its internal concerns according to its own will, and where the laws of the central Government, strictly confined to matters of national jurisdiction, apply with equal force to all the people of every section. That such is not the present "state of the Union" is a melancholy fact. . . .

I am aware it is assumed that this system of government for the Southern States is not to be perpetual. It is true this military government is to be only provisional, but it is through this temporary evil that a greater evil is to be made perpetual. If the guaranties of the Constitution can be broken provisionally to serve a temporary purpose, and in a part only of the country, we can destroy them everywhere and for all time. . . .

It is manifestly and avowedly the object of these [Reconstruction] laws to confer upon Negroes the privilege of voting and to disfranchise such a number of white citizens as will give the former a clear majority at all elections in the Southern States. . . .

The blacks in the South are entitled to be well and humanely governed, and to have the protection of just laws for all their rights of person and property. . . . It is not proposed merely that they shall govern themselves, but that they shall rule the white race, make and administer State laws, elect Presidents and members of Congress, and shape to a greater or less extent the future destiny of the whole country. Would such a trust and power be safe in such hands?

. . . But if anything can be proved by known facts, if all reasoning upon evidence is not abandoned, it must be acknowledged that in the progress of nations Negroes have shown less capacity for government than any other race of people. No independent government of any form has ever been successful in their hands. On the contrary, wherever they have been left to their own devices they have shown a constant tendency to relapse into barbarism. In the Southern States, however, Congress has undertaken to confer upon them the privilege of the ballot. Just released from slavery, it may be doubted whether as a class they know more than their ancestors how to organize and regulate civil society.

The plan of putting the Southern States wholly and the General Government partially into the hands of Negroes is proposed at a time peculiarly unpropitious. The foundations of society have been broken up by civil war. Industry must be reorganized, justice reestablished, public credit maintained, and order brought out of confusion. To accomplish these ends would require all the wisdom and virtue of the great men who formed our institutions originally. I confidently believe that their descendants will be equal to the arduous task before them, but it is worse than madness to expect that Negroes will perform it for us. Certainly we ought not to ask their assistance till we despair of our own competency.

The great interests of the country require immediate relief from these enactments. Business in the South is paralyzed by a sense of general insecurity, by the terror of confiscation, and the dread of Negro supremacy. . . .

. . . The expenses of the United States, including interest on the public debt, are more than six times as much as they were seven years ago. To collect and disburse this vast amount requires careful supervision as well as systematic vigilance. The system, never perfected, was much disorganized by the "tenure-of-office bill," which has almost destroyed official accountability. The President may be thoroughly convinced that an officer is incapable, dishonest, or unfaithful to the Constitution, but under the law which I have named the utmost he can do is to complain to the Senate and ask the privilege of supplying his place with a better man. If the Senate be regarded as personally or politically hostile to the President, it is natural, and not altogether unreasonable, for the officer to expect that it will take his part as far as possible, restore him to his place, and give him a triumph over his Executive superior. . . .

The Constitution invests the President with authority to *decide* whether a removal should be made in any given case; the act of Congress declares in substance that he shall only *accuse* such as he supposes to be unworthy of their trust. The Constitution makes him sole *judge* in the premises, but the statute takes away his jurisdiction, transfers it to the Senate, and leaves him nothing but the odious and sometimes impracticable duty of becoming a *prosecutor*. The prosecution is to be conducted before a tribunal whose members are not, like him, responsible to the whole people, but to separate constituent bodies, and who may hear his accusation with great disfavor. The law does not define what shall be deemed good cause for removal. It is impossible even to conjecture what may or may not be so considered by the Senate. The nature of the subject forbids clear proof. If the charge be incapacity, what evidence will support it? . . .

▦   ▦   ▦

It will hardly be necessary to call the attention of Congress to the subject of providing for the payment to Russia of the sum stipulated in the treaty for the cession of Alaska. Possession having been formally delivered to our commissioner, the territory remains for the present in care of a military force, awaiting such civil organization as shall be directed by Congress. . . .

ANDREW JOHNSON
FOURTH STATE-OF-THE-UNION MESSAGE
WASHINGTON, *December 9, 1868*

Fellow-Citizens of the Senate and House of Representatives:

Upon the reassembling of Congress it again becomes my duty to call your attention to the state of the Union and to its continued disorganized condition under the various laws which have been passed upon the subject of reconstruction.

. . . After a fair trial they have substantially failed and proved pernicious in their results, and there seems to be no good reason why they should longer remain upon the statute book. States to which the Constitution guarantees a republican form of government have been reduced to military dependencies, in each of which the people have been made subject to the arbitrary will of the commanding general. . . .

Under the influence of party passion and sectional prejudice, other acts have been passed not warranted by the Constitution. Congress has already been made familiar with my views respecting the "tenure-of-office bill." Experience has proved that its repeal is demanded by the best interests of the country, and that while it remains in force the President can not enjoin that rigid accountability of public officers so essential to an honest and efficient execution of the laws. . . .

The condition of our finances demands the early and earnest consideration of Congress. Compared with the growth of our population, the public expenditures have reached an amount unprecedented in our history.

The population of the United States in 1790 was nearly 4,000,000 people. Increasing each decade about 33 per cent, it reached in 1860 31,000,000, an increase of 700 per cent on the population in 1790. In 1869 it is estimated that it will reach 38,000,000, or an increase of 868 per cent in seventy-nine years.

The annual expenditures of the Federal Government in 1791 were $4,200,000; in 1820, $18,200,000; in 1850, forty-one millions; in 1860, sixty-three millions; in 1865, nearly thirteen hundred millions; and in 1869 it is estimated by the Secretary of the Treasury, in his last annual report, that they will be three hundred and seventy-two millions.

By comparing the public disbursements of 1869, as estimated, with those of 1791, it will be seen that the increase of expenditure since the beginning of the Government has been 8,618 per cent, while the increase of the population for the same period was only 868 per cent. Again, the expenses of the Government in 1860, the year of peace immediately preceding the war, were only sixty-three millions, while in 1869, the year of peace three years after the war, it is estimated they will be three hundred and seventy-two millions, an increase of 489 per cent, while the increase of population was only 21 per cent for the same period.

     🏴   🏴   🏴

. . . We now pride ourselves upon having given freedom to 4,000,000 of the colored race; it will then be our shame that 40,000,000 of people, by their own toleration of usurpation and profligacy, have suffered themselves to become enslaved, and merely exchanged slave owners for new taskmasters in the shape of bondholders and taxgatherers. . . .

     🏴   🏴   🏴

It can not be long before it will become necessary for this Government to lend some effective aid to the solution of the political and social problems which are continually kept before the world by the two Republics of the island of St. Domingo, and which are now disclosing themselves more distinctly than heretofore in the island of Cuba.

     🏴   🏴   🏴

I renew the recommendation contained in my communication to Congress dated the 18th July last that the judgment of the people should be taken on the propriety of so amending the Federal Constitution that it shall provide—

First. For an election of President and Vice-President by a direct vote of the people, and making them ineligible for reelection to a second term.

Second. For a distinct designation of the person who shall discharge the duties of President in the event of a vacancy in that office, by the death, resignation, or removal of both the President and Vice-President.

Third. For the election of Senators of the United States directly by the people of the several States, instead of by the legislatures; and

Fourth. For the limitation to a period of years of the terms of Federal judges.

. . . Let us earnestly hope that before the expiration of our respective terms of service, now rapidly drawing to a close, an all-wise Providence will so guide our counsels as to strengthen and preserve the Federal Union, inspire reverence for the Constitution, restore prosperity and happiness to our whole people, and promote "on earth peace, good will toward men."

ULYSSES S. GRANT
(1869–1877)

*"Failures have been
errors of judgment,
not of intent"*

The mightiest figure to emerge from the Civil War was a short, bearded, stubborn fighter, *Ulysses S. Grant,* who, on March 4, 1869, became eighteenth President of the United States. Magnanimous conqueror was Grant, but lame statesman and worse politician. He despised war, politics, and show-off; he tabooed dirty jokes.

To this blunt fighting man and former Democrat, the National Union Republican Party turned for leadership in the presidential campaign of 1868. Political issues were drowned out in the furor of "Grant enthusiasm," as the boys in blue lined up in solid ranks to vote for their old commander in chief. In accepting the nomination, Grant used four words, "Let us have peace," which became the Republican campaign slogan and are today carved on his magnificent tomb in New York City overlooking the Hudson.

The Democrats picked a sincere but innocuous candidate, former Governor Horatio Seymour of New York, hoping to rehabilitate their party and clear their skirts of past sins. Grant was swept into office, although, strangely, except for some 700,000 Negro votes, he might have lost it.

His administration ushered in a shocking era of government corruption, rascality in high places, bribery, graft, and dishonesty. He packed his Cabinet with low-graders, three of whom were forced to resign in disgrace. Public morals sank to the lowest level in American history. Confidence in government was all but shattered. The nation was agitated to its depths. Members of Congress, Vice President Colfax, and the Speaker of the House were implicated wholesale in the infamous Crédit Mobilier whose stock was distributed "where it would do the most good" for a government-subsidized construction company. A plundering clique, the Whiskey Ring, mulcted the government of millions of dollars in taxes. Grant's private secretary, General Orville Babcock, was deeply involved in this dishonest scheme. Duped by two Wall Street slickers, Jim Fisk and Jay Gould, Grant unconsciously fell in with manipulations in gold that brought on Black Friday in 1872. He came out of this affair slightly tarnished.

On the constructive side, Grant's administration witnessed one of America's great leaps forward. American genius began pouring out a dazzling stream of new, labor-saving inventions and processes that would revolutionize life and industry not only in America but throughout the world, bring untold expansion to the nation, and thousands of comforts to American living.

In a single year of Grant's administration, 13,622 patents were issued by the government, including that for multiplex telegraphy, the first major invention to spring from the prolific brain of young Thomas Alva Edison.

May 10, 1869, saw the dream of a continental railroad come true when, at Promontory Point, Utah, the East and West were joined by bands of steel. The Transcontinental Railroad Act, signed by President Lincoln in 1862, and the hopes of the Congress that had subsidized the building of this road with $60,000,000 and 100,000,000 acres of land, had been justified.

In 1876, the nation was invited to come to the Centennial Exhibition at Philadelphia and gaze on the marvels of invention and industry America had produced in the first hundred years since the Declaration of Independence gave her birth.

In 1872, the Republicans nominated Grant to succeed himself while the Democrats turned to baby-faced editor-reformer Horace Greeley of the New York *Tribune* to lead the nation out of the morass of corruption. They had a good battle cry—"Turn the rascals out!"—but failed to override the Union veterans and Negro voters, who, still faithful to Grant, snowed Greeley even deeper than they had Seymour in 1868. Three weeks after election Greeley died.

The year 1873 brought hard times to the nation and panic to Wall

Street. Armies of unemployed roamed the streets. With a fateful crash Jay Cooke & Company, the famed banking house that had shown President Lincoln how to apply high-pressure promotion to selling millions of Civil War bonds, went under. Credit was paralyzed. Over 23,000 business firms went to the wall. Grant got the blame.

Grant's State-of-the-Union Messages are typical of the man—blunt and as readily understandable as was his "unconditional surrender" at Fort Donelson in 1862. They cover a variety of events and are most informative.

In his first message he took his stand for sound currency, thus anticipating his veto of the inflation bill of 1874, which would have flooded the nation with additional millions of greenbacks, and the Resumption of Specie Act in 1875. (His veto of the inflation bill led to creation of the Greenback Party, which put three presidential candidates in the field, polled one million votes in the congressional election of 1878, and shortly passed into deserved oblivion.)

In his second message, Grant heralded the advent of much-needed civil-service reform by asking Congress for a law establishing the merit (personal fitness) system in civil appointments. Wide-spread dishonesty and bad government in vast measure had stemmed from the partisan appointment policy spawned by Andrew Jackson forty years before. Grant's efforts lagged, but he had at least spotlighted the problem.

His attempts to annex San Domingo and his reasons therefor are fully given in his messages. Cuba, with its annoying impact on the United States, also came in for full-scale treatment.

Unintentionally perhaps, in his 1869 State-of-the-Union Message, Grant offered a suggestion that backfired and swept away Republican control of the House in the 1874 elections. He suggested that Congress raise the salaries of the "important offices" of the government. Congress later took him at his word, doubled the President's salary and raised their own from $5,000 to $7,500. The "Salary Grab" Bill was the last straw for a disgusted electorate. Denounced by the press, as well as by state legislatures, as an unjustifiable raid on the Treasury, this bill led to a Democratic landslide in 1874. For the first time since the Civil War, Democrats took control of the House.

In his eighth and last message Grant made a most startling utterance. He apologized for the shortcomings of his long tenure of office. Perhaps mindful of the maelstrom of political slush that had characterized his administrations, he said, "Failures have been errors of judgment, not of intent."

ULYSSES S. GRANT

FIRST STATE-OF-THE-UNION MESSAGE

WASHINGTON, D.C., *December 6, 1869*

To the Senate and House of Representatives:

In coming before you for the first time as Chief Magistrate of this great nation, it is with gratitude to the Giver of All Good for the many benefits we enjoy. Happily, harmony is being rapidly restored within our own borders. . . .

Seven States which passed ordinances of secession have been fully restored to their places in the Union. The eighth [Georgia] held an election at which she ratified her constitution, republican in form, elected a governor, Members of Congress, a State legislature, and all other officers required. . . . Subsequently, however, in violation of the constitution which they had just ratified they unseated the colored members of the legislature. . . . Under these circumstances I would submit to you whether it would not be wise, without delay, to enact a law authorizing the governor of Georgia to convene the members originally elected to the legislature, requiring each member to take the oath prescribed by the reconstruction acts, and none to be admitted who are ineligible under the fourteenth amendment.

Among the evils growing out of the rebellion, and not yet referred to, is that of an irredeemable currency. It is an evil which I hope will receive your most earnest attention. It is a duty, and one of the highest duties, of Government to secure to the citizen a medium of exchange of fixed, unvarying value. This implies a return to a specie basis, and no substitute for it can be devised.

For more than a year a valuable province of Spain, and a near neighbor of ours . . . has been struggling for independence and freedom. The people and Government of the United States entertain . . . warm feelings and sympathies for the people of Cuba

. . . but the contest has at no time assumed the conditions which amount to a war in the sense of international law, or which would show the existence of a *de facto* political organization of the insurgents sufficient to justify a recognition of belligerency.

The subject of an interoceanic canal to connect the Atlantic and Pacific oceans through the Isthmus of Darien is one in which commerce is greatly interested. Instructions have been given to our minister to the Republic of the United States of Colombia to endeavor to obtain authority for a survey by this Government, in order to determine the practicability of such an undertaking, and a charter for the right of way to build, by private enterprise, such a work, if the survey proves it to be practicable.

🐘   🐘   🐘

Toward the close of the last Administration a convention was signed at London for the settlement of all outstanding claims [the Alabama Claims] between Great Britain and the United States, which failed to receive the advice and consent of the Senate to its ratification. The injuries resulting to the United States by reason of the course adopted by Great Britain during our late civil war . . . could not be adjusted and satisfied as ordinary commercial claims. . . . They differ more widely in the gravity of their character. Not a word was found in the treaty, and not an inference could be drawn from it, to remove the sense of the unfriendliness of the course of Great Britain in our struggle for existence, which had so deeply and universally impressed itself upon the people of this country.

. . . I hope that the time may soon arrive when the two Governments can approach the solution of this momentous question. . . . This is now the only grave question which the United States has with any foreign nation.

🐘   🐘   🐘

On my assuming the responsible duties of Chief Magistrate of the United States it was with the conviction that three things were essential to its peace, prosperity, and fullest development. First among these is strict integrity in fulfilling all our obligations; second, to secure protection to the person and property of the citizen of the United States in each and every portion of our common country . . . third, union of all the States, with equal rights, indestructible by any constitutional means.

🐘 🐘 🐘

It may be well to mention here the embarrassment possible to arise from leaving on the statute books the so-called "tenure-of-office acts," and to earnestly recommend their total repeal.

🐘 🐘 🐘

I desire respectfully to call the attention of Congress to the inadequate salaries of a number of the most important offices of the Government. In this message I will not enumerate them, but will specify only the justices of the Supreme Court. No change has been made in their salaries for fifteen years. Within that time the labors of the court have largely increased and the expenses of living have at least doubled. . . .

ULYSSES S. GRANT
SECOND STATE-OF-THE-UNION MESSAGE
EXECUTIVE MANSION, *December 5, 1870*

To the Senate and House of Representatives:

A year of peace and general prosperity to this nation has passed since the last assembling of Congress. . . . It is to be regretted, however, that a free exercise of the elective franchise has by violence and intimidation been denied to citizens in exceptional cases in several of the States lately in rebellion, and the verdict of the people has thereby been reversed. The States of Virginia, Mississippi, and Texas have been restored to representation in our national councils. Georgia, the only State now without representation, may confidently be expected to take her place there also at the beginning of the new year. . . .

🐘 🐘 🐘

During the last session of Congress a treaty for the annexation of the Republic of San Domingo to the United States failed to receive the requisite two-thirds vote of the Senate. . . . The people of San Domingo yearn for the protection of our free institutions and laws, our progress and civilization. Shall we refuse them? The acquisition of San Domingo is an adherence to the "Monroe Doctrine"; it is a measure of national protection; it is asserting our just claim to a controlling influence over the great commercial traffic soon to flow from west to east by way of the Isthmus of Darien.

🐘 🐘 🐘

Always favoring practical reforms, I respectfully call your attention to one abuse of long standing which I would like to see remedied by this Congress. It is a reform in the civil service of the country. . . . I would have it govern, not the tenure, but the manner of making all appointments. . . . The present system does not secure the best men, and often not even fit men, for public place. The elevation and purification of the civil service of the Government will be hailed with approval by the whole people of the United States.

🐘 🐘 🐘

During the year ending September 30, 1870, there were filed in the Patent Office 19,411 applications for patents, 3,374 caveats, and 160 applications for the extension of patents. Thirteen thousand six hundred and twenty-two patents, including reissues and designs, were issued, 1,010 extended, and 1,089 allowed, but not issued by reason of the nonpayment of the final fees. . . .

🐘 🐘 🐘

The subjects of education and agriculture are of great interest to the success of our republican institutions, happiness, and grandeur as a nation. In the interest of one a bureau has been established in the Interior Department—the Bureau of Education; and in the interest of the other, a separate Department, that of Agriculture. . . .

In conclusion I would sum up the policy of the Administration to be a thorough enforcement of every law; a faithful collection of every tax provided for; economy in the disbursement of the same; a prompt payment of every debt of the nation; a reduction of taxes as rapidly as the requirements of the country will admit; reductions of taxation and tariff, to be so arranged as to afford the greatest relief to the greatest number; honest and fair dealings with all other peoples, to the end that war, with all its blighting consequences, may be avoided, but without surrendering any right or obligation due to us; a reform in the treatment of Indians and in the whole civil service of the country; and, finally in securing a pure, untrammeled ballot, where every man entitled to cast a vote may do so, just once at each election, without fear of molestation or proscription on account of his political faith, nativity, or color.

ULYSSES S. GRANT
THIRD STATE-OF-THE-UNION MESSAGE
EXECUTIVE MANSION, *December 4, 1871*

To the Senate and House of Representatives:

The past year has, under a wise Providence, been one of general prosperity to the nation. . . .

The relations of the United States with foreign powers continue to be friendly. The year has been an eventful one in witnessing two great nations, speaking one language and having one lineage, settling by peaceful arbitration disputes [the Alabama Claims] of long standing and liable at any time to bring those nations into bloody and costly conflict.

🐘　🐘　🐘

It is to be regretted that the disturbed condition of the island of Cuba continues to be a source of annoyance and of anxiety. The existence of a protracted struggle in such close proximity to our own territory, . . . can not be other than an object of concern to a people . . . who naturally desire to see every country in the undisturbed enjoyment of peace, liberty, and the blessings of free institutions.

🐘　🐘　🐘

Continued fluctuations in the value of gold, as compared with the national currency, has a most damaging effect upon the increase and development of the country, in keeping up prices of all articles necessary in everyday life. It fosters a spirit of gambling, prejudicial alike to national morals and the national finances. If the question can be met as to how to get a fixed value to our currency, that value constantly and uniformly approaching par with specie, a very desirable object will be gained.

There has been imposed upon the executive branch of the Government the execution of the act of Congress approved April 20, 1871, and commonly known as the Ku Klux law, in a portion of the State of South Carolina. . . .

It was ascertained that in nine counties of that State such combinations were active and powerful, embracing a sufficient portion of the citizens to control the local authority, and having, among other things, the object of depriving the emancipated class of the substantial benefits of freedom and of preventing the free political action of those citizens who did not sympathize with their own views. Among their operations were frequent scourgings and occasional assassinations, generally perpetrated at night by disguised persons, the victims in almost all cases being citizens of different political sentiments from their own or freed persons who had shown a disposition to claim equal rights with other citizens. . . .

Direction was given that within the counties so designated persons supposed, upon creditable information, to be members of such unlawful combinations should be arrested by the military forces of the United States and delivered to the marshal, to be dealt with according to law. In two of said counties, York and Spartanburg, many arrests have been made. . . .

In Utah there still remains a remnant of barbarism, repugnant to civilization, to decency, and to the laws of the United States. Neither polygamy nor any other violation of existing statutes will be permitted within the territory of the United States.

More than six years having elapsed since the last hostile gun was fired between the armies then arrayed against each other— one for the perpetuation, the other for the destruction, of the

Union—it may well be considered whether it is not now time that the disabilities imposed by the fourteenth amendment should be removed. That amendment does not exclude the ballot, but only imposes the disability to hold offices upon certain classes. When the purity of the ballot is secure, majorities are sure to elect officers reflecting the views of the majority.

🐘 🐘 🐘

The number of immigrants ignorant of our laws, habits, etc., coming into our country annually has become so great and the impositions practiced upon them so numerous and flagrant that I suggest Congressional action for their protection. It seems to me a fair subject of legislation by Congress. . . .

ULYSSES S. GRANT
FOURTH STATE-OF-THE-UNION MESSAGE
EXECUTIVE MANSION, *December 2, 1872*

To the Senate and House of Representatives:
    When Congress adjourned in June last, a question had been raised by Great Britain, and was then pending, which for a time seriously imperiled the settlement by friendly arbitration of the grave differences between this Government and that of Her Britannic Majesty, which by the Treaty of Washington had been referred to the tribunal of arbitration which had met at Geneva, in Switzerland. . . .
    The tribunal . . . awarded the sum of $15,500,000 in gold as the indemnity to be paid by Great Britain to the United States for the satisfaction of all the claims referred to its consideration.

🐘 🐘 🐘

It is with regret that I have again to announce a continuance of the disturbed condition of the island of Cuba. . . . This contest has lasted now for more than four years. Were its scene at a distance from our neighborhood, we might be indifferent to its result, although humanity could not be unmoved by many of its incidents wherever they might occur. It is, however, at our door.

The whole number of soldiers enlisted in [the Union Army in] the War of the Rebellion was 2,688,523. The total number of claims for invalid pensions is 176,000, being but 6 per cent of the whole number of enlisted men. . . . On the 30th of June, 1872, there were on the rolls the names of 95,405 invalid military pensioners, 113,518 widows, orphans, and dependent relatives, making an aggregate of 208,923 army pensioners.

In accordance with the terms of the act of Congress approved March 3, 1871, providing for the celebration of the one hundredth anniversary of American independence, a commission has been organized, consisting of two members from each of the States and Territories. . . . It will be the duty of the commission at your coming session to transmit a full report of the progress made, and to lay before you the details relating to the exhibition of American and foreign arts, products, and manufactures, which by the terms of the act is to be held under the auspices of the Government of the United States in the city of Philadelphia in the year 1876.

ULYSSES S. GRANT
FIFTH STATE-OF-THE-UNION MESSAGE
EXECUTIVE MANSION, *December 1, 1873*

To the Senate and House of Representatives:
        The year that has passed since the submission of my last message to Congress has, especially during the latter part of it, been an eventful one to the country. In the midst of great national prosperity a financial crisis has occurred that has brought low fortunes of gigantic proportions; political partisanship has almost ceased to exist, especially in the agricultural regions; and, finally, the capture upon the high seas of a vessel bearing our flag has for a time threatened the most serious consequences, and has agitated the public mind from one end of the country to the other. . . .

The embargoing of American estates in Cuba, cruelty to American citizens detected in no act of hostility to the Spanish Government, the murdering of prisoners taken with arms in their hands, and, finally, the capture upon the high seas of a vessel [*Virginios*] sailing under the United States flag and bearing a United States registry have culminated in an outburst of indignation that has seemed for a time to threaten war. Pending negotiations between the United States and the Government of Spain on the subject of this capture, I have authorized the Secretary of the Navy to put our Navy on a war footing. . . .

The development of the mines of precious metals during the past year and the prospective development of them for years to come are gratifying in their results. Could but one-half of the gold extracted from the mines be retained at home, our advance toward specie payments would be rapid.

The experience of the present panic has proven that the currency of the country, based, as it is, upon the credit of the country, is the best that has ever been devised. Usually in times of such trials currency has become worthless. . . . Everyone holding it has been anxious to dispose of it on any terms. Now we witness the reverse. Holders of currency hoard it as they did gold in former experiences of a like nature.

In three successive messages to Congress I have called attention to the subject of "civil-service reform." Action has been taken so far as to authorize the appointment of a board to devise rules governing methods of making appointments and promotions, but there never has been any action making these rules, or any rules, binding, or even entitled to observance, where persons desire the appointment of a friend or the removal of an official who may be disagreeable to them.

To have any rules effective they must have the acquiescence of Congress as well as of the Executive. I commend, therefore, the subject to your attention, and suggest that a special committee of Congress might confer with the Civil-Service Board during the present session for the purpose of devising such rules as can be maintained, and which will secure the services of honest and capable officials, and which will also protect them in a degree of independence while in office. . . .

ULYSSES S. GRANT
SIXTH STATE-OF-THE-UNION MESSAGE
EXECUTIVE MANSION, *December 7, 1874*

To the Senate and House of Representatives:
          Since the convening of Congress one year ago the nation has undergone a prostration in business and industries such as has not been witnessed with us for many years. . . .

Gold and silver are now the recognized medium of exchange the civilized world over, and to this we should return with the least practicable delay. In view of the pledges of the American Congress when our present legal-tender system was adopted, and debt contracted, there should be no delay—certainly no unnecessary delay—in fixing by legislation a method by which we will return to specie. To the accomplishment of this end I invite your special attention. I believe firmly that there can be no prosperous and permanent revival of business and industries until a policy is adopted—with legislation to carry it out—looking to a return to a specie basis. I believe it is in the power of Congress at this session to devise such legislation as will renew confidence, revive all the industries, start us on a career of prosperity to last for many years and to save the credit of the nation and of the people. . . .

Education of the people entitled to exercise the right of franchise I regard essential to general prosperity everywhere, and especially so in republics, where birth, education, or previous condition does not enter into account in giving suffrage. Next to the public school, the post-office is the great agent of education over our vast territory. . . .

The deplorable strife in Cuba continues without any marked

change in the relative advantages of the contending forces. The insurrection continues, but Spain has gained no superiority. Six years of strife give to the insurrection a significance which can not be denied. Its duration and the tenacity of its adherents, together with the absence of manifested power of suppression on the part of Spain, can not be controverted, and may make some positive steps on the part of other powers a matter of self-necessity. . . .

I regret to say that with preparations for the late election decided indications appeared in some localities in the Southern States of a determination, by acts of violence and intimidation, to deprive citizens of the freedom of the ballot because of their political opinions. Bands of men, masked and armed, made their appearance; White Leagues and other societies were formed; large quantities of arms and ammunition were imported and distributed to these organizations; military drills, with menacing demonstrations, were held, and with all these murders enough were committed to spread terror among those whose political action was to be suppressed, if possible, by these intolerant and criminal proceedings. In some places colored laborers were compelled to vote according to the wishes of their employers, under threats of discharge if they acted otherwise; and there are too many instances in which, when these threats were disregarded, they were remorselessly executed by those who made them. . . .

. . . Under existing conditions the Negro votes the Republican ticket because he knows his friends are of that party. Many a good citizen votes the opposite, not because he agrees with the great principles of state which separate parties, but because, generally, he is opposed to Negro rule. This is a most delusive cry. Treat the Negro as a citizen and a voter, as he is and must remain, and soon parties will be divided, not on the color line, but on principle. Then we shall have no complaint of sectional interference.

I have stated that three elements of prosperity to the nation—capital, labor, skilled and unskilled, and products of the soil—still remain with us. To direct the employment of these is a problem deserving the most serious attention of Congress. If employment can be given to all the labor offering itself, prosperity necessarily follows. I have expressed the opinion, and repeat it, that the first requisite to the accomplishment of this end is the substitution of a sound currency in place of one of a fluctuating value. . . .

ULYSSES S. GRANT
SEVENTH STATE-OF-THE-UNION MESSAGE
EXECUTIVE MANSION, *December 7, 1875*

To the Senate and House of Representatives:

In submitting my seventh annual message to Congress, in this centennial year of our national existence as a free and independent people, it affords me great pleasure to recur to the advancement that has been made from the time of the colonies, one hundred years ago. We were then a people numbering only 3,000,-000. Now we number more than 40,000,000. Then industries were confined almost exclusively to the tillage of the soil. Now manufacturies absorb much of the labor of the country. . . .

One hundred years ago the cotton gin, the steamship, the railroad, the telegraph, the reaping, sewing, and modern printing machines, and numerous other inventions of scarcely less value to our business and happiness were entirely unknown.

. . . Our merchants in the last hundred years have had a success and have established a reputation for enterprise, sagacity, progress, and integrity unsurpassed by peoples of older nationalities. This "good name" is not confined to their homes, but goes out upon every sea and into every port where commerce enters. With equal pride we can point to our progress in all of the learned professions. . . . As the primary step, therefore, to our advancement in all that has marked our progress in the past century, I suggest for your earnest consideration, and most earnestly recommend it, that a constitutional amendment be submitted to the legislatures of the several States for ratification, making it the duty of each of the several States to establish and forever maintain free public schools adequate to the education of all the children in the rudimentary branches within their respective limits, irrespective of sex, color, birthplace, or religions; forbidding the teaching in said schools of religious, atheistic, or pagan tenets; and prohibiting the granting of any school funds or school taxes, or any part thereof, either by legislative, municipal, or other authority, for the benefit or in aid, directly or indirectly, of any religious sect or denomination, or in aid or for the benefit of any other object of any nature or kind whatever.

In 1850, I believe, the church property of the United States which paid no tax, municipal or State, amounted to about $83,000,000. In 1860 the amount had doubled; in 1875 it is about $1,000,000,000. By 1900, without check, it is safe to say this property will reach a sum exceeding $3,000,000,000. So vast a sum, receiving all the protection and benefits of Government without bearing its proportion of the burdens and expenses of the same, will not be looked upon acquiescently by those who have to pay the taxes. . . .

I would suggest the taxation of all property equally, whether church or corporation, exempting only the last resting place of the dead and possibly, with proper restrictions, church edifices.

🐘 🐘 🐘

The past year has furnished no evidence of an approaching termination of the ruinous conflict which has been raging for seven years in the neighboring island of Cuba. . . . A recognition of the independence of Cuba being, in my opinion, impracticable and indefensible, the question which next presents itself is that of the recognition of belligerent rights in the parties to the contest. . . . Considered as a question of expediency, I regard the accordance of belligerent rights still to be as unwise and premature as I regard it to be, at present, indefensible as a measure of right.

🐘 🐘 🐘

As this will be the last annual message which I shall have the honor of presenting to Congress before my successor is chosen, I will repeat or recapitulate the questions which I deem of vital importance which may be legislated upon and settled at this session:

First. That the States shall be required to afford the opportunity of a good common-school education to every child within their limits.

Second. No sectarian tenets shall ever be taught in any school supported in whole or in part by the State, nation, or by the proceeds of any tax levied upon any community. Make education compulsory so far as to deprive all persons who can not read and write from becoming voters after the year 1890, disfranchising none, however, on grounds of illiteracy who may be voters at the time this amendment takes effect.

Third. Declare church and state forever separate and distinct, but each free within their proper spheres; and that all church property shall bear its own proportion of taxation.

Fourth. Drive out licensed immorality, such as polygamy and the importation of women for illegitimate purposes. To recur again to the centennial year, it would seem as though now, as we are about to begin the second century of our national existence, would be a most fitting time for these reforms.

Fifth. Enact such laws as will insure a speedy return to a sound currency, such as will command the respect of the world.

ULYSSES S. GRANT
EIGHTH STATE-OF-THE-UNION MESSAGE
EXECUTIVE MANSION, *December 5, 1876*

To the Senate and House of Representatives:
        In submitting my eighth and last annual message to Congress, it seems proper that I should refer to and in some degree recapitulate the events and official acts of the past eight years.

It was my fortune, or misfortune, to be called to the office of Chief Executive without any previous political training. From the age of 17 I had never even witnessed the excitement attending a Presidential campaign but twice antecedent to my own candidacy, and at but one of them was I eligible as a voter.

Under such circumstances it is but reasonable to suppose that errors of judgment must have occurred. Even had they not, differences of opinion between the Executive, bound by an oath to the strict performance of his duties, and writers and debaters must have arisen. It is not necessarily evidence of blunder on the part of the Executive because there are these differences of views. Mistakes have been made, as all can see and I admit, but it seems to me oftener in the selections made of the assistants appointed to aid in carrying out the various duties of administering the Government—in nearly every case selected without a personal acquaintance with the appointee, but upon recommendations of the representatives chosen directly by the people. It is impossible, where so many trusts are to be allotted, that the right parties should be chosen in every instance. History shows that no Administration from the time of Washington to the present has been free from these mistakes. But I leave comparisons to history, claiming only that I have acted in every instance from a conscientious desire to do what was right, constitutional, within the law, and for the very best interests of the whole people. Failures have been errors of judgment, not of intent.

Immediately on the cessation of hostilities the then noble President, who had carried the country so far through its perils, fell a martyr to his patriotism at the hands of an assassin.

The intervening time to my first inauguration was filled up with wranglings between Congress and the new Executive as to the best mode of "reconstruction," or, to speak plainly, as to whether the control of the Government should be thrown immediately into the hands of those who had so recently and persistently tried to destroy it, or whether the victors should continue to have an equal voice with them in this control. Reconstruction, as finally agreed upon, means this and only this, except that the late slave was enfranchised, giving an increase, as was supposed, to the Union-loving and Union-supporting votes.

If free in the full sense of the word, they would not disappoint this expectation. Hence at the beginning of my first Administration the work of reconstruction, much embarrassed by the long delay, virtually commenced. It was the work of the legislative branch of the government. My province was wholly in approving their acts, which I did most heartily, urging the legislatures of the States that had not yet done so to ratify the Fifteenth Amendment to the Constitution. The country was laboring under an enormous debt, contracted in suppression of rebellion, and taxation was so oppressive as to discourage production. Another danger also threatened us—a foreign war. This last difficulty had to be adjusted, and was adjusted without a war, in a manner highly honorable to all parties concerned. Taxes have been reduced within the last seven years nearly $300 million and the national debt has been reduced in the same time over $435 million. . . .

🐘 🐘 🐘

With the present term of Congress my official life terminates. It is not probable that public affairs will ever again receive attention from me further than as a citizen of the Republic, always taking a deep interest in the honor, integrity and prosperity of the whole land. . . .

RUTHERFORD B. HAYES
(1877–1881)

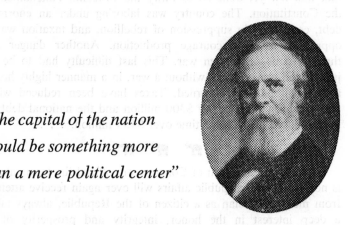

*"The capital of the nation
should be something more
than a mere political center"*

In the campaign of 1876 to elect a successor to Ulysses S. Grant, the Republicans fanned the dying embers of the Civil War by festooning the nation with the bloody shirt. They hoped thereby to becloud the issue of a party honeycombed with incapacity, waste and fraud, and the mountainous corruption of Grant's administrations. Thus would they stem the political tide that presaged Democratic control of both houses of Congress in 1879.

In 1876, the Republicans needed a man of unimpeachable integrity; "a man who is spotless as a star," said golden-voiced Robert G. Ingersoll, who, in a speech at the Republican convention, nominated James G. Blaine, the magnetic Man from Maine. On this occasion Ingersoll adorned Blaine with his bombastic peroration, "Like an armed warrior, like a plumed knight, James G. Blaine marched down the halls of the American Congress," and so on, to no avail. The ghosts of "loans" and railroad bonds accepted by the plumed knight were too much for the convention that turned to a spotless dark horse, *Rutherford B. Hayes,* former Governor of Ohio, who possessed both integrity and courage. As a major general in the Civil War, Hayes had an outstanding fighting record.

The Democrats picked Samuel J. Tilden, a rich corporation lawyer, who, while Governor of New York, had smashed the notorious Tweed Ring in New York City.

268

On the morning after the election the returns indicated that Tilden had won, with 250,000 more popular votes than Hayes and 196 electorals to Hayes' 173. The Republicans promptly challenged the returns from Oregon, Louisiana, South Carolina, and Florida. The returning boards in the last three states were still under carpetbag control. In a day or so, it became clear that Tilden had roped in 184 undisputed votes, one less than needed for election, to Hayes' 165.

Congress finally stepped into the tangle of claims and counterclaims and set up a fifteen-man electoral commission (eight Republicans and seven Democrats) to decide who actually won. In a big sideshow, pictorially resembling the trial of Andrew Johnson, the commission voted eight to seven to seat Hayes in the President's chair. The Democrats howled "steal," though 'twas whispered that Tilden's friends simply failed to "git thar fustest with the mostest money." But such is politics.

Hayes was inaugurated Monday, March 5, 1877, but since March 4 was a Sunday, he was sworn in Saturday night, March 3. During the welcoming dinner at the White House, Grant and Hayes slipped into the Red Room where Chief Justice Waite administered the oath. Hayes took office with three top-drawer policies: to harmonize the North and South, to reform the civil service, and to maintain the gold standard as imperative to the nation's business revival.

Hayes promptly achieved his harmony objective by withdrawing federal occupation troops from the South. His action restored home rule to the whites in the South and sent the last carpetbaggers scurrying northward. His own party attacked him bitterly for his temperate policy toward the South, but Hayes stood his ground and stated his case succinctly in his First State-of-the-Union Message. Determined to uphold the gold standard, he courageously vetoed the Bland-Allison Silver Coinage Act, which directed the Treasury to buy at least $2,000,000 worth of silver bullion a month and mint it into dollars. Congress promptly passed it over his veto. For the next twenty years Congress would be deluged with oratory and schemes for monetizing silver, led by famed Richard (Silver Dick) Bland of Missouri.

Hayes' civil-service-reform program, well covered in his first message, got off to a bad start when he ordered government workers to refuse to pay party assessments. It earned him the bitter hatred of Republican spoilsmen. On his appointment of Southerners to political office, he was accused of party treason. His followers were tagged as "Half-Breeds"; those older leaders who revolted against him called themselves "Stalwarts."

"The very serious riots" to which Hayes referred in his first message was the bloodshed occasioned by the "Great Strike" of railroad employees in 1877, induced by wage cuts resulting from the Depression of 1873. It was the bloodiest labor disturbance ever seen in the United States. Hayes despatched federal troops to the trouble spots in Maryland, West Virginia, Pennsylvania, Illinois, and Missouri to quell the eruptions.

In this same message he pioneered the need of a new building adequate for the vast collections and treasures of the Library of Congress. His suggestion bore fruit, though not in his time; it presaged the beautiful building that is today one of the showplaces of the nation's capital.

RUTHERFORD B. HAYES
FIRST STATE-OF-THE-UNION MESSAGE
December 3, 1877

Fellow-Citizens of the Senate and House of Representatives:

To complete and make permanent the pacification of the country continues to be the most important of all our national interests. . . .

. . . Opinions have differed widely as to the measures best calculated to secure this great end. The measures adopted by the Administration have been subjected to severe and varied criticism. These measures were, in my judgment, such as were most in harmony with the Constitution and with the genius of our people. . . . The discontinuance of the use of the Army for the purpose of upholding local governments in two States of the Union was no less a constitutional duty and requirement, under the circumstances existing at the time, than it was a much-needed measure for the restoration of local self-government and the promotion of national harmony. The withdrawal of the troops from such employment was effected deliberately, and with solicitous care for the peace and good order of society and the protection of the property and persons and every right of all classes of citizens.

Among the other subjects of great and general importance to the people of this country, I can not be mistaken, I think, in regarding as preeminent the policy and measures which are designed to secure the restoration of the currency to that normal and healthful condition in which, by the resumption of specie payments, our internal trade and foreign commerce may be brought into harmony with the system of exchanges which is based upon the precious metals as the intrinsic money of the world. . . .

Closely connected with this general subject of the resumption of specie payments is one of subordinate, but still of grave, importance; I mean the readjustment of our coinage system by the renewal of the silver dollars as an element in our specie currency, endowed by legislation with the quality of legal tender to a greater or less extent. . . .

The organization of the civil service of the country has for a number of years attracted more and more of the public attention. . . . I have endeavored to reduce the number of changes in subordinate places usually made upon the change of the general administration, and shall most heartily cooperate with Congress in the better systematizing of such methods and rules of admission to the public service and of promotion within it as may promise to be most successful in making thorough competency, efficiency, and character the decisive tests in these matters.

The very serious riots which occurred in several of the States in July last rendered necessary the employment of a considerable portion of the Army to preserve the peace and maintain order. In the States of West Virginia, Maryland, Pennsylvania, and Illinois these disturbances were so formidable as to defy the local and State authorities, and the National Executive was called upon, in the mode provided by the Constitution and laws, to furnish military aid. . . .

The question of providing for the preservation and growth of the Library of Congress is also one of national importance. As the depository of all copyright publications and records, this library has outgrown the provisions for its accommodation; and the erection, on such site as the judgment of Congress may approve, of a fireproof library building, to preserve the treasures and enlarge the usefulness of this valuable collection, is recommended. . . .

The capital of the nation should be something more than a mere political center. We should avail ourselves of all the opportunities which Providence has here placed at our command to promote the general intelligence of the people and increase the conditions most favorable to the success and perpetuity of our institutions.

RUTHERFORD B. HAYES
SECOND STATE-OF-THE-UNION MESSAGE
EXECUTIVE MANSION, *December 2, 1878*

Fellow-Citizens of the Senate and House of Representatives:
        The permanent pacification of the country by the complete protection of all citizens in every civil and political right continues to be of paramount interest with the great body of our people. . . . The recent Congressional elections have furnished a direct and trustworthy test of the advance thus far made in the practical establishment of the right of suffrage secured by the Constitution to the liberated race in the Southern States. All disturbing influences, real or imaginary, had been removed from all of these States.
        The three constitutional amendments which conferred freedom and equality of civil and political rights upon the colored people of the South were adopted by the concurrent action of the great body of good citizens who maintained the authority of the National Government and the integrity and perpetuity of the Union at such a cost of treasure and life, as a wise and necessary embodiment in the organic law of the just results of the war. . . . By

these constitutional amendments the southern section of the Union obtained a large increase of political power in Congress and in the electoral college, and the country justly expected that elections would proceed, as to the enfranchised race, upon the same circumstances of legal and constitutional freedom and protection which obtained in all the other States of the Union.

The Spanish Government has officially announced the termination of the insurrection in Cuba and the restoration of peace throughout that island. Confident expectations are expressed of a revival of trade and prosperity, which it is earnestly hoped may prove well founded. . . .

RUTHERFORD B. HAYES
THIRD STATE-OF-THE-UNION MESSAGE
EXECUTIVE MANSION, *December 1, 1879*

Fellow-Citizens of the Senate and House of Representatives:
    The most interesting events which have occurred in our public affairs since my last annual message to Congress are connected with the financial operations of the Government, directly affecting the business interests of the country. I congratulate Congress on the successful execution of the resumption act. . . .

The resumption of specie payments has been followed by a very great revival of business. The increasing foreign demand for our manufactures and agricultural products has caused a large balance of trade in our favor, which has been paid in gold. . . .

The continued deliberate violation by a large number of the prominent and influential citizens of the Territory of Utah of the laws of the United States for the prosecution and punishment of polygamy demands the attention of every department of the Government. This Territory has a population sufficient to entitle it to admission as a State. . . . This important change will not, however, be approved by the country while the citizens of Utah in very considerable number uphold a practice which is condemned as a crime by the laws of all civilized communities throughout the world.

🐘 🐘 🐘

. . . The views I have heretofore expressed concerning the defects and abuses in our civil administration remain unchanged, except in so far as an enlarged experience has deepened my sense of the duty both of officers and of the people themselves to co-operate for their removal. The grave evils and perils of a partisan spoils system of appointment to office and of office tenure are now generally recognized. . . . The gravity of these evils has been pointed out and the need of their reform has been admitted. . . .

🐘 🐘 🐘

The joint commission created by the act of Congress of August 2, 1876, for the purpose of supervising and directing the completion of the Washington National Monument has given careful attention to this subject, and already the strengthening of the foundation has so far progressed as to insure the entire success of this part of the work. . . .

RUTHERFORD B. HAYES
FOURTH STATE-OF-THE-UNION MESSAGE
EXECUTIVE MANSION, *December 6, 1880*

Fellow-Citizens of the Senate and House of Representatives:

In my former annual messages I have asked the attention of Congress to the urgent necessity of a reformation of the civil-service system of the Government. My views concerning the dangers of patronage, or appointments for personal or partisan considerations, have been strengthened by my observation and experience in the Executive office, and I believe these dangers threaten the stability of the Government. Abuses so serious in their nature can not be permanently tolerated. . . .

Competitive examinations in aid of impartial appointments and promotions have been conducted for some years past in several of the Executive Departments and by my direction this system has been adopted in the custom-houses and post-offices of the larger cities of the country. In the city of New York over 2,000 positions in the civil service have been subject in their appointments and tenure of place to the operation of published rules for this purpose during the past two years. The results of these practical trials have been very satisfactory, and have confirmed my opinion in favor of this system of selection. . . .

I also recommend such legislation as, while leaving every officer as free as any other citizen to express his political opinions and to use his means for their advancement, shall also enable him to feel as safe as any private citizen in refusing all demands upon his salary for political purposes.

The most serious obstacle, however, to an improvement of the civil service, and especially to a reform in the method of appointment and removal, has been found to be the practice, under what is known as the spoils system, by which the appointing power has been so largely encroached upon by members of Congress. The first step in the reform of the civil service must be a complete divorce between Congress and the Executive in the matter of appointments. . . .

The relations between this Government and that of the United States of Colombia have engaged public attention during the past year, mainly by reason of the project of an interoceanic canal across the Isthmus of Panama, to be built by private capital under a concession [to a French concern] from the Colombian Government for that purpose. The treaty obligations subsisting between the United States and Colombia, by which we guarantee the neutrality of the transit and the sovereignty and property of Colombia in the Isthmus, make it necessary that the conditions under which so stupendous a change in the region embraced in this guaranty should be effected—transforming, as it would, this Isthmus from a barrier between the Atlantic and Pacific oceans into a gateway and thoroughfare between them for the navies and the merchant ships of the world—should receive the approval of this Government, as being compatible with the discharge of these obligations on our part and consistent with our interests as the principal commercial power of the Western Hemisphere. . . .

🐘 🐘 🐘

. . . The Constitution in express terms recognizes both gold and silver as the only true legal-tender money. The United States produces more silver than any other country, and is directly interested in maintaining it as one of the two precious metals which furnish the coinage of the world. It will, in my judgment, contribute to this result if Congress will repeal so much of existing legislation as required the coinage of silver dollars containing only 412½ grains of silver, and in its stead will authorize the Secretary of the Treasury to coin silver dollars of equivalent value, as bullion, with gold dollars. This will defraud no man, and will be in accordance with familiar precedents.

🐘 🐘 🐘

The two great rivers of the North American continent, the Mississippi and the Columbia, have their navigable waters wholly within the limits of the United States, and are of vast importance to our internal and foreign commerce. The permanency of the important work on the South Pass of the Mississippi River seems now to be assured. There has been no failure whatever in the maintenance of the maximum channel during the six months ended August 9 last. This experiment has opened a broad, deep highway to the ocean, and is an improvement upon the permanent success of which congratulations may be exchanged among people abroad and at home, and especially among the communities of the Mississippi Valley, whose commercial exchanges float in an unobstructed channel safely to and from the sea.

🐘 🐘 🐘

The conduct of the Indians throughout the country during the past year, with but few noteworthy exceptions, has been orderly and peaceful. The guerrilla warfare carried on for two years by Victoria and his band of Southern Apaches has virtually come to an end by the death of that chief and most of his followers on

Mexican soil. The disturbances caused on our northern frontier by Sitting Bull and his men, who had taken refuge in the British dominions, are also likely to cease. A large majority of his followers have surrendered to our military forces, and the remainder are apparently in process of disintegration. . . .

CHESTER A. ARTHUR
(1881–1885)

*"Appointments should
be based upon
ascertained fitness"*

The year 1880 gave birth to the Solid South—the most powerful
political bloc ever created in America—and the man who presided over
this accouchement was the Union general Winfield Scott Hancock, who,
at Gettysburg, had commanded the Second Corps that repulsed
Pickett's spectacular charge and crushed the last best hope of Southern
independence. Quite an oddity.

Ulysses Grant had returned from two years of globe-trotting hankering for a third term in the White House. At the Republican convention that year Senator Roscoe Conkling, spokesman for the Stalwarts
and New York's Republican spoils boss, put Grant's name in nomination with his powerhouse "He hails from Appomattox with its famous
appletree" speech that well-nigh stampeded the delegates. But the conventionites were somewhat suspicious of a third term for Grant and
worked out a compromise that threw the nomination to dark horse
James A. Garfield, Union veteran and Senator-elect from Ohio. Moaned
Grant, "My friends have not been honest with me. I can not afford
to be defeated."

For Vice-President, the Republicans selected *Chester A. Arthur,*
former Collector of the Port of New York and hander-out for Roscoe
Conkling.

To oppose Garfield, the Democrats named Hancock, who was no
campaigner but had polled substantial votes in the 1868 and 1876

278

conventions. Handsome and forthright, he was considered acceptable to the South in spite of his triumph at Gettysburg. As Reconstruction Governor of Military District Five (Texas and Louisiana) he had administered his duties so justly as to win the respect and confidence of thousands of Southerners and to alienate the Radical Republicans in Washington who forced his recall. He was an ideal drawing card for Southern voters.

The tariff emerged as the big issue of the campaign. The Republicans plunked for higher protective tariff; the Democrats pledged a tariff for revenue only. Hancock immortalized his campaign with six injudicious words—"The tariff is a local issue"—a great tactical blunder which set off explosions of ridicule. How could a presidential candidate speak so disrespectfully of the sacred tariff cow? And the New York *Sun* did not help matters when it said Hancock was "a good man weighing 250 pounds."

Hancock lost by less than 10,000 popular votes in the then-largest voting spree. Of 10,000,000 votes cast, Garfield received 4,449,053, Hancock 4,442,035. In the electoral college, Garfield ran off with 214, Hancock 155. The eleven former Confederate States solidified behind Hancock and gave him 95 electorals.

James A. Garfield, third American President born in a log cabin, was fatally shot by a disappointed office seeker four months after taking office, a martyr to the spoils system.

Vice President Arthur was promptly inducted into the highest office. Historians have brushed Arthur off as somewhat of a nonentity, but, on the contrary, he turned in a competent performance, for which the nation should be grateful, if only for the creation of the new American navy that won the Spanish-American War. Fond of the luxuries of life, associate of the rich and aristocratic, Arthur rivaled Martin Van Buren as the fashion plate of the presidential parade. His wardrobe included seventy-five suits of clothes and one hundred pairs of shoes. Upstanding, six-feet-two, adorned with fascinating side whiskers, he looked the role he played. His taste for grandeur ran to gold wallpaper in his dining room. A sumptuous entertainer, his midnight champagne suppers were the talk of the town. He held the first White House rummage sale, selling off twenty-four cartloads of historic furnishings.

Arthur was the only President to die presumably of a broken heart because his party refused to renominate him. He died at his home in New York City, November 18, 1886.

Arthur had the vision and the courage to father the Pendleton Act (which really established the merit system in passing out government jobs and is the basic model of today's civil-service system), to prosecute members of his own party in the Star Route frauds, to launch the construction of America's modern steel navy (the White Squadron), and to acquire Pearl Harbor as a naval base in the Pacific. Not until 1883 did the nation, under Arthur's prodding, profit by the *Merrimack-Monitor* ironclad lesson of the sixties. His first message pioneered for the nation's first four steel cruisers, the so-called ABCD ships, *Atlanta, Boston, Chicago,* and *Dolphin.*

In this same message he requested legislation clarifying the clause in the Constitution in respect to the death, inability, or resignation of a President—which spelled out the Presidential Succession Act of 1886. At the same time he gave the nation a laugh by asking Congress what to do about a gang of cowboys who were shooting up small towns in Arizona. The local sheriffs had found things too hot to handle and had written to ask President Arthur what to do about it.

In his last message, Arthur asked Congress to restore General Grant to rank in the army with retirement on full pay. Grant's plunge into Wall Street high finance had pauperized him overnight. Congress complied, and Arthur signed the bill just before going out of office. The nation commended him heartily for this act of kindness. Grant was dead seven months later.

CHESTER A. ARTHUR
FIRST STATE-OF-THE-UNION MESSAGE
WASHINGTON, *December 6, 1881*

To the Senate and House of Representatives of the United States:
An appalling calamity has befallen the American people since their chosen representatives last met in the halls where you are now assembled. To that mysterious exercise of His will which has taken from us the loved and illustrious citizen who was but lately the head of the nation we bow in sorrow and submission.

🐘 🐘 🐘

The intimacy between our own country and Japan, the most advanced of the Eastern nations, continues to be cordial. I am advised that the Emperor contemplates the establishment of full constitutional government, and that he has already summoned a parliamentary congress for the purpose of effecting the change. . . .

It is a matter for congratulation that the business of the country has been so prosperous during the past year as to yield by taxation a large surplus of income to the Government. In 1860, just prior to the institution of our internal-revenue system, our population but slightly exceeded 30,000,000; by the census of 1880 it is now found to exceed 50,000,000. . . .

In view, however, of the heavy load of taxation which our people have already borne, we may well consider whether it is not the part of wisdom to reduce the revenues, even if we delay a little the payment of the [national] debt.

I can not too strongly urge upon you my conviction that every consideration of national safety, economy, and honor imperatively demands a thorough rehabilitation of our Navy. . . .

No danger from abroad now threatens this people, nor have we any cause to distrust the friendly professions of other governments. But for avoiding as well as for repelling dangers that may threaten us in the future we must be prepared to enforce any policy which we think wise to adopt.

The Acting Attorney General also calls attention to the disturbance of the public tranquillity during the past year in the Territory of Arizona. A band of armed desperadoes known as "Cowboys," probably numbering from fifty to one hundred men, have been engaged for months in committing acts of lawlessness and brutality which the local authorities have been unable to repress. The depredations of these "Cowboys" have also extended into Mexico, which the marauders reach from the Arizona frontier. With every disposition to meet the exigencies of the case, I am embarrassed by lack of authority to deal with them effectually. In view of the speedy assembling of your body I have preferred to await such legislation as in your wisdom the occasion may seem to demand.

We have had to deal with the appalling fact that though thousands of lives have been sacrificed and hundreds of millions of dollars expended in the attempt to solve the Indian problem, it has until within the past few years seemed scarcely nearer a solution than it was half a century ago. But the Government has of late been cautiously but steadily feeling its way to the adoption of a policy which has already produced gratifying results. . . .

In my letter accepting the nomination for the vice-presidency I stated that in my judgment—

No man should be the incumbent of an office the duties of which he is for any cause unfit to perform; who is lacking in the ability, fidelity, or integrity which a proper administration of such office demands. Original appointments should be based upon ascertained fitness.

The tenure of office should be stable.

Positions of responsibility should, so far as practicable, be filled by the promotion of worthy and efficient officers.

The investigation of all complaints and the punishment of all official misconduct should be prompt and thorough.

The views expressed in the foregoing letter are those which will govern my administration of the executive office. . . .

There are very many characteristics which go to make a model civil servant. Prominent among them are probity, industry, good sense, good habits, good temper, patience, order, courtesy, tact, self-reliance, manly deference to superior officers, and manly consideration for inferiors. The absence of these traits is not supplied by wide knowledge of books, or by promptitude in answering questions, or by any other quality likely to be brought to light by competitive examination.

The importance of timely legislation with respect to the ascertainment and declaration of the vote for Presidential electors was sharply called to the attention of the people more than four years ago. Questions which concern the very existence of the Government and the liberties of the people were suggested by the prolonged illness of the late President and his consequent incapacity to perform the functions of his office.

It is provided by the second article of the Constitution, in the fifth clause of its first section, that "in case of the removal of the President from office, or of his death, resignation, or inability to discharge the powers and duties of the said office, the same shall devolve on the Vice President."

What is the intendment of the Constitution in its specification of "inability to discharge the powers and duties of the said office" as one of the contingencies which calls the Vice President to the exercise of Presidential functions?

Is the inability limited in its nature to long-continued intellectual incapacity, or has it a broader import?

What must be its extent and duration?

How must its existence be established?

🐘 🐘 🐘

If the inability proves to be temporary in its nature, and during its continuance the Vice President lawfully exercises the functions of the Executive, by what tenure does he hold his office?

Does he continue as President for the remainder of the four years' term?

Or would the elected President, if his inability should cease in the interval, be empowered to resume his office?

And if, having such lawful authority, he should exercise it, would the Vice President be thereupon empowered to resume his powers and duties as such?

I can not doubt that these important questions will receive your early and thoughtful consideration. . . .

CHESTER A. ARTHUR
SECOND STATE-OF-THE-UNION MESSAGE
WASHINGTON, *December 4, 1882*

To the Senate and House of Representatives of the United States:
. . . I first call your attention to the gratifying condition of our foreign affairs. Our intercourse with other powers has continued to be of the most friendly character.

A comparison between the respective amounts of silver-dollar circulation on November 1, 1882, shows a slight increase of a million and a half of dollars. . . . Of the one hundred and twenty-eight millions thus far minted, little more than thirty-five millions are in circulation. The mass of accumulated coin has grown so great that the vault room at present available for storage is scarcely sufficient to contain it. It is not apparent why it is desirable to continue this coinage, now so enormously in excess of the public demand.

It appears by the [Navy] Secretary's report that the available naval force of the United States consists of 37 cruisers, 14 single-turreted monitors, built during the rebellion, a large number of smoothbore guns and Parrott rifles, and 87 rifled cannon.
The cruising vessels should be gradually replaced by iron or steel ships, the monitors by modern armored vessels, and the armament by high-power rifled guns.

The regulation of interstate commerce has already been the subject of your deliberations. One of the incidents of the marvelous extension of the railway system of the country has been the adoption of such measures by the corporations which own or control the roads as have tended to impair the advantages of healthful competition and to make hurtful discriminations in the adjustment of freightage.

The civil list now comprises about 100,000 persons, far the larger part of whom must, under the terms of the Constitution, be selected by the President either directly or through his own appointees.

In the early years of the administration of the Government the personal direction of appointments to the civil service may not have been an irksome task for the Executive, but now that the burden has increased fully a hundredfold it has become greater than he ought to bear. . . .

As to the most appropriate term and tenure of the official life of the subordinate employees of the Government, it seems to be generally agreed that, whatever their extent or character, the one should be definite and the other stable, and that neither should be regulated by zeal in the service of party or fidelity to the fortunes of an individual.

Among the questions which have been the topic of recent debate in the halls of Congress none are of greater gravity than those relating to the ascertainment of the vote for Presidential electors and the intendment of the Constitution in its provisions for devolving Executive functions upon the Vice President when the President suffers from inability to discharge the powers and duties of his office.

I trust that no embarrassments may result from a failure to determine these questions before another national election. . . .

CHESTER A. ARTHUR
THIRD STATE-OF-THE-UNION MESSAGE
WASHINGTON, *December 4, 1883*

To the Congress of the United States:

Questions have arisen touching the rights of American and other foreign manufacturers in China under the provisions of treaties which permit aliens to exercise their industries in that country. On this specific point our own treaty is silent, but under the operation of the most-favored-nation clause we have like privileges with those of other powers. While it is the duty of the Government to see that our citizens have the full enjoyment of every benefit secured by treaty, I doubt the expediency of leading in a movement to constrain China to admit an interpretation which we have only an indirect treaty right to exact. . . .

The rich and populous valley of the Congo is being opened to commerce by a society called the International African Association, of which the King of the Belgians is the president and a citizen of the United States the chief executive officer. . . . The objects of the society are philanthropic. It does not aim at permanent political control, but seeks the neutrality of the valley. The United States can not be indifferent to this work nor to the interests of their citizens involved in it.

I again call your attention to the present condition of our extended seacoast, upon which are so many large cities whose wealth and importance to the country would in time of war invite attack from modern armored ships, against which our existing defensive works could give no adequate protection. Those works were built before the introduction of modern heavy rifled guns into maritime warfare, and if they are not put in an efficient condition we may easily be subjected to humiliation by a hostile power greatly inferior to ourselves. As germane to this subject, I call your attention to the importance of perfecting our submarine-torpedo defenses. . . .

The Secretary of the Navy reports that the work of strengthening our Navy by the construction of modern vessels has been auspiciously begun. Three cruisers are in process of construction—the *Chicago,* of 4,500 tons displacement, and the *Boston* and *Atlanta,* each of 2,500 tons. They are to be built of steel. A fourth vessel, the *Dolphin,* is to be constructed of similar material, and is intended to serve as a fleet dispatch boat.

I feel bound to impress upon the attention of Congress the necessity of continued progress in the reconstruction of the Navy. . . . That our naval strength should be made adequate for the defense of our harbors, the protection of our commercial interests, and the maintenance of our national honor is a proposition from which no patriotic citizen can withhold his assent.

I trust that Congress will not fail at its present session to put Alaska under the protection of law. Its people have repeatedly remonstrated against our neglect to afford them the maintenance and protection expressly guaranteed by the terms of the treaty whereby that Territory was ceded to the United States. . . .

🐘 🐘 🐘

At the time when the present Executive entered upon his office his death, removal, resignation, or inability to discharge his duties would have left the Government without a constitutional head.

It is possible, of course, that a similar contingency may again arise unless the wisdom of Congress shall provide against its recurrence. . . .

The clause of the Constitution upon which must depend any law regulating the Presidential succession presents also for solution other questions of paramount importance. These questions relate to the proper interpretation of the phrase "inability to discharge the powers and duties of said office," our organic law providing that when the President shall suffer from such inability the Presidential office shall devolve upon the Vice President, who must himself under like circumstances give place to such officer as Congress may by law appoint to act as President. . . .

CHESTER A. ARTHUR
FOURTH STATE-OF-THE-UNION MESSAGE
WASHINGTON, *December 1, 1884*

To the Congress of the United States:

Eight years have passed since a controversy concerning the result of a national election sharply called the attention of the Congress to the necessity of providing more precise and definite regulations for counting the electoral vote.

It is of the gravest importance that this question be solved before conflicting claims to the Presidency shall again distract the country, and I am persuaded that by the people at large any of the measures of relief thus far proposed would be preferred to continued inaction.

Our relations with all foreign powers continue to be amicable. With France the traditional cordial relationship continues. The colossal statue of Liberty Enlightening the World, the generous gift of the people of France, is expected to reach New York in May next. I suggest that Congressional action be taken in recognition of the spirit which has prompted this gift and in aid of the timely completion of the pedestal upon which it is to be placed.

I concur with the Secretary of the Treasury in recommending the immediate suspension of the coinage of silver dollars and of the issuance of silver certificates. This is a matter to which in former communications I have more than once invoked the attention of the National Legislature.

The report of the Secretary of the Navy exhibits the progress which has been made on the new steel cruisers. Of the four vessels under contract, one, the *Chicago,* of 4,500 tons, is more than half finished; the *Atlanta,* of 3,000 tons, has been successfully launched, and her machinery is now fitting; the *Boston,* also of 3,000 tons, is ready for launching, and the *Dolphin,* a dispatch steamer of 1,500 tons, is ready for delivery.

In this the last of the stated messages that I shall have the honor to transmit to the Congress of the United States I can not too strongly urge upon its attention the duty of restoring our Navy as rapidly as possible to the high state of efficiency which formerly characterized it. . . .

I recommend that in recognition of the eminent services of Ulysses S. Grant, late General of the armies of the United States and twice President of this nation, the Congress confer upon him a suitable pension.

As the time draws nigh when I am to retire from the public service, I can not refrain from expressing to the members of the National Legislature with whom I have been brought into personal and official intercourse my sincere appreciation of their unfailing courtesy and of their harmonious cooperation with the Executive in so many measures calculated to promote the best interests of the nation. . . .

GROVER CLEVELAND
(1885–1889)

*"It is a condition
which confronts us,
not a theory"*

Grover Cleveland used this historic phrase in his Third State-of-the-Union Message, December, 1887, in emphasizing his four-square stand on the tariff, the issue then besetting Congress and the nation. Two simple traits, honesty and truth, made up Cleveland's code of life. Nowhere were they more clearly illustrated than in his making the tariff the sole subject of this message, which not only fixed the main issue in the coming election, but assured his renomination.

Cleveland's popularity was based on his rugged independence. When his campaign managers said he would lessen his chances of election by opposing the prevailing high customs duties, he replied, "I care more for principle than the presidency" wherein he paraphrased Henry Clay's "I'd rather be right than President."

In the violent, colorful campaign of 1884, no holds were barred, no scandals left unbared. In mid-campaign the Republicans suddenly blasted off with "A Terrible Tale" about an illegitimate child hidden somewhere in Cleveland's past. His managers threw up their hands in despair. "Tell them the truth," said Cleveland, who promptly admitted the paternity of the child—an admission that brought down much wrath on his head.

Pitted against Cleveland was James G. Blaine, who in many ways was the nimblest, most resourceful actor in American politics. His

290

party had nominated him by acclamation. To several million Republicans, Blaine was still the Plumed Knight on whom Robert G. Ingersoll had pinned that questionable accolade, but a sizable bloc of Republicans, the so-called Mugwumps, unable to stomach Blaine's unworthy transactions, threw their support to Cleveland.

A week before election Blaine had an unfortunate break. He failed to contradict three words used by a Protestant clergyman, spokesman for a group that came to see Blaine at his New York hotel. In reassuring Blaine of their loyalty, Dr. Samuel Burchard tagged the Democrats as the party of Rum, Romanism and Rebellion—a sidewise anti-Catholic slap which Blaine failed to notice. The Democrats promptly crucified him, interpreting his silence as an insult to the Catholic Church—and so did the voters on Election Day.

For the American people it was a choice between a man who had acknowledged fathering an illegitimate child, but who was honest to the core, and a man tarred with dishonesty in high places, which he had tried to hide. Cleveland won by a narrow majority. Both parties accepted the tariff and civil-service reform as the chief issues.

Cleveland was the only President ever to deliver his Inaugural Address *ex tempore* and the first Democratic President since the Civil War. His inaugural drew immense crowds (estimated at 200,000), the greatest assembled for the induction of a President up to his time. The South turned up *en masse.*

Pictures of Cleveland in 1884 reveal a bulky, bull-necked man almost as huge (265 pounds) as future President William H. Taft. At forty-eight he entered the White House a lonely bachelor, but he remedied this condition in 1886, when he was married in the White House, to pretty Frances Folsom. He was one of the most industrious Presidents.

He came to the presidency at an expansive time. The frontiers were vanishing. Gone were the hunters and trappers. The cattle kings and cowboys were taking over. Across the grassy Western plains, ancient home of Indian and buffalo, civilization was advancing like an inexorable wall. The red man had made his last spectacular stand at Little Big Horn in Montana. After the Custer massacre the Indian kept up a forlorn, rearguard fight before retiring to reservations and white man's ways.

The South had risen from defeat and ashes. Alexander Graham Bell had bestowed his boon, the telephone, on mankind. Out of Edison's laboratory came the phonograph and electric light. From the teeming genius of this one man came other devices, including the streetcar and the motion picture. Basic industries—steel, coal, electricity, oil, railroads, and others were making mighty impacts on the nation's economy while labor opened its long, arduous crusade for the rights of the working man and an eight-hour day. Napoleons of Finance, Coal Barons, Steel Kings, Railway Magnates, and Oil Czars were assuming roles for good or evil in the nation's economy.

American interests were reaching out around the globe, and the United States was emerging from an isolated continent into a world power. Tornadoes of debate swept Capitol Hill on the protective tariff, and the twenty-five-year tussle between the Silver Democrats and Gold Republicans was rising to a high pitch.

Immigration in 1882 had reached its nineteenth-century high of almost 790,000 people entering the country in a single year, a figure not to be equaled until 1903. Advertising, formerly employed only by patent medicine and circus, was being sampled gingerly by manufacturers of household products. The bicycle craze was speeding on. The American woman was still tightly encased in corsets, but the bathtub was no longer a luxury of the wealthy. John L. Sullivan, the Boston Strong Boy, was the new heavyweight champion.

Cleveland startled the country by devoting his entire Third State-of-the-Union Message to the imperative need of action on the tariff. His first message, December, 1885, had endorsed tariff reduction somewhat casually; his 1886 message was more definite; his 1887 message was an electrifying call for action. His whole idea was tariff for revenue only. Congress took the hint and complied.

His collision with the Grand Army of the Republic (a Union Army veterans' association formed in 1866 for the "defense of the late soldiery of the United States morally, socially, and politically") over veterans' pensions was well told in his messages. He was not unsympathetic to the actual needs of veterans, but he would not permit the United States to be defrauded by hundreds of false pension claims. In a single year he vetoed over three hundred special pension bills. In 1887, he vetoed the General Pension Bill. From then on out the G.A.R. hated him cordially.

In mentioning the dedication of the "Colossal Statue of Liberty Enlightening the World" in New York Harbor, he failed to say that he himself officiated at the dedication of this statue that has brought hope to thousands seeking new homes in a new world.

GROVER CLEVELAND
FIRST STATE-OF-THE-UNION MESSAGE
WASHINGTON, *December 8, 1885*

To the Congress of the United States:

Emergencies growing out of civil war in the United States of Colombia demanded of the Government at the beginning of this Administration the employment of armed forces to fulfill its guaranties under the thirty-fifth article of the treaty of 1846, in order to keep the transit open across the Isthmus of Panama. . . .

🦌 🦌 🦌

The condition of the Chinese question in the Western States and Territories is . . . far from being satisfactory. The recent outbreak in Wyoming Territory, where numbers of unoffending Chinamen, indisputably within the protection of the treaties and the law, were murdered by a mob, and the still more recent threatened outbreak of the same character in Washington Territory, are fresh in the minds of all, and there is apprehension lest the bitterness of feeling against the Mongolian race on the Pacific Slope may find vent in similar lawless demonstrations. All the power of this Government should be exerted to maintain the amplest good faith toward China in the treatment of these men, and the inflexible sternness of the law in bringing the wrongdoers to justice should be insisted upon. . . .

Race prejudice is the chief factor in originating these disturbances, and it exists in a large part of our domain, jeopardizing our domestic peace and the good relationship we strive to maintain with China.

🦌 🦌 🦌

The fact that our revenues are in excess of the actual needs of an economical administration of the Government justified a reduction in the amount exacted from the people for its support. . . .

The proposition with which we have to deal is the reduction of the revenue received by the Government, and indirectly paid by the people, from customs duties. The question of free trade is not involved. Nor is there now any occasion for the general discussion of the wisdom or expediency of a protective system. . . .

I think the reduction should be made in the revenue derived from a tax upon the imported necessaries of life. We thus directly lessen the cost of living in every family of the land and release to the people in every humble home a larger measure of the rewards of frugal industry.

Nothing more important than the present condition of our currency and coinage can claim your attention.

🐴 🐴 🐴

The desire to utilize the silver product of the country should not lead to a misuse or the perversion of this power. Every month two millions of gold in the public Treasury are paid out for two millions or more of silver dollars, to be added to the idle mass already accumulated.

If continued long enough, this operation will result in the substitution of silver for all the gold the Government owns applicable to its general purposes. . . .

We have now on hand all the silver dollars necessary to supply the present needs of the people. That disaster has not already overtaken us furnishes no proof that danger does not wait upon a continuation of the present silver coinage. Prosperity hesitates upon our threshold because of the dangers and uncertainties surrounding this question.

As a necessary consequence, labor lacks employment and suffering and distress are visited upon a portion of our fellow-citizens especially entitled to the careful consideration of those charged with the duties of legislation. No interest appeals to us so strongly for a safe and stable currency as the vast army of the unemployed.

🐴 🐴 🐴

Troops were sent to Rock Springs, in Wyoming Territory, after the massacre of Chinese there, to prevent further disturbance, and afterwards to Seattle, in Washington Territory, to avert a threatened attack upon Chinese laborers and domestic violence there. In both cases the mere presence of the troops had the desired effect.

🐴 🐴 🐴

The Military Academy at West Point is reported as being in a high state of efficiency and well equipped for the satisfactory accomplishment of the purposes of its maintenance.

🐕 🐕 🐕

Congress at its last session authorized the construction of two additional new cruisers and two gunboats, at a cost not exceeding in the aggregate $2,995,000. . . . All must admit the importance of an effective navy to a nation like ours, having such an extended seacoast to protect; and yet we have not a single vessel of war that could keep the seas against a first-class vessel of any important power. Such a condition ought not longer to continue. The nation that can not resist aggression is constantly exposed to it. . . .

🐕 🐕 🐕

It appears from the report of the Commissioner of Pensions that there were on the 1st day of July, 1885, 345,125 persons borne upon the pension rolls. . . .

While there is no expenditure of the public funds which the people more cheerfully approve than that made in recognition of the services of our soldiers living and dead, the sentiment underlying the subject should not be vitiated by the introduction of any fraudulent practices. Therefore it is fully as important that the rolls should be cleansed of all those who by fraud have secured a place thereon as that meritorious claims should be speedily examined and adjusted.

🐕 🐕 🐕

In the Territory of Utah the law of the United States passed for the suppression of polygamy has been energetically and faithfully executed during the past year, with measurably good results. . . .

🐕 🐕 🐕

I am inclined to think that there is no sentiment more general in the minds of the people of our country than a conviction of the correctness of the principle upon which the law enforcing civil-service reform is based. . . .

The allurements of an immense number of offices and places

exhibited to the voters of the land, and the promise of their bestowal in recognition of partisan activity, debauch the suffrage and rob political action of its thoughtful and deliberative character. . . .

Civil-service reform enforced by law came none too soon to check the progress of demoralization. . . .

One of its effects, not enough regarded, is the freedom it brings to the political action of those conservative and sober men who, in fear of the confusion and risk attending an arbitrary and sudden change in all the public offices with a change of party rule, cast their ballots against such a change.

Parties seem to be necessary, and will long continue to exist; nor can it be now denied that there are legitimate advantages, not disconnected with office holding, which follow party supremacy. The civil-service law does not prevent the discharge of the indolent or incompetent clerk, but it does prevent supplying his place with the unfit party worker. . . .

🐗 🐗 🐗

The present condition of the law relating to the succession to the Presidency in the event of the death, disability, or removal of both the President and Vice President is such as to require immediate amendment. . . .

In conclusion I commend to the wise care and thoughtful attention of Congress the needs, the welfare, and the aspirations of an intelligent and generous nation. . . .

GROVER CLEVELAND
SECOND STATE-OF-THE-UNION MESSAGE
WASHINGTON, *December 6, 1886*

To the Congress of the United States:

In discharge of a constitutional duty, and following a well-established precedent in the Executive office, I herewith transmit to the Congress at its reassembling certain information concerning the state of the Union. . . .

The sympathy between the people of the United States and France, born during our colonial struggle for independence and continuing today, has received a fresh impulse in the successful completion and dedication of the colossal statue of "Liberty Enlightening the World" in New York Harbor—the gift of Frenchmen to Americans.

🐐 🐐 🐐

I express my unhesitating conviction that the intimacy of our relations with Hawaii should be emphasized. As a result of the reciprocity treaty of 1875, those islands, on the highway of Oriental and Australasian traffic, are virtually an outpost of American commerce and a stepping-stone to the growing trade of the Pacific. The Polynesian Island groups have been so absorbed by other and more powerful governments that the Hawaiian Islands are left almost alone in the enjoyment of their autonomy. . . .

🐐 🐐 🐐

In my last annual message to the Congress attention was directed to the fact that the revenues of the Government exceeded its actual needs, and it was suggested that legislative action should be taken to relieve the people from the unnecessary burden of taxation thus made apparent. . . .

Those who toil for daily wages are beginning to understand that capital, though sometimes vaunting its importance and clamoring for the protection and favor of the Government, is dull and sluggish till, touched by the magical hand of labor, it springs into activity, furnishing an occasion for Federal taxation and gaining the value which enables it to bear its burden. And the laboring man is thoughtfully inquiring whether in these circumstances, and considering the tribute he constantly pays into the public Treasury as he supplies his daily wants, he receives his fair share of advantages.

🐐 🐐 🐐

In September and October last the hostile Apaches who, under the leadership of Geronimo, had for eighteen months been on the war path, and during that time had committed many murders and been the cause of constant terror to the settlers of Arizona, surrendered to General Miles, the military commander who succeeded General Crook in the management and direction of their pursuit.

🐐 🐐 🐐

The total amount paid for pensions since 1861 is $808,624,-811.57. . . .

The American people, with a patriotic and grateful regard for our ex-soldiers, too broad and too sacred to be monopolized by any special advocates, are not only willing but anxious that equal and exact justice should be done to all honest claimants for pensions. . . .

. . . Yielding to no one in the desire to indulge this feeling of consideration, I can not rid myself of the conviction that if these ex-soldiers are to be relieved they and their cause are entitled to the benefit of an enactment under which relief may be claimed as a right, and that such relief should be granted under the sanction of law, not in evasion of it; nor should such worthy objects of care, all equally entitled, be remitted to the unequal operation of sympathy or the tender mercies of social and political influence, with their unjust discriminations. . . .

GROVER CLEVELAND
THIRD STATE-OF-THE-UNION MESSAGE
WASHINGTON, *December 6, 1887*

To the Congress of the United States:

You are confronted at the threshold of your legislative duties with a condition of the national finances which imperatively demands immediate and careful consideration.

The amount of money annually exacted, through the operation of present laws, from the industries and necessities of the people largely exceeds the sum necessary to meet the expenses of the Government.

. . . The public Treasury, which should only exist as a conduit conveying the people's tribute to its legitimate objects of expenditure, becomes a hoarding place for money needlessly withdrawn from trade and the people's use, thus crippling our national energies, suspending our country's development, preventing investment in productive enterprise, threatening financial disturbance, and inviting schemes of public plunder.

🐕 🐕 🐕

. . . Our present tariff laws, the vicious, inequitable, and illogical source of unnecessary taxation, ought to be at once revised and amended. . . .

It is not proposed to entirely relieve the country of this taxation. It must be extensively continued as the source of the Government's income; and in a readjustment of our tariff the interests of American labor engaged in manufacture should be carefully considered, as well as the preservation of our manufacturers. . . .

The standard of our laborers' life should not be measured by that of any other country less favored, and they are entitled to their full share of all our advantages.

But the reduction of taxation demanded should be so measured as not to necessitate or justify either the loss of employment by the workingman or the lessening of his wages; and the profits still remaining to the manufacturer after a necessary readjustment should furnish no excuse for the sacrifice of the interests of his employees, either in their opportunity to work or in the diminution of their compensation. . . .

🐕 🐕 🐕

Under our present laws more than 4,000 articles are subject to duty. Many of these do not in any way compete with our own manufactures, and many are hardly worth attention as subjects of revenue. A considerable reduction can be made in the aggregate by adding them to the free list. The taxation of luxuries presents no features of hardship; but the necessaries of life used and consumed by all the people, the duty upon which adds to the cost of living in every home, should be greatly cheapened.

🐕 🐕 🐕

Our progress toward a wise conclusion will not be improved by dwelling upon the theories of protection and free trade. This savors too much of bandying epithets. It is a *condition* which confronts us, not a theory. Relief from this condition may involve a slight reduction of the advantages which we award our home productions, but the entire withdrawal of such advantages should not be contemplated. The question of free trade is absolutely irrelevant, and the persistent claim made in certain quarters that all the efforts to relieve the people from unjust and unnecessary taxation are schemes of so-called free traders is mischievous and far removed from any consideration for the public good.

The simple and plain duty which we owe the people is to reduce taxation to the necessary expenses of an economical operation of the Government and to restore to the business of the country the money which we hold in the Treasury through the perversion of governmental powers. . . .

The Constitution provides that the President "shall from time to time give to the Congress information on the state of the Union." I am so much impressed with the paramount importance of the subject to which this communication has thus far been devoted that I shall forego the addition of any other topic, and only urge upon your immediate consideration the "state of the Union" as shown in the present condition of our Treasury and our general fiscal situation, upon which every element of our safety and prosperity depends.

GROVER CLEVELAND
FOURTH STATE-OF-THE-UNION MESSAGE
WASHINGTON, *December 3, 1888*

To the Congress of the United States:

As you assemble for the discharge of the duties you have assumed as the representatives of a free and generous people, your meeting is marked by an interesting and impressive incident. With the expiration of the present session of the Congress the first century of our constitutional existence as a nation will be completed.

Our survival for one hundred years is not sufficient to assure us that we no longer have dangers to fear in the maintenance, with all its promised blessings, of a government founded upon the freedom of the people. . . .

🦌   🦌   🦌

A century has passed. Our cities are the abiding places of wealth and luxury; our manufactories yield fortunes never dreamed of by the fathers of the Republic; our businessmen are madly striving in the race for riches, and immense aggregations of capital outrun the imagination in the magnitude of their undertakings.

We view with pride and satisfaction this bright picture of our country's growth and prosperity, while only a closer scrutiny develops a somber shading. Upon more careful inspection we find the wealth and luxury of our cities mingled with poverty and wretchedness and unremunerative toil. . . .

We discover that the fortunes realized by our manufacturers are no longer solely the reward of sturdy industry and enlightened foresight, but that they result from the discriminating favor of the Government and are largely built upon undue exactions from the masses of our people. The gulf between employers and the employed is constantly widening, and classes are rapidly forming, one comprising the very rich and powerful, while in another are found the toiling poor.

As we view the achievements of aggregated capital, we discover the existence of trusts, combinations, and monopolies, while the citizen is struggling far in the rear or is trampled to death beneath an iron heel. Corporations, which should be the carefully restrained creatures of the law and the servants of the people, are fast becoming the people's masters.

🦌   🦌   🦌

Instead of limiting the tribute drawn from our citizens to the necessities of its economical administration, the Government persists in exacting from the substance of the people millions which, unapplied and useless, lie dormant in its Treasury. . . .

Under the same laws by which these results are produced the Government permits many millions more to be added to the cost of living of our people and to be taken from our consumers, which unreasonably swell the profits of a small but powerful minority.

The people must still be taxed for the support of the Government under the operation of tariff laws. . . .

This is not equality before the law.

The existing situation is injurious to the health of our entire body politic. It stifles in those for whose benefit it is permitted all patriotic love of country, and substitutes in its place selfish greed and grasping avarice. . . .

🐃 🐃 🐃

Our workingmen, enfranchised from all delusions and no longer frightened by the cry that their wages are endangered by a just revision of our tariff laws, will reasonably demand through such revision steadier employment, cheaper means of living in their homes, freedom for themselves and their children from the doom of perpetual servitude, and an open door to their advancement beyond the limits of a laboring class. . . .

🐃 🐃 🐃

Communism is a hateful thing and a menace to peace and organized government; but the communism of combined wealth and capital, the outgrowth of overweening cupidity and selfishness, which insidiously undermines the justice and integrity of free institutions, is not less dangerous than the communism of oppressed poverty and toil, which, exasperated by injustice and discontent, attacks with wild disorder the citadel of rule.

He mocks the people who proposes that the Government shall protect the rich and that they in turn will care for the laboring poor. Any intermediary between the people and their Government or the least delegation of the care and protection the Government owes to the humblest citizen in the land makes the boast of free institutions a glittering delusion and the pretended boon of American citizenship a shameless imposition.

A just and sensible revision of our tariff laws should be made for the relief of those of our countrymen who suffer under present conditions. . . . The cause for which the battle is waged is comprised within lines clearly and distinctly defined. . . . It should never be compromised. It is the people's cause.

BENJAMIN HARRISON
(1889–1893)

"There are

no near frontiers

to our possible development"

The Fifty-first Congress that convened in December, 1889, to hear *Benjamin Harrison*'s First State-of-the-Union Message well deserved its popular nickname, "the billion-dollar Congress." It was the first Congress to achieve fame by spending the taxpayer's hard-earned dollars in ten figures. It had taken exactly one hundred years of constitutional government to reach this then-appalling plateau of expenditures. To the friend who chided Speaker Tom Reed for the Fifty-first Congress' spending a billion dollars, he quipped, "Yes, but this is a billion-dollar country."

In this Congress the Republicans had a majority of three, representing barely a quorum and one so narrow they could not even adopt new rules if the Democratic minority refused to cooperate. It meant that the Democrats, by simply sitting still and saying nothing, could veto all legislation.

For the first time in ten years, the Republicans controlled both houses of Congress. They had campaign pledges to redeem. The Treasury had a $97,000,000 surplus the Republicans wanted to spend (and did spend), mostly by increasing pensions for Union Army veterans and adding over 200,000 pensioners to the overstuffed rolls. They hoped to enact the federal-elections bill, the so-called force bill, giving the government power to supervise congressional elections in the South and use military force to do it. Most of all, the Republicans wanted a new protective tariff. Increasing the purchase of silver and an antitrust act rated high on their agenda. Yet, these measures were all hobbled by a Democratic no-quorum yoke in the House.

In a battle reminiscent of the turbulent antebellum debates, Speaker Reed overturned the traditional method of counting a quorum and set a new precedent by simply counting those Democrats he could see, who were sitting in the House but engaging in the pleasant fiction of being physically present and vocally absent when their names came up on roll call. He took unto himself power to declare a quorum whenever those voting and those present but refusing to vote added up to a majority. It brought fiery repercussions, but Reed stood fast while the public applauded. Reed, incidentally, was a masterful man-mountain, six feet three and more than three hundred pounds, whose wit and sarcasm has never heard its match in the House.

Actually, Speaker Reed's battle on Capitol Hill took the play away from new President Benjamin Harrison, who sat in the White House waiting for Congress to pass a few bills for him to sign and to enact one he wanted most of all, a sky-high protective tariff.

Backed by the biggest campaign fund then on record, Harrison had nosed out Cleveland whom the Democrats had renominated by acclamation. Rich merchant John Wanamaker of Philadelphia, whom Harrison appointed Postmaster General, reputedly dropped $400,000 into the Republican campaign till.

Harrison, former United States Senator from Indiana, Union veteran, and grandson of William Henry Harrison, the ninth President, was a frigid man. The saying went in Washington, "Harrison sweats ice water." Often told was the story of a tiff between Harrison and Senator Matt Quay of Pennsylvania, Republican party boss, who virtually put Harrison in the White House. Quay, so the story went, asked Harrison for a government job for his son. To Quay's surprise, Harrison refused, whereupon Quay asked, "Harrison, who made you President of the United States?" To this the President replied, "The Almighty and the American people." "Well," said Quay, "wait and see what the Almighty and the American people do to you at the next election."

Prophetic, indeed, was Harrison's First State-of-the-Union Message. He plunked for higher tariffs immediately. To Representative William McKinley, chairman of the Ways and Means Committee, was assigned the task of raising the tariff. He did so well his constituents refused to reelect him. The American consumers raised a terrific outcry that brought revenge at the next presidential election in 1892.

This same message presaged passage of the Sherman Antitrust Act a year later. It was fathered by Senator John Sherman, brother of the great Civil War general. This much-embattled act outlawed combinations of big business, or trusts, to restrain trade and free competition. The act, mostly a gesture by the Republican majority, was enforced feebly, but it is still the cornerstone of government action against monopolies.

The purchase of the Cherokee Strip from the Indians, which Harrison revealed in his third message, set the stage for the last colorful "Rush" in 1893 for free land on America's vanishing frontier.

Harrison's flirtation with Hawaii is shown in his fourth message. With the connivance of the American Minister to the Islands, famed Queen Liliuokalani was deposed and a Hawaiian commission rushed to Washington with an annexation treaty. Harrison approved it and sent the treaty to the Senate. It arrived too late. Harrison's term was near its end. Hawaiian annexation must wait—as it did until 1898.

BENJAMIN HARRISON
FIRST STATE-OF-THE-UNION MESSAGE
WASHINGTON, *December 3, 1889*

To the Senate and House of Representatives:

I recommend a revision of our tariff law both in its administration features and in the schedules. The need of the former is generally conceded and an agreement upon the evils and inconveniences to be remedied and the best methods for their correction will probably not be difficult. Uniformity of valuation at all our ports is essential and measures should be taken to secure it. . . .

Earnest attention should be given by Congress to a consideration of the question how far the restraint of those combinations of capital commonly called "trusts" is a matter of Federal jurisdiction. When organized, as they often are, to crush out all healthy competition and to monopolize the production or sale of an article of commerce and general necessity, they are dangerous conspiracies against the public good, and should be made the subject of prohibitory and even penal legislation.

Under the agreement made between the United States and the Muscogee (or Creek) Nation of Indians on the 19th day of January, 1889, an absolute title was secured by the United States to about 3,500,000 acres of land. . . .

. . . In view of the fact that several thousand persons, many of them with their families, had gathered upon the borders of the Indian Territory with a view to securing homesteads on the ceded lands, and that delay would involve them in much loss and suffering, I did on the 23d day of March last issue a proclamation declaring that the lands therein described would be open to settlement under the provisions of the law on the 22d day of April following at 12 o'clock noon. . . .

. . . It is estimated that there are now in the Territory about 60,000 people, and several considerable towns have sprung up, for which temporary municipal governments have been organized. Guthrie is said to have now a population of almost 8,000. Eleven schools and nine churches have been established, and three daily and five weekly newspapers are published in this city, whose charter and ordinances have only the sanction of the voluntary acquiescence of the people from day to day.

The advent of four new States—South Dakota, North Dakota, Montana, and Washington—into the Union under the Constitution in the same month, and the admission of their duly chosen representatives to our National Congress at the same session, is an event as unexampled as it is interesting.

The interest of the General Government in the education of the people found an early expression, not only in the thoughtful and sometimes warning utterances of our ablest statesmen, but in liberal appropriations from the common resources for the support of education in the new States. . . . National aid to education has heretofore taken the form of land grants, and in that form the constitutional power of Congress to promote the education of the people is not seriously questioned. I do not think it can be successfully questioned when the form is changed to that of a direct grant of money from the public Treasury.

The colored people did not intrude themselves upon us. They were brought here in chains and held in the communities where they are now chiefly found by a cruel slave code. Happily for both races, they are now free. . . .

But notwithstanding all this, in many parts of our country where the colored population is large the people of that race are by various devices deprived of any effective exercise of their political rights and of many of their civil rights.

It has been the hope of every patriot that a sense of justice and of respect for the law would work a gradual cure of these flagrant evils. . . . If it is said that these communities must work out this problem for themselves, we have a right to ask whether they are at work upon it. Do they suggest any solution? When and under what conditions is the black man to have a free ballot? When is he in fact to have those full civil rights which have so long been his in law? When is that equality of influence which our form of government was intended to secure to the electors to be restored? No question in our country can be at rest except upon the firm base of justice and of the law. . . .

BENJAMIN HARRISON
SECOND STATE-OF-THE-UNION MESSAGE
EXECUTIVE MANSION, *December 1, 1890*

To the Senate and House of Representatives:

The admission of the States of Wyoming and Idaho to the Union are events full of interest and congratulation, not only to the people of those States now happily endowed with a full participation in our privileges and responsibilities, but to all our people. Another belt of States stretches from the Atlantic to the Pacific.

I congratulate the Congress and the country upon the passage at the first session of the Fifty-first Congress of an unusual number

taken up by settlers in a single day. The rush for these lands was accompanied by a great deal of excitement, but was happily free from incidents of violence.

The grain crop of this year was the largest in our history—50 per cent greater than that of last year—and yet the new markets that have been opened and the larger demand resulting from short crops in Europe have sustained prices to such an extent that the enormous surplus of meats and breadstuffs will be marketed at good prices, bringing relief and prosperity to an industry that was much depressed. . . .

I have twice before urgently called the attention of Congress to the necessity of legislation for the protection of the lives of railroad employees, but nothing has yet been done. During the year ending June 30, 1890, 369 brakemen were killed and 7,841 maimed while engaged in coupling cars. The total number of railroad employees killed during the year was 2,451 and the number injured 22,390. This is a cruel and largely needless sacrifice. . . . A law requiring of every railroad engaged in interstate commerce the equipment each year of a given per cent of its freight cars with automatic couplers and air brakes would compel an agreement between the roads as to the kind of brakes and couplers to be used, and would very soon and very greatly reduce the present fearful death rate among railroad employees.

I have been greatly rejoiced to notice many evidences of the increased unification of our people and of a revived national spirit. The vista that now opens to us is wider and more glorious than ever before. Gratification and amazement struggle for supremacy as we contemplate the population, wealth, and moral strength of our country. . . .

BENJAMIN HARRISON
FOURTH STATE-OF-THE-UNION MESSAGE
EXECUTIVE MANSION, *December 6, 1892*

To the Senate and House of Representatives:

In submitting my annual message to Congress I have great satisfaction in being able to say that the general conditions affecting the commercial and industrial interests of the United States are in the highest degree favorable. . . .

The total wealth of the country in 1860 was $16,159,616,068. In 1890 it amounted to $62,610,000,000, an increase of 287 per cent.

🐘 🐘 🐘

The official returns of the Eleventh Census and those of the Tenth Census for seventy-five leading cities furnish the basis for the following comparisons:

In 1880 the capital invested in manufacturing was $1,232,-839,670.

In 1890 the capital invested in manufacturing was $2,900,-735,884.

In 1880 the number of employees was 1,301,388.

In 1890 the number of employees was 2,251,134.

In 1880 the wages earned were $501,965,778.

In 1890 the wages earned were $1,221,170,454.

In 1880 the value of the product was $2,711,579,899.

In 1890 the value of the product was $4,860,286,837.

I believe that the protective system, which has now for something more than thirty years continuously prevailed in our legislation, has been a mighty instrument for the development of our national wealth and a most powerful agency in protecting the homes of our workingmen from the invasion of want. I have felt a most solicitous interest to preserve to our working people rates of wages that would not only give daily bread, but supply a comfortable margin for those home attractions and family comforts and enjoyments without which life is neither hopeful nor sweet.

. . . We must assume that the present tariff, constructed upon the lines of protection, is to be repealed and that there is to be substituted for it a tariff law constructed solely with reference to revenues, that no duty is to be higher because the increase will keep open an American mill or keep up the wages of an American workman, but that in every case such a rate of duty is to be imposed as will bring to the Treasury of the United States the largest returns of revenue. . . .

Our relations with Hawaii have been such as to attract an increased interest, and must continue to do so. I deem it of great importance that the projected submarine cable, a survey for which has been made, should be promoted. Both for naval and commercial uses we should have quick communication with Honolulu. . . .

🐘 🐘 🐘

Lawlessness is not less such, but more, where it usurps the functions of the peace officer and of the courts. The frequent lynching of colored people accused of crime is without the excuse, which has sometimes been urged by mobs for a failure to pursue the appointed methods for the punishment of crime, that the accused have an undue influence over courts and juries. Such acts are a reproach to the community where they occur, and so far as they can be made the subject of Federal jurisdiction the strongest repressive legislation is demanded. . . .

. . . There is no reason why the national influence, power, and prosperity should not observe the same rates of increase that have characterized the past thirty years. We carry the great impulse and increase of these years into the future. There is no reason why in many lines of production we should not surpass all other nations, as we have already done in some. There are no near frontiers to our possible development. Retrogression would be a crime. . . .

GROVER CLEVELAND

(1893–1897)

"Cuba

is again

gravely disturbed"

In 1893 *Grover Cleveland* moved back into the White House as casually as if he had not moved out four years before. After his defeat by Harrison in 1888, he had opined, "Why should I have any desire or purpose of returning to the Presidency? I made a creditable showing during my first term, and I might lose whatever character or reputation I have already gained by it. I do not feel I can take the risk involved in a second term."

But the second-term bug always bites deep, and in 1892 Cleveland changed his mind. He took the risk, and won, in spite of a million votes drawn off by the new Populist Party, rampant for free silver, greenbacks, and government ownership of almost everything. In his reelection campaign Cleveland made the tariff a living issue. He also demanded return to sound currency by restoration of the gold standard in defiance of the free-silver wing of his party. His first major proposal to Congress after election was that they repeal the Sherman Silver Purchase Act of 1890, passed by the preceding administration. Cleveland laid the blame for the economic disaster about to strike the nation on this act. By so doing he split his party and ushered in a magnificent spellbinder, William Jennings Bryan, who would thrice lead the Democratic party to defeat with the major issue of free and unlimited coinage of silver.

The year 1893 witnessed the opening of the Columbian Exposition,

313

better known as the Chicago World's Fair, to celebrate the four-hundredth anniversary of the discovery of America. The world was invited to visit this panorama of beauty and magnificence and gaze on what the nation had achieved since Columbus set foot on the New World. Hit of the Fair, and best remembered, was the Egyptian Village's hootchy-kootchy girls, whose sensuous wriggles and swaying hips became the Fair's "must" for the male segment of visitors.

Cleveland's second term was overshadowed by party conflict and national disaster. Hardly had he taken office when the nation was plunged into depression. It was a repeat of the 1873 debacle. Factories shut down, armies of breadwinners lost their jobs, hundreds of banks closed, scores of railroads quit running. Farmers faced ruin with grain prices scraping the bottom. Thanks to the Silver Purchase Act that ordered the Treasury to pass out gold to buy silver, the nation's gold reserves shrank so low that, in order to maintain the gold standard and replenish the Treasury, the government was compelled to call on a syndicate of banks to lend enough gold to relieve the strain and tide the nation over the crisis. For a while Tom Reed's "billion-dollar country" trembled on a precipice.

Depression brought wage cutting, strikes, and labor disorders. In Chicago, violence flared at the Pullman Company's plant, trains were plundered, and United States mails interrupted. Cleveland ordered Federal troops to the scene. When Illinois' governor protested against the use of the army to break the strike, Cleveland replied character-istically, "If it takes the entire Army and Navy of the United States to deliver a postcard in Chicago, that card will be delivered."

Cleveland's State-of-the-Union Messages reflect his four-square stand on all issues. In his first message he struck again at the recurring frauds in the Pension Bureau with the same vehemence shown by his vetoes during his first administration.

Significantly, he listed the vessels of the new navy ready for service and those nearing completion, among the latter the ill-fated battleship *Maine*. Virtually every ship he named served in the war just over the horizon.

Cleveland's last two messages spelled out war with Spain, which he apparently sought to avert as long as he was in the White House. War would land full-blown in the next administration's lap. His comments on the perplexities of the Cuban situation are timely. His words, "Cuba is again gravely disturbed," might well apply to what is happening today in the Pearl of the Antilles.

In his first message he called for tariff reduction, an issue on which he collided head-on with a powerful bloc of protectionist Democratic Senators whom he blasted in his famous "Party dishonor and perfidy" letter. The Wilson-Gorman tariff, which Cleveland wanted, was watered down considerably, but it was an improvement on the McKinley Tariff of 1890. Cleveland let it become a law without his signature.

In his 1895 message he gave a clear exposition of the Venezuela affair. England's bullying tactics in the Venezuela-British Guiana boundary dispute and her arbitrary extension of the boundary far beyond her rightful claims led Cleveland to invoke the Monroe Doctrine. For days war clouds hovered, but Cleveland stood firm and in the end arbitration prevailed.

GROVER CLEVELAND
FIRST STATE-OF-THE-UNION MESSAGE
WASHINGTON, *December 4, 1893*

To the Congress of the United States:

The recent repeal of the provision of law requiring the purchase of silver bullion by the Government as a feature of our monetary scheme has made an entire change in the complexion of our currency affairs. I do not doubt that the ultimate result of this action will be most salutary and far-reaching. . . .

The Superintendent of Immigration, through the Secretary of the Treasury, reports that during the last fiscal year there arrived at our ports 440,793 immigrants. Of these, 1,063 were not permitted to land under the limitations of the law and 577 were returned to the countries from whence they came by reason of their having become public charges. The total arrivals were 141,034 less than for the previous year.

🐀 🐀 🐀

The following vessels of the new Navy have been completed and are now ready for service: The double-turreted coast-defense monitor *Miantonomoh,* the double-turreted coast-defense monitor *Monterey, Chicago, Philadelphia, Newark, San Francisco, Charleston, Atlanta,* and *Boston,* the cruiser *Detroit,* the gunboats *York-*

town, Concord, Bennington, Machias, Castine, and *Petrel,* the dispatch vessel *Bancroft,* and the dynamite gunboat *Vesuvius.*

The following vessels are in process of construction: The battleships *Maine* and *Texas,* the cruisers *Montgomery* and *Marblehead,* and the coast-defense monitors *Terror, Puritan, Amphitrite,* and *Monadnock,* all of which will be completed within one year; the harbor-defense ram *Katahdin* and the protected cruisers *Columbia, Minneapolis, Olympia, Cincinnati,* and *Raleigh,* all of which will be completed prior to July 1, 1895; the first-class battleships *Iowa, Indiana, Massachusetts,* and *Oregon,* which will be completed February 1, 1896, and the armored cruiser *Brooklyn,* which will be completed by August 1 of that year. It is also expected that the three gunboats authorized by the last Congress will be completed in less than two years.

🐐　🐐　🐐

. . . The discovery having been made that many names had been put upon the pension roll by means of wholesale and gigantic frauds, the Commissioner suspended payments upon a number of pensions which seemed to be fraudulent or unauthorized pending a complete examination, giving notice to the pensioners, in order that they might have an opportunity to establish, if possible, the justice of their claims notwithstanding apparent invalidity.

I am unable to understand why frauds in the pension rolls should not be exposed and corrected with thoroughness and vigor. Every name fraudulently put upon these rolls is a wicked imposition upon the kindly sentiment in which pensions have their origin; every fraudulent pensioner has become a bad citizen; every false oath in support of a pension has made perjury more common, and false and undeserving pensioners rob the people not only of their money, but of the patriotic sentiment which the survivors of a war fought for the preservation of the Union ought to inspire. Thousands of neighborhoods have their well-known fraudulent pensioners, and recent developments by the Bureau establish appalling conspiracies to accomplish pension frauds. By no means the least wrong done is to brave and deserving pensioners, who certainly ought not to be condemned to such association.

🐐　🐐　🐐

Our Indians number about 248,000. Most of them are located on 161 reservations, containing 86,116,531 acres of land. About 110,000 of these Indians have to large degree adopted civilized customs. Lands in severalty have been allotted to many of them. Such allotments have been made to 10,000 individuals during the last fiscal year, embracing about 1,000,000 acres. The number of Indian Government schools opened during the year was 195, an increase of 12 over the preceding year. Of this total 170 were on reservations, of which 73 were boarding schools and 97 were day schools. Twenty boarding schools and 5 day schools supported by the Government were not located on reservations. The total number of Indian children enrolled during the year as attendants of all schools was 21,138, an increase of 1,231 over the enrollment for the previous year.

🐺 🐺 🐺

. . . The recent opening to settlement of the lands in the Cherokee Outlet, embracing an area of 6,500,000 acres, notwithstanding the utmost care in framing the regulations governing the selection of locations and notwithstanding the presence of United States troops, furnished an exhibition, though perhaps in a modified degree, of the mad scramble, the violence, and the fraudulent occupation which have accompanied previous openings of public land.

I concur with the Secretary [of the Interior] in the belief that these outrageous incidents can not be entirely prevented without a change in the laws on the subject, and I hope his recommendations in that direction will be favorably considered.

🐺 🐺 🐺

The course of civil-service reform in this country instructively and interestingly illustrated how strong a hold a movement gains upon our people which has underlying it a sentiment of justice and right and which at the same time promises better administration of their Government.

🐺 🐺 🐺

After a hard struggle tariff reform is directly before us. Nothing so important claims our attention and nothing so clearly presents itself as both an opportunity and a duty, an opportunity to deserve the gratitude of our fellow-citizens and a duty imposed upon us by our oft-repeated professions and by the emphatic mandate of the people. . . . Manifestly if we are to aid the people directly through tariff reform, one of its most obvious features should be a reduction in present tariff charges upon the necessaries of life. The benefits of such a reduction would be palpable and substantial, seen and felt by thousands who would be better fed and better clothed and better sheltered. These gifts should be the willing benefactions of a Government whose highest function is the promotion of the welfare of the people.

GROVER CLEVELAND
SECOND STATE-OF-THE-UNION MESSAGE
EXECUTIVE MANSION, *December 3, 1894*

To the Congress of the United States:

. . . Although the war between China and Japan endangers no policy of the United States, it deserves our gravest consideration by reason of its disturbance of our growing commercial interests in the two countries and the increased dangers which may result to our citizens domiciled or sojourning in the interior of China.

Acting under a stipulation in our treaty with Korea (the first [she has] concluded with a Western power), I felt constrained at the beginning of the controversy to tender our good offices to induce an amicable arrangement of the initial difficulty growing out of the Japanese demands for administrative reforms in Korea, but the unhappy precipitation of actual hostilities defeated this kindly purpose.

🐐   🐐   🐐

The boundary of British Guiana still remains in dispute between Great Britain and Venezuela. Believing that its early settlement on some just basis alike honorable to both parties is in the line of our established policy to remove from this hemisphere all causes of difference with powers beyond the sea, I shall renew the efforts heretofore made to bring about a restoration of diplomatic relations between the disputants and to induce a reference to arbitration. . . .

It is hardly necessary to recall the fact that in obedience to the commands of the Constitution and the laws, and for the purpose of protecting the property of the United States, aiding the process of Federal courts, and removing lawless obstructions to the performance by the Government of its legitimate functions, it became necessary in various localities during the year to employ a considerable portion of the regular troops. The duty was discharged promptly, courageously, and with marked discretion by the officers and men. . . .

🐴 🐴 🐴

The bare-faced and extensive pension frauds exposed under the direction of the courageous and generous veteran soldier now at the head of the Bureau [William H. Lochren, Commissioner of Pensions] leave no room for the claim that no purgation of our pension rolls was needed or that continued vigilance and prompt action are not necessary to the same end.

🐴 🐴 🐴

With the advent of a new tariff policy not only calculated to relieve the consumers of our land in the cost of their daily life, but to invite a better development of American thrift and create for us closer and more profitable commercial relations with the rest of the world, it follows as a logical and imperative necessity that we should at once remove the chief if not the only obstacle which has so long prevented our participation in the foreign carrying trade of the sea. . . .

GROVER CLEVELAND
THIRD STATE-OF-THE-UNION MESSAGE
EXECUTIVE MANSION, *December 2, 1895*

To the Congress of the United States:

The present assemblage of the legislative branch of our Government occurs at a time when the interests of our people and the needs of the country give especial prominence to the condition of our foreign relations and the exigencies of our national finances. . . .

🐎 🐎 🐎

It being apparent that the boundary dispute between Great Britain and the Republic of Venezuela concerning the limits of British Guiana was approaching an acute stage, a definite statement of the interest and policy of the United States as regards the controversy seemed to be required both on its own account and in view of its relations with the friendly powers directly concerned. . . . This Government is firmly opposed to a forcible increase by any European power of its territorial possessions on this continent; . . . the United States is bound to protest against the enlargement of the area of British Guiana in derogation of the rights and against the will of Venezuela; considering the disparity in strength of Great Britain and Venezuela the territorial dispute between them can be reasonably settled only by friendly and impartial arbitration. And that the resort to such arbitration should include the whole controversy.

🐎 🐎 🐎

Cuba is again gravely disturbed. An insurrection in some respects more active than the last preceding revolt, which continued from 1868 to 1878, now exists in a large part of the eastern interior of the island, menacing even some populations on the coast. . . .

Whatever may be the traditional sympathy of our countrymen as individuals with a people who seem to be struggling for larger autonomy and greater freedom, . . . yet the plain duty of their

Government is to observe in good faith the recognized obligations of international relationships.

🐐 🐐 🐐

The compulsory purchase and coinage of silver by the Government, unchecked and unregulated by business conditions and heedless of our currency needs, which for more than fifteen years diluted our circulating medium, undermined confidence abroad in our financial ability, and at last culminated in distress and panic at home, has been recently stopped by the repeal of the laws which forced this reckless scheme upon the country.

. . . [Because of] the unnatural infusion of silver into our currency and the increasing agitation for its free and unlimited coinage, which have created apprehension as to our disposition or ability to continue gold payments; the consequent hoarding of gold at home and the stoppage of investments of foreign capital . . . the gold reserve on the 1st day of February, 1894, was reduced to $65,438,377, having lost more than $31,000,000 during the preceding nine months, or since April, 1893. Its replenishment being necessary and no other manner of accomplishing it being possible, resort was had to the issue and sale of bonds provided for by the resumption act of 1875.

🐐 🐐 🐐

This depressed condition grew worse. . . . In February, 1895, the situation was exceedingly critical. With a reserve perilously low and a refusal of Congressional aid, everything indicated that the end of gold payments by the Government was imminent. . . .

In this emergency, and in view of its surrounding perplexities, it became entirely apparent to those upon whom the struggle for safety was devolved not only that our gold reserve must, for the third time in less than thirteen months, be restored by another issue and sale of bonds bearing a high rate of interest and badly suited to the purpose, but that a plan must be adopted for their disposition promising better results than those realized on previous sales. . . . An agreement was therefore made with a number of financiers and bankers whereby it was stipulated that bonds described in the resumption act of 1875, payable in coin thirty years after their date, bearing interest at the rate of 4 per cent per annum, and amounting to about $62,000,000, should be exchanged for gold, receivable by weight, amounting to a little more than $65,000,000.

. . . I have never had the slightest misgiving concerning the wisdom or propriety of this arrangement, and am quite willing to answer for my full share of responsibility for its promotion. I believe it averted a disaster the imminence of which was, fortunately, not at the time generally understood by our people.

🐐　🐐　🐐

It is neither unfair nor unjust to charge a large share of our present financial perplexities and dangers to the operation of the laws of 1878 and 1890 compelling the purchase of silver by the Government, which not only furnished a new Treasury obligation upon which its gold could be withdrawn, but so increased the fear of an overwhelming flood of silver and a forced descent to silver payments that even the repeal of these laws did not entirely cure the evils of their existence.

🐐　🐐　🐐

No government, no human contrivance or act of legislation, has ever been able to hold the two metals together in free coinage at a ratio appreciably different from that which is established in the markets of the world.

Those who believe that our independent free coinage of silver at an artificial ratio with gold of 16 to 1 would restore the parity between the metals, and consequently between the coins, oppose an unsupported and improbable theory to the general belief and practice of other nations. . . .

🐐　🐐　🐐

Those who advocate a blind and headlong plunge to free coinage in the name of bimetalism, and professing the belief, contrary to all experience, that we could thus establish a double standard and a concurrent circulation of both metals in our coinage, are certainly reckoning from a cloudy standpoint. . . .

In conclusion I especially entreat the people's representatives in the Congress, who are charged with the responsibility of inaugurating measures for the safety and prosperity of our common country, to promptly and effectively consider the ills of our critical financial plight. . . .

GROVER CLEVELAND
FOURTH STATE-OF-THE-UNION MESSAGE
EXECUTIVE MANSION, *December 7, 1896*

To the Congress of the United States:
. . . A political contest involving momentous consequences, fraught with feverish apprehension, and creating aggressiveness so intense as to approach bitterness and passion has been waged throughout our land and determined by the decree of free and independent suffrage without disturbance of our tranquillity or the least sign of weakness in our national structure.

🐂 🐂 🐂

The insurrection in Cuba still continues with all its perplexities. . . . If Spain still holds Havana and the seaports and all the considerable towns, the insurgents still roam at will over at least two-thirds of the inland country.

The spectacle of the utter ruin of an adjoining country, by nature one of the most fertile and charming on the globe, would engage the serious attention of the Government and people of the United States in any circumstances. . . . It lies so near to us as to be hardly separated from our territory. Our actual pecuniary interest in it is second only to that of the people and Government of Spain. . . .

These inevitable entanglements of the United States with the rebellion in Cuba, the large American property interests affected, and considerations of philanthropy and humanity in general have led to a vehement demand in various quarters for some sort of positive intervention on the part of the United States. . . . It is urged finally that, all other methods failing, the existing internecine strife in Cuba should be terminated by our intervention, even at the cost of a war between the United States and Spain—a war which its advocates confidently prophesy could neither be large in its proportions nor doubtful in its issue.

The correctness of this forecast need be neither affirmed nor denied. The United States has, nevertheless, a character to maintain as a nation, which plainly dictates that right and not might should be the rule of its conduct.

🐾 🐾 🐾

In my opinion . . . the abuses which have been allowed to creep into our pension system have done incalculable harm in demoralizing our people and undermining good citizenship. I have endeavored within my sphere of official duty to protect our pension roll and make it what it should be, a roll of honor, containing the names of those disabled in their country's service and worthy of their country's affectionate remembrance. . . .

🐾 🐾 🐾

The progress made in civil-service reform furnishes a cause for the utmost congratulation. It has survived the doubts of its friends as well as the rancor of its enemies and has gained a permanent place among the agencies destined to cleanse our politics and to improve, economize, and elevate the public service.

🐾 🐾 🐾

Another topic in which our people rightfully take a deep interest may be here briefly considered. I refer to the existence of trusts and other huge aggregations of capital the object of which is to secure the monopoly of some particular branch of trade, industry, or commerce and to stifle wholesome competition. When these are defended, it is usually on the ground that though they increase profits they also reduce prices, and thus may benefit the public. It must be remembered, however, that a reduction of prices to the people is not one of the real objects of these organizations. If it occurs in a particular case it is only because it accords with the purposes or interests of those managing the scheme.

Such occasional results fall far short of compensating the palpable evils charged to the account of trusts and monopolies. Their tendency is to crush out individual independence and to hinder or prevent the free use of human faculties and the full development of human character. . . .

Though Congress has attempted to deal with this matter by legislation, the laws passed for that purpose thus far have proved ineffective. If the insufficiencies of existing laws can be remedied by further legislation, it should be done. . . .

𝔂 𝔂 𝔂

In concluding this communication its last words shall be an appeal to the Congress for the most rigid economy in the expenditure of the money it holds in trust for the people. The way to perplexing extravagance is easy, but a return to frugality is difficult. . . .

WILLIAM McKINLEY

(1897–1901)

"Cuba is

a constant menace

to our peace"

In 1896 the mounting crescendo of *Cuba Libre!* resounded across the land. At the same time the American people were subjected to one of the most absurd political campaigns the nation has ever witnessed.

This was the battle-royal for the presidency between the Gold Republicans and the Silver Democrats. It is safe to say that a goodly segment of the people never understood what the politicians were talking about during this unbelievable contest. Legions of good folk believed that each silver dollar they owned would, magically, be transmuted into sixteen dollars if the eloquent Boy Orator of the Platte, William Jennings Bryan, bore the Democratic banner to victory. With his persuasive "Cross of Gold and Crown of Thorns" appeal to the twenty thousand conventionites at Chicago, he had captured the nomination and forced adoption of a free-silver plank as the main prop of the Democratic platform.

On an unprecedented whirlwind tour of the country Bryan poured out his silver-tongued oratory to more than five million Americans. People flocked to him, if only to hear his superb voice. It looked as if he would sweep the election.

In sharp contrast, the Republican nominee, *William McKinley*, former Ohio Governor, put on a conservative front-porch act that plunked for the gold standard, sound money, big protective tariff, and big business. By a process as old as cupidity, the election proved again that man preferred gold to silver. Bryan was defeated, but, like Henry Clay, he tried twice again before giving up.

When McKinley entered the White House, it was inevitable he would be a war President. War fever was rising. Congress had blood in its eye. Cuba's rebellion against Spain, now in its third year, was deluging the island with blood and destruction right at this nation's threshold. With the fervor of Crusaders setting out to redeem the Holy Sepulcher, politicians called for a holy war to rescue Cuba from the "Spanish barbarians."

Screaming headlines, souped-up pictures and cartoons hurtled the American people toward intervention in Cuba and war against Spain. The build-up for the ten-week war harked back a century. Oceans of political sobs and wrathful outpourings had risen from the Capitol, but Congress never had sufficient backbone to support any of the Presidents who proposed to settle the problem for good and all by purchase or force. Statesmen had eloquently pursued the now-apparent jack-o'-lantern of setting Cuba afloat on the "shining sea of freedom."

To protect American citizens and property in Cuba, President McKinley dispatched the new battleship *Maine* to Havana. She arrived on January 25, 1898. On the night of February 15 she was blown up at her anchorage with a loss of 260 officers and seamen. Thus was the die cast for war, and the nation had its slogan—"Remember the Maine!"

On April 11, 1898, McKinley sent his War Message to Congress. Capitol Hill replied on April 20 with a Joint Resolution that launched America into the shortest war in her history.

McKinley's War Message (somewhat briefed here) left nothing unsaid. But he did not want war. Apparently he wrote two messages, one accepting Spain's last-minute concessions that eased the situation somewhat. But he lacked the nerve to resist a war-whooping House of Representatives, the yellow press, and the jingo sentiment racing across the nation, so he sent up the War Message.

Cuba, the Philippines, and their aftermath dominate McKinley's State-of-the-Union Messages. In his first, however, he broke the secrecy clamped by the Senate on the annexation of the Republic of Hawaii, which McKinley characterized by his historic observation, "Annexation is not a change; it is a consummation."

His third message posed the still-disturbing question of what to do about Cuba and the Philippines. The Cuban question was supposedly resolved on March 2, 1901, by passage of the Platt Amendment that offered eight alterations to the new constitution the Cubans were drawing up under the supervision of U.S. military government. The hottest issue was Section VII that gave to the United States the Guantanamo Bay naval base (two bases, in fact; one was given up) that today moves madman Castro to dire threats against this foothold on Cuba. This provision drove the Democrats into hysterics against the Platt Amendment, but calmer minds prevailed. Cuba's alliance with Russia demonstrates the wisdom of this amendment and the unwisdom of ever having let Cuba go in the first place. McKinley was right as rain when he said this nation had "assumed a grave responsibility" in pledging future good government in Cuba.

In 1900, William McKinley was reelected with a catchy slogan of "Four More Years of the Full Dinner Pail." It proved unbeatable. This campaign saw a dynamic young fighter, Theodore Roosevelt, step into the political ring as candidate for Vice President.

McKinley's third message contains a tragic reference to the coming Pan-American Exposition at Buffalo, at which, a year later the President was to be assassinated by a "professed anarchist influenced by the teachings of professed anarchists."

WILLIAM McKINLEY
FIRST STATE-OF-THE-UNION MESSAGE
EXECUTIVE MANSION, *December 6, 1897*

To the Senate and House of Representatives:

The most important problem with which this Government is now called upon to deal pertaining to its foreign relations concerns its duty toward Spain and the Cuban insurrection. The story of Cuba for many years has been one of unrest, growing discontent, an effort toward a larger enjoyment of liberty and self-control, of organized resistance to the mother country, of depression after distress and warfare, and of ineffectual settlement to be followed by renewed revolt. . . .

The present insurrection broke out in February, 1895. . . . The revolt and the efforts to subdue it carried destruction to every quarter of the island, developing wide proportions and defying the efforts of Spain for its suppression. . . .

. . . There is no desire on the part of our people to profit by the misfortunes of Spain. We have only the desire to see the Cubans prosperous and contented, enjoying that measure of self-control which is the inalienable right of man, protected in their right to reap the benefit of the exhaustless treasures of their country.

The cruel policy of concentration was initiated February 16, 1896. The productive districts controlled by the Spanish armies were depopulated. The agricultural inhabitants were herded in and about the garrison towns, their lands laid waste and their dwellings destroyed. This policy the late cabinet of Spain justified as a necessary measure of war and as a means of cutting off supplies from the insurgents. It has utterly failed as a war measure. It was not civilized warfare. It was extermination.

Against this abuse of the rights of war I have felt constrained on repeated occasions to enter the firm and earnest protest of this Government. . . .

Of the untried measures there remain only: Recognition of the insurgents as belligerents; recognition of the independence of Cuba; neutral intervention to end the war by imposing a rational compromise between the contestants, and intervention in favor of one or the other party. I speak not of forcible annexation, for that can not be thought of. That, by our code of morality, would be criminal aggression.

By a special message dated the 16th day of June last, I laid before the Senate a treaty signed that day by the plenipotentiaries of the United States and of the Republic of Hawaii, having for its purpose the incorporation of the Hawaiian Islands as an integral part of the United States and under its sovereignty. The Senate having removed the injunction of secrecy, although the treaty is still pending before that body, the subject may be properly referred to in this Message because the necessary action of the Congress is required to determine by legislation many details of the eventual union should the fact of annexation be accomplished, as I believe it should be.

The present immediately effective force of the Navy consists of four battle ships of the first class, two of the second, and forty-eight other vessels, ranging from armored cruisers to torpedo boats. There are under construction five battle ships of the first class, sixteen torpedo boats, and one submarine boat. . . .

The Library building provided for by the act of Congress approved April 15, 1886, has been completed and opened to the public. It should be a matter of congratulation that through the foresight and munificence of Congress the nation possesses this noble treasurehouse of knowledge. . . .

WILLIAM McKINLEY
SPECIAL WAR MESSAGE
EXECUTIVE MANSION, *April 11, 1898*

To the Congress of the United States:
Obedient to that precept of the Constitution which commands the President to give from time to time to the Congress information of the state of the Union and to recommend to their consideration such measures as he shall judge necessary and expedient, it becomes my duty to now address your body with regard to the grave crisis that has arisen in the relations of the United States to Spain by reason of the warfare that for more than three years has raged in the neighboring island of Cuba.

I do so because of the intimate connection of the Cuban question with the state of our own Union and the grave relation the course which it is now incumbent upon the nation to adopt must needs bear to the traditional policy of our Government if it is to accord with the precepts laid down by the founders of the Republic and religiously observed by succeeding Administrations to the present day.

X X X

Since the present revolution began, in February, 1895, this country has seen the fertile domain at our threshold ravaged by fire and sword in the course of a struggle unequaled in the history of the island and rarely paralleled as to the numbers of the combatants and the bitterness of the contest by any revolution of modern times where a dependent people striving to be free have been opposed by the power of the sovereign state.

Our people have beheld a once prosperous community reduced to comparative want, its lucrative commerce virtually paralyzed, its exceptional productiveness diminished, its fields laid waste, its mills in ruins, and its people perishing by tens of thousands from hunger and destitution. . . .

Our trade has suffered, the capital invested by our citizens in Cuba has been largely lost, and the temper and forbearance of our people have been so sorely tried as to beget a perilous unrest among our own citizens. . . .

✗ ✗ ✗

The war in Cuba is of such a nature that, short of subjugation or extermination, a final military victory for either side seems impracticable. The alternative lies in the physical exhaustion of the one or the other party, or perhaps of both—a condition which in effect ended the ten years' war by the truce of Zanjon. The prospect of such a protraction and conclusion of the present strife is a contingency hardly to be contemplated with equanimity by the civilized world, and least of all by the United States, affected and injured as we are, deeply and intimately, by its very existence.

✗ ✗ ✗

There remain the alternative forms of intervention to end the war, either as an impartial neutral, by imposing a rational compromise between the contestants, or as the active ally of the one party or the other.

✗ ✗ ✗

The grounds for such intervention may be briefly summarized as follows:

First. In the cause of humanity and to put an end to the barbarities, bloodshed, starvation, and horrible miseries now existing there, and which the parties to the conflict are either unable or unwilling to stop or mitigate. . . .

Second. We owe it to our citizens in Cuba to afford them that protection and indemnity for life and property which no government there can or will afford, and to that end to terminate the conditions that deprive them of legal protection.

Third. The right to intervene may be justified by the very serious injury to the commerce, trade, and business of our people and by the wanton destruction of property and devastation of the island.

Fourth, and which is of the utmost importance. The present condition of affairs in Cuba is a constant menace to our peace and entails upon this Government an enormous expense. . . .

These elements of danger and disorder already pointed out have been strikingly illustrated by a tragic event which has deeply and justly moved the American people. I have already transmitted to Congress the report of the naval court of inquiry on the destruction of the battle ship *Maine* in the harbor of Havana during the night of the 15th of February. The destruction of that noble vessel has filled the national heart with inexpressible horror. Two hundred and fifty-eight brave sailors and marines and two officers of our Navy, reposing in the fancied security of a friendly harbor, have been hurled to death, grief and want brought to their homes and sorrow to the nation.

The naval court of inquiry, which, it is needless to say, commands the unqualified confidence of the Government, was unanimous in its conclusion that the destruction of the *Maine* was caused by an exterior explosion—that of a submarine mine. It did not assume to place the responsibility. That remains to be fixed.

✠   ✠   ✠

The long trial has proved that the object for which Spain has waged the war can not be attained. The fire of insurrection may flame or may smolder with varying seasons, but it has not been and it is plain that it can not be extinguished by present methods. The only hope of relief and repose from a condition which can no longer be endured is the enforced pacification of Cuba. In the name of humanity, in the name of civilization, in behalf of endangered American interests which give us the right and the duty to speak and to act, the war in Cuba must stop.

In view of these facts and of these considerations I ask the Congress to authorize and empower the President to take measures to secure a full and final termination of hostilities between the Government of Spain and the people of Cuba, and to secure in the island the establishment of a stable government, capable of maintaining order and observing its international obligations, insuring peace and tranquillity and the security of its citizens as well as our own, and to use the military and naval forces of the United States as may be necessary for these purposes.

And in the interest of humanity and to aid in preserving the lives of the starving people of the island I recommend that the distribution of food and supplies be continued and that an appropriation be made out of the public Treasury to supplement the charity of our citizens.

The issue is now with the Congress. It is a solemn responsibility. I have exhausted every effort to relieve the intolerable condition of affairs which is at our doors. Prepared to execute every obligation imposed upon me by the Constitution and the law, I await your action.

WILLIAM McKINLEY
SECOND STATE-OF-THE-UNION MESSAGE
EXECUTIVE MANSION, *December 5, 1898*

To the Senate and House of Representatives:
    Notwithstanding the added burdens rendered necessary by the war, our people rejoice in a very satisfactory and steadily increasing degree of prosperity, evidenced by the largest volume of business ever recorded. . . .

                    ✂ ✂ ✂

The effect of this remarkable victory [Manila Bay] upon the spirit of our people and upon the fortunes of the war was instant. A prestige of invincibility thereby attached to our arms which continued throughout the struggle. Reenforcements were hurried to Manila under the command of Major-General Merritt and firmly established within sight of the capital, which lay helpless before our guns.

. . . The nation's profoundest gratitude is due to all of these brave men who by their skill and devotion in a few short hours crushed the sea power of Spain [at Santiago Bay] and wrought a triumph whose decisiveness and far-reaching consequences can scarcely be measured. . . .

On August 7, forty-six days from the date of the landing of General Shafter's army in Cuba and twenty-one days from the surrender of Santiago, the United States troops commenced embarkation for home, and our entire force was returned to the United States as early as August 24. They were absent from the United States only two months.

X   X   X

On the 26th of July, M. Cambon presented a communication signed by the Duke of Almodóvar, the Spanish minister of state, inviting the United States to state the terms upon which it would be willing to make peace. . . . On the afternoon of August 12, M. Cambon, as the plenipotentiary of Spain, and the Secretary of State, as the plenipotentiary of the United States, signed a protocol providing—

ARTICLE   I. Spain will relinquish all claim of sovereignty over and title to Cuba.

ARTICLE   II. Spain will cede to the United States the island of Puerto Rico and other islands now under Spanish sovereignty in the West Indies, and also an island in the Ladrones to be selected by the United States.

ARTICLE III. The United States will occupy and hold the city, bay, and harbor of Manila pending the conclusion of a treaty of peace which shall determine the control, disposition, and government of the Philippines.

X   X   X

As soon as we are in possession of Cuba and have pacified the island it will be necessary to give aid and direction to its people to form a government for themselves. . . .

Spanish rule must be replaced by a just, benevolent, and humane government, created by the people of Cuba, capable of performing all international obligations. . . . Neither revenge nor passion should have a place in the new government. Until there is complete tranquillity in the island and a stable government inaugurated military occupation will be continued.

WILLIAM McKINLEY
THIRD STATE-OF-THE-UNION MESSAGE
EXECUTIVE MANSION, *December 5, 1899*

To the Senate and House of Representatives:

I urgently recommend that to support the existing gold standard, and to maintain "the parity in value of the coins of the two metals (gold and silver) and the equal power of every dollar at all times in the market and in the payment of debts," the Secretary of the Treasury be given additional power and charged with the duty to sell United States bonds and to employ such other effective means as may be necessary to these ends. . . . The financial transactions of the Government are conducted upon a gold basis. We receive gold when we sell United States bonds and use gold for their payment. We are maintaining the parity of all the money issued or coined by authority of the Government. We are doing these things with the means at hand. Happily at the present time we are not compelled to resort to loans to supply gold.

Combinations of capital organized into trusts to control the conditions of trade among our citizens, to stifle competition, limit production, and determine the prices of products used and consumed by the people, are justly provoking public discussion, and should early claim the attention of the Congress.

This nation has assumed before the world a grave responsibility for the future good government of Cuba. . . . Whatever be the outcome, we must see to it that free Cuba be a reality, not a name, a perfect entity, not a hasty experiment bearing within itself the elements of failure. . . .

The act to encourage the holding of the Pan-American Exposition on the Niagara frontier, within the county of Erie or Niagara, in the State of New York, in the year 1901, was approved on March 3, 1899. This exposition, which will be held in the city of

Buffalo, in the near vicinity of the great Niagara cataract, and within a day's journey of which reside 40,000,000 of our people, will be confined entirely to the Western Hemisphere.

🐘 🐘 🐘

On the 10th of December, 1898, the treaty of peace between the United States and Spain was signed. It provided, among other things, that Spain should cede to the United States the archipelago known as the Philippine Islands, that the United States should pay to Spain the sum of twenty millions of dollars, and that the civil rights and political status of the native inhabitants of the territories thus ceded to the United States should be determined by the Congress. . . .

🐘 🐘 🐘

On the 21st of January, I announced my intention of dispatching to Manila a commission composed of three gentlemen of the highest character and distinction, thoroughly acquainted with the Orient, who, in association with Admiral Dewey and Major-General Otis, were instructed "to facilitate the most humane and effective extension of authority throughout the islands. . . ."

But before their arrival at Manila the sinister ambition of a few leaders of the Filipinos had created a situation full of embarrassment for us and most grievous in its consequences to themselves. This was the unhappy condition of affairs which confronted our Commissioners on their arrival in Manila. . . .

The course thus clearly indicated has been unflinchingly pursued. The rebellion must be put down. Civil government cannot be thoroughly established until order is restored. . . .

The future government of the Philippines rests with the Congress of the United States. . . . The islands lie under the shelter of our flag. . . . If we desert them we leave them at once to anarchy and finally to barbarism. . . . Until Congress shall have made known the formal expression of its will I shall use the authority vested in me by the Constitution and the statutes to uphold the sovereignty of the United States in those distant islands as in all other places where our flag rightfully floats. . . . Our flag has never waved over any community but in blessing. I believe the

Filipinos will soon recognize the fact that it has not lost its gift of benediction in its world-wide journey to their shores.

🐘 🐘 🐘

A necessity for immediate legislative relief exists in the Territory of Alaska. . . . The increase in population by immigration during the past few years, consequent upon the discovery of gold, has produced such a condition as calls for more ample facilities for local self-government and more numerous conveniences of civil and judicial administration. . . .

🐘 🐘 🐘

The 14th of December will be the One Hundredth Anniversary of the death of Washington. For a hundred years the Republic has had the priceless advantage of the lofty standard of character and conduct which he bequeathed to the American people. It is an inheritance which time, instead of wasting, continually increases and enriches. We may justly hope that in the years to come the benignant influence of the Father of his Country may be even more potent for good than in the century which is drawing to a close. . . .

Presented to this Congress are great opportunities. With them come great responsibilities. The power confided to us increases the weight of our obligations to the people, and we must be profoundly sensible of them as we contemplate the new and grave problems which confront us. Aiming only at the public good, we cannot err. . . .

WILLIAM McKINLEY
FOURTH STATE-OF-THE-UNION MESSAGE
EXECUTIVE MANSION, *December 3, 1900*

To the Senate and House of Representatives:

At the outgoing of the old and the incoming of the new century you begin the last session of the Fifty-sixth Congress with evidences on every hand of individual and national prosperity and with proof of the growing strength and increasing power for good of Republican institutions. . . .

When the Sixth Congress assembled in November, 1800, the
population of the United States was 5,308,483. It is now 76,-
304,799. Then we had sixteen States. Now we have forty-five.
Then our territory consisted of 909,050 square miles. It is now
3,846,595 square miles. Education, religion, and morality have
kept pace with our advancement. . . .

In our foreign intercourse the dominant question has been the
treatment of the Chinese problem. Apart from this our relations
with the powers have been happy.

The recent troubles in China spring from the antiforeign agitation which for the past three years has gained strength in the
northern provinces. Their origin lies deep in the character of the
Chinese races and in the traditions of their Government. . . .

The sect, commonly styled the Boxers, developed greatly in the
provinces north of the Yang-Tse, and with the collusion of many
notable officials, including some in the immediate councils of the
Throne itself, became alarmingly aggressive. No foreigner's life,
outside of the protected treaty ports, was safe. No foreign interest
was secure from spoliation. The Chinese Government proved, however, unable to check the rising strength of the Boxers and appeared to be a prey to internal dissensions. . . .

. . . At this critical juncture, in the early spring of this year, a
proposal was made by the other powers that a combined fleet
should be assembled in Chinese waters as a moral demonstration,
under cover of which to exact of the Chinese Government respect
for foreign treaty rights and the suppression of the Boxers.

The United States, while not participating in the joint demonstration, promptly sent from the Philippines all ships that could
be spared for service on the Chinese coast. A small force of
marines was landed at Taku and sent to Peking for the protection
of the American legation. Other powers took similar action, until
some four hundred men were assembled in the capital as legation
guards.

Still the peril increased. The legations reported the development of the seditious movement in Peking and the need of increased provision for defense against it. . . .

Severance of communication with Peking followed, and a combined force of additional guards, which was advancing to Peking by the Pei-Ho, was checked at Langfang. The isolation of the legations was complete. . . .

By June 19 the legations were cut off.

This news stimulated the preparations for a joint relief expedition. . . . The United States contingent amounted to some 5,000 men, under the able command first of the lamented Colonel Liscum and afterwards of General Chaffee. . . .

Toward the end of July the movement began. A severe conflict followed at Tientsin, in which Colonel Liscum was killed. The city was stormed and partly destroyed. Its capture afforded the base of operations from which to make the final advance, which began in the first days of August, the expedition being made up of Japanese, Russian, British, and American troops at the outset. . . .

On August 14, the capital was reached. After a brief conflict beneath the walls the relief column entered and the legations were saved. . . .

The policy of the United States through all this trying period was clearly announced and scrupulously carried out. . . . Our declared aims involved no war against the Chinese nation. We adhered to the legitimate office of rescuing the imperiled legation, obtaining redress for wrongs already suffered, securing wherever possible the safety of American life and property in China, and preventing a spread of the disorders or their recurrence.

🐘 🐘 🐘

In my last annual message I dwelt at some length upon the condition of affairs in the Philippines. . . .

I have on another occasion called the Filipinos "the wards of the nation." Our obligation as guardian was not lightly assumed; it must not be otherwise than honestly fulfilled, aiming first of all to benefit those who have come under our fostering care. It is our duty so to treat them that our flag . . . shall be a revered symbol of liberty, enlightenment, and progress in every avenue of development.

We now have in Cuba between 5000 and 6000 troops. For the present our troops in that island cannot be withdrawn or materially diminished. . . .

We will be required to keep a considerable force in the Philippine Islands for some time to come. From the best information obtainable we will need there for the immediate future from 45,000 to 60,000 men. The number may be reduced as the insurgents come to acknowledge the authority of the United States of which there are assuring indications.

🐘 🐘 🐘

The transfer of the Government to this city is a fact of great historical interest. Among the people there is a feeling of genuine pride in the Capital of the Republic. It is a matter of interest in this connection that in 1800 the population of the District of Columbia was 14,093; to-day it is 278,718. The population of the city of Washington was then 3,210; to-day it is 218,196.

🐘 🐘 🐘

. . . In this era of great business activity and opportunity, caution is not untimely. It will not abate, but strengthen, confidence. It will not retard, but promote, legitimate industrial and commercial expansion. Our growing power brings with it temptations and perils requiring constant vigilance to avoid. . . . Let us keep always in mind that the foundation of our Government is liberty; its superstructure peace.

THEODORE ROOSEVELT
(1901–1909)

*"Whatever affects Cuba
for good or for ill
affects us also"*

Vice President *Theodore Roosevelt* was projected into the presidency by the assassin's bullet that brought death to President McKinley at Buffalo, New York, September 14, 1901. Aged forty-three, Roosevelt was the youngest Chief Executive up to that time.

Colorful and ebullient, Theodore Roosevelt soon qualified as a new-look, extrovert President. Bold, fearless, outspoken, often indiscreet, he put himself in closer touch with the American people than any other Chief Magistrate, not excepting even Abraham Lincoln.

Shortly after taking office he said: "I enjoy being President. I like to do the work and have my hand on the lever." His apt size-up of a President's day-by-day existence—"You don't live in the White House; you are only Exhibit A to the country"—has never been bettered.

Advocate of the strenuous life—"I preach to you, my countrymen, that your country calls not for the life of ease, but for the life of strenuous endeavor"—he practiced what he preached: as cowboy, big-game hunter, horseman, globetrotter, explorer, tennis player, wrestler, boxer, mountain climber, all-round athlete, and fighting Rough Rider in the Spanish-American War.

He began life as a puny boy whose ambition was to rise above his physical handicap and attain body fitness. From Harvard he went to the Dakotas, where he rounded up longhorns and led the hard, outdoor life of a cowboy. He came back East brimming with energy and

341

plunged into New York politics with such vigor that he rocketed from civil-service reformer to crime-busting police commissioner of New York City to Governor of the state of New York. In 1896 McKinley picked him for Assistant Secretary of the Navy. So disgusted was he with McKinley's pussyfooting in making war on Spain that he blurted, "McKinley has no more backbone than a chocolate éclair." In 1898, he organized and led a regiment of volunteer cavalry, the Rough Riders, to Cuba and on to glory at San Juan Hill. In 1900, the Republicans brought him forward as running mate for McKinley's bid for a second term.

Theodore Roosevelt had a knack of popularizing his ideas by catchwords and phrases that caught on with the public. His administration was flecked with verbal barbs—"Malefactors of great wealth, Muckrakers, Square Deal"—that he applied to those he felt deserved them. People went "Wild, simply wild," over Teddy with his famous toothy smile and effervescent "Bully!" and "Dee-lighted!" Up to his time Presidents had shunned the limelight. He changed all that, and reveled in having his picture taken. News photographers never had a better or more willing political subject.

Cartoonists had a field day with his "big stick," which became the emblem of his political philosophy. His big-stick philosophy dated back to 1900 when he said: "I have always been fond of the West African proverb—'Speak softly and carry a big stick; you will go far.'" He brandished his big stick often. For example, in 1906 he sent the American war fleet around the world to show off the prowess of the navy—one of America's "big sticks." With another "big stick" he fought corruption and injustice, broke up monopolies, prosecuted oversized trusts and pursued "malefactors of great wealth."

Theodore Roosevelt's administrations saw much progress: man's conquest of air by the Wright Brothers in 1903; words flying through space without wires; great shovels digging the Panama Canal; automobiles crowding the horse off the nation's roads and streets; countless new inventions and appliances developed for the comfort of man.

In 1904, he was reelected over an innocuous Democratic candidate, Alton B. Parker, who raised the cry of "Executive usurpation" against the aggressive Roosevelt, but to no avail. For mediating peace between Russia and Japan in 1905, he was awarded the Nobel Prize for Peace, the first American to win this coveted award. In 1912, after lion-shooting in Africa and exploring the River of Doubt in Brazil, he came home, like Ulysses Grant, hankering for a third term. Finding Republican party leaders nonreceptive, he split the party by organizing his own Bull Moose (Progressive Party) that drew off enough votes in the three-way 1912 election to throw it to Woodrow Wilson.

Theodore Roosevelt's State-of-the-Union Messages contain lessons in good government and ideas for bettering the condition of his adored America. They are among the longest of the State-of-the-Union procession. He offered no finespun theories or philosophies. Some of his suggestions that proved too radical for the public palate then will be found in today's pattern of American government.

His first message created a sensation by launching his eight-year unrelenting attack on trusts, corporations, and "accumulations of great wealth." He announced his intention of prosecuting "bad" trusts and curbing "bad" business by giving sharper teeth to the Sherman Antitrust Act already on the books. In doing so he broke with Republican boss and president-maker Senator Marcus Hanna of Ohio and other trust-builders.

In the same message he leveled his big stick at the leading powers of Europe by proclaiming that he would enforce the Monroe Doctrine with the biggest navy he could build. In his message of December, 1904, he enunciated what was called the Roosevelt Corollary: that "chronic wrongdoing" by Latin-American nations might ultimately require the United States, in adhering to the Monroe Doctrine, "to exercise international police power."

First President to attack deforestation in America, his first message rang with urgings to Congress to stop wasting the nation's forests and natural resources. His words were prophetic of the Reclamation Act of 1902 that gave the President authority to create national parks and forests from the nation's domain and to undertake big-scale conservation by irrigation, dams, and reservoirs. He preached the gospel of conservation so clearly that the masses understood and backed it.

He recommended creation of a Department of Commerce and Industry. Two months after this message (December, 1901), Congress enacted into law the formation of the Department of Commerce and Labor with Cabinet status, the ninth such department.

Cuba, where Roosevelt and his Rough Riders had performed on San Juan Hill, assumed a prominent place in three of Roosevelt's State-of-the-Union Messages. He stated clearly the relationship between that troubled island and the United States.

His third message spelled out his role in the acquisition of the Panama Canal Zone. It was here he gave his celebrated summary of the "revolutions, rebellions, insurrections, riots and other outbreaks" that had occurred on the isthmus. Said he, "They number fifty-three for the fifty-seven years" since the United States made its first treaty with New Granada (later Colombia).

THEODORE ROOSEVELT
FIRST STATE-OF-THE-UNION MESSAGE
WHITE HOUSE, *December 3, 1901*

To the Senate and House of Representatives:

The Congress assembles this year under the shadow of a great calamity. On the sixth of September, President McKinley was shot by an anarchist while attending the Pan-American Exposition at Buffalo, and died in that city on the fourteenth of that month.

Of the last seven elected Presidents, he is the third who has been murdered, and the bare recital of this fact is sufficient to justify grave alarm among all loyal American citizens. . . . The blow was aimed not at this President, but at all Presidents. . . .

🐘 🐘 🐘

The growth of cities has gone on beyond comparison faster than the growth of the country, and the upbuilding of the great industrial centers has meant a startling increase, not merely in the aggregate of wealth, but in the number of very large individual, and especially of very large corporate, fortunes. . . .

The process has aroused much antagonism, a great part of which is wholly without warrant. It is not true that as the rich have grown richer the poor have grown poorer. On the contrary, never before has the average man, the wage-worker, the farmer, the small trader, been so well off as in this country and at the present time. There have been abuses connected with the accumulation of wealth; yet it remains true that a fortune accumulated in legitimate business can be accumulated by the person specially benefited only on condition of conferring immense incidental benefits upon others. . . .

There is a widespread conviction in the minds of the American people that the great corporations known as trusts are in certain of their features and tendencies hurtful to the general welfare. . . .

The first essential in determining how to deal with the great industrial combinations is knowledge of the facts—publicity. In the interest of the public, the Government should have the right to inspect and examine the workings of the great corporations engaged in interstate business. . . . The first requisite is knowledge, full and complete—knowledge which may be made public to the world.

There should be created a Cabinet officer, to be known as Secretary of Commerce and Industries, as provided in the bill introduced at the last session of the Congress. It should be his province to deal with commerce in its broadest sense, including among many other things whatever concerns labor and all matters affecting the great business corporations and our merchant marine.

The most vital problem with which this country, and for that matter the whole civilized world, has to deal, is the problem which has for one side the betterment of social conditions, moral and physical, in large cities, and for another side the effort to deal with that tangle of far-reaching questions which we group together when we speak of "labor." The chief factor in the success of each man—wage-worker, farmer, and capitalist alike—must ever be the sum total of his own individual qualities and abilities. Second only to this comes the power of acting in combination or association with others. . . .

In 1887 a measure was enacted for the regulation of interstate railways, commonly known as the Interstate Commerce Act. The cardinal provisions of that act were that railway rates should be just and reasonable and that all shippers, localities, and commodities should be accorded equal treatment. . . .

The act should be amended. The railway is a public servant. Its rates should be just to and open to all shippers alike. The Government should see to it that within its jurisdiction this is so and should provide a speedy, inexpensive, and effective remedy to that end. At the same time it must not be forgotten that our railways are the arteries through which the commercial lifeblood of this Nation flows. . . .

🐘   🐘   🐘

The preservation of our forests is an imperative business necessity. We have come to see clearly that whatever destroys the forest, except to make way for agriculture, threatens our well-being. . . .

The wise administration of the forest reserves will be not less helpful to the interests which depend on water than to those which depend on wood and grass. The water supply itself depends upon the forest.

🐘   🐘   🐘

In Hawaii our aim must be to develop the Territory on the traditional American lines. We do not wish a region of large estates tilled by cheap labor; we wish a healthy American community of men who themselves till the farms they own. All our legislation for the islands should be shaped with this end in view. . . .

In Cuba such progress has been made toward putting the independent government of the island upon a firm footing that before the present session of the Congress closes this will be an accomplished fact. Cuba will then start as her own mistress; and to the beautiful Queen of the Antilles, as she unfolds this new page of her destiny, we extend our heartiest greetings and good wishes. . . .

In the Philippines our problem is larger. They are very rich tropical islands, inhabited by many varying tribes, representing widely different stages of progress toward civilization. Our earnest effort is to help these people upward along the stony and difficult path that leads to self-government. . . .

No single great material work which remains to be undertaken on this continent is of such consequence to the American people as the building of a canal across the Isthmus connecting North and South America. Its importance to the Nation is by no means limited merely to its material effects upon our business prosperity; and yet with view to these effects alone it would be to the last degree important for us immediately to begin it. . . .

🐘   🐘   🐘

The Monroe Doctrine should be the cardinal feature of the foreign policy of all the nations of the two Americas, as it is of the United States. . . . The Monroe Doctrine is a declaration that there must be no territorial aggrandizement by any non-American power at the expense of any American power on American soil. It is in no wise intended as hostile to any nation in the Old World. Still less is it intended to give cover to any aggression by one New World power at the expense of any other. . . .

🐘   🐘   🐘

This doctrine has nothing to do with the commercial relations of any American power, save that it in truth allows each of them to form such as it desires. In other words, it is really a guaranty of the commercial independence of the Americans. We do not ask under this doctrine for any exclusive commercial dealings with any other American state. We do not guarantee any state against punishment if it misconducts itself, provided that punishment does not take the form of the acquisition of territory by any non-American power.

Our people intend to abide by the Monroe Doctrine and to insist upon it as the one sure means of securing the peace of the Western Hemisphere. The Navy offers us the only means of making our insistence upon the Monroe Doctrine anything but a subject of derision to whatever nation chooses to disregard it. We desire the peace which comes as of right to the just man armed; not the peace granted on terms of ignominy to the craven and the weakling.

Our attitude in Cuba is a sufficient guaranty of our own good faith. We have not the slightest desire to secure any territory at the expense of any of our neighbors. . . .

🐘   🐘   🐘

Our present Navy was begun in 1882. At that period our Navy consisted of a collection of antiquated wooden ships, already almost as out of place against modern war vessels as the galleys of

Alcibiades and Hamilcar—certainly as the ships of Tromp and Blake. Nor at that time did we have men fit to handle a modern man-of-war. Under the wise legislation of the Congress and the successful administration of a succession of patriotic Secretaries of the Navy, belonging to both political parties, the work of up-building the Navy went on. . . . The result was seen in the short war with Spain, which was decided with such rapidity because of the infinitely greater preparedness of our Navy than of the Spanish Navy.

🐘 🐘 🐘

Perhaps the most characteristic educational movement of the past fifty years is that which has created the modern public library and developed it into broad and active service. There are now over five thousand public libraries in the United States. . . .

The Library of Congress is the one national library of the United States. Already the largest single collection of books on the Western Hemisphere . . . this library has a unique opportunity to render to the libraries of this country—to American scholarship—service of the highest importance. . . .

THEODORE ROOSEVELT
SECOND STATE-OF-THE-UNION MESSAGE
WHITE HOUSE, *December 2, 1902*

To the Senate and House of Representatives:

We still continue in a period of unbounded prosperity. . . . Our people, the sons of the men of the Civil War, the sons of the men who had iron in their blood, rejoice in the present and face the future high of heart and resolute of will. Ours is not the creed of the weakling and the coward; ours is the gospel of hope and of triumphant endeavor. . . .

In my Message to the present Congress at its first session I discussed the question of the regulation of those big corporations commonly doing an interstate business, often with some tendency to monopoly, which are popularly known as trusts.

No more important subject can come before the Congress than

this of the regulation of interstate business. The power of the Congress to regulate interstate commerce is an absolute and unqualified grant, and without limitations other than those prescribed by the Constitution. . . .

How to secure fair treatment alike for labor and for capital, how to hold in check the unscrupulous man, whether employer or employee, without weakening individual initiative, without hampering and cramping the industrial development of the country, is a problem fraught with great difficulties. . . . Organized capital and organized labor alike should remember that in the long run the interest of each must be brought into harmony with the interest of the general public. . . .

On May 20 last the United States kept its promise to the island by formally vacating Cuban soil and turning Cuba over to those whom her own people had chosen as the first officials of the new Republic. Cuba lies at our doors, and whatever affects her for good or for ill affects us also. So much have our people felt this that in the Platt Amendment we definitely took the ground that Cuba must hereafter have closer political relations with us than with any other power. Thus in a sense Cuba has become a part of our international political system. . . .

The Congress has wisely provided that we shall build at once an isthmian canal, if possible at Panama. . . . Negotiations are now pending with Colombia to secure her assent to our building the canal. This canal will be one of the greatest engineering feats of the twentieth century; a greater engineering feat than has yet been accomplished during the history of mankind. . . .

I especially urge upon the Congress the need of wise legislation for Alaska. It is not to our credit as a nation that Alaska, which has been ours for thirty-five years, should still have as poor a system of laws as is the case. No country has a more valuable possession—in mineral wealth, in fisheries, furs, forests, and also in land available for certain kinds of farming and stock-growing. . . .

Through a wise provision of the Congress at its last session the

White House, which had become disfigured by incongruous additions and changes, has now been restored to what it was planned to be by Washington. In making the restorations the utmost care has been exercised to come as near as possible to the early plans and to supplement these plans by a careful study of such buildings as that of the University of Virginia, which was built by Jefferson. The White House is the property of the Nation, and so far as is compatible with living therein it should be kept as it originally was, for the same reasons that we keep Mount Vernon as it originally was. The stately simplicity of its architecture is an expression of the character of the period in which it was built, and is in accord with the purposes it was designed to serve. It is a good thing to preserve such buildings as historic monuments which keep alive our sense of continuity with the Nation's past.

THEODORE ROOSEVELT
THIRD STATE-OF-THE-UNION MESSAGE
WHITE HOUSE, *December 7, 1903*

To the Senate and House of Representatives:

    With a nation as with a man the most important things are those of the household, and therefore the country is especially to be congratulated on what has been accomplished in the direction of providing for the exercise of supervision over the great corporations and combinations of corporations engaged in interstate commerce. The Congress has created the Department of Commerce and Labor, including the Bureau of Corporations, with for the first time authority to secure proper publicity of such proceedings of these great corporations as the public has the right to know. . . .

    By the act of June 28, 1902, the Congress authorized the President to enter into treaty with Colombia for the building of the canal across the Isthmus of Panama. . . . I am enabled to lay before the Senate a treaty providing for the building of the canal across the Isthmus of Panama. . . .

In the year 1846 this Government entered into a treaty with New Granada, the predecessor upon the Isthmus of the Republic of Colombia and of the present Republic of Panama, by which treaty it was provided that the Government and citizens of the United States should always have free and open right of way or transit across the Isthmus of Panama. . . . A new Republic, that of Panama, which was at one time a sovereign state . . . has now succeeded to the rights which first one and then the other formerly exercised over the Isthmus. . . .

Immediately after the adjournment of the Congress a revolution broke out in Panama. The people of Panama had long been discontented with the Republic of Colombia, and they had been kept quiet only by the prospect of the conclusion of the treaty, which was to them a matter of vital concern. When it became evident that the treaty was hopelessly lost, the people of Panama rose literally as one man. Not a shot was fired by a single man on the Isthmus in the interest of the Colombian Government. Not a life was lost in the accomplishment of the revolution. The Colombian troops stationed on the Isthmus, who had long been unpaid, made common cause with the people of Panama, and with astonishing unanimity the new Republic was started. The duty of the United States in the premises was clear. . . . The United States gave notice that it would permit the landing of no expeditionary force, the arrival of which would mean chaos and destruction along the line of the railroad and of the proposed canal, and an interruption of transit as an inevitable consequence. . . .

When these events happened, fifty-seven years had elapsed since the United States had entered into its treaty with New Granada. During that time the Governments of New Granada and of its successor, Colombia, have been in a constant state of flux. [Here President Roosevelt provided a "partial list of the disturbances on the Isthmus of Panama during the period in question as reported to us by our consuls."]

The above is only a partial list of the revolutions, rebellions, insurrections, riots, and other outbreaks that have occurred during the period in question; yet they number 53 for the 57 years.

Under such circumstances the Government of the United States would have been guilty of folly and weakness, amounting in their sum to a crime against the Nation, had it acted otherwise than it did when the revolution of November 3 last took place in Panama. . . . The possession of a territory fraught with such peculiar capacities as the Isthmus in question carries with it obligations to mankind. The course of events has shown that this canal can not be built by private enterprise, or by any other nation than our own; therefore it must be built by the United States.

. . . The new Republic of Panama immediately offered to negotiate a treaty with us. This treaty I herewith submit. . . . By the provisions of the treaty the United States guarantees and will maintain the independence of the Republic of Panama. There is granted to the United States in perpetuity the use, occupation, and control of a strip ten miles wide and extending three nautical miles into the sea at either terminal, with all lands lying outside of the zone necessary for the construction of the canal or for its auxiliary works. and with the islands in the Bay of Panama. . . .

THEODORE ROOSEVELT
FOURTH STATE-OF-THE-UNION MESSAGE
WHITE HOUSE, *December 6, 1904*

To the Senate and House of Representatives:

In the vast and complicated mechanism of our modern civilized life the dominant note is the note of industrialism; and the relations of capital and labor, and especially of organized capital and organized labor, to each other and to the public at large come second in importance only to the intimate questions of family life. . . .

. . . There are in this country some labor unions which have habitually, and other labor unions which have often, been among the most effective agents in working for good citizenship and for uplifting the condition of those whose welfare should be closest to our hearts. But when any labor union seeks improper ends, or seeks to achieve proper ends by improper means, all good citizens and more especially all honorable public servants must oppose the wrongdoing as resolutely as they would oppose the wrongdoing of any great corporation. Wage-workers have an entire right to organize and by all peaceful and honorable means to endeavor to persuade their fellows to join with them in organizations. They have a legal right, which, according to circumstances, may or may not be a moral right, to refuse to work in company with men who decline to join their organizations. They have under no circumstances the right to commit violence upon those, whether capitalists or wage-workers, who refuse to support their organizations, or who side with those with whom they are at odds; for mob rule is intolerable in any form.

Above all else, we must strive to keep the highways of commerce open to all on equal terms; and to do this it is necessary to put a complete stop to all rebates. Whether the shipper or the railroad is to blame makes no difference; the rebate must be stopped, the abuses of the private car and private terminal-track and side-track systems must be stopped. . . .

. . . No Christian and civilized community can afford to show a happy-go-lucky lack of concern for the youth of to-day; for, if so, the community will have to pay a terrible penalty of financial burden and social degradation in the to-morrow. There should be severe child-labor and factory-inspection laws. It is very desirable that married women should not work in factories. The prime duty of the man is to work, to be the breadwinner; the prime duty of the woman is to be the mother, the housewife. . . .

It is mortifying to remember that Washington has no compulsory school attendance law and that careful inquiries indicate the habitual absence from school of some twenty per cent of all children between the ages of eight and fourteen. It must be evident to all who consider the problems of neglected child life or the benefits of compulsory education in other cities that one of the most urgent needs of the National Capital is a law requiring the school attendance of all children. . . .

Public playgrounds are necessary means for the development

of wholesome citizenship in modern cities. It is important that the work inaugurated here through voluntary efforts should be taken up and extended through Congressional appropriation of funds sufficient to equip and maintain numerous convenient small playgrounds upon land which can be secured without purchase or rental. . . .

There are certain offenders, whose criminality takes the shape of brutality and cruelty towards the weak, who need a special type of punishment. The wife-beater, for example, is inadequately punished by imprisonment; for imprisonment may often mean nothing to him, while it may cause hunger and want to the wife and children who have been the victims of his brutality. Probably some form of corporal punishment would be the most adequate way of meeting this kind of crime.

🐘 🐘 🐘

The forest policy of the Government is just now a subject of vivid public interest throughout the West and to the people of the United States in general. The forest reserves themselves are of extreme value to the present as well as to the future welfare of all the western public-land States. They powerfully affect the use and disposal of the public lands. . . .

🐘 🐘 🐘

Alaska, like all our Territorial acquisitions, has proved resourceful beyond the expectations of those who made the purchase. It has become the home of many hardy, industrious, and thrifty American citizens. Alaska should have a Delegate in the Congress.

🐘 🐘 🐘

It is not true that the United States feels any land hunger or entertains any projects as regards the other nations of the Western Hemisphere save such as are for their welfare. All that this country desires is to see the neighboring countries stable, orderly, and prosperous. Any country whose people conduct themselves well can count upon our hearty friendship. . . . Chronic wrongdoing, or an impotence which results in a general loosening of the ties of civilized society, may in America, as elsewhere, ultimately require intervention by some civilized nation, and in the Western Hemisphere the adherence of the United States to the Monroe Doctrine may force the United States, however reluctantly, in flagrant cases of such wrongdoing or impotence, to the exercise of an international police power. If every country washed by the Caribbean Sea would show the progress in stable and just civilization which, with the aid of the Platt Amendment, Cuba has shown since our troops left the island, and which so many of the republics in both Americas are constantly and brilliantly showing, all question of interference by this Nation with their affairs would be at an end. Our interests and those of our southern neighbors are in reality identical.

The strong arm of the Government in enforcing respect for its just rights in international matters is the Navy of the United States. I most earnestly recommend that there be no halt in the work of upbuilding the American Navy. . . . We have undertaken to build the Isthmian Canal. We have undertaken to secure for ourselves our just share in the trade of the Orient. We have undertaken to protect our citizens from improper treatment in foreign lands. We continue steadily to insist on the application of the Monroe Doctrine to the Western Hemisphere. . . .

. . . Our people must keep steadily before their minds the fact that the justification for our stay in the Philippines must ultimately rest chiefly upon the good we are able to do in the islands. . . .
. . . Unfortunately hitherto those of our people here at home who have specially claimed to be the champions of the Filipinos have in reality been their worst enemies. This will continue to be the case as long as they strive to make the Filipinos independent, and stop all industrial development of the islands by crying out against the laws which would bring it on the ground that capitalists must not "exploit" the islands. Such proceedings are not only unwise, but are most harmful to the Filipinos, who do not need independence at all, but who do need good laws, good public servants, and industrial development. . . .

THEODORE ROOSEVELT
FIFTH STATE-OF-THE-UNION MESSAGE
WHITE HOUSE, *December 5, 1905*

To the Senate and House of Representatives:

. . . In order to insure a healthy social and industrial life, every big corporation should be held responsible by, and be accountable to, some sovereign strong enough to control its conduct. I am in no sense hostile to corporations. This is an age of combination and any effort to prevent all combination will be not only useless, but in the end vicious, because of the contempt for law which the failure to enforce law inevitably produces. . . . The corporation has come to stay, just as the trade union has come to stay. Each can do and has done great good. Each should be favored so long as it does good. But each should be sharply checked where it acts against law and justice.

🐘   🐘   🐘

I renew the recommendation I made in my last annual message for an investigation by the Department of Commerce and Labor of general labor conditions, especial attention to be paid to the conditions of child labor and child-labor legislation in the several States. . . .

The Department of Commerce and Labor should also make a thorough investigation of the conditions of women in industry. Over five million American women are now engaged in gainful occupations. . . . The introduction of women into industry is working change and disturbance in the domestic and social life of the Nation. The decrease in marriage, and especially in the birth rate, has been coincident with it. . . . This whole matter in reality forms one of the greatest sociological phenomena of our time. . . .

The question of securing a healthy, self-respecting, and mutually sympathetic attitude as between employer and employee capitalist and wage-worker, is a difficult one. All phases of the labor problem prove difficult when approached. We can get justice and right dealing only if we put as of paramount importance the principle of

treating a man on his worth, as a man rather than with reference
to his social position, his occupation or the class to which he
belongs. . . .

🐘   🐘   🐘

One of the most effective instruments for peace is the Monroe
Doctrine as it has been and is being gradually developed by this
Nation and accepted by other nations. No other policy could have
been as efficient in promoting peace in the Western Hemisphere
and in giving to each nation thereon the chance to develop along
its own lines. . . .

That our rights and interests are deeply concerned in the maintenance of the doctrine is so clear as hardly to need argument.
This is especially true in view of the construction of the Panama
Canal. As a mere matter of self-defense we must exercise a close
watch over the approaches to this canal; and this means that we
must be thoroughly alive to our interests in the Caribbean Sea.

🐘   🐘   🐘

The question of immigration is of vital interest to this country.
In the year ending June 30, 1905, there came to the United States
1,026,000 alien immigrants. In other words, in the single year
that has just elapsed there came to this country a greater number
of people than came here during the one hundred and sixty-nine
years of our Colonial life, which intervened between the first landing at Jamestown and the Declaration of Independence. It is
clearly shown in the report of the Commissioner General of Immigration that while much of this enormous immigration is undoubt-
edly healthy and natural, a considerable proportion is undesirable
for one reason or another. . . .

If the man who seeks to come here is from the moral and social
standpoint of such a character as to bid fair to add value to the
community he should be heartily welcomed. . . . We cannot afford to consider whether he is Catholic or Protestant, Jew or
Gentile; whether he is Englishman or Irishman, Frenchman or
German, Japanese, Italian, Scandinavian, Slav, or Magyar. What

we should desire to find out is the individual quality of the individual man. . . .

🐘 🐘 🐘

I recommend that a law be enacted to regulate inter-State commerce in misbranded and adulterated foods, drinks, and drugs. Such law would protect legitimate manufacture and commerce, and would tend to secure the health and welfare of the consuming public. Traffic in foodstuffs which have been debased or adulterated so as to injure health or to deceive purchasers should be forbidden.

🐘 🐘 🐘

I call your attention to the generous act of the State of California in conferring upon the United States Government the ownership of the Yosemite Valley and the Mariposa Big Tree Grove. . . . There are certain mighty natural features of our land which should be preserved in perpetuity for our children and our children's children. In my judgment, the Grand Canyon of the Colorado should be made into a National park. . . .

🐘 🐘 🐘

The most characteristic animal of the Western plains was the great, shaggy-maned wild ox, the bison, commonly known as buffalo. Small fragments of herds exist in a domesticated state here and there, a few of them in the Yellowstone Park. Such a herd as that on the Flathead Reservation should not be allowed to go out of existence. . . .

The treaty between the United States and the Republic of Panama, under which the construction of the Panama Canal was made possible, went into effect with its ratification by the United States Senate on February 23, 1904. . . . Active work in canal construction, mainly preparatory, has been in progress for less than a year and a half. The canal will be built on the Isthmus of Panama. . . .

THEODORE ROOSEVELT
SIXTH STATE-OF-THE-UNION MESSAGE
WHITE HOUSE, *December 3, 1906*

To the Senate and House of Representatives:

    I again recommend a law prohibiting all corporations from contributing to the campaign expenses of any party. Such a bill has already passed one House of Congress. Let individuals contribute as they desire; but let us prohibit in effective fashion all corporations from making contributions for any political purpose, directly or indirectly.

🐘 🐘 🐘

    In connection with the delays of the law, I call your attention and the attention of the Nation to the prevalence of crime among us, and above all to the epidemic of lynching and mob violence that springs up, now in one part of our country, now in another. . . . A great many white men are lynched, but the crime is peculiarly frequent in respect to black men. The greatest existing cause of lynching is the perpetration, especially by black men, of the hideous crime of rape—the most abominable in all the category of crimes, even worse than murder. Mobs frequently avenge the commission of this crime by themselves torturing to death the man committing it; thus avenging in bestial fashion a bestial deed, and reducing themselves to a level with the criminal. . . .

    Let justice be both sure and swift; but let it be justice under the law, and not the wild and crooked savagery of a mob.

🐘 🐘 🐘

. . . The free public school, the chance for each boy or girl to get a good elementary education, lies at the foundation of our whole political situation. In every community the poorest citizens, those who need the schools most, would be deprived of them if they only received school facilities proportioned to the taxes they paid. This is as true of one portion of our country as of another. It is as true for the Negro as for the white man. The white man, if he is wise, will decline to allow the Negroes in a mass to grow to manhood and womanhood without education. Unquestionably education such as is obtained in our public schools does not do everything towards making a man a good citizen; but it does much. . . .

🐘 🐘 🐘

In dealing with both labor and capital, with the questions affecting both corporations and trade unions, there is one matter more important to remember than aught else, and that is the infinite harm done by preachers of mere discontent. These are the men who seek to excite a violent class hatred against all men of wealth. They seek to turn wise and proper movements for the better control of corporations and for doing away with the abuses connected with wealth, into a campaign of hysterical excitement and falsehood in which the aim is to inflame to madness the brutal passions of mankind. . . . All this is to commit a crime against the body politic and to be false to every worthy principle and tradition of American national life. . . .

🐘 🐘 🐘

When home ties are loosened; when men and women cease to regard a worthy family life, with all its duties fully performed, and all its responsibilities lived up to, as the life best worth living; then evil days for the commonwealth are at hand. There are regions in our land, and classes of our population, where the birth rate has sunk below the death rate. Surely it should need no demonstration to show that wilful sterility is, from the standpoint of the nation, from the standpoint of the human race, the one sin for which the penalty is national death, race death; a sin for which there is no atonement. No man, no woman, can shirk the primary duties of life, whether for love of ease and pleasure, or for any other cause, and retain his or her self-respect.

🐘 🐘 🐘

I most earnestly hope that the bill to provide a lower tariff for, or else absolute free trade in, Philippine products will become a law. . . . Let us also see to it that they are given free access to our markets. This nation owes no more imperative duty to itself and mankind than the duty of managing the affairs of all the islands under the American flag—the Philippines, Puerto Rico, and Hawaii—so as to make it evident that it is in every way to their advantage that the flag should fly over them. . . .

Last August an insurrection broke out in Cuba which it speedily grew evident that the existing Cuban Government was powerless to quell. Thanks to the preparedness of our Navy, I was able immediately to send enough ships to Cuba to prevent the situation from becoming hopeless.

. . . I take this opportunity of expressing upon behalf of the American people, with all possible solemnity, our most earnest hope that the people of Cuba will realize the imperative need of preserving justice and keeping order in the Island. The United States wishes nothing of Cuba except that it shall prosper morally and materially, and wishes nothing of the Cubans save that they shall be able to preserve order among themselves and therefore to preserve their independence. . . .

THEODORE ROOSEVELT
SEVENTH STATE-OF-THE-UNION MESSAGE
WHITE HOUSE, *December 3, 1907*

To the Senate and House of Representatives:

No nation has greater resources than ours, and I think it can be truthfully said that the citizens of no nation possess greater energy and industrial ability. In no nation are the fundamental business conditions sounder than in ours at this very moment; and it is foolish, when such is the case, for people to hoard money instead of keeping it in sound banks; for it is such hoarding that is the immediate occasion of money stringency. . . .

Those who fear, from any reason, the extension of Federal activity will do well to study the history not only of the national banking act but of the Pure-Food law, and notably the meat-inspection law recently enacted. The Pure-Food law was opposed so violently that its passage was delayed for a decade; yet it has worked unmixed and immediate good. . . .

This country is definitely committed to the protective system and any effort to uproot it could not but cause widespread industrial disaster. In other words, the principle of the present tariff law could not with wisdom be changed. . . .

The Congress should consider the extension of the eight-hour law. The constitutionality of the present law has recently been called into question, and the Supreme Court has decided that the existing legislation is unquestionably within the powers of the Congress. . . .

I renew my previous recommendation that the Congress favorably consider the matter of creating the machinery for compulsory investigation of such industrial controversies as are of sufficient magnitude and of sufficient concern to the people of the country as a whole to warrant the Federal Government in taking action.

Our school system is gravely defective in so far as it puts a premium upon mere literary training and tends therefore to train the boy away from the farm and the workshop. Nothing is more needed than the best type of industrial school, the school for mechanical industries in the city, the school for practically teaching agriculture in the country. The calling of the skilled tiller of the soil, the calling of the skilled mechanic, should alike be recognized as professions, just as emphatically as the callings of lawyer, doctor, merchant, or clerk. . . .

No growth of cities, no growth of wealth, can make up for any loss in either the number or the character of the farming population. . . . We can not afford to lose that preeminently typical American, the farmer who owns his own medium-sized farm. . . .

There should be a National gallery of art established in the capital city of this country. This is important not merely to the artistic but to the material welfare of the country. . . .

🐘 🐘 🐘

Among the [Army] officers there should be severe examinations to weed out the unfit up to the grade of major. From that position on, appointments should be solely by selection. The practice marches and field maneuvers of the last two or three years have been invaluable to the Army. They should be continued and extended. A rigid and not a perfunctory examination of physical capacity has been provided for the higher-grade officers. Unless an officer has a good physique, unless he can stand hardship, ride well, and walk fairly, he is not fit for any position, even after he has become a colonel. I hope speedily to see introduced into the Army a far more rigid and thoroughgoing test of horsemanship for all field officers than at present. There should be a Chief of Cavalry just as there is a Chief of Artillery.

🐘 🐘 🐘

. . . The battle fleet is about starting by the Straits of Magellan to visit the Pacific coast. Sixteen battleships are going under the command of Rear-Admiral Evans, while eight armored cruisers and two other battleships will meet him at San Francisco, whither certain torpedo destroyers are also going. No fleet of such size has ever made such a voyage, and it will be of very great educational use to all engaged in it. . . . Moreover, the only way to find out our actual needs is to perform in time of peace whatever maneuvers might be necessary in time of war. After war is declared it is too late to find out the needs; that means to invite disaster. . . .

🐘 🐘 🐘

A year ago in consequence of a revolutionary movement in Cuba which threatened the immediate return to chaos of the island, the United States intervened, sending down an army and establishing a provisional government. Absolute quiet and prosperity have returned to the island because of this action. We are now taking steps to provide for elections in the island and our expectation is within the coming year to be able to turn the island over again to a government chosen by the people thereof. Cuba is at our doors. It is not possible that this Nation should permit Cuba again to sink into the condition from which we rescued it. . . .

THEODORE ROOSEVELT
EIGHTH STATE-OF-THE-UNION MESSAGE
WHITE HOUSE, *December 8, 1908*

To the Senate and House of Representatives:

At the last election certain leaders of organized labor made a violent and sweeping attack upon the entire judiciary of the country, an attack couched in such terms as to include the most upright, honest and broad-minded judges, no less than those of narrower mind and more restricted outlook. Last year, before the House Committee on the Judiciary, these same labor leaders formulated their demands, specifying the bill that contained them, refusing all compromise. . . . This bill legalized black-listing and boycotting in every form . . . while the right to carry on a business was explicitly taken out from under that protection which the law throws over property. . . .

The wage-workers, the workingmen, the laboring men of the country, by the way in which they repudiated the effort to get them to cast their votes in response to an appeal to class hatred, have emphasized their sound patriotism and Americanism. The whole country has cause to feel pride in this attitude of sturdy independence, in this uncompromising insistence upon acting simply as good citizens, as good Americans, without regard to fancied—and improper—class interests. Such an attitude is an object-lesson in good citizenship to the entire nation.

If there is any one duty which more than another we owe it to our children and our children's children to perform at once, it is to save the forests of this country, for they constitute the first and most important element in the conservation of the natural resources of the country. . . . The lesson of deforestation in China

is a lesson which mankind should have learned many times already
from what has occurred in other places. . . .

. . . Nothing should be permitted to stand in the way of the
preservation of the forests, and it is criminal to permit individuals
to purchase a little gain for themselves through the destruction of
forests when this destruction is fatal to the well-being of the whole
country in the future.

🐘   🐘   🐘

The work on the Panama Canal is being done with a speed,
efficiency and entire devotion to duty which make it a model for
all work of the kind. No task of such magnitude has ever before
been undertaken by any nation; and no task of the kind has ever
been better performed. . . .

Real progress toward self-government is being made in the
Philippine Islands. The gathering of a Philippine legislative body
and Philippine assembly marks a process absolutely new in Asia,
always excepting the striking and wonderful example afforded by
the great Empire of Japan; it opens an entirely new departure
when compared with anything which has happened among Asiatic
powers which are their own masters. But no one can prophesy the
exact date when it will be wise to consider independence as a fixed
and definite policy. . . .

In Cuba our occupancy will cease in about two months' time;
the Cubans have in orderly manner elected their own governmental
authorities, and the island will be turned over to them. Our occupation on this occasion has lasted a little over two years, and Cuba
has thriven and prospered under it. . . .

Nothing better for the Navy from every standpoint has ever
occurred than the cruise of the battle fleet around the world. The
improvement of the ships in every way has been extraordinary,
and they have gained far more experience in battle tactics than
they would have gained if they had stayed in the Atlantic waters.
The American people have cause for profound gratification, both
in view of the excellent condition of the fleet as shown by this
cruise, and in view of the improvement the cruise has worked in
this already high condition. I do not believe that there is any
other service in the world in which the average of character and

efficiency in the enlisted men is as high as is now the case in our own. I believe that the same statement can be made as to our officers, taken as a whole; but there must be a reservation made in regard to those in the highest ranks—as to which I have already spoken—and in regard to those who have just entered the service; because we do not now get full benefit from our excellent naval school at Annapolis. It is absurd not to graduate the midshipmen as ensigns. In the academy itself, every first classman should be required in turn to serve as petty officer and officer; his ability to discharge his duties as such should be a prerequisite to his going into the line, and his success in commanding should largely determine his standing at graduation. . . .

WILLIAM HOWARD TAFT
(1909–1913)

"The most important naval
base in the West Indies
is Guantanamo"

The year 1908 witnessed a reenactment of the old Jackson-to-Van Buren routine when Theodore Roosevelt hand-picked *William Howard Taft* of Ohio to succeed him in the White House.

Taft's Democratic opponent, William Jennings Bryan, was making his last hopeless bid for the Nation's top job, but his free-silver act had lost its magic. No longer did wide-eyed folk flock to hear his siren voice dangle gold and silver before their eyes. Taft's election was bagged before he started.

Taft was a lovable, genial, six-foot-two 350-pounder, with a broad smile, a head that required a bucket-sized hat, and a stance like a battleship. His magnificent handle-bar mustache measured seven inches across. He was the largest of the Presidents and a prodigious worker. The best gauge of his feelings about the presidency was his late-in-life comment, "I don't remember I was ever President." His chief accomplishment lay in directions other than running the office of Chief Magistrate, which he characterized as the "loneliest place in the world."

President McKinley gave Taft his start up the presidential ladder in 1900 by appointing him first Governor of the Philippine Islands, which were ceded to the United States after the war with Spain. He apparently won the affection of the Filipinos, whom he called "my little brown brothers." In 1904, Roosevelt recalled him to join his Cabinet

367

as Secretary of War, a task he performed with merit. Incidentally, much of the supervision of building the Panama Canal fell to Taft as War Secretary.

Taft's regime witnessed mighty interparty battles on Capitol Hill. The so-called "Insurgents"—led by progressives like Robert M. La-Follette of Wisconsin, George Norris of Nebraska, William Borah of Idaho, and Hiram Johnson of California—ran riot, upsetting party plans and jamming through an amazing amount of legislation that augured well for the nation. They prestidigitated two constitutional amendments: the Sixteenth that legalized the income-tax collector's yearly dip into America's pocketbook, and the Seventeenth, that took the election of United States Senators from State legislatures and handed it over to the people. For good measure, the insurgents forced enactment of the parcel-post system and postal-savings-bank bills. They also deserve their share of credit for teaming up with the Democrats to overthrow hard-boiled, poker-playing Speaker Joseph Gurney Cannon, who had "czared" it over House legislation for eight years.

Having pledged himself to carry on Theodore Roosevelt's program, Taft tried his best. A year later, however, he was writing the former President that he was having a hard time "carrying out your policies . . . my method of doing so has not worked out too well." Thus began the internecine Taft-Roosevelt rift that led to Theodore Roosevelt's break with the Republicans (who refused to nominate him for a third term) and his creation of the Bull Moose party. The entry of a third party in the 1912 contest assured Wilson as Taft's successor.

WILLIAM HOWARD TAFT
FIRST STATE-OF-THE-UNION MESSAGE
WHITE HOUSE, *December 7, 1909*

. . . I have thus, in a message compressed as much as the subjects will permit, referred to many of the legislative needs of the country, with the exceptions already noted. Speaking generally, the country is in a high state of prosperity. There is every reason to believe that we are on the eve of a substantial business expansion, and we have just garnered a harvest unexampled in the market value of our agricultural products. The high prices which such products bring mean great prosperity for the farming community, but on the other hand they mean a very considerably increased burden upon those classes in the community whose yearly compensation does not expand with the improvement in business and the general prosperity. Various reasons are given for the high prices. The proportionate increase in the output of gold, which to-day is the chief medium of exchange and is in some respects a measure of value, furnishes a substantial explanation of at least a part of the increase in prices. The increase in population and the more expensive mode of living of the people, which have not been accompanied by a proportionate increase in acreage production, may furnish a further reason. It is well to note that the increase in the cost of living is not confined to this country, but prevails the world over, and that those who would charge increases in prices to the existing protective tariff must meet the fact that the rise in prices has taken place almost wholly in those products of the factory and farm in respect to which there has been either no increase in the tariff or in many instances a very considerable reduction.

WILLIAM HOWARD TAFT
SECOND STATE-OF-THE-UNION MESSAGE
WHITE HOUSE, *December 6, 1910*

During the past year the foreign relations of the United States have continued upon a basis of friendship and good understanding.

Among questions arising for present solution is whether the Canal shall be fortified. I have already stated to the Congress that I strongly favor fortification and I now reiterate this opinion and ask your consideration of the subject in the light of the report already before you made by a competent board.

If, in our discretion, we believe modern fortifications to be necessary to the adequate protection and policing of the Canal, then it is our duty to construct them. We have built the Canal. It is our property. By convention we have indicated our desire for, and indeed undertaken, its universal and equal use. It is also well known that one of the chief objects in the construction of the

Canal has been to increase the military effectiveness of our navy.

Failure to fortify the Canal would make the attainment of both these aims depend upon the mere moral obligations of the whole international public—obligations which we would be powerless to enforce.

The Secretary points out that the most important naval base in the West Indies is Guantanamo, in the southeastern part of Cuba. Its geographical situation is admirably adapted to protect the commercial paths to the Panama Canal and he shows that by the expenditure of less than half a million dollars, with the machinery which he shall take from other navy yards, he can create a naval station at Guantanamo of sufficient size and equipment to serve the purpose of an emergency naval base.

🐘 🐘 🐘

The complete success of our country in Arctic exploration should not remain unnoticed. . . . The unparalleled accomplishment of an American in reaching the North Pole, April 6, 1909, approved by critical examination of the most expert scientists, has added to the distinction of our navy, to which he belongs, and reflects credit upon his country. His unique success has received generous acknowledgment from scientific bodies and institutions of learning in Europe and America. I recommend fitting recognition by Congress of the great achievement of Robert Edwin Peary.

Our national parks have become so extensive and involve so much detail of action in their control that it seems to me there ought to be legislation creating a bureau for their care and control. The greatest natural wonder of this country and the surrounding territory should be included in another national park. I refer to the Grand Canyon of the Colorado.

WILLIAM HOWARD TAFT
THIRD STATE-OF-THE-UNION MESSAGE
WHITE HOUSE, *December 7, 1911*

. . . The fur-seal controversy, which for nearly twenty-five years has been the source of serious friction between the United

States and the powers bordering upon the north Pacific Ocean, whose subjects have been permitted to engage in pelagic sealing against the fur-seal herds having breeding grounds within the jurisdiction of the United States, has at last been satisfactorily adjusted by the conclusion of the north Pacific sealing convention entered into between the United States, Great Britain, Japan, and Russia on the 7th of July last. . . .

WILLIAM HOWARD TAFT
FOURTH STATE-OF-THE-UNION MESSAGE
WHITE HOUSE, *December 3, 1912*

At the beginning of the present administration the United States, having fully entered upon its position as a world power, with the responsibilities thrust upon it by the results of the Spanish-American War, and already engaged in laying the groundwork of a vast foreign trade upon which it should one day become more and more dependent, found itself without the machinery for giving thorough attention to, and taking effective action upon, a mass of intricate business vital to American interests in every country in the world.

The Department of State was an archaic and inadequate machine lacking most of the attributes of the foreign office of any great modern power. With an appropriation made upon my recommendation by the Congress on August 5, 1909, the Department of State was completely reorganized.

For two years revolution and counter-revolution has distraught the neighboring Republic of Mexico. . . . Throughout this trying period, the policy of the United States has been one of patient nonintervention, steadfast recognition of constituted authority in the neighboring nation, and the exertion of every effort to care for American interests. I profoundly hope that the Mexican nation may soon resume the path of order, prosperity, and progress.

The Republic of Cuba last May was in the throes of a lawless uprising that for a time threatened the destruction of a great deal of valuable property—much of it owned by Americans and other foreigners—as well as the existence of the government itself. The armed forces of Cuba being inadequate to guard property from attack and at the same time properly to operate against the rebels, a force of American Marines was dispatched from our naval station of Guantanamo into the Province of Oriente for the protection of Americans and other foreign life and property. The Cuban government was thus able to use all its forces in putting down the outbreak, which it succeeded in doing in a period of six weeks. The presence of two American warships in the harbor of Havana during the most critical period of this disturbance contributed in a great measure to allay the fears of the inhabitants, including a large foreign colony.

A bill is pending in Congress which revolutionizes the carefully worked out scheme of government under which the Philippine Islands are now governed and which proposes to render them virtually autonomous at once and absolutely independent in eight years. . . .

Our true course is to pursue steadily and courageously the path we have thus far followed; to guide the Filipinos into self-sustaining pursuits; to continue the cultivation of sound political habits through education and political practice; to encourage the diversification of industries, and to realize the advantages of their industrial education by conservatively approved cooperative methods, at once checking the dangers of concentrated wealth and building up a sturdy, independent citizenship. We should do all this with a disinterested endeavor to secure for the Filipinos economic independence and to fit them for complete self-government. . . . A present declaration even of future independence would retard progress by the dissension and disorder it would arouse.

From time to time there is considerable agitation in Washington in favor of granting the citizens of the city the franchise and constituting an elective government. I am strongly opposed to this change. The history of Washington discloses a number of experiments of this kind, which have always been abandoned as unsatisfactory. The truth is this is a city governed by a popular body, to wit, the Congress of the United States, selected from the people of the United States, who own Washington.

The construction of the Lincoln Memorial and of a memorial bridge from the base of the Lincoln Monument to Arlington would be an appropriate and symbolic expression of the union of the North and the South at the Capital of the Nation. I urge upon Congress the appointment of a commission to undertake these national improvements, and to submit a plan for their execution; and when the plan has been submitted and approved, and the work carried out, Washington will really become what it ought to be— the most beautiful city in the world. . . .

WOODROW WILSON
(1913–1921)

*"The world
must be made safe
for democracy"*

Of the millions and millions of words uttered and written by *Woodrow Wilson* during his eight years in the White House, the eight quoted above, which adorned his War Message of April 2, 1917, will be longest remembered.

Yet, had there been no war in Europe, Wilson would probably have gone into history as a one-term "Professor" President, whose State-of-the-Union Messages and other speeches were clothed in the smoothest, most elegant rhetoric of all the Chief Executives. He owed his reelection in 1916 to an unidentified word-slinger in the Democratic high command who at the right moment came up with the campaign slogan, "Vote for Wilson—He kept us out of war!" Even so, he was reelected in 1916 by a slim 23 electoral-vote majority or, as some claimed, by a handshake or the lack of it.

Wilson was a drama-maker. Hardly had he taken office before he astonished the nation by dramatically scrapping the precedent established by Thomas Jefferson, his party's founder, of simply sending his written message to Capitol Hill, and reviving the original custom of appearing in person before Congress to deliver his State-of-the-Union Message and other speeches. Presidents have done so ever since.

In 1912, Woodrow Wilson brought to the White House the first of three Democratic catch-plans tagged with the word "New"—New Freedom, New Deal, and New Frontier. Thus, he gave the Democratic party its dramatic, fresh approach to the common man and his wants and blazed for his successors a new trail that could be summed up in a single word, REFORM. He also demonstrated the persuasive power of the word NEW.

Riding the wave of his New Freedom, Woodrow Wilson, during his first twenty months in office, wangled through Congress more constructive legislation than any other President up to his time was able to. Using spur and whip on the Democratic majorities in House and Senate, he managed to get the Underwood tariff bill, which reduced duties on 958 articles; the Federal Reserve Act, which gave government control of the nation's credit system; the Federal Trade Commission Act, by which the national government could crack down on unfair competition in business, and other salutary enactments which brought him great acclaim.

The New Freedom was booming along when, in 1914, World War I exploded in Europe and the nation suddenly faced new, grave problems: How could it keep neutral in a world on fire, and how defend itself if it were drawn into war as seemed inevitable to those with vision? For three years Wilson clung to his policy of "splendid isolation," but it wouldn't work. In 1917, with disaster hovering over the Allies, Germany went berserk in an effort to deliver a final, knockout blow. To this end, Germany opened undeclared submarine war on American shipping, which quickly brought America to the brink of war. The hour of decision struck when Woodrow Wilson, on April 2, 1917, appeared before Congress and asked a declaration of war against the Imperial German government. To this War Message he committed eight words—"The world must be made safe for democracy"— that still wing across the world in these later hours when the red shadow of thermonuclear war threatens man's very existence. Under Wilson's war leadership, America threw her might into the struggle against Germany and her satellites. It turned the tide, and Germany capitulated to the Allies in November, 1918.

But the task was not yet done. Wilson immediately hurried to Paris for the Peace Conference. His famous Fourteen Points, which he had laid down as the basis of a "just and holy" peace with Germany and her satellites, were hacked beyond recognition by shrewd European diplomats who were past masters in the art of selfish peace-making. Wilson came home with the Treaty of Versailles. In it was firmly imbedded his pet covenant of the League of Nations, forerunner of the United Nations, that would, he thought, make future war impossible. But the Senate cold-shouldered it. Hoping to whip up public support for the treaty, Wilson took his cause to the people on a swing westward. Forty speeches in twenty-eight days brought him to the end of the line. At Pueblo, Colorado, he was stricken with paralysis. From then on, he was only a shadow of the former leader. Back in Washington, he remained secluded in the White House for the rest of his term. On November 19, 1919, while Wilson lay helpless, the treaty finally came to a vote in the Senate and was rejected. On March 4, 1921, he handed the reins to his successor, Warren G. Harding of Ohio.

Wilson began his First State-of-the-Union Message hopefully. The New Freedom was on its way. He saw but "one cloud on our horizon": that was Mexico, where General Victoriano Huerta had usurped the presidency and set himself up as dictator. Wilson refused to recognize Huerta, whom he called a "desperate brute," and thus began an endurance contest which Wilson designated "watchful waiting"—a policy decidedly unpopular with most Americans. It was resolved by Huerta's going into exile.

This message also spelled out passage of the Adamson Act, which provided an eight-hour day for railroad employees with pro-rata pay for overtime. It was widely heralded as labor's Magna Carta.

World War I was in its fourth month when Wilson appeared on December 8, 1914, with his second message. War was fast overrunning the world and America's thoughts had turned to national defense, but Wilson was loath to embark on a program of military preparedness. Instead, he proposed expansion of the National Guard as sufficient to cope with eventualities. With war excitement spreading, the New Freedom band wagon slowed down. Domestic reform came almost to a full stop.

By 1915 war was coming closer. The torpedoing of the *Lusitania* had shocked the civilized world. Woodrow Wilson, on December 7, 1915, in his Third State-of-the-Union Message, replaced his policy of non-preparedness with an "absolutely imperative" program for enlarging both army and navy.

His December, 1916, State-of-the-Union Message gave little hint of America's entrance into World War I. That step was taken by his War Message on April 2, 1917, the chief components of which are reprinted here.

In his message of December, 1917, Woodrow Wilson enunciated the terms of a "just and holy" peace by giving a preview of his famous Fourteen Points. He followed quickly with his Special Message of January 8, 1918, which elaborated these terms in fourteen brief paragraphs, to which the world pinned the insignia, "Fourteen Points."

In December, 1918, Wilson delivered his Sixth State-of-the-Union Message to a cheering Congress and galleries packed with diplomats from the world over. He stood at the high-water mark of his career. He highlighted this dramatic appearance on Capitol Hill by announcing his departure shortly for Paris to take part in the upcoming Peace Conference, and by his recommendation that Congress, in gratitude for woman's share in victory, extend universal suffrage to the women of America.

His December, 1919, message was written from his sickroom in the White House and sent to Congress by messenger. The Senate had barely three weeks before it killed the Treaty of Versailles with its covenant of the League of Nations.

In December, 1920, an awed Congress received Wilson's last State-of-the-Union Message—the so-called Message of Faith which he began by quoting Abraham Lincoln.

It is worth noting that not a word appears in Wilson's State-of-the-Union Messages about the Eighteenth Amendment to the Constitution, ratified in 1919, forbidding the use of intoxicating liquors, nor about the Volstead Enforcement Act, which he vetoed because of its definition of an intoxicating beverage—one-half of one per cent alcohol. It was carried over his veto, and America embarked on the futile "noble experiment."

WOODROW WILSON
FIRST STATE-OF-THE-UNION MESSAGE
December 2, 1913

In pursuance of my constitutional duty to "give to the Congress information of the state of the Union," I take the liberty of addressing you on several matters which ought, as it seems to me, particularly to engage the attention of your honorable bodies, as of all who study the welfare and progress of the Nation.

🐎 🐎 🐎

There is but one cloud upon our horizon. That has shown itself to the south of us, and hangs over Mexico. There can be no certain prospect of peace in America until General Huerta has surrendered his usurped authority in Mexico; until it is understood on all hands, indeed, that such pretended governments will not be countenanced or dealt with by the Government of the United States. . . . Even if the usurper had succeeded in his purposes, he has forfeited the respect and the moral support even of those who were at one time willing to see him succeed. Little by little he has been completely isolated. By a little every day his power and prestige are crumbling and the collapse is not far away. We shall not, I believe, be obliged to alter our policy of watchful waiting. . . .

I turn to matters of domestic concern. You already have under consideration a bill for the reform of our system of banking and currency. . . . I need not say how earnestly I hope for its early enactment into law. I present to you, in addition, the urgent necessity that special provisions be made also for facilitating the credits needed by the farmers of this country. The pending currency bill does the farmers a great service; and upon its passage they will find themselves quit of many of the difficulties which now hamper them in the field of credit. . . .

. . . I think it will be easily agreed that we should let the Sherman antitrust law stand, unaltered, as it is, with its debatable ground about it, but that we should as much as possible reduce the area of that debatable ground by further and more explicit legislation. . . .

☙ ☙ ☙

. . . We can satisfy the obligations of generous justice toward the people of Puerto Rico by giving them ample and familiar rights and privileges accorded our own citizens in our own territories and our obligations toward the people of Hawaii by perfecting the provisions for self-government already granted them, but in the Philippines we must go further. We must hold in view their ultimate independence. . . .

. . . The people of Alaska should be given the full territorial form of government, and Alaska, as a storehouse, should be unlocked. One key to it is a system of railways. These the Government must build and administer. We must use the resources of Alaska, not lock them up.

☙ ☙ ☙

We owe it, in mere justice to the railway employees of the country, to provide for them a fair and effective employers' liability act; and a law we can stand by in this matter will be no less to the advantage of those who administer the railroads of the country than to the advantage of those whom they employ. . . .

🐴 🐴 🐴

May I not express the very real pleasure I have experienced in cooperating with this Congress and sharing with it the labors of common service to which it has devoted itself so unreservedly during the past seven months of uncomplaining concentration upon the business of legislation? Surely it is a proper and pertinent part of my report on "the state of the Union" to express my admiration for the diligence, the good temper, and the full comprehension of public duty which has already been manifested by both the Houses; and I hope that it may not be deemed an impertinent intrusion of myself into the picture if I say with how much and how constant satisfaction I have availed myself of the privilege of putting my time and energy at their disposal alike in counsel and in action.

WOODROW WILSON
SECOND STATE-OF-THE-UNION MESSAGE
December 8, 1914

. . . Our thoughts are now more of the future than of the past. While we have worked at our tasks of peace the circumstances of the whole age have been altered by war. . . .

War has interrupted the means of trade not only but also the processes of production. In Europe it is destroying men and resources wholesale and upon a scale unprecedented and appalling. There is reason to fear that the time is near, if it be not already at hand, when several of the countries of Europe will find it difficult to do for their people what they have hitherto been always easily able to do. . . . They will need our help and our manifold services as they have never needed them before; and we should be ready, more fit and ready than we have ever been.

🐴 🐴 🐴

To speak plainly, we have grossly erred in the way in which we have stunted and hindered the development of our merchant marine. And now, when we need ships, we have not got them. . . . I have come to ask you to remedy and correct these mistakes and omissions. . . .

And there is another great piece of legislation which awaits and should receive the sanction of the Senate: I mean the bill which gives a larger measure of self-government to the people of the Philippines. . . .

The great subject of rural credits still remains to be dealt with, and it is a matter of deep regret that the difficulties of the subject have seemed to render it impossible to complete a bill for passage at this session. . . .

🐂 🐂 🐂

The other topic I shall take leave to mention goes deeper into the principles of our national life and policy. It is the subject of national defense. . . .

From the first we have had a clear and settled policy with regard to military establishments. We never have had, and while we retain our present principles and ideals we never shall have, a large standing army. If asked, Are you ready to defend yourselves? we reply, Most assuredly, to the utmost; and yet we shall not turn America into a military camp. We will not ask our young men to spend the best years of their lives making soldiers of themselves. . . .

. . . We must depend in every time of national peril, in the future as in the past, not upon a standing army, nor yet upon a reserve army, but upon a citizenry trained and accustomed to arms. It will be right enough, right American policy, based upon our accustomed principles and practices, to provide a system by which every citizen who will volunteer for the training may be made familiar with the use of modern arms. . . . It is right, too, that the National Guard of the States should be developed and strengthened by every means which is not inconsistent with our obligations to our own people or with the established policy of our Government. . . .

More than this carries with it a reversal of the whole history and character of our polity. More than this, proposed at this time, permit me to say, would mean merely that we had lost our self-possession, that we had been thrown off our balance by a war with which we have nothing to do, whose causes can not touch us. . . .

🐕 🐕 🐕

I close, as I began, by reminding you of the great tasks and duties of peace which challenge our best powers and invite us to build what will last, the tasks to which we can address ourselves now and at all times with free-hearted zest and with all the finest gifts of constructive wisdom we possess. . . .

WOODROW WILSON
THIRD STATE-OF-THE-UNION MESSAGE
December 7, 1915

Since I last had the privilege of addressing you on the state of the Union the war of nations on the other side of the sea, which had then only begun to disclose its portentous proportions, has extended its threatening and sinister scope until it has swept within its flame some portion of every quarter of the globe. . . .

We have stood apart, studiously neutral. It was our manifest duty to do so. It was necessary, if a universal catastrophe was to be avoided . . . that some part of the great family of nations should keep the processes of peace alive.

🐕 🐕 🐕

There was a time in the early days of our own great nation and of the republics fighting their way to independence in Central and South America when the government of the United States looked upon itself as in some sort the guardian of the republics to the south of her as against any encroachments or efforts at political control from the other side of the water. . . . Our concern for the dependence and prosperity of the states of Central and South America is not altered. We retain unabated the spirit that has inspired us throughout the whole life of our government and which was so frankly put into words by President Monroe. . . .

The moral is, that the states of America are not hostile rivals, but cooperating friends. . . . Separated they are subject to all the cross-currents of the confused politics of a world of hostile rivalries; united in spirit and purpose they cannot be disappointed of their peaceful destiny.

This is Pan-Americanism. It has none of the spirit of empire in it. It is the embodiment, the effectual embodiment, of the spirit of law and independence and liberty and mutual service.

🐎 🐎 🐎

But war has never been a mere matter of men and guns. It is a thing of disciplined might. If our citizens are ever to fight effectively upon a sudden summons, they must know how modern fighting is done. . . .

It is with these ideals in mind that the plans of the Department of War for more adequate national defense were conceived which will be laid before you and which I urge you to sanction. . . .

They contemplate an increase of the standing force of the regular army from its present strength of 5,023 officers and 102,985 enlisted men of all services to a strength of 7,136 officers and 134,707 enlisted men, or 141,843, all told, all services, rank and file. . . .

By way of making the country ready to assert some part of its real power promptly and upon a larger scale, should occasion arise, the plan also contemplates supplementing the army by a force of four hundred thousand disciplined citizens, raised in increments of one hundred and thirty-three thousand a year throughout a period of three years. . . .

🐎 🐎 🐎

The program to be laid before you by the Secretary of the Navy contemplates the construction within five years of ten battleships, six battle-cruisers, ten scout-cruisers, fifty destroyers, fifteen fleet submarines, eighty-five coast submarines, four gunboats, one hospital ship, two ammunition ships, two fuel-oil ships, and one repair ship. . . .

The Secretary of the Navy is asking also for the immediate addition to the personnel of the navy of seven thousand five hundred sailors, twenty-five hundred apprentice seamen, and fifteen hundred marines. . . .

🐐 🐐 🐐

For what we are seeking now, what in my mind is the single thought of this message, is national efficiency and security. We serve a great nation. We should serve it in the spirit of its peculiar genius. It is the genius of common men for self-government, industry, justice, liberty and peace. We should see to it that it lacks no instrument, no facility or vigor of law, to make it sufficient to play its part with energy, safety, and assured success. In this we are no partisans but heralds and prophets of a new age.

WOODROW WILSON
FOURTH STATE-OF-THE-UNION MESSAGE
December 5, 1916

Three matters of capital importance await the action of the Senate which have already been acted upon by the House of Representatives: the bill which seeks to extend greater freedom of combination to those engaged in promoting the foreign commerce of the country than is now thought by some to be legal under the terms of the laws against monopoly; the bill amending the present organic law of Puerto Rico; and the bill proposing a more thorough and systematic regulation of the expenditure of money in elections, commonly called the Corrupt Practices Act. . . .

🐐 🐐 🐐

Inasmuch as this is, Gentlemen, probably the last occasion I shall have to address the Sixty-fourth Congress, I hope that you will permit me to say with what genuine pleasure and satisfaction I have cooperated with you in the many measures of constructive policy with which you have enriched the legislative annals of the country. It has been a privilege to labour in such company. I take the liberty of congratulating you upon the completion of a record of rare serviceableness and distinction.

WOODROW WILSON
SPECIAL WAR MESSAGE ASKING DECLARATION OF WAR
AGAINST THE GERMAN EMPIRE
April 2, 1917

I have called the Congress into extraordinary session because there are serious, very serious, choices of policy to be made,
and made immediately, which it was neither right nor constitutionally permissible that I should assume the responsibility of
making.

On the third of February last I officially laid before you the
extraordinary announcement of the Imperial German Government
that on and after the first day of February it was its purpose to
put aside all restraints of law or of humanity and use its submarines to sink every vessel that sought to approach either the
ports of Great Britain and Ireland or the western coasts of Europe
or any of the ports controlled by the enemies of Germany within
the Mediterranean. . . . The new policy has swept every restriction aside. Vessels of every kind, whatever their flag, their character, their cargo, their destination, their errand, have been ruthlessly
sent to the bottom without warning and without thought of help
or mercy for those on board, the vessels of friendly neutrals along
with those of belligerents. . . .

✂ ✂ ✂

. . . I am not now thinking of the loss of property involved, immense and serious as that is, but only of the wanton and wholesale
destruction of the lives of non-combatants, men, women, and
children, engaged in pursuits which have always, even in the
darkest periods of modern history, been deemed innocent and
legitimate. Property can be paid for; the lives of peaceful and
innocent people cannot be. The present German submarine warfare against commerce is a warfare against mankind.

✂ ✂ ✂

It is a war against all nations. American ships have been sunk,
American lives taken, in ways which it has stirred us very deeply
to learn of, but the ships and people of other neutral and friendly
nations have been sunk and overwhelmed in the waters in the

same way. There has been no discrimination. The challenge is to all mankind.

When I addressed the Congress on the twenty-sixth of February last I thought that it would suffice to assert our neutral rights with arms, our right to use the seas against unlawful interference, our right to keep our people safe against unlawful violence. But armed neutrality, it now appears, is impracticable. . . .

With a profound sense of the solemn and even tragical character of the step I am taking and of the grave responsibilities which it involves, but in unhesitating obedience to what I deem my constitutional duty, I advise that the Congress declare the recent course of the Imperial German Government to be in fact nothing less than war against the government and people of the United States; that it formally accept the status of belligerent which has thus been thrust upon it; and that it take immediate steps not only to put the country in a more thorough state of defense but also to exert all its power and employ all its resources to bring the Government of the German Empire to terms and end the war.

❊ ❊ ❊

We have no quarrel with the German people. We have no feeling towards them but one of sympathy and friendship. It was not upon their impulse that their government acted in entering this war. It was not with their previous knowledge or approval. It was a war determined upon as wars used to be determined upon in the old, unhappy days when peoples were nowhere consulted by their rulers and wars were provoked and waged in the interest of dynasties or of little groups of ambitious men who were accustomed to use their fellow men as pawns and tools. . . .

❊ ❊ ❊

Does not every American feel that assurance has been added to our hope for the future peace of the world by the wonderful and heartening things that have been happening within the last few weeks in Russia? . . . The autocracy that crowned the summit of her political structure, long as it had stood and terrible as was the reality of its power, was not in fact Russian in origin, character, or purpose; and now it has been shaken off and the great, generous Russian people have been added in all their naïve majesty and might to the forces that are fighting for freedom in the world, for justice, and for peace. Here is a fit partner for a League of Honour.

✗   ✗   ✗

. . . We are now about to accept gage of battle with this natural foe to liberty and shall, if necessary, spend the whole force of the nation to check and nullify its pretensions and its power. We are glad, now that we see the facts with no veil of false pretence about them, to fight thus for the ultimate peace of the world and for the liberation of its peoples, the German peoples included: for the rights of nations great and small and the privilege of men everywhere to choose their way of life and of obedience. The world must be made safe for democracy. Its peace must be planted upon the tested foundations of political liberty. We have no selfish ends to serve. We desire no conquest, no dominion. We seek no indemnities for ourselves, no material compensation for the sacrifices we shall freely make. We are but one of the champions of the rights of mankind. . . .

✗   ✗   ✗

It is a distressing and oppressive duty, Gentlemen of the Congress, which I have performed in thus addressing you. There are, it may be, many months of fiery trial and sacrifice ahead of us. It is a fearful thing to lead this great peaceful people into war, into the most terrible and disastrous of all wars, civilization itself seeming to be in the balance. But the right is more precious than peace, and we shall fight for the things which we have always carried nearest our hearts, for democracy, for the right of those who submit to authority to have a voice in their own governments, for the rights and liberties of small nations, for a universal dominion of right by such a concert of free peoples as shall bring peace and safety to all nations and make the world itself at last free. To such a task we can dedicate our lives and our fortunes, everything that we are and everything that we have, with the pride of those who know that the day has come when America is privileged to spend her blood and her might for the principles that gave her birth and happiness and the peace which she has treasured. God helping her, she can do no other.

WOODROW WILSON
FIFTH STATE-OF-THE-UNION MESSAGE
December 4, 1917

I shall not go back to debate the causes of the war. . . .
But I shall ask you to consider again and with a very grave scrutiny our objectives and the measures by which we mean to attain
them. Our object is, of course, to win the war; and we shall not
slacken or suffer ourselves to be diverted until it is won. But it is
worth while asking and answering the question, When shall we
consider the war won?

. . . We shall regard the war as won only when the German people say to us that they are ready to agree to a settlement based
upon justice and the reparation of the wrongs their rulers have
done. They have done a great wrong to Belgium which must be
repaired. They have established a power over other lands and
peoples than their own—over the great Empire of Austria-
Hungary, over hitherto free Balkan States, over Turkey and within
Asia—which must be relinquished.

✗ ✗ ✗

We owe it, however, to ourselves to say that we do not wish in
any way to impair or to rearrange the Austro-Hungarian Empire.
. . . One very embarrassing obstacle that stands in our way is that
we are at war with Germany, but not with her allies. I therefore
very earnestly recommend that the Congress immediately declare
the United States in a state of war with Austria-Hungary. Does it
seem strange to you that this should be the conclusion of the argument I have just addressed to you? It is not. It is, in fact, the inevitable logic of what I have said. Austria-Hungary is for the time
being not her own mistress, but simply the vassal of the German
Government. We must face the facts as they are and act upon
them without sentiment in this stern business. . . .

✗ ✗ ✗

. . . The cause being just and holy, the settlement must be of
like motive and quality. For this we can fight, but for nothing less
noble or less worthy of our traditions. For this cause we entered

the war and for this cause will we battle until the last gun is fired. . . . A supreme moment of history has come. The eyes of the people have been opened and they see. The hand of God is laid upon the nations. He will show them favor, I devoutly believe, only if they rise to the clear heights of His own justice and mercy.

WOODROW WILSON
SIXTH STATE-OF-THE-UNION MESSAGE
December 2, 1918

The year that has elapsed since I last stood before you to fulfil my constitutional duty to give to the Congress from time to time information on the state of the Union has been so crowded with great events, great processes and great results that I cannot hope to give you an adequate picture of its transactions or of the far-reaching changes which have been wrought in the life of our nation and of the world. You have yourselves witnessed these things, as I have. . . .

What we all thank God for with deepest gratitude is that our men went in force into the line of battle just at the critical moment when the whole fate of the world seemed to hang in the balance and threw their fresh strength into the ranks of freedom in time to turn the whole tide and sweep of the fateful struggle,— turn it once for all, so that thenceforth it was back, back, back for their enemies, always back, never again forward! . . .

And what shall we say of the women,—of their instant intelligence, quickening every task that they touched; their capacity for organization and cooperation, which gave their action discipline and enhanced the effectiveness of everything they attempted; their aptitude at tasks to which they had never before set their hands; their utter self-sacrifice alike in what they did and in what they gave? They have added a new lustre to the annals of American womanhood.

The least tribute we can pay them is to make them the equals of men in political rights as they have proved themselves their equals in every field of practical work they have entered, whether for themselves or for their country. These great days of completed achievement would be sadly marred were we to omit that act of justice. . . .

And now we are sure of the great triumph for which every sacrifice was made. With the pride and inspiration of these days of achievement quick within us we turn to the tasks of peace again. . . . We are about to give order and organization to this peace not only for ourselves but for the other peoples of the world as well, so far as they will suffer us to serve them. . . .

🐂 🐂 🐂

I welcome this occasion to announce to the Congress my purpose to join in Paris the representatives of the governments with which we have been associated in the war against the Central Empires for the purpose of discussing with them the main features of the treaty of peace. I shall be in close touch with you and with affairs on this side of the water, and you will know all that I do. . . .

May I not hope, Gentlemen of the Congress, that in the delicate tasks I shall have to perform on the other side of the sea, in my efforts truly and faithfully to interpret the principles and purposes of the country we love, I may have the encouragement and the added strength of your united support? I realize the magnitude and difficulty of the duty I am undertaking; I am poignantly aware of its grave responsibilities. I am the servant of the nation. . . . The cables and the wireless will render me available for any counsel or service you may desire of me, and I shall be happy in the thought that I am constantly in touch with the weighty matters of domestic policy with which we shall have to deal. I shall make my absence as brief as possible and shall hope to return with the happy assurance that it has been possible to translate into action the great ideals for which America has striven.

WOODROW WILSON
SEVENTH STATE-OF-THE-UNION MESSAGE
December 2, 1919

I sincerely regret that I cannot be present at the opening of this session of the Congress. I am thus prevented from presenting in as direct a way as I could wish the many questions that are pressing for solution at this time. . . .

🐴 🐴 🐴

. . . A fundamental change has taken place with reference to the position of America in the world's affairs. . . . Before the war America was heavily the debtor of the rest of the world, and the interest payments she had to make to foreign countries on American securities held abroad, the expenditures of American travelers abroad and the ocean freight charges she had to pay to others, about balanced the value of her pre-war favorable balance of trade. During the war America's exports have been greatly stimulated and increased prices have increased their value. On the other hand, she has purchased a large proportion of the American securities previously held abroad, has loaned some $9,000,000,000 to foreign governments, and has built her own ships. Our favorable balance of trade has thus been greatly increased and Europe has been deprived of the means of meeting it heretofore existing. . . .

. . . If we want to sell, we must be prepared to buy. Whatever, therefore, may have been our views during the period of growth of American business concerning tariff legislation, we must now adjust our own economic life to a changed condition growing out of the fact that American business is full grown and that America is the greatest capitalist in the world.

No policy of isolation will satisfy the growing needs and opportunities of America. The recent war has ended our isolation and thrown upon us a great duty and responsibility. The United States must share the expanding world market. . . .

The great unrest throughout the world, out of which has emerged a demand for an immediate consideration of the difficulties be-

tween capital and labour, bids us put our own house in order. . . .
Frankly, there can be no permanent and lasting settlements between capital and labour which do not recognize the fundamental
concepts for which labour has been struggling through the years.

🐂 🐂 🐂

Governments must recognize the right of men collectively to
bargain for humane objects that have at their base the mutual protection and welfare of those engaged in all industries. Labour must
not be longer treated as a commodity. It must be regarded as the
activity of human beings, possessed of deep yearnings and desires.
. . . The right of labour to live in peace and comfort must be
recognized by governments, and America should be the first to lay
the foundation stones upon which industrial peace shall be built.

🐂 🐂 🐂

This is the hour of test and trial for America. By her prowess
and strength, she demonstrated her power to vindicate on foreign
battlefields her conceptions of liberty and justice. Let not her
influence as a mediator between capital and labour be weakened
and her own failure to settle matters of purely domestic concern
be proclaimed to the world. There are those in this country who
threaten direct action to force their will upon a majority. Russia
to-day, with its blood and terror, is a painful object lesson of the
power of minorities. It makes little difference what minority it is;
whether capital or labour, or any other class; no sort of privilege
will ever be permitted to dominate this country. We are a partner-
ship or nothing that is worth while. We are a democracy, where
the majority are the masters, or all the hopes and purposes of the
men who founded this government have been defeated and forgotten. . . .

WOODROW WILSON
EIGHTH STATE-OF-THE-UNION MESSAGE
December 7, 1920

When I addressed myself to performing the duty laid upon
the President by the Constitution to present to you an annual report of the State of the Union, I found my thought dominated by
an immortal sentence of Abraham Lincoln's,

"Let us have faith that right makes might, and in that faith let
us dare to do our duty as we understand it,"—a sentence immortal
because it embodies in a form of utter simplicity and purity the essential faith of the nation, the faith in which it was conceived and
the faith in which it has grown to glory and power. With that faith
and the birth of a nation founded upon it came the hope into the
world that a new order would prevail throughout the affairs of
mankind, an order in which reason and right would take precedence of covetousness and force, and I believe that I express the
wish and purpose of every thoughtful American when I say that
this sentence marks for us in the plainest manner the part we
should play alike in the arrangement of our domestic affairs and
in our exercise of influence upon the affairs of the world. By this
faith, and by this faith alone, can the world be lifted out of its
present confusion and despair. It was this faith which prevailed
over the wicked force of Germany. You will remember that the
beginning of the end of the war came when the German people
found themselves face to face with the conscience of the world and
realized that right was everywhere arrayed against the wrong which
their government was attempting to perpetrate. I think, therefore,
that it is true to say that this was the faith which won the war.
Certainly this was the faith with which our gallant men went into
the field and out upon the seas to make sure of victory.

This is the mission upon which democracy came into the world.
Democracy is an assertion of the rights of the individual to live
and to be treated justly as against any attempt on the part of any
combination of individuals to make laws which will overburden or
which will destroy his equality among his fellows in the matter of
right or privilege, and I think we all realize that the day has come

when democracy is being put upon its final test. . . . This is the time of all others when democracy should prove its purity and its spiritual power to prevail. It is surely the manifest destiny of the United States to lead in the attempt to make this spirit prevail.

✡ ✡ ✡

I have not so much laid before you a series of recommendations, gentlemen, as sought to utter a confession of faith, of the faith in which I was bred and which it is my solemn purpose to stand by until my last fighting day. I believe this to be the faith of America, the faith of the future, and of all the victories which await national action in the days to come, whether in America or elsewhere.

WARREN G. HARDING
(1921–1923)

*"A world hope
is centered
on this Capital City"*

Warren G. Harding was swept into the White House by the election of 1920 on a wave of weariness. The American people were weary of war and its austerity, weary of Europe, weary of the world's worries, and weary of being dinned at by leather-lunged politicians about the dead-duck League of Nations which the Democrats embalmed and displayed as the chief issue of the 1920 presidential campaign.

The people wanted a change. Harding promised them a "return to normalcy," a sort of political Shangri-la where they would never hear another word about reform, reconstruction, crisis, war, Prohibition, or the League of Nations. It sounded most alluring to a huge majority of voting Americans, who promptly deserted the New Freedom band wagon and leaped aboard the Harding Special for Normalcy. Harding also pledged himself to clean up the messy governmental debris left by the war.

Harding was a handsome, poker-loving, small-town newspaper publisher whose handshaking ability, impressive appearance, and willingness to serve his party leaders had carried him far. In 1915 he reached the United States Senate. In 1920 he just fitted the needs of his party's President-makers. His nomination was witch-doctored at Chicago by the classic, smoke-filled-room routine. Taking his cue from McKinley, Harding put on a front-porch campaign from his home at Marion, Ohio. With his "return to normalcy" sideshow he could probably have won without another word. His running mate was quiet, thrifty Governor Calvin Coolidge of Massachusetts, who had crashed the nation's headlines in 1919 by his dramatic call-out of the militia to put Boston under martial law and suppress the Boston policemen's strike. The Harding-Coolidge team won in a landslide over the Democratic James Cox-F. D. Roosevelt ticket.

Harding's Cabinet appointments were unfortunate. Three of them later faced charges of graft and bribery. In 1923, with the greasy Teapot Dome scandals breaking over his head, hoping to clear his own skirts, he headed West on a speaking tour. Harding himself was honest, but some of his friends and federal appointees were not. His trip carried him to the West Coast and up to Alaska. On his return journey he became ill in San Francisco and died August 2, 1923.

During his campaign Harding had promised to promote international peace. He redeemed that pledge by calling on the great powers to convene at Washington for the Limitation of Armament Conference that met in November, 1922. Out of the meeting emerged various peace-promoting pacts. The most important was an agreement to scrap a lot of first-class battleships and freeze the Britain, United States, and Japan battlewagons at a ratio of 5–5–3. It said nothing about building ships in secret. Uncle Sam outsunk all the others; Britain and Japan went only halfway. The second pact promised to halt Japan's aggression in China. The conference was acclaimed by the world. There would be no more war. For a brief spell Harding was hailed as the great peacemaker.

The *chef d'oeuvre* of Harding's tragic half term was the Budget and Accounting Act, his one lasting contribution to improvement in government. Prohibition was in the saddle when Harding took office. Bathtub gin, bootleggers, speakeasies, and "dry-wet" politicians were spurring the nation on to better and bigger "Prohibition."

WARREN G. HARDING
FIRST STATE-OF-THE-UNION MESSAGE
December 6, 1921

It is not my purpose to bring to you a program of world restoration. In the main, such a program must be worked out by the nations more directly concerned. They must themselves turn to the heroic remedies for the menacing conditions under which they are struggling; then we can help, and we mean to help. . . .

It has been perhaps the proudest claim of our American civilization that in dealing with human relationships it has constantly moved toward such justice in distributing the product of human energy that it has improved continuously the economic status of the mass of people. Ours has been a highly productive social organization. On the way up from the elemental stages of society we have eliminated slavery and serfdom and are now far on the way to the elimination of poverty.

Through the eradication of illiteracy and the diffusion of education mankind has reached a stage where we may fairly say that in the United States equality of opportunity has been attained, though all are not prepared to embrace it.

In the case of the corporation which enjoys the privilege of limited liability of stockholders, particularly when engaged in the public service, it is recognized that the outside public has a large concern which must be protected; and so we provide regulations, restrictions, and in some cases detailed supervision. Likewise, in the case of labor organizations, we might well apply similar and equally well-defined principles of regulation and supervision in order to conserve the public's interests as affected by their operations.

While we are thinking of promoting the fortunes of our own people, I am sure there is room in the sympathetic thought of America for fellow human beings who are suffering and dying of starvation in Russia. A severe drought in the Valley of the Volga has plunged 15,000,000 people into grievous famine. Our voluntary agencies are exerting themselves to the utmost to save the lives of children in this area, but it is now evident that unless relief is afforded the loss of life will extend into many millions. America can not be deaf to such a call as that.

We do not recognize the government of Russia, nor tolerate the propaganda which emanates therefrom, but we do not forget the traditions of Russian friendship. We may put aside our consideration of all international politics and fundamental differences in government. The big thing is the call of the suffering and the dying. . . .

🐘 🐘 🐘

. . . I think our tax problems, the tendency of wealth to seek nontaxable investment, and the menacing increase of public debt, Federal, State, and municipal—all justify a proposal to change the Constitution so as to end the issue of nontaxable bonds. No action can change the status of the many billions outstanding, but we can guard against future encouragement of capital's paralysis, while a halt in the growth of public indebtedness would be beneficial throughout our whole land.

Such a change in the Constitution must be very thoroughly considered before submission. There ought to be known what influence it will have on the inevitable refunding of our vast national debt, how it will operate on the necessary refunding of State and municipal debt, how the advantages of Nation over State and municipality, or the contrary, may be avoided. Clearly the States would not ratify to their own apparent disadvantage. I suggest the consideration because the drift of wealth into nontaxable securities is hindering the flow of large capital to our industries, manufacturing, agricultural, and carrying, until we are discouraging the very activities which make our wealth.

Agreeable to your expressed desire and in complete accord with the purposes of the executive branch of the Government, there is in Washington, as you happily know, an International Conference now most earnestly at work on plans for the limitation of armament, a naval holiday, and the just settlement of problems which might develop into causes of international disagreement.

It is easy to believe a world hope is centered on this Capital City. A most gratifying world accomplishment is not improbable.

WARREN G. HARDING
SECOND STATE-OF-THE-UNION MESSAGE
December 8, 1922

It is four years since the World War ended, but the inevitable readjustment of the social and economic order is not more than barely begun. . . .

If the sober and deliberate appraisal of pre-war civilization makes it seem a worth-while inheritance, then with patience and good courage it will be preserved. There never again will be precisely the old order; indeed, I know of no one who thinks it to be desirable. For out of the old order came the war itself, and the new order, established and made secure, never will permit its recurrence.

It is no figure of speech to say we have come to the test of our civilization. The world has been passing—is to-day passing—through a great crisis. The conduct of war itself is not more difficult than the solution of the problems which necessarily follow. . . .

Manifestly, we have need to begin on plans to coordinate all transportation facilities. We should more effectively connect up our rail lines with our carriers by sea. We ought to reap some benefit from the hundreds of millions expended on inland waterways, proving our capacity to utilize as well as expend. We ought to turn the motor truck into a railway feeder and distributor instead of a destroying competitor.

. . . With full recognition of motor-car transportation we must turn it to the most practical use. It can not supersede the railway lines, no matter how generously we afford it highways out of the Public Treasury. If freight traffic by motor were charged with its proper and proportionate share of highway construction, we should find much of it wasteful and more costly than like service by rail. Yet we have paralleled the railways, a most natural line of construction, and thereby taken away from the agency of expected service much of its profitable traffic, for which the taxpayers have been providing the highways, whose cost of maintenance is not yet realized.

. . . Let men who are rending the moral fiber of the Republic through easy contempt for the prohibition law, because they think it restricts their personal liberty, remember that they set the example and breed a contempt for law which will ultimately destroy the Republic.

Constitutional prohibition has been adopted by the Nation. It is the supreme law of the land. In plain speaking, there are conditions relating to its enforcement which savor of nation-wide scandal. It is the most demoralizing factor in our public life.

. . . It is distracting the public mind and prejudicing the judgment of the electorate.

The day is unlikely to come when the eighteenth amendment will be repealed. The fact may as well be recognized and our course adapted accordingly. If the statutory provisions for its enforcement are contrary to deliberate public opinion, which I do not believe, the rigorous and literal enforcement will concentrate public attention on any requisite modification. Such a course conforms with the law and saves the humiliation of the Government and the humiliation of our people before the world, and challenges the destructive forces engaged in widespread violation, official corruption, and individual demoralization.

. . . I believe in the co-operation of the national authority to stimulate, encourage, and broaden the work of the local authorities. But it is the especial obligation of the Federal Government to devise means and effectively assist in the education of the newcomer from foreign lands, so that the level of American education may be made the highest that is humanly possible.

Closely related to this problem of education is the abolition of child labor. Twice Congress has attempted the correction of the evils incident to child employment. The decision of the Supreme Court has put this problem outside the proper domain of Federal regulation until the Constitution is so amended as to give the Congress indubitable authority. I recommend the submission of such an amendment.

Whether all nations signatory ratify all the treaties growing out of the Washington Conference on Limitation of Armament or some withhold approval, the underlying policy of limiting naval armament has the sanction of the larger naval powers, and naval competition is suspended. Of course, unanimous ratification is much to be desired.

The four-power pact, which abolishes every probability of war on the Pacific, has brought new confidence in a maintained peace, and I can well believe it might be made a model for like assurances wherever in the world any common interests are concerned.

CALVIN COOLIDGE

(1923–1929)

*"To reduce war taxes
is to give
every home a better chance"*

Calvin Coolidge was a product of the granite hills of Vermont where he was born. On the night of August 3, 1923, he assumed the presidency in a scene so truly American that it could have been enacted in no other country in the world.

At two-thirty that morning Vice President Coolidge was awakened with the news that President Harding had died at San Francisco. Thirteen minutes later, with his wife at his side, Coolidge was sworn in by his father, Colonel John Coolidge, as the thirtieth President of the United States. The brief ceremony took place by the light of a coal-oil lamp in the parlor of the old family homestead at Plymouth Notch, Vermont, directly across the road from the house in which he was born.

Thrifty, taciturn, gifted with native Yankee wit, Coolidge brought integrity and lots of it to the White House. Behind him lay years of hard work in his slow, sure climb up the political ladder to the governorship of Massachusetts. In 1919 he had become a national figure overnight when he broke the Boston police strike with his stern dictum—"There is no right to strike against the public safety by anybody, anywhere, at any time"—and backed it up by calling out the militia.

From the Harding administration Coolidge inherited a quagmire of corruption in high places rivaling the saddest days of President Grant's

401

regime. Most flagrant of these scandals was the notorious sell-out of the nation's oil reserves at Teapot Dome, Wyoming. With characteristic honesty, President Coolidge rode out the storm and cleaned up the mess. Meanwhile, the postwar boom rose higher and higher. Industry surged and wages soared. Peace reigned. Credit was easy, and speculation, as inevitable as man's urge to bet, mounted sky-high.

The Roaring Twenties reached their best and worst during Coolidge's six years in the White House. Radio, jazz, short skirts, flappers, women's knees, speakeasies, tin Lizzies, tango, and crazy songs—"Yes, We Have No Bananas" for one—ran riot. Happiest achievement of the Coolidge era was Charles Lindbergh's historic solo flight across the Atlantic to Paris.

Meanwhile, hand in hand with Prohibition, the noble experiment, bootlegging and crime flourished like cancer on the body politic. America's status symbol was the hip-pocket flask. With boot and spur and a specious appeal to religion, the temperance groups invaded every nook and cranny of national life. "Wet" and "dry" politicians packed both Houses of Congress.

On the world scene, the Kellogg-Briand Pact was engineered at Paris by Secretary of State Kellogg and Premier Aristide Briand of France. This useless gesture that outlawed war "as an instrument of national policy" was not worth the paper it was written on.

The underlying theme of President Coolidge's six State-of-the-Union Messages was economy in government and reduction of taxes.

CALVIN COOLIDGE
FIRST STATE-OF-THE-UNION MESSAGE
December 6, 1923

For us peace reigns everywhere. We desire to perpetuate it always by granting full justice to others and requiring of others full justice to ourselves. . . . Our country has definitely refused to adopt or ratify the covenant of the League of Nations. I am not proposing any change in this policy; nor is the Senate. The incident, as far as we are concerned, is closed. The League exists as a foreign agency. We hope it will be helpful. But the United States sees no reason to limit its own freedom and independence of action by joining it. We shall do well to recognize this basic fact in all national affairs and govern ourselves accordingly.

Being opposed to war taxes in time of peace I am not in favor of excess profits taxes. A very great service could be rendered through immediate enactment of legislation relievable[ing] the people of taxation. To reduce war taxes is to give every home a better chance.

For seven years the people have borne with uncomplaining courage the tremendous burden of national and local taxation. These must both be reduced. The taxes of the Nation must be reduced now as much as prudence will permit, and expenditures must be reduced accordingly. High taxes reach everywhere and burden everybody. They bear most heavily on the poor. They diminish industry and commerce. They make agriculture unprofitable. They increase rates on transportation. They are a charge on every necessary of life. Of all services which the Congress can render to the country, I have no hesitation in declaring this one to be paramount. To neglect it, to postpone it, to obstruct it by unsound proposals, is to become unworthy of public confidence and untrue to public trust. The country wants this measure to have the right of way over all others.

Another reform which is urgent in our fiscal system is the abolition of the right to issue tax-exempt securities. The existing system not only permits a large amount of the wealth of the nation to escape its just burden, but acts as a continual stimulant to municipal extravagance. All the wealth of the nation ought to contribute its fair share to the expenses of the nation.

🐘 🐘 🐘

It is 100 years since our country announced the Monroe Doctrine. This principle has been ever since, and is now, one of the main foundations of our foreign relations. It must be maintained. But in maintaining it we must not be forgetful that a great change has taken place. We are no longer a weak nation, thinking mainly of defense, dreading foreign imposition. We are great and powerful. New powers bring new responsibilities. Our duty then was to protect ourselves. Added to that our duty now is to help give stability to the world. Our authority among the nations must be represented by justice and mercy. It is necessary not only to have faith, but to make sacrifices for our faith. The spiritual forces of the world make all its final determinations. It is with these voices that America should speak. America has taken her place in the world as a Republic—free, independent, powerful. The best service that can be rendered to humanity is the assurance that this place will be maintained.

CALVIN COOLIDGE
SECOND STATE-OF-THE-UNION MESSAGE
December 3, 1924

Our domestic problems are mostly economic. We have an enormous debt to pay, and we are paying it. We have the high cost of government to diminish, and we are diminishing it. We have a heavy burden of taxation to reduce, and we are reducing it. . . .

In my opinion the Government can do more to remedy the economic ills of the people by a system of rigid economy in public expenditure than can be accomplished through any other action. . . .

CALVIN COOLIDGE
THIRD STATE-OF-THE-UNION MESSAGE
December 7, 1925

It is a fundamental principle of our country that the people are sovereign. While they recognize the undeniable authority of the State they have established as its instrument a Government of limited powers. They hold inviolate in their own hands the jurisdiction over their own freedom and the ownership of their own property. Neither of these can be impaired except by due process of law. The wealth of our country is not public wealth, but private wealth. It does not belong to the Government, it belongs to the people. The Government has no justification in taking private property except for a public purpose. It is always necessary to keep these principles in mind in laying taxes and making of appropriations. No right exists to levy on a dollar, or to order the expenditure of a dollar of the money of the people, except for a necessary public purpose duly authorized by the Constitution. The power over the purse is the power over liberty.

Under the orderly processes of our fundamental institutions the Constitution was lately amended providing for national prohibition. The Congress passed an act for its enforcement, and similar acts have been passed by most of the States. It is the law of the land. It is the duty of all who come under its jurisdiction to observe the spirit of that law, and it is the duty of the Department of Justice and the Treasury Department to enforce it. . . .

CALVIN COOLIDGE
FOURTH STATE-OF-THE-UNION MESSAGE
December 7, 1926

In reporting to the Congress on the State of the Union I find it impossible to characterize it other than one of general peace and prosperity. In some quarters our diplomacy is vexed with difficult and yet unsolved problems, but nowhere are we met with armed conflict. If some occupations and areas are not flourishing, in none does there remain any acute chronic depression. What the country needs is not so much new policies as a steady continuation of those which are already being crowned with such abundant success. . . .

Our present state of prosperity has been greatly promoted by three important causes, one of which is economy resulting in reduction and reform in national taxation. Another is the elimination of many kinds of waste. The third is a general raising of the standards of efficiency. . .

CALVIN COOLIDGE
FIFTH STATE-OF-THE-UNION MESSAGE
December 5, 1927

Being a nation relying not on force, but on fair dealing and good-will to maintain peace with others, we have provided a moderate military force in a form adapted solely to defense. . . . While our army is small prudence requires it should be kept in a high state of efficiency and provided with such supplies as would permit immediate expansion.

Our Navy is likewise a weapon of defense. We have a foreign commerce and ocean lines of trade unsurpassed by any other country. We have outlying territory in two great oceans and long stretches of seacoast studded with the richest cities in the world. We are charged with an international duty of defending the Panama Canal. To meet these responsibilities we need a very substantial sea armament. . . .

We have one treaty secured by an unprecedented attitude of generosity on our part for a limitation of naval armament. Any future treaty of limitation will call on us for more warships. It should be made clear to all the world that lacking a definite agreement the attitude of any other nation is not to be permitted to alter our own policy. Where there is no treaty limitation the size of the Navy which America is to have will be solely for America to determine. No outside influence should enlarge it or diminish it. But it should be known to all that our military power holds no threat of aggrandizement. It is a guaranty of peace and security at home, and when it goes abroad it is an instrument for the protection of the legal rights of our citizens under international law, a refuge in time of disorder, and always the servant of world peace. Where our flag goes the rights of humanity increase. . . .

CALVIN COOLIDGE
SIXTH STATE-OF-THE-UNION MESSAGE
December 4, 1928

We have been coming into a period which may be fairly characterized as a conservation of our national resources. We have substituted for the vicious circle of increasing expenditures, increasing tax rates and diminishing profits the charmed circle of diminishing expenditures, diminishing tax rates and increasing profits. Four times have we made a drastic revision in our internal revenue system, abolishing many taxes and substantially reducing almost all others. One third of the national debt has been paid. . . . This is constructive economy in the highest degree. It is the cornerstone of prosperity. It should not fail to be continued.

🐘 🐘 🐘

One of the most important treaties ever laid before the Senate of the United States will be that which the fifteen nations have recently signed at Paris [the Kellogg-Briand Pact], renouncing war as a national policy and agreeing to resort only to peaceful means for the settlement of international differences. It is the most solemn declaration against war, the most positive adherence to peace, that it is possible for sovereign nations to make. It is a new standard in the world around which can rally the informed and enlightened opinion of nations to prevent their governments from being forced into hostile actions by temporary outbreaks of international animosities. The observance of this covenant, so simple and so straightforward, promises more for the peace of the world than any other agreement ever negotiated among the nations.

HERBERT HOOVER

(1929–1933)

*"Economic depression
cannot be cured by
legislative action or
Executive pronouncement"*

Herbert Hoover was the first President born west of the Mississippi
River. Son of a blacksmith, he first saw light in a two-room farmhouse
at West Branch, Iowa. His family were Quakers. Sturdy, independent,
ambitious, at seventeen he entered Leland Stanford University, earning his way and graduating in mining engineering and geology.

His rise to eminence in his profession was phenomenal. His career
and his much-sought-after services carried him to faraway places all
over the world. At forty, by dint of hard work and scientific application, he had accumulated a fortune.

In 1917, President Wilson selected Hoover as Food Administrator
during World War I. In this work Hoover captured popular imagination more strongly, perhaps, than any other figure of that era. He had
already played the top role in organizing and heading the Commission
for the Relief of Belgium. As Secretary of Commerce under Presidents
Harding and Coolidge, his nomination by the Republicans in 1928
was virtually assured when President Coolidge brushed aside the
nomination with his succinct, "I do not choose to run for President
in nineteen twenty-eight."

In this election Hoover broke the Solid South, the second Repub-
lican nominee to do so. He carried five states below the Mason and
Dixon Line. When at fifty-four, President Hoover entered the White
House on March 4, 1929, the nation's business picture was the rosiest

in a generation. The economic goose hung high, that is, until a certain Black Thursday, October 24, 1929, when the spiraling stock market went into a tailspin and crashed with a universal roar. The long speculative boom collapsed, carrying with it the economy, first of America and then of the world. With promises of "prosperity just around the corner" the nation's economy kept fading away like a jack-o'-lantern.

President Hoover's State-of-the-Union Messages deal mostly with stemming the Depression that swept the nation's economy from bad to worse. Farm prices sank to record low levels, business failures ran as high as thirty thousand a month, millions of unemployed walked the streets. Breadlines lengthened. Crops wilted under the impact of prolonged drought. By the end of Hoover's term more than five thousand banks had closed their doors.

Of the many stop-gap measures offered by Hoover to cope with the bottomless prostration of business, the Reconstruction Finance Corporation was the most far-reaching. Before it passed into limbo in 1952, this agency had loaned billions of dollars to help tide over and resuscitate banks, states, railroads, cities, and businesses large and small.

Today, Herbert Hoover, as ex-President for thirty years, has outdistanced ex-President John Adams, who up to five years ago held the record for having lived the longest time after holding the presidential office. John Adams, however, still holds the presidential longevity record—he was ninety-one when he died, two years older than Hoover is now in 1963.

HERBERT HOOVER
FIRST STATE-OF-THE-UNION MESSAGE
December 2, 1929

The country has enjoyed a large degree of prosperity and sound progress during the past year with steady improvement in methods of production and distribution and consequent advancement in the standards of living.

. . . The long upward trend of fundamental progress, however, gave rise to overoptimism as to profits, which translated itself into a wave of uncontrolled speculation in securities, resulting in diversion of capital from business to the stock market and the inevitable crash. The natural consequence has been a reduction in the consumption of luxuries and seminecessities by those who have met with losses, and a number of persons thrown temporarily out of employment. Prices of agricultural products dealt in upon the great markets have been affected in sympathy with the stock crash.

Fortunately, the Federal Reserve System had taken measures to strengthen the position against the day when speculation would break, which, together with the strong position of the banks, has carried the credit system through the crisis without impairment. The capital which has hitherto been absorbed in stock-market loans for speculative purposes is now returning to normal channels of business. There has been no inflation in the prices of commodities. . . .

The sudden threat of unemployment and especially the recollection of the economic consequences of previous crashes under a much less secured financial system created unwarranted pessimism and fear. It was recalled that past storms of a similar character had resulted in retrenchment of construction, reduction of wages and laying off of workers. The natural result was the tendency of business agencies throughout the country to pause in their plans and proposals for continuation and extension of their businesses, and this hesitation unchecked could in itself intensify into a depression with widespread unemployment and suffering.

I have, therefore, instituted systematic voluntary measures of cooperation with business institutions and with State and municipal authorities to make certain that fundamental businesses of the country shall continue as usual, that wages and therefore consuming power shall not be reduced, and that a special effort shall be made to expand construction work in order to assist in equalizing other deficits in employment. . . . We have canvassed the Federal government and instituted measures of prudent expansion in such work that should be helpful.

I am convinced that through these measures we have reestablished confidence. Wages should remain stable. A large degree of industrial unemployment and suffering which would otherwise have occurred has been prevented. Agricultural prices have reflected the returning confidence. The measures taken must be vigorously pursued until normal conditions are restored.

HERBERT HOOVER
SECOND STATE-OF-THE-UNION MESSAGE
December 2, 1930

During the past twelve months we have suffered with other
nations from economic depression. The origins of this depression
lie to some extent within our own borders through a speculative
period which diverted capital and energy into speculation rather
than constructive enterprise. Had overspeculation in securities been
the only forces operating we should have seen recovery many
months ago. . . .

Other deep-seated causes have been in action, chiefly the world-
wide over-production beyond the demand of prosperous times
. . . world-wide causes, overproduction of certain commodities
abroad, financial crises in many countries, political agitation in
Asia, revolutions in South America, political unrest in some European States, methods of sale by Russia of her agricultural exports.
In the larger view the major forces of depression lie outside the
United States. Fear and apprehension are created by these outside
forces.

🐘 🐘 🐘

. . . We should remember that these occasions have been met
many times before, that they are but temporary, that our country is
today stronger and richer in resources, in equipment, in skill, than
ever in its history. We are in an extraordinary degree self-sustaining and we will overcome world influences and will lead the march
to prosperity as we have always done hitherto.

Economic depression cannot be cured by legislative action or
Executive pronouncement. Economic wounds must be healed by
the action of the cells of the economic body, the producers and
consumers themselves. Recovery can be expedited and its effects
mitigated by cooperative action. . . .

We have as a nation a definite duty to see that no deserving person in our country suffers from hunger and cold. I have set up a
more extensive organization to relieve individual distress. The
Federal Government is engaged upon the greatest program of im-

provement in all our history. . . . I favor still further temporary
expansion of these activities in aid to unemployment. . . . We
have had a most severe drought. . . . In order that the government may meet its full obligation toward our countrymen in distress I recommend an appropriation for purpose of seed and
feed. . . . The Red Cross can relieve the cases of individual distress.

HERBERT HOOVER
THIRD STATE-OF-THE-UNION MESSAGE
December 8, 1931

The chief influence affecting the State of the Union during
the past year has been the continued world-wide economic disturbance. Our national concern has been to meet the emergencies
it has created for us and to lay the foundations for recovery. . . .

The economic depression has deepened in every part of the
world. In many countries political instability, excessive armaments,
debts, governmental expenditures and taxes have resulted in revolutions, in unbalanced budgets and monetary collapse and financial
panics, in dumping goods upon world markets, and in diminished
consumption of commodities.

Within two years there have been revolutions or acute social disorders in nineteen countries, embracing more than half the population of the world. Ten countries have been unable to meet their
external obligations. In fourteen countries, embracing a quarter of
the world's population, former monetary standards have been temporarily abandoned. In numbers of countries there have been acute
financial panics or compulsory restraints upon banking. These disturbances have many roots in the dislocations from the World
War. Every one of them has reacted upon us. They have sharply
affected the markets and prices of our agricultural and industrial
products. They have increased unemployment and greatly embarrassed our financial and credit system.

As our difficulties during the past year have plainly originated in
large degree from these sources, any effort to bring about our own

recuperation has dictated the necessity of co-operation by us with other nations in reasonable effort to restore world confidence and economic stability.

🐘 🐘 🐘

The first requirement of confidence and economic recovery is the financial stability of the United States Government. . . . We must have insistent and determined reduction in government expenses. We must face a temporary increase in taxes.

🐘 🐘 🐘

Our people have a right to a banking system in which their deposits shall be safeguarded and the flow of credit less subject to storms. The need of a sounder system is plainly shown by the extent of bank failures. I recommend the prompt improvement of the banking laws. Changed financial conditions and commercial practices must be met. . . .

HERBERT HOOVER
FOURTH STATE-OF-THE-UNION MESSAGE
December 6, 1932

Our major difficulties during the past two years find their origins in the shocks from economic collapse abroad, which in turn are the aftermath of the Great War. If we are to secure rapid and assured recovery and protection for the future we must cooperate with foreign nations in many measures.

🐘 🐘 🐘

We are participating in the formulation of a World Economic Conference, successful results from which would contribute much to advance in agricultural prices, employment and business. Currency depreciation and correlated forces have contributed greatly to decrease in price levels. Moreover, from these origins rise most of the destructive trade barriers now stifling the commerce of the world. We could by successful action increase security and expand trade through stability in international exchange and monetary values. By such action world confidence could be restored. . . .

The creation of the Reconstruction Finance Corporation and the amendments to the Federal Reserve Act served to defend the nation in a great crisis. They are not remedies: they are relief. It is inconceivable that the Reconstruction Corporation, which has extended aid to nearly 6000 institutions and is manifestly but a temporary device, can go on indefinitely.

. . . There is no reason why a solution should not be found at the present session of Congress. Inflation of currency or government conduct of banking can have no part in these reforms. Parallel with reform in the banking laws must be changes in the Federal Farm Loan Banking System and in the Joint Stock Land Banks. Some of these changes should be directed to permanent improvement and some to emergency aid to our people where they wish to fight to save their farms and homes.

I wish again to emphasize this view—that these widespread banking reforms are a national necessity and are the first requisites for further recovery in agriculture and business. They should have immediate consideration as steps greatly needed to further recovery.

FRANKLIN DELANO ROOSEVELT
(1933–1945)

*"A date
which will live
in infamy"*

Franklin Delano Roosevelt, thirty-first President of the United States, was, like Jefferson, a tradition-breaker. His reelection in 1940, after two terms in the White House, and again in 1944, shattered the long-mooted, no-third-term tradition established by Washington, relayed on by his successors, and sought after unsuccessfully by Ulysses Grant and Theodore Roosevelt.

Gifted with a superb, lyrical voice and an intimate, heart-reaching style of delivery, Franklin Roosevelt combined with these the added genius of committing his convictions and ideas to words that seldom, if ever, overshot the heads of the millions of citizens who eagerly hovered before their radio sets to drink in his State-of-the-Union Messages and Fireside Chats.

When Roosevelt took office in 1933, economic paralysis held the nation in a crushing vise. The election year 1932 saw thirteen million unemployed wondering where they would get the next meal. To carry out his New Deal for the "Forgotten Man," he was speedily endowed by Congress with the broadest peacetime powers ever granted a President. Thus equipped, he plunged into the task of leading the nation out of the depression that had followed the stock-market crash of 1929.

415

Later, as Commander in Chief of America's fighting forces and armed with almost dictatorial powers, he first turned the nation into the Arsenal of Democracy and then hurled her whole might into the struggle against Axis aggression.

His State-of-the-Union Messages reflect virtually every significant event and act of his twelve years in the White House. They are clothed for the most part in simple but moving rhetoric and imagery.

His First State-of-the-Union Message (1934) reminded the nation that he intended to carry out the "mandate from the whole people" in building a new and better national structure on the ruins of the past. He stressed the word "recovery," as he was often to do in later messages. He said the seeds for recovery were sown. If the nation cultivated the sprouting plant, full economic recovery must follow. In his 1935 message he reminded the nation to be patient, that change was the order of the day.

In his 1936 message he struck out at his critics and those who sought to block his policies and plans. It led him to repeat that he had a mandate from the people, whose thousands of letters urged him to keep up what he was doing.

His 1937 message was delivered to the first Congress to assemble under the Twentieth (Lame Duck) Amendment to the Constitution, which pushed the opening of the new Congress from the traditional March 4 to January 3 and the inauguration of the newly elected President from March 4 to January 20. Congress was overwhelmingly Democratic. For the first time since James Monroe (114 years), a President had the advantage of a majority of his own party in both houses of Congress for eight years.

Roosevelt's 1938 message, delivered against the backdrop of the Recession of 1937, stressed the necessity of increasing national buying power. He added, "I do not propose to let the people down."

In 1939, President Roosevelt blasted off his first warning to dictator nations; he saw "storm signals from across the sea." The year 1938 had witnessed ominous events abroad—Germany had annexed Austria; Hitler and Mussolini had solidified the Rome-Berlin Axis; Japan had extended her grip on China; Czechoslovakia was partitioned; Hitler and his minions were boasting of force enough to overrun central and eastern Europe. The outbreak of World War II was still eight months off.

Without mincing words, Roosevelt struck directly at the aggressor nations and their "new philosophy of force." He warned that force would be met with force, and he urged his own country to arm quickly.

His 1940 message again warned that the well-being of 130,000,000 Americans was deeply affected by the "well-being or the ill-being" of the rest of the world. Defense was the theme in this message.

His January 6, 1941, message was perhaps the most significant and far-reaching of his twelve State-of-the-Union Messages. In stirring words he enunciated his justly celebrated "Four Essential Human Freedoms," on which future world security must be based. In unequivocal words he defied the Axis powers, denounced appeasement, and summoned the nation to all-out aid for the fighting democracies. Unconsciously, perhaps, he foretold the Pearl Harbor sneak attack and debacle in these prophetic words: "When the dictators are ready to make war upon us, they will not wait for an act of war on our part."

Then came Monday, December 8, 1941. Ten thousand miles from the Capitol, death and desolation bespoke the fury of Sunday's sudden Japanese air attack at Pearl Harbor in the Hawaiian Islands. The core and pride of the American Pacific fleet wallowed in crumpled masses of steel at the bottom of the harbor. More than two thousand American soldiers, sailors, and civilians lay dead or wounded. At noon this day members of Congress, Cabinet, and Supreme Court met in grim, solemn assemblage in the House chamber. At precisely 12:23 P.M., President Roosevelt, stern-faced and pale, entered the chamber and walked slowly down the center aisle. Across the nation 130,000,000 people hung over their radios. Mounting the rostrum, he turned and faced the chamber. In a voice clear but shot with emotion he asked that the United States declare war against the Japanese empire. He spoke exactly six minutes and thirty seconds. It is the shortest War Message on record.

On January 6, 1942, thirty days after Pearl Harbor and America's entrance into the global conflict, President Roosevelt appeared before Congress with a deeply stirring call to arms. By now, Japan had overrun most of the American bases in the Pacific and was invading the Philippines.

Forty-five times he was interrupted by applause as he delivered his State-of-the-Union Message on January 7, 1943. The galleries were seas of color with diplomats from all the United Nations in full, brilliant regalia, listening eagerly as President Roosevelt unfolded his hopes and aspirations for the postwar world that could come only after utter victory.

On January 11, 1944, in his Eleventh State-of-the-Union Message, President Roosevelt gave a blueprint of his legislative program to help win the war. Calling on Congress to explore what he called the new Economic Bill of Rights, he said, "Our fighting men abroad and their families at home expect such a program and have the right to insist upon it." But his proposed postwar National Service Act brought sharp controversy that doomed its passage.

FRANKLIN DELANO ROOSEVELT (1933–1945)
FIRST STATE-OF-THE-UNION MESSAGE
January 3, 1934

Mr. President, Mr. Speaker, Senators, and Representatives in Congress, I come before you at the opening of the regular session of the Seventy-third Congress not to make requests for special or detailed items of legislation; I come, rather, to counsel with you, who, like myself, have been selected to carry out a mandate of the whole people, in order that without partisanship you and I may cooperate to continue the restoration of our national well-being and, equally important, to build on the ruins of the past a new structure designed better to meet the present problems of modern civilization.

☙ ☙ ☙

Civilization cannot go back; civilization must not stand still. We have undertaken new methods. It is our task to perfect, to improve, to alter when necessary, but in all cases to go forward. To consolidate what we are doing, to make our economic and social structure capable of dealing with modern life, is the joint task of the legislative, the judicial, and the executive branches of the National Government.

Without regard to party, the overwhelming majority of our people seek a greater opportunity for humanity to prosper and find happiness. They recognize that human welfare has not increased, and does not increase, through mere materialism and luxury, but that it does progress through integrity, unselfishness, responsibility, and justice.

In the past few months, as a result of our action, we have demanded of many citizens that they surrender certain licenses to do as they please in their business relationships; but we have asked this in exchange for the protection which the state can give against exploitation by their fellow men or by combinations of their fellow men.

🐐 🐐 🐐

The adoption of the Twenty-first Amendment should give material aid to the elimination of those new forms of crime which came from the illegal traffic in liquor.

I shall continue to regard it as my duty to use whatever means may be necessary to supplement State, local, and private agencies for the relief of suffering caused by unemployment. With respect to this question, I have recognized the dangers inherent in the direct giving of relief and have sought the means to provide not mere relief but the opportunity for useful and remunerative work. We shall, in the process of recovery, seek to move as rapidly as possible from direct relief to publicly supported work and from that to the rapid restoration of private employment.

🐐 🐐 🐐

We have plowed the furrow and planted the good seed; the hard beginning is over. If we would reap the full harvest, we must cultivate the soil where this good seed is sprouting and the plant is reaching up to mature growth. . . .

FRANKLIN DELANO ROOSEVELT
SECOND STATE-OF-THE-UNION MESSAGE
January 4, 1935

We have undertaken a new order of things, yet we progress to it under the framework and in the spirit and intent of the American Constitution. We have proceeded throughout the Nation a measurable distance on the road toward this new order. Materially, I can report to you substantial benefits to our agricultural population, increased industrial activity, and profits to our merchants. Of equal moment, there is evident a restoration of that spirit of confidence and faith which marks the American character. . . .

Throughout the world change is the order of the day. In every nation economic problems, long in the making, have brought crises of many kinds for which the masters of old practice and theory were unprepared. In most nations social justice, no longer a distant ideal, has become a definite goal, and ancient governments are beginning to heed the call.

Thus, the American people do not stand alone in the world in their desire for change. We seek it through tested liberal traditions, through processes which retain all of the deep essentials of that republican form of representative government first given to a troubled world by the United States.

🦌   🦌   🦌

We find our population suffering from old inequalities, little changed by past sporadic remedies. In spite of our efforts and in spite of our talk we have not weeded out the overprivileged and we have not effectively lifted up the underprivileged. No wise man has any intention of destroying what is known as the "profit motive," because by the profit motive we mean the right by work to earn a decent livelihood for ourselves and for our families.

We have, however, a clear mandate from the people, that Americans must forswear that conception of the acquisition of wealth which, through excessive profits, creates undue private power over private affairs and, to our misfortune, over public affairs as well. In building toward this end we do not destroy ambition, nor do we seek to divide our wealth into equal shares on stated occasions. We continue to recognize the greater ability of some to earn more than others. But we do assert that the ambition of the individual to obtain for him and his a proper security, a reasonable leisure, and a decent living throughout life is an ambition to be preferred to the appetite for great wealth and great power.

In defining immediate factors which enter into our quest, I have spoken to the Congress and the people of three great divisions:

First. The security of a livelihood through the better use of the national resources of the land in which we live.

Second. The security against the major hazards and vicissitudes of life.

Third. The security of decent homes.

🐴 🐴 🐴

But the stark fact before us is that great numbers still remain unemployed. A large proportion of these unemployed and their dependents have been forced on the relief rolls. The burden on the Federal Government has grown with great rapidity. We have here a human as well as an economic problem. When humane considerations are concerned, Americans give them precedence. The lessons of history, confirmed by the evidence immediately before me, show conclusively that continued dependence upon relief induces a spiritual and moral disintegration fundamentally destructive to the national fiber. To dole out relief in this way is to administer a narcotic, a subtle destroyer of the human spirit. It is inimical to the dictates of sound policy. It is in violation of the traditions of America. Work must be found for able-bodied but destitute workers.

The Federal Government must and shall quit this business of relief.

I am not willing that the vitality of our people be further sapped by the giving of cash, of market baskets, of a few hours of weekly work cutting grass, raking leaves, or picking up papers in the public parks. We must preserve not only the bodies of the unemployed from destitution but also their self-respect, their self-reliance, and courage and determination.

🐴 🐴 🐴

I cannot with candor tell you that general international relationships outside the borders of the United States are improved. On the surface of things many old jealousies are resurrected, old passions aroused; new strivings for armament and power, in more than one land, rear their ugly heads. I hope that calm counsel and constructive leadership will provide the steadying influence and the time necessary for the coming of new and more practical forms of representative government throughout the world wherein privilege and power will occupy a lesser place and world welfare a greater. . . .

FRANKLIN DELANO ROOSEVELT
THIRD STATE-OF-THE-UNION MESSAGE
January 3, 1936

You will remember on that 4th of March 1933 the world picture was an image of substantial peace. International consultation and widespread hope for the bettering of relations between the nations gave to all of us a reasonable expectation that the barriers to mutual confidence, to increased trade, and to the peaceful settlement of disputes could be progressively removed. In fact, my only reference to the field of world policy in that address was in these words: "I would dedicate this Nation to the policy of the good neighbor—the neighbor who resolutely respects himself and, because he does so, respects the rights of others—a neighbor who respects his obligations and respects the sanctity of his agreements in and with a world of neighbors."

🐴 🐴 🐴

This policy of the good neighbor among the Americas is no longer a hope—no longer an objective remaining to be accomplished—it is a fact, active, present, pertinent, and effective. In this achievement every American nation takes an understanding part. There is neither war, nor rumor of war, nor desire for war. The inhabitants of this vast area, 250,000,000 strong, spreading more than 8,000 miles from the Arctic to the Antarctic, believe in, and propose to follow, the policy of the good neighbor; and they wish with all their heart that the rest of the world might do likewise.

The rest of the world—ah! there is the rub.

Were I today to deliver an inaugural address to the people of the United States, I could not limit my comments on world affairs to one paragraph. With much regret I should be compelled to devote the greater part to world affairs. Since the summer of that same year of 1933 the temper and the purposes of the rulers of many of the great populations in Europe and Asia have not pointed the way either to peace or to good will among men. Not only have peace and good will among men grown more remote in those areas of the earth during this period, but a point has been reached where the people of the Americas must take cognizance of growing ill will, of marked trends toward aggression, of increasing armaments, of shortening tempers—a situation which has in it many of the elements that lead to the tragedy of general war.

🐃 🐃 🐃

I cannot better end this message on the state of the Union than by repeating the words of a wise philosopher at whose feet I sat many years ago:

"What great crises teach all men whom the example and counsel of the brave inspire is this lesson: Fear not, view all the tasks of life as sacred, have faith in the triumph of the ideal, give daily all that you have to give, be loyal and rejoice whenever you find yourselves part of a great ideal enterprise. You, at this moment, have the honor to belong to a generation whose lips are touched by fire. You live in a land that now enjoys the blessings of peace. But let nothing human be wholly alien to you. The human race now passes through one of its great crises. New ideas, new issues— a new call for men to carry on the work of righteousness, of charity, of courage, of patience, and of loyalty. However memory brings back this moment to your minds, let it be able to say to you: That was a great moment. It was the beginning of a new era. This world in its crisis called for volunteers, for men of faith in life, of patience in service, of charity, and of insight. I responded to the call however I could. I volunteered to give myself to my Master— the cause of humane and brave living. I studied, I loved, I labored, unsparingly and hopefully, to be worthy of my generation."

FRANKLIN DELANO ROOSEVELT
FOURTH STATE-OF-THE-UNION MESSAGE
WASHINGTON, D.C., *January 6, 1937*

For the first time in our national history a President delivers his Annual Message to a new Congress within a fortnight of the expiration of his term of office. While there is no change in the Presidency this year, change will occur in future years. It is my belief that under this new constitutional practice, the President should in every fourth year, in so far as seems reasonable, review the existing state of our national affairs and outline broad future problems, leaving specific recommendations for future legislation to be made by the President about to be inaugurated.

🦌 🦌 🦌

In March, 1933, the problems which faced our Nation and which only our national Government had the resources to meet were more serious even than appeared on the surface.

It was not only that the visible mechanism of economic life had broken down. More disturbing was the fact that long neglect of the needs of the underprivileged had brought too many of our people to the verge of doubt as to the successful adaptation of our historic traditions to the complex modern world. In that lay a challenge to our democratic form of Government itself.

Ours was the task to prove that democracy could be made to function in the world of today as effectively as in the simpler world of a hundred years ago. . . .

🦌 🦌 🦌

That cooperation of the past four years between the Congress and the President has aimed at the fulfillment of a twofold policy; first, economic recovery through many kinds of assistance to agriculture, industry and banking; and, second, deliberate improvement in the personal security and opportunity of the great mass of our people.

The recovery we sought was not to be merely temporary. It was to be a recovery protected from the causes of previous disasters.

Nor was the recovery we sought merely a purposeless whirring of machinery. It is not enough that the wheels turn. They must carry us in the direction of a greater satisfaction in life for the average man. . . .

FRANKLIN DELANO ROOSEVELT
FIFTH STATE-OF-THE-UNION MESSAGE
January 3, 1938

In spite of the determination of this Nation for peace, it has become clear that acts and policies of nations in other parts of the world have far-reaching effects not only upon their immediate neighbors but also on us.

. . . In a world where stable civilization is actually threatened, it becomes the responsibility of each nation which strives for peace at home and peace with and among others to be strong enough to assure the observance of those fundamentals of peaceful solution of conflicts which are the only ultimate basis for orderly existence.

Resolute in our determination to respect the rights of others, and to command respect for the rights of ourselves, we must keep ourselves adequately strong in self-defense.

🐾 🐾 🐾

We have raised the Nation's income from $38,000,000,000 in the year 1932 to about $68,000,000,000 in the year 1937. Our goal, our objective, is to raise it to ninety or one hundred billion dollars. . . .

To many who have pleaded with me for an immediate balancing of the budget by a sharp curtailment or even elimination of Government functions, I have asked the question, "What present expenditures would you reduce or eliminate?" And the invariable answer has been, "That is not my business; I know nothing of the details, but I am sure that it could be done." That is not what you or I would call helpful citizenship.

On only one point do most of them have a suggestion. They think that relief for the unemployed by the giving of work is wasteful, and when I pin them down I discover that at heart they are actually in favor of substituting a dole in place of useful work. To that neither I nor, I am confident, the Senators and Representatives in the Congress will ever consent.

⊠ ⊠ ⊠

As a nation we have rejected any radical revolutionary program. For a permanent correction of grave weaknesses in our economic system we have relied on new applications of old democratic processes. It is not necessary to recount what has been accomplished in preserving the homes and livelihood of millions of workers on farms and in cities, in reconstructing a sound banking and credit system, in reviving trade and industry, in reestablishing security of life and property. All we need today is to look upon the fundamental, sound economic conditions to know that this business recession causes more perplexity than fear on the part of most people and to contrast our prevailing mental attitude with the terror and despair of five years ago.

Government has a final responsibility for the well-being of its citizenship. If private cooperative endeavor fails to provide work for willing hands and relief for the unfortunate, those suffering hardship from no fault of their own have a right to call upon the Government for aid; and a government worthy of its name must make fitting response. . . .

That presupposes on the part of the representatives of the people, a program, its enactment and its administration.

Not because of the pledges of party programs alone, not because of the clear policies of the past five years, but chiefly because of the need of national unity in ending the mistakes of the past and meeting the necessities of today, we must carry on.

I do not propose to let the people down.

I am sure the Congress of the United States will not let the people down.

FRANKLIN DELANO ROOSEVELT
SIXTH STATE-OF-THE-UNION MESSAGE
WASHINGTON, D.C., *January 4, 1939*

In reporting on the state of the Nation, I have felt it necessary on previous occasions to advise the Congress of disturbance abroad and of the need of putting our own house in order in the face of storm signals from across the seas. As this Seventy-sixth Congress opens there is need for further warning.

A war which threatened to envelop the world in flames has been averted; but it has become increasingly clear that world peace is not assured.

All about us rage undeclared wars—military and economic. All about us grow more deadly armaments—military and economic.

Storms from abroad directly challenge three institutions indispensable to Americans, now as always. The first is religion. It is the source of the other two—democracy and international good faith.

🦌   🦌   🦌

Where freedom of religion has been attacked, the attack has come from sources opposed to democracy. Where democracy has been overthrown, the spirit of free worship has disappeared. And where religion and democracy have vanished, good faith and reason in international affairs have given way to strident ambition and brute force. . . .

There comes a time in the affairs of men when they must prepare to defend, not their homes alone, but the tenets of faith and humanity on which their churches, their governments and their very civilization are founded. . . .

We know what might happen to us of the United States if the new philosophies of force were to encompass the other continents and invade our own. . . . That Hemisphere, that peace, and that ideal we propose to do our share in protecting against storms from any quarter. Our people and our resources are pledged to secure that protection. From that determination no American flinches.

🦌   🦌   🦌

For if any government bristling with implements of war insists on policies of force, weapons of defense give the only safety. . . .

We have learned that survival cannot be guaranteed by arming after the attack begins—for there is new range and speed to offense. . . .

And we have learned something else—the old, old lesson that probability of attack is mightily decreased by the assurance of an ever ready defense. Since 1931, nearly eight years ago, world events of thunderous import have moved with lightning speed. During these eight years many of our people clung to the hope that the innate decency of mankind would protect the unprepared who showed their innate trust in mankind. Today we are all wiser —and sadder.

✳ ✳ ✳

In meeting the troubles of the world we must meet them as one people—with a unity born of the fact that for generations those who have come to our shores, representing many kindreds and tongues, have been welded by common opportunity into a united patriotism. If another form of government can present a united front in its attack on a democracy, the attack must and will be met by a united democracy. Such a democracy can and must exist in the United States.

✳ ✳ ✳

Once I prophesied that this generation of Americans had a rendezvous with destiny. That prophecy comes true. To us much is given; more is expected.

This generation will "nobly save or meanly lose the last best hope of earth. . . ." The way is plain, peaceful, generous, just— a way which if followed the world will forever applaud and God must forever bless.

FRANKLIN DELANO ROOSEVELT
SEVENTH STATE-OF-THE-UNION MESSAGE
January 3, 1940

As the Congress reassembles, the impact of wars abroad makes it natural to approach "the state of the union" through a discussion of foreign affairs. . . .

The social and economic forces which have been mismanaged abroad until they have resulted in revolution, dictatorship, and war are the same as those which we here are struggling to adjust peacefully at home.

You are well aware that dictatorships—and the philosophy of force which justifies and accompanies dictatorships—have originated in almost every case in the necessity for drastic action to improve internal conditions where democratic action for one reason or another has failed to respond to modern needs and modern demands.

It was with farsighted wisdom that the framers of the Constitution brought together in one magnificent phrase three great concepts—"common defense," "general welfare," and "domestic tranquility."

More than a century and a half later we still believe with them that our best defense is the promotion of our general welfare and domestic tranquility.

In previous messages to the Congress I have repeatedly warned that, whether we like it or not, the daily lives of American citizens will, of necessity, feel the shock of events on other continents. This is no longer mere theory, for it has been definitely proved by the facts of yesterday and today.

Already the crash of swiftly moving events over the earth has made us all think with a longer view. Fortunately, that thinking cannot be controlled by partisanship. The time is long past when any political party or any particular group can curry and capture public favor by labeling itself the "peace party" or the "peace bloc." That label belongs to the whole United States and to every right-thinking man, woman, and child within it.

🐂   🐂   🐂

We must look ahead and see the possibilities for our children if the rest of the world comes to be dominated by concentrated force alone—even though today we are a very great and a very powerful nation.

We must look ahead and see the effect on our own future if all the small nations throughout the world have their independence snatched from them or become mere appendages to relatively vast and powerful military systems.

We must look ahead and see the kind of lives our children would have to lead if a large part of the rest of the world were compelled to worship the god imposed by a military ruler, or were forbidden to worship God at all; if the rest of the world were forbidden to read and hear the facts—the daily news of their own and other nations—if they were deprived of the truth which makes men free.

We must look ahead and see the effect on our future generations if world trade is controlled by any nation or group of nations which sets up that control through military force.

It is, of course, true that the record of past centuries includes destruction of small nations, enslavement of peoples, and building of empires on the foundation of force. But wholly apart from the greater international morality which we seek today, we recognize the practical fact that with modern weapons and modern conditions, modern man can no longer live a civilized life if we are to go back to the practice of wars and conquests of the seventeenth and eighteenth centuries.

Summing up this need of looking ahead, and in words of common sense and good American citizenship, I hope that we will have fewer American ostriches in our midst. It is not good for the ultimate health of ostriches to bury their heads in the sand.

Only an ostrich would look upon these wars through the eyes of cynicism or ridicule.

🐐 🐐 🐐

I emphasize the leadership which this Nation can take when the time comes for a renewal of world peace. Such an influence will be greatly weakened if this Government becomes a dog in the manger of trade selfishness.

The first President of the United States warned us against entangling foreign alliances. The present President of the United States subscribes to and follows that precept.

🐿 🐿 🐿

As will appear in the annual Budget tomorrow, the only important increase in any part of the Budget is the estimate for national defense. Practically all other important items show a reduction. Therefore, in the hope that we can continue in these days of increasing economic prosperity to reduce the Federal deficit, I am asking the Congress to levy sufficient additional taxes to meet the emergency spending for national defense.

Behind the Army and Navy, of course, lies our ultimate line of defense—"the general welfare" of our people. We cannot report, despite all the progress we have made in our domestic problems—despite the fact that production is back to 1929 levels—that all our problems are solved. The fact of unemployment of millions of men and women remains a symptom of a number of difficulties in our economic system not yet adjusted.

While the number of the unemployed has decreased, while their immediate needs for food and clothing—as far as the Federal Government is concerned—have been largely met, while their morale has been kept alive by giving them useful public work, we have not yet found a way to employ the surplus of our labor which the efficiency of our industrial processes has created.

🐿 🐿 🐿

The permanent security of America in the present crisis does not lie in armed force alone. What we face is a set of world-wide forces of disintegration—vicious, ruthless, destructive of all the moral, religious, and political standards which mankind, after centuries of struggle, has come to cherish most. . . .

We must as a united people keep ablaze on this continent the flames of human liberty, of reason, of democracy, and of fair play as living things to be preserved for the better world that is to come. . . .

FRANKLIN DELANO ROOSEVELT
EIGHTH STATE-OF-THE-UNION MESSAGE
WASHINGTON, D.C., *January 6, 1941*

I address you, the Members of the Seventy-seventh Congress, at a moment unprecedented in the history of the Union. I use the word "unprecedented," because at no previous time has American security been as seriously threatened from without as it is today. . . .

Every realist knows that the democratic way of life is at this moment being directly assailed in every part of the world—assailed either by arms, or by secret spreading of poisonous propaganda, by those who seek to destroy unity and promote discord in nations still at peace.

During sixteen months this assault has blotted out the whole pattern of democratic life in an appalling number of independent nations, great and small. The assailants are still on the march, threatening other nations, great and small.

🐃 🐃 🐃

Armed defense of democratic existence is now being gallantly waged in four continents. If that defense fails, all the population and all the resources of Europe, Asia, Africa and Australasia will be dominated by the conquerors. The total of those populations and their resources greatly exceeds the sum total of the population and resources of the whole of the Western Hemisphere—many times over.

🐃 🐃 🐃

But we learn much from the lessons of the past years in Europe—particularly the lesson of Norway, whose essential seaports were captured by treachery and surprise built up over a series of years.

The first phase of the invasion of this Hemisphere would not be the landing of regular troops. The necessary strategic points would be occupied by secret agents and their dupes—and great numbers of them are already here, and in Latin America.

As long as the aggressor nations maintain the offensive, they—

not we—will choose the time and the place and the method of their attack.

That is why the future of all American Republics is today in serious danger.

🐂   🐂   🐂

That is why this Annual Message to the Congress is unique in our history.

Our national policy is this:

First, by an impressive expression of the public will and without regard to partisanship, we are committed to all-inclusive national defense.

Second, by an impressive expression of the public will and without regard to partisanship, we are committed to full support of all those resolute peoples, everywhere, who are resisting aggression and are thereby keeping war away from our Hemisphere. . . .

Therefore, the immediate need is a swift and driving increase in our armament production. . . .

I also ask this Congress for authority and for funds sufficient to manufacture additional munitions and war supplies of many kinds, to be turned over to those nations which are now in actual war with aggressor nations.

Our most useful and immediate role is to act as an arsenal for them as well as for ourselves. They do not need manpower. They do need billions of dollars' worth of the weapons of defense. . . .

In fulfillment of this purpose we will not be intimidated by the threats of dictators that they will regard as a breach of international law and as an act of war our aid to the democracies which dare to resist their aggression. Such aid is not an act of war, even if a dictator should unilaterally proclaim it so to be.

When the dictators are ready to make war upon us, they will not wait for an act of war on our part. They did not wait for Norway or Belgium or the Netherlands to commit an act of war.

. . . The happiness of future generations of Americans may well depend upon how effective and how immediate we can make our aid felt. No one can tell the exact character of the emergency

situations that we may be called upon to meet. The Nation's
hands must not be tied when the Nation's life is in danger.

🦌 🦌 🦌

In the future days, which we seek to make secure, we look forward to a world founded upon four essential human freedoms.

The first is freedom of speech and expression—everywhere in
the world.

The second is freedom of every person to worship God in his
own way—everywhere in the world.

The third is freedom from want—which, translated into world
terms, means economic understandings which will secure to every
nation a healthy peacetime life for its inhabitants—everywhere in
the world.

The fourth is freedom from fear—which, translated into world
terms, means a world-wide reduction of armaments to such a point
and in such a thorough fashion that no nation will be in a position
to commit an act of physical aggression against any neighbor—
anywhere in the world.

That is no vision of a distant millennium. It is a definite basis
for a kind of world attainable in our own time and generation.
That kind of world is the very antithesis of the so-called new order
of tyranny which the dictators seek to create with the crash of a
bomb.

To that new order we oppose the greater conception—the moral
order. A good society is able to face schemes of world domination
and foreign revolutions alike without fear.

Since the beginning of our American history we have been engaged in change—in a perpetual peaceful revolution—a revolution which goes on steadily, quietly adjusting itself to changing
conditions—without the concentration camp or the quick-lime in
the ditch. The world order which we seek is the cooperation of free
countries, working together in a friendly, civilized society.

This Nation has placed its destiny in the hands and heads and
hearts of its millions of free men and women; and its faith in freedom under the guidance of God. Freedom means the supremacy
of human rights everywhere. Our support goes to those who

struggle to gain those rights or keep them. Our strength is in our unity of purpose.

To that high concept there can be no end save victory.

FRANKLIN DELANO ROOSEVELT
WAR MESSAGE TO CONGRESS
WASHINGTON, D.C., *December 8, 1941*

Yesterday, December 7, 1941—a date which will live in infamy—the United States of America was suddenly and deliberately attacked by naval and air forces of the Empire of Japan.

The United States was at peace with that nation and, at the solicitation of Japan, was still in conversation with its government and its Emperor looking toward the maintenance of peace in the Pacific. Indeed, one hour after Japanese air squadrons had commenced bombing in Oahu, the Japanese ambassador to the United States and his colleague delivered to the Secretary of State a formal reply to a recent American message. While this reply stated that it seemed useless to continue the existing diplomatic negotiations, it contained no threat or hint of war or armed attack.

It will be recorded that the distance of Hawaii from Japan makes it obvious that the attack was deliberately planned many days or even weeks ago. During the intervening time the Japanese Government has deliberately sought to deceive the United States by false statements and expressions of hope for continued peace.

The attack yesterday on the Hawaiian Islands has caused severe damage to American naval and military forces. Very many American lives have been lost. In addition, American ships have been reported torpedoed on the high seas between San Francisco and Honolulu.

Yesterday the Japanese government also launched an attack against Malaya.

Last night Japanese forces attacked Hong Kong.

Last night Japanese forces attacked Guam.

Last night Japanese forces attacked the Philippine Islands.

Last night the Japanese attacked Wake Island.

Japan has, therefore, undertaken a surprise offensive extending throughout the Pacific area. The facts of yesterday speak for themselves. The people of the United States have already formed their opinions and well understood the implications to the very life and safety of our nation.

As Commander in Chief of the Army and Navy, I have directed that all measures be taken for our defense.

Always will we remember the character of the onslaught against us.

No matter how long it may take us to overcome this premeditated invasion, the American people in their righteous might will win through to absolute victory.

I believe I interpret the will of the Congress and of the people when I assert that we will not only defend ourselves to the uttermost but will make very certain that this form of treachery shall never endanger us again.

Hostilities exist. There is no blinking at the fact that our people, our territory and our interests are in grave danger.

With confidence in our armed forces—with the unbounding determination of our people—we will gain the inevitable triumph—so help us God.

I ask that the Congress declare that since the unprovoked and dastardly attack by Japan on Sunday, December 7th, a state of war has existed between the United States and the Japanese Empire.

FRANKLIN DELANO ROOSEVELT
NINTH STATE-OF-THE-UNION MESSAGE
January 6, 1942

In fulfilling my duty to report upon the state of the Union, I am proud to say to you that the spirit of the American people was never higher than it is today—the Union was never more closely knit together—this country was never more deeply determined to face the solemn tasks before it.

The response of the American people has been instantaneous. It will be sustained until our security is assured.

Exactly one year ago today I said to this Congress:

When the dictators are ready to make war upon us, they will not wait for an act of war on our part. They—not we—will choose the time and the place and the method of their attack.

We now know their choice of the time: a peaceful Sunday morning—December 7th, 1941.

✗ ✗ ✗

The plan failed in its purpose. We have not been stunned. We have not been terrified or confused. This reassembling of the Seventy-seventh Congress is proof of that; for the mood of quiet, grim resolution which here prevails bodes ill for those who conspired and collaborated to murder world peace. . . .

Admittedly, we have been faced with hard choices. It was bitter, for example, not to be able to relieve the heroic and historic defenders of Wake Island. It was bitter for us not to be able to land a million men and a thousand ships in the Philippine Islands.

But this adds only to our determination to see to it that the Stars and Stripes will fly again over Wake and Guam, and that the brave people of the Philippines will be rid of Japanese imperialism, and will live in freedom, security, and independence.

✗ ✗ ✗

I have just sent a letter of directive to the appropriate departments and agencies of our Government, ordering that immediate steps be taken:

1. To increase our production rate of airplanes so rapidly that in this year, 1942, we shall produce 60,000 planes, 10,000 more than the goal set a year and a half ago. This includes 45,000 combat planes—bombers, dive-bombers, pursuit planes. The rate of increase will be continued, so that next year, 1943, we shall produce 125,000 airplanes, including 100,000 combat planes.

2. To increase our production rate of tanks so rapidly that in this year, 1942, we shall produce 45,000 tanks; and to continue that increase so that next year, 1943, we shall produce 75,000 tanks.

3. To increase our production rate of antiaircraft guns so rapidly that in this year, 1942, we shall produce 20,000 of them; and to continue that increase so that next year, 1943, we shall produce 35,000 antiaircraft guns.

4. To increase our production rate of merchant ships so rapidly that in this year, 1942, we shall build 8,000,000 deadweight tons as compared with a 1941 production of 1,100,000. We shall continue that increase so that next year, 1943, we shall build 10,-000,000 tons.

These figures and similar figures for a multitude of other implements of war will give the Japanese and Nazis a little idea of just what they accomplished in the attack on Pearl Harbor.

✗ ✗ ✗

Production for war is based on men and women—the human hands and brains which collectively we call labor. Our workers stand ready to work long hours; to turn out more in a day's work; to keep the wheels turning and the fires burning 24 hours a day, and 7 days a week. They realize well that on the speed and efficiency of their work depend the lives of their sons and their brothers on the fighting fronts.

✗ ✗ ✗

We must guard against complacency. We must not underrate the enemy. He is powerful and cunning—and cruel and ruthless. He will stop at nothing which gives him a chance to kill and to destroy. He has trained his people to believe that their highest perfection is achieved by waging war. For many years he has prepared for this very conflict—planning, plotting, training, arming, fighting. We have already tasted defeat. We may suffer further setbacks. We must face the fact of a hard war, a long war, a bloody war, a costly war.

✗ ✗ ✗

Many people ask, "When will this war end?" There is only one answer to that. It will end just as soon as we make it end, by our combined efforts, our combined strength, our combined determination to fight through and work through until the end—the end of militarism in Germany and Italy and Japan. Most certainly we shall not settle for less. . . .

We are fighting today for security, for progress and for peace, not only for ourselves, but for all men, not only for one generation but for all generations. We are fighting to cleanse the world of ancient evils, ancient ills.

Our enemies are guided by brutal cynicism, by unholy contempt for the human race. We are inspired by a faith which goes back through all the years to the first chapter of the Book of Genesis: "God created man in His own image."

We on our side are striving to be true to that divine heritage. We are fighting as our fathers have fought, to uphold the doctrine that all men are equal in the sight of God. Those on the other side are striving to destroy this deep belief and to create a world in their own image—a world of tyranny and cruelty and serfdom.

That is the conflict that day and night now pervades our lives. No compromise can end that conflict. There never has been—there never can be—successful compromise between good and evil. Only total victory can reward the champions of tolerance, and decency, and freedom, and faith.

FRANKLIN DELANO ROOSEVELT
TENTH STATE-OF-THE-UNION MESSAGE
WASHINGTON, D.C., *January 7, 1943*

The Seventy-eighth Congress assembles in one of the great moments in the history of this Nation. The past year was perhaps the most crucial for modern civilization; the coming year will be filled with violent conflict—yet with high promise of better things.

We must appraise the events of 1942 according to their relative importance; we must exercise a sense of proportion. . . .

The Axis Powers knew that they must win the war in 1942—or eventually lose everything. I do not need to tell you that our enemies did not win this war in 1942.

✕   ✕   ✕

Our forward progress in this war has depended upon our progress on the production front.

✕   ✕   ✕

The arsenal of democracy is making good.

✕   ✕   ✕

Two years ago I spoke in my Annual Message of Four Free-doms. The blessings of two of them—Freedom of Speech and Freedom of Religion—are an essential part of the very life of this Nation; and we hope that these blessings will be granted to all men everywhere.

The people at home and the people at the front—men and women—are wondering about the Third Freedom—Freedom from Want. To them it means that when they are mustered out, when war production is converted to the economy of peace, they will have the right to expect full employment—for themselves and for all able-bodied men and women in America who want to work.

They expect the opportunity to work, to run their farms, their stores, to earn decent wages. They are eager to face the risks inherent in our system of free enterprise.

They do not want a post-war America which suffers from under-nourishment or slums—or the dole. They want no get-rich-quick era of bogus "prosperity" which will end for them in selling apples on a street corner, as happened after the bursting of the boom in 1929.

When you talk with our young men and women, you will find they want to work for themselves and their families; they consider they have the right to work; and they know that after the last war their fathers did not gain that right.

✕   ✕   ✕

I have been told that this is no time to speak of a better America after the war. I am told it is a grave error on my part.

I dissent.

I say this now to this Seventy-eighth Congress, because it is wholly possible that Freedom from Want—the right of employment and the right of assurance against life's hazards—will loom very large as a task of America during the coming two years.

✕   ✕   ✕

In this war of survival we must keep before our minds not only the evil things we fight against but the good things we are fighting for. We fight to retain a great past—and we fight to gain a greater future. . . .

Victory in this war is the first and greatest goal before us. Victory in the peace is the next. That means striving toward the enlargement of the security of man here and throughout the world—and, finally, striving for the Fourth Freedom—Freedom from Fear.

ℵ ℵ ℵ

I do not prophesy when this war will end.

But I do believe that this year of 1943 will give to the United Nations a very substantial advance along the roads that lead to Berlin and Rome and Tokyo.

I tell you it is within the realm of possibility that this Seventy-eighth Congress may have the historic privilege of helping greatly to save the world from future fear.

Therefore, let us—all of us—have confidence, let us redouble our efforts.

A tremendous, costly, long-enduring task in peace as well as in war is still ahead of us.

But, as we face that continuing task, we may know that the state of this Nation is good—the heart of this Nation is sound—the spirit of this Nation is strong—the faith of this Nation is eternal.

FRANKLIN DELANO ROOSEVELT
ELEVENTH STATE-OF-THE-UNION MESSAGE
WASHINGTON, D.C., *January 11, 1944*

This nation in the past two years has become an active partner in the world's greatest war against human slavery.

We have joined with like-minded people in order to defend ourselves in a world that has been gravely threatened with gangster rule. . . .

We are united in determination that this war shall not be followed by another interim which leads to new disaster—that we shall not repeat the tragic errors of ostrich isolationism—that we shall not repeat the excesses of the wild Twenties when this Nation went for a joy-ride on a roller coaster which ended in a tragic crash.

x   x   x

It is our duty now to begin to lay plans and determine the strategy for the winning of a lasting peace and the establishment of an American standard of living higher than ever before known. We cannot be content, no matter how high that general standard of living may be, if some fraction of our people—whether it be one-third or one-fifth or one-tenth—is ill-fed, ill-clothed, ill-housed, and insecure. . . .

We have come to a clear realization of the fact that true individual freedom cannot exist without economic security and independence. "Necessitous men are not free men." People who are hungry and out of a job are the stuff of which dictatorships are made.

In our day these economic truths have become accepted as self-evident. We have accepted, so to speak, a second Bill of Rights under which a new basis of security and prosperity can be established for all—regardless of station, race or creed.

Among these are:

The right to a useful and remunerative job in the industries or shops or farms or mines of the nation;

The right to earn enough to provide adequate food and clothing and recreation;

The right of every farmer to raise and sell his products at a return which will give him and his family a decent living;

The right of every businessman, large and small, to trade in an atmosphere of freedom from unfair competition and domination by monopolies at home or abroad;

The right of every family to a decent home;

The right to adequate medical care and the opportunity to achieve and enjoy good health;

The right to adequate protection from the economic fears of old age, sickness, accident and unemployment;

The right to a good education.

All of these rights spell security. And after this war is won we must be prepared to move forward, in the implementation of these rights, to new goals of human happiness and well-being.

✗ ✗ ✗

I ask the Congress to explore the means for implementing this economic Bill of Rights—for it is definitely the responsibility of Congress so to do. . . .

Our fighting men abroad—and their families at home—expect such a program and have the right to insist upon it. . . .

The foreign policy that we have been following—a policy that guided us at Moscow, Cairo and Teheran—is based on the common sense principle which was best expressed by Benjamin Franklin on July fourth, 1776: "We must all hang together, or assuredly we shall all hang separately.". . .

FRANKLIN DELANO ROOSEVELT
TWELFTH STATE-OF-THE-UNION MESSAGE
WASHINGTON, D.C., *January 6, 1945*

In considering the State of the Union, the war and the peace that is to follow are naturally uppermost in the minds of all of us.

This war must be waged—it is being waged—with the greatest and most persistent intensity. Everything we are and have is at stake. Everything we are and have will be given. American men, fighting far from home, have already won victories which the world will never forget.

We have no question of the ultimate victory. We have no question of the cost. Our losses will be heavy.

We and our allies will go on fighting together to ultimate total victory. . . .

The nearer we come to vanquishing our enemies the more we inevitably become conscious of differences among the victors.

We must not let those differences divide us and blind us to our more important common and continuing interests in winning the war and building the peace.

International cooperation on which enduring peace must be based is not a one-way street.

❊ ❊ ❊

This new year of 1945 can be the greatest year of achievement in human history.

Nineteen forty-five can see the final ending of the Nazi-Fascist reign of terror in Europe.

Nineteen forty-five can see the closing in of the forces of retribution about the center of the malignant power of imperialistic Japan.

Most important of all—1945 can and must see the substantial beginning of the organization of world peace. . . . It must be the justification of all the sacrifices that have been made—of all the dreadful misery that this world has endured.

We Americans of today, together with our allies, are making history—and I hope it will be better history than ever has been made before.

We pray that we may be worthy of the unlimited opportunities that God has given us.

HARRY S. TRUMAN

(1945–1953)

*"Every individual has a right
to expect from our Government a fair deal"*

On President *Harry S. Truman*—living example of farm boy to President—devolved responsibility for the most portentous act in world
history. All else that he accomplished during his almost eight years as
Chief Magistrate fades into the background because this act—ordered
by him in early August, 1945—ushered in the Atomic Age that today,
by its chain reaction, threatens the continued existence of life on this
planet.

On April 12, 1945, this country boy from Missouri who rose to
Vice President, was projected into the presidency by the death of
Franklin D. Roosevelt. The day after assuming the awesome power
and grave responsibility of the Chief Magistrate's office, he said to
reporters: "When they told me what had happened yesterday I felt as
if the moon, the stars and all the planets had fallen on me. I've got the
most awful responsibility a man ever had."

Within three months he was called upon to activate this "most awful
responsibility." By July, 1945, General Douglas MacArthur had
liberated the Philippines; Germany was battered into submission; the
United Nations Charter was given birth at San Francisco. Only Japan
held out. Wrote Truman: "It was my responsibility as President to
force the Japanese warlords to come to terms as quickly as possible
with the minimum loss of lives. I then made my final decision."

That final, courageous decision was executed on August 6, 1945, by

445

an American plane. Acting under orders from President Truman, the *Enola Gay* dropped a 400-pound atomic bomb over Hiroshima, Japan. In the blinding flash and immeasurable heat of that bomb, 78,150 Japanese died and more than 200,000 were left burned, maimed, missing, destitute, in a wholesale destruction far more devastating than expected even by the scientists who had developed the bomb at Alamogordo, New Mexico. On August 16, 1945, Japan surrendered totally. Hiroshima had proven that man had at last discovered the means of extinguishing life on our earth.

Of Truman's State-of-the-Union Messages his eighth and last, January 7, 1953, was his best. After recapitulating the achievements of his administrations, he issued a last stern warning against communism and stressed the awfulness of nuclear warfare, adverting to "that great white flash of light, man-made at Alamogordo."

In 1947, Congress, at the behest of President Truman, created the Marshall Plan for rehabilitation of the European countries devastated by the war. In 1950 the nation plunged into the second most unpopular war in her history—the Korean Affair that cost the country so many lives and so much blood only to end in a stalemate. Truman's administration saw the Russian-American entente of World War II transmuted into the cold war, a new kind of war front of nerves and propaganda.

In his 1949 message (after winning an upset victory by his famous whistle-stop campaign that confounded all the so-called experts who had counted him out) he originated the phrase "Fair Deal," which he used to identify his program of reform and betterment. It was probable he hoped for political gain by hitching his program to the tail of Franklin D. Roosevelt's New Deal kite. For Truman's Fair Deal was actually a restatement, with modification, of the "progressive and humane principles of the New Deal." That phrase—Fair Deal—incidentally, occurred near the end of this message. It was not originally written in capital letters, but it sounded good and was elevated to the status of slogan for his program in the upcoming new term in the White House.

His First State-of-the-Union Message—1946—was the longest on record, running to over twenty-five thousand words. It fairly defies abridging, for therein he set the stage for America's task of helping in global reconstruction and promoting peace through the United Nations, and presaged his Point-Four program for assistance to underdeveloped countries that he would propose in 1949.

HARRY S. TRUMAN
FIRST STATE-OF-THE-UNION MESSAGE
January 21, 1946

In his last message on the State of the Union, delivered one year ago, President Roosevelt said:

"This new year of 1945 can be the greatest year of achievement in human history.

"Nineteen forty-five can see the final ending of the Nazi-Fascist reign of terror in Europe.

"Nineteen forty-five can see the closing in of the forces of retribution about the center of the malignant power of imperialistic Japan.

"Most important of all—1945 can and must see the substantial beginning of the organization of world peace."

All those hopes, and more were fulfilled in the year 1945. It was the greatest year of achievement in human history. It saw the end of the Nazi-Fascist terror in Europe, and also the end of the malignant power of Japan. And it saw the substantial beginning of world organization for peace. These momentous events became realities because of the steadfast purpose of the United Nations and of the forces that fought for freedom under their flags. The plain fact is that civilization was saved in 1945 by the United Nations.

🐕 🐕 🐕

The United Nations Organization now being established represents a minimum essential beginning. It must be developed rapidly and steadily. Its work must be amplified to fill in the whole pattern that has been outlined. Economic collaboration, for example, already charted, now must be carried on as carefully and as comprehensively as the political and security measures.

It is important that the nations come together as States in the Assembly and in the Security Council and in the other specialized assemblies and councils that have been and will be arranged. But this is not enough. Our ultimate security requires more than a process of consultation and compromise.

It requires that we begin now to develop the United Nations Organization as the representative of the world as one society. The United Nations Organization, if we have the will adequately to staff it and to make it work as it should, will provide a great voice to speak constantly and responsibly in terms of world collaboration and world well-being.

🐕 🐕 🐕

The year 1945 brought with it the final defeat of our enemies. There lies before us now the work of building a just and enduring peace.

Our most immediate task toward that end is to deprive our enemies completely and forever of their power to start another war. Of even greater importance to the preservation of international peace is the need to preserve the wartime agreement of the United Nations and to direct it into the ways of peace.

🐕 🐕 🐕

The great and dominant objective of United States foreign policy is to build and preserve a just peace. The peace we seek is not peace for 20 years. It is permanent peace. At a time when massive changes are occurring with lightning speed throughout the world, it is often difficult to perceive how this central objective is best served in one isolated complex situation or another. Despite this very real difficulty, there are certain basic propositions to which the United States adheres and to which we shall continue to adhere.

One proposition is that lasting peace requires genuine understanding and active cooperation among the most powerful nations. Another is that even the support of the strongest nations cannot guarantee a peace unless it is infused with the quality of justice for all nations.

On October 27, 1945, I made, in New York City, the following public statement of my understanding of the fundamental foreign policy of the United States:

1. We seek no territorial expansion or selfish advantage. We have no plans for aggression against any other state, large or small. We have no objective which need clash with the peaceful aims of any other nation.

2. We believe in the eventual return of sovereign rights and self-government to all peoples who have been deprived of them by force.

3. We shall approve no territorial changes in any friendly part of the world unless they accord with the freely expressed wishes of the people concerned.

4. We believe that all peoples who are prepared for self-government should be permitted to choose their own form of government by their own freely expressed choice, without interference from any foreign source.

5. By the combined and cooperative action of our war allies, we shall help the defeated enemy states establish peaceful democratic governments of their own free choice.

6. We shall refuse to recognize any government imposed upon any nation by the force of any foreign power.

7. We believe that all nations should have the freedom of the seas and equal rights to the navigation of boundary rivers and waterways which pass through more than one country.

8. We believe that all states which are accepted in the society of nations should have access on equal terms to the trade and the raw materials of the world.

9. We believe that the sovereign states of the Western Hemisphere, without interference from outside the Western Hemisphere, must work together as good neighbors in the solution of their common problems.

10. We believe that full economic collaboration between all nations, great and small, is essential to the improvement of living conditions all over the world, and to the establishment of freedom from fear and freedom from want.

11. We shall continue to strive to promote freedom of expression and freedom of religion throughout the peace-loving areas of the world.

12. We are convinced that the preservation of peace between nations requires a United Nations Organization composed of all the peace-loving nations of the world who are willing jointly to use force, if necessary, to insure peace.

That is our foreign policy.

HARRY S. TRUMAN
SECOND STATE-OF-THE-UNION MESSAGE
January 6, 1947

. . . Today I shall outline five major economic policies which I believe the Government should pursue during 1947. These policies are designed to meet our immediate needs and, at the same time, to provide for the long-range welfare of our free-enterprise system:

First. Promotion of greater harmony between labor and management.

Second. Restriction of monopoly and unfair business practices; assistance to small business; and the promotion of the free competitive system of private enterprise.

Third. Continuation of an aggressive program of home construction.

Fourth. The balancing of the budget in the next fiscal year, and the achieving of a substantial surplus to be applied to the reduction of the public debt.

Fifth. Protection of a fair level of return to farmers in postwar agriculture.

🐴 🐴 🐴

The United States has taken the lead in the endeavor to put atomic energy under effective international control. We seek no monopoly for ourselves or for any group of nations. We ask only that there be safeguards sufficient to insure that no nation will be able to use this power for military purposes. So long as all governments are not agreed on means of international control of atomic energy, the shadow of fear will obscure the bright prospects for the peaceful use of this enormous power.

🐴 🐴 🐴

This is an age when unforeseen attack could come with unprecedented speed. We must be strong enough to defeat, and thus to forestall any such attack. . . . When a system of collective security under the United Nations has been established, we shall be willing to lead in collective disarmament, but, until such a system becomes a reality, we must not again allow our weakness to invite attack.

HARRY S. TRUMAN
THIRD STATE-OF-THE-UNION MESSAGE
January 7, 1948

. . . As we examine the state of our Union today, we can benefit from viewing it on a basis of the accomplishments of the last decade and our goals for the next. How far have we come during the last 10 years and how far can we go during the next 10?

🐎 🐎 🐎

Our first goal is to secure fully the essential human rights of our citizens. . . .

Our second goal is to protect and develop our human resources. . . .

Our third goal is to conserve and use our natural resources so that they can contribute most effectively to the welfare of our people.

Our fourth goal is to lift the standard of living for all our people by strengthening our economic system and sharing more broadly among our people the goods we produce. . . .

Our fifth goal is to achieve world peace based on principles of freedom and justice and the equality of all nations.

Twice within our generation, world wars have taught us that we cannot isolate ourselves from the rest of the world. . . .

Our present major effort toward economic reconstruction is to support the program for recovery developed by the countries of Europe.

🐎 🐎 🐎

I consider it of the highest importance that the Congress should authorize support for the European recovery program for the period from April 1, 1948, to June 30, 1952, with an initial amount for the first 15 months of $6,800,000,000. I urge the Con-

gress to act promptly on this vital measure of our foreign policy—
on this decisive contribution to world peace.

We are following a sound, constructive, and practical course in
carrying out our determination to achieve peace.

We are fighting poverty, hunger, and suffering.

This leads to peace—not war.

We are building toward a world where all nations, large and
small alike, may live free from the fear of aggression.

This leads to peace—not war.

Above all else, we are striving to achieve a concord among the
peoples of the world based upon the dignity of the individual and
the brotherhood of man.

This leads to peace—not war.

🐎 🐎 🐎

I recommend, therefore, that, effective January 1, 1948, a cost-
of-living tax credit be extended to our people consisting of a credit
of $40 to each individual taxpayer and an additional credit of $40
for each dependent. Thus the income tax of a man with a wife and
two children would be reduced $160. The credit would be ex-
tended to all taxpayers, but it would be particularly helpful to
those in the low-income group.

This is the proper method of tax relief at this time. It gives relief to those who need it most. . . .

We are determined that every citizen of this Nation shall have
an equal right and equal opportunity to grow in wisdom and in
stature and to take his place in the control of his Nation's destiny.

We are determined that the productive resources of the Nation
shall be used wisely and fully for the benefit of all. . . .

HARRY S. TRUMAN
FOURTH STATE-OF-THE-UNION MESSAGE
January 5, 1949

In this society we are conservative about the values and principles which we cherish; but we are forward-looking in protecting
those values and principles and in extending their benefits. We have

rejected the discredited theory that the fortunes of the Nation should be in the hands of a privileged few. We have abandoned the "trickle down" concept of national prosperity. Instead, we believe that our economic system should rest on a democratic foundation and that wealth should be created for the benefit of all.

The recent election shows that the American people are in favor of this kind of society and want to go on improving it.

🐴 🐴 🐴

But, great as our progress has been, we still have a long way to go.

As we look around the country, many of our shortcomings stand out in bold relief.

We are suffering from excessively high prices.

Our production is still not large enough to satisfy our demands.

Our minimum wages are far too low.

Small business is losing ground to growing monopoly.

Our farmers still face an uncertain future. And too many of them lack the benefits of our modern civilization.

Some of our natural resources are still being wasted.

We are acutely short of electric power, although the means for developing such power are abundant.

Five million families are still living in slums and firetraps. Three million families share their homes with others.

Our health is far behind the progress of medical science. Proper medical care is so expensive that it is out of reach of the great majority of our citizens.

Our schools, in many localities, are utterly inadequate.

Our democratic ideals are often thwarted by prejudice and intolerance.

Each of these shortcomings is also an opportunity—an opportunity for the Congress and the President to work for the good of the people.

Our first great opportunity is to protect our economy against the evils of "boom and bust."

🐴 🐴 🐴

We stand at the opening of an era which can mean either great achievement or terrible catastrophe for ourselves and for all mankind.

The strength of our Nation must continue to be used in the interest of all our people rather than a privileged few. It must continue to be used unselfishly in the struggle for world peace and the betterment of mankind the world over.

This is the task before us.

It is not an easy one. It has many complications, and there will be strong opposition from selfish interests.

I hope for cooperation from farmers, from labor, and from business. Every segment of our population and every individual has a right to expect from our Government a fair deal. . . .

HARRY S. TRUMAN
FIFTH STATE-OF-THE-UNION MESSAGE
January 4, 1950

A year ago I reported to this Congress that the state of the Union was good. I am happy to be able to report to you today that the state of the Union continues to be good. . . .

We are now, in this year of 1950, nearing the midpoint of the twentieth century.

The first half of this century will be known as the most turbulent and eventful period in recorded history. The swift pace of events promises to make the next 50 years decisive in the history of man on this planet.

The scientific and industrial revolution which began two centuries ago has, in the last 50 years, caught up the peoples of the globe in a common destiny. Two world-shattering wars have proved that no corner of the earth can be isolated from the affairs of mankind.

We must create the moral and legal framework for the world which will insure that his new powers are used for good and not for evil. In shaping the outcome, the people of the United States will play a leading role.

🐃   🐃   🐃

We shall continue to give our wholehearted support to the United Nations. We believe that this organization can ultimately provide the framework of international law and morality without which mankind cannot survive. It has already set up new standards for the conduct of nations in the Declaration of Human Rights and the Convention of Genocide. It is moving ahead to give meaning to the concept of world brotherhood through a wide variety of cultural, economic, and technical activities.

The events of the past year again showed the value of the United Nations in bringing about the peaceful adjustment of tense international controversies. In Indonesia and in Palestine, the efforts of the United Nations have put a stop to bloodshed and paved the way to peaceful settlements.

We are working toward the time when the United Nations will control weapons of mass destruction and will have the forces to preserve international law and order. While the world remains unsettled, however, and as long as our own security and the security of the free world require, we will maintain a strong and well-balanced defense organization. The selective service system is an essential part of our defense plans, and it must be continued.

🐐   🐐   🐐

We shall continue our efforts for world economic recovery, because world prosperity is the only sure foundation for permanent peace.

As an immediate means to this end, we must continue our support of the European recovery program. . . .

As we move forward into the second half of the twentieth century we must always bear in mind the central purpose of our national life. We do not seek material prosperity for ourselves because we love luxury. We do not aid other nations because we wish to increase our power. We have not devised programs for the security and well-being of our people because we are afraid or unwilling to take risks. This is not the meaning of our past history or our present course.

We work for a better life for all, so that all men may put to good use the great gifts with which they have been endowed by their Creator. We seek to establish those material conditions of life in which, without exception, men may live in dignity, perform useful work, serve their communities, and worship God as they see fit. . . .

HARRY S. TRUMAN
SIXTH STATE-OF-THE-UNION MESSAGE
January 8, 1951

This Eighty-second Congress faces as grave a task as any Congress in the history of our Republic. . . .

As we meet here today, American soldiers are fighting a bitter campaign in Korea.

We pay tribute to their courage, devotion, and gallantry.

Our men are fighting, alongside their United Nations allies, because they know, as we do, that the aggression in Korea is part of the attempt of the Russian Communist dictatorship to take over the world, step by step.

Our men are fighting a long way from home, but they are fighting for our lives and our liberties. They are fighting to protect our right to meet here today—our right to govern ourselves as a free nation.

🦌 🦌 🦌

The imperialism of the Czars has been replaced by the even more ambitious, more crafty, and more menacing imperialism of the rulers of the Soviet Union.

This new imperialism has powerful military forces. It is keeping millions of men under arms. It has a large air force and a strong submarine force. It has complete control of the men and equipment of its satellites. It has kept its subject peoples and its economy in a state of perpetual mobilization.

The present rulers of the Soviet Union have shown that they are willing to use this power to destroy the free nations and win domination over the whole world.

🦌 🦌 🦌

If Western Europe were to fall to Soviet Russia, it would double the Soviet supply of coal and triple the Soviet supply of steel. If the free countries of Asia and Africa should fall to Soviet Russia, we would lose the sources of many of our most vital raw materials, including uranium, which is the basis of our atomic power. And Soviet command of the manpower of the free nations of Europe and Asia would confront us with military forces which we could never hope to equal.

In such a situation, the Soviet Union could impose its demands on the world, without resort to conflict, simply through the preponderance of its economic and military power. The Soviet Union does not have to attack the United States to secure domination of the world. It can achieve its ends by isolating us and swallowing up all our allies. Therefore, even if we were craven enough, and I do not believe that we could be—I say even if we were craven enough to abandon our ideals, it would be disastrous for us to withdraw from the community of free nations.

🐐 🐐 🐐

This country has a practical, realistic program of action for meeting this challenge.

First, we shall have to extend economic assistance, where it can be effective. The best way to stop subversion by the Kremlin is to strike at the roots of social injustice and economic disorder. People who have jobs, homes, and hopes for the future will defend themselves against the underground agents of the Kremlin. Our programs of economic aid have done much to turn back communism.

🐐 🐐 🐐

Korea has tremendous significance for the world. It means that free nations, acting through the United Nations, are fighting together against aggression. . . .

The principles for which we are fighting in Korea are right and just. They are the foundations of collective security and of the future of free nations. Korea is not only a country undergoing the torment of aggression; it is also a symbol. It stands for right and justice in the world against oppression and slavery. The free world must always stand for these principles—and we will stand with the free world.

As the third part of our program, we will continue to work for peaceful settlements of international disputes. We will support the United Nations and remain loyal to the great principles of international cooperation laid down in its Charter.

We are willing, as we have always been, to negotiate honorable settlements with the Soviet Union. But we will not engage in appeasement.

🐴 🐴 🐴

I ask the Congress for unity in these crucial days.

Make no mistake about my meaning. I do not ask, or expect, unanimity. I do not ask for an end to debate. Only by debate can we arrive at decisions which are wise, and which reflect the desires of the American people. We do not have dictatorship in this country, and we will never have one in this country. . . .

HARRY S. TRUMAN
SEVENTH STATE-OF-THE-UNION MESSAGE
January 9, 1952

We are moving through a perilous time. Faced with a terrible threat of aggression, our Nation has embarked upon a great effort to help establish the kind of world in which peace shall be secure. Peace is our goal—not peace at any price, but a peace based on freedom and justice. We are now in the midst of our effort to reach that goal. On the whole, we have been doing very well.

🐴 🐴 🐴

Peace depends upon the free nations sticking together, and making a combined effort to check aggression and prevent war. In this respect, 1951 was a year of great achievement.

In Korea, the forces of the United Nations turned back the Chinese Communist invasion—and did it without widening the area of conflict. The action of the United Nations in Korea has been a powerful deterrent to a third world war. However, the situation in Korea remains very hazardous. The outcome of the armistice negotiations is still uncertain.

🐐 🐐 🐐

At the present session of the United Nations in Paris, we, together with the British and the French, offered a plan to reduce and control all armaments under a fool-proof inspection system. This is a concrete, practical proposal for disarmament.

But what happened? Vishinsky laughed at it. Listen to what he said: "I could hardly sleep at all last night. I could not sleep because I kept laughing." The world will be a long time forgetting the spectacle of that fellow laughing at disarmament.

Disarmament is not a joke. Vishinsky's laughter met with shock and anger from people all over the world. And, as a result, Mr. Stalin's representative received orders to stop laughing and start talking.

🐐 🐐 🐐

But if there are any among us who think we ought to ease up in the fight for peace, I want to remind them of three things—just three things.

First. The threat of world war is still very real. We had one Pearl Harbor—let us not get caught off guard again. If you do not think the threat of Communist armies is real, talk to some of our men back from Korea.

Second. If the United States had to try to stand alone against a Soviet-dominated world, it would destroy the life we know and the ideals we hold dear. Our allies are essential to us, just as we are essential to them. The more shoulders there are to bear the burden the lighter it will be.

Third. The things we believe in most deeply are under relentless attack. We have the great responsibility of saving the basic moral and spiritual values of our civilization. We have started out well—with a program for peace that is unparalleled in history. If we believe in ourselves and the faith we profess, we will stick to the job.

🐐 🐐 🐐

We should do all we can to help and encourage the move toward a strong and united Europe.

In Asia, the new Communist empire is a daily threat to millions of people. The peoples of Asia want to be free to follow their own way of life. They want to preserve their culture and their traditions against communism, just as much as we want to preserve ours. They are laboring under terrific handicaps—poverty, ill health, feudal systems of land ownership, and the threat of internal subversion or external attack. We can and must increase our help to them.

That means military aid, especially to those places like Indochina which might be hardest hit by some new Communist attack.

It also means economic aid, both technical know-how and capital investment. . . .

To meet the crisis which now hangs over the world, we need many different kinds of strength—military, economic, political, and moral. And of all these, I am convinced that moral strength is the most vital. . . .

In all we do, we should remember who we are and what we stand for. We are Americans. Our forefathers had far greater obstacles than we have, and much poorer chances of success. They did not lose heart, or turn aside from their goals. In that darkest of all winters in American history, at Valley Forge, George Washington said: "We must not in so great a contest, expect to meet with nothing but sunshine." With that spirit, they won their fight for freedom. . . .

HARRY S. TRUMAN
EIGHTH STATE-OF-THE-UNION MESSAGE
January 7, 1953

I have the honor to report to the Congress on the state of the Union. . . .

The President-elect is about to take up the greatest burdens, the most compelling responsibilities, given to any man. And I, with you and all Americans, wish for him all possible success in undertaking the tasks that will so soon be his.

What are these tasks? The President is Chief of State, elected representative of all the people, national spokesman for them and to them. He is Commander in Chief of our Armed Forces. He is charged with the conduct of our foreign relations. He is Chief Executive of the Nation's largest civilian organization. He must select and nominate all top officials of the executive branch and all Federal judges. And on the legislative side, he has the obligation and the opportunity to recommend, and to approve or veto legislation. Besides all this, it is to him that a great political party turns naturally for leadership, and that, too, he must provide as President.

🐂 🐂 🐂

But our times are not easy; they are hard—as hard and complex, perhaps, as any in our history. Now, the President not only has to carry on these tasks in such a way that our democracy may grow and flourish and our people prosper, but he also has to lead the whole free world in overcoming the Communist menace—and all this under the shadow of the atomic bomb.

This is a huge challenge to the human being who occupies the Presidential office. But it is not a challenge to him alone, for in reality he cannot meet it alone. The challenge runs not just to him but to his whole administration, to the Congress, to the country.

🐂 🐂 🐂

It has been my privilege to hold the Presidential office for nearly 8 years now, and much has been done in which I take great pride. But this is not personal pride. It is pride in the people, in the Nation. It is pride in our political system and our form of government—balky sometimes, mechanically deficient perhaps, in many ways—but enormously alive and vigorous; able through these years to keep the Republic on the right course, rising to the great occasions, accomplishing the essentials, meeting the basic challenge of our times.

🐂 🐂 🐂

I took the oath of office on April 12, 1945. In May of that same year, the Nazis surrendered. Then, in July, that great white flash of light, man-made at Alamogordo, heralded swift and final victory in World War II—and opened the doorway to the atomic age. . . . From 1945 to 1949, the United States was sole possessor of the atomic bomb. That was a great deterrent and protection in itself.

But when the Soviets produced an atomic explosion—as they were bound to do in time—we had to broaden the whole basis of our strength. We had to endeavor to keep our lead in atomic weapons. We had to strengthen our Armed Forces generally and to enlarge our productive capacity—our mobilization base. Historically, it was the Soviet atomic explosion in the fall of 1949, 9 months before the aggression in Korea, which stimulated the planning for our program of defense mobilization. . . .

War today between the Soviet empire and the free nations might dig the grave not only of our Stalinist opponents, but of our own society, our world as well as theirs.

This transformation has been brought to pass in the 7 years from Alamogordo to Eniwetok. It is only 7 years, but the new force of atomic energy has turned the world into a very different kind of place.

🐾 🐾 🐾

We in this Government realized, even before the first successful atomic explosion, that this new force spelled terrible danger for all mankind unless it were brought under international control. We promptly advanced proposals in the United Nations to take this new source of energy out of the arena of national rivalries, to make it impossible to use as a weapon of war. These proposals, so pregnant with benefit for all humanity, were rebuffed by the rulers of the Soviet Union. . . .

The war of the future would be one in which man could extinguish millions of lives at one blow, demolish the great cities of the world, wipe out the cultural achievements of the past, and destroy the very structure of a civilization that has been slowly and painfully built up through hundreds of generations.

Such a war is not a possible policy for rational men. We know this, but we dare not assume that others would not yield to the temptation science is now placing in their hands. . . .

It is no wonder that some people wish that we had never succeeded in splitting the atom. But atomic power, like any other
force of nature, is not evil in itself. Properly used, it is an instrumentality for human betterment. As a source of power, as a
tool of scientific inquiry, it has untold possibilities. We are already
making good progress in the constructive use of atomic power. We
could do much more if we were free to concentrate on its peaceful
uses exclusively.

☙ ☙ ☙

The Communists cannot deprive us of our liberties—fear can.
The Communists cannot stamp out our faith in human dignity—
fear can. Fear is an enemy within ourselves, and if we do not
root it out, it may destroy the very way of life we are so anxious
to protect.

DWIGHT D. EISENHOWER

(1953–1961)

*"Our sons no longer die
on the distant mountains
of Korea"*

Dwight D. Eisenhower, thirty-third President, hailed from the nation's midriff—born in Texas and raised in Abilene, Kansas. He was the tenth American general to become President.

Like victorious Union Commander in Chief Ulysses Grant (who had no political ambition other than running for Mayor of Galena, Illinois, and fixing the sidewalk between his home and the station—until the Republicans drafted him in 1868), Dwight Eisenhower scorned political office—"I have no political ambitions whatever"—until he was drafted by the Republicans in 1952.

Leader of the crusade in Europe that demolished the Nazi war machine, Eisenhower came home in 1945 to a hero's welcome. In 1950 he returned to Europe as Supreme Commander of the North Atlantic Treaty Organization (NATO) forces to hold the line against Soviet aggression on that continent.

Elected President in 1952 by the greatest popular vote in history, Eisenhower carried out in record time his campaign promise to end the bloody, unpopular war in Korea. He opened his Second State-of-the-Union Message by pointing to the welcome fact that "Our sons no longer die on the distant mountains of Korea." In 1956, he was re-elected by an even greater plurality of ten million votes over his second-time opponent, Adlai Stevenson.

Eisenhower's administrations witnessed a sharp turn for the worse in

464

the free world's search for peace and security. Temperature of the conflict with Russia rose higher as the thermonuclear race picked up ominous speed. In 1949, the Soviets announced the exploding of their first atom bomb, a power over which the United States had previously had exclusive control. In 1952, the United States exploded its first thermonuclear hydrogen bomb over Eniwetok in the Pacific. In 1954, Russia countered by announcing that they, too, had penetrated the thermonuclear mysteries.

The Eisenhower years brought staccato, startling developments. In July, 1955, the heads of government of the United States, Russia, Great Britain, and France held a summit meeting at Geneva, Switzerland, hoping to devise a means of lessening tension in the world. It got nowhere. In 1956, Soviet tanks brutally crushed the Hungarian uprising. In 1957, the free world was caught off balance as Soviet satellite Sputnik I soared into orbit around the earth, thus opening the Space Age and presaging man's flight into outer space. In 1958, Nikita Khrushchev became Premier of Russia. His demand that the Allied powers withdraw their troops from West Berlin and abrogate the four-power occupation of that city, brought on the Berlin Crisis that is still unresolved.

The year 1959 saw Fidel Castro and his bearded mob overthrow the Batista government in Cuba. Hardly had Castro clenched his hold on the Pearl of the Antilles before he seized the vast American properties on the island, while the American government looked on complacently, hardly emitting a feeble squeal. To crown the ignominy heaped on America, Castro reached across the seas and allied Cuba with the Communist government of Russia, thus precipitating an enduring crisis for the American people.

Three themes run through President Eisenhower's State-of-the-Union Messages: strengthening the nation's defenses, keeping the American economy strong while doing so, and protecting the free nations against the encroachment of communism.

DWIGHT D. EISENHOWER
FIRST STATE-OF-THE-UNION MESSAGE
February 2, 1953

It is manifestly the joint purpose of the congressional leadership and of this administration to justify the summons to governmental responsibility issued last November by the American people.

The grand labors of this leadership will involve: Application of America's influence in world affairs with such fortitude and such foresight that it will deter aggression and eventually secure peace.

Establishment of a national administration of such integrity and such efficiency that its honor at home will insure respect abroad.

Encouragement of those incentives that inspire creative initiative in our economy, so that its productivity may fortify freedom everywhere; and

Dedication to the well-being of all our citizens and to the attainment of equality of opportunity for all, so that our Nation will ever act with the strength of unity in every task to which it is called.

This administration has . . . begun the definition of a new positive foreign policy. . . . The policy we embrace must be a coherent global policy. The freedom we cherish and defend in Europe and in the Americas is no different from the freedom that is imperilled in Asia. . . .

I have referred to the inescapable need for economic health and strength if we are to maintain adequate military power. . . . Our immediate task is to chart a fiscal and economic policy that can: First, Reduce the planned deficits and then balance the budget, which means, among other things, reducing Federal expenditures to the safe minimum.

Our civil and social rights form a central part of the heritage we are striving to defend on all fronts and with all our strength. I believe with all my heart that our vigilant guarding of these rights is a sacred obligation binding upon our citizens. A cardinal ideal in this heritage we cherish is the equality of rights of all citizens of every race and color and creed.

DWIGHT D. EISENHOWER
SECOND STATE-OF-THE-UNION MESSAGE
January 7, 1954

Much for which we may be thankful has happened during the past year.

First of all we are deeply grateful that our sons no longer die on the distant mountains of Korea. Although they are still called from our homes to military service, they are no longer called to the field of battle.

The Nation has just completed the most prosperous year in its history. The damaging effect of inflation on the wages, pensions, salaries, and savings of us all has been brought under control. Taxes have begun to go down. The cost of our Government has been reduced and its work proceeds with some 183,000 fewer employees; thus the discouraging trend of modern governments toward their own limitless expansion has in our case been reversed. The cost of armaments becomes less oppressive as we near our defense goals; yet we are militarily stronger every day. During the year, creation of the new Cabinet Department of Health, Education, and Welfare symbolized the Government's permanent concern with the human problems of our citizens.

Segregation in the Armed Forces and other Federal activities is on the way out. We have also made progress toward its abolition in the District of Columbia. These are steps in the continuing effort to eliminate interracial difficulty.

American freedom is threatened so long as the world Communist conspiracy exists in its present scope, power, and hostility. More closely than ever before, American freedom is interlocked with the freedom of other people. In the unity of the free world lies our best chance to reduce the Communist threat without war. . . .

As we maintain our military strength during the coming year and draw closer the bonds with our allies, we shall be in an improved position to discuss outstanding issues with the Soviet Union. Indeed, we shall be glad to do so whenever there is a reasonable prospect of constructive results. In this spirit the atomic-energy proposals of the United States were recently presented to the United Nations General Assembly. A truly constructive Soviet reaction will make possible a new start toward an era of peace, and away from the fatal road toward atomic war.

I am flatly opposed to the socialization of medicine. The great need for hospital and medical services can best be met by the initiative of private plans. But it is unfortunately a fact that medical costs are rising and already impose severe hardships on many families. The Federal Government can do many helpful things and still avoid the socialization of medicine.

In the District of Columbia, the time is long overdue for granting national suffrage to its citizens and also applying the principle of local self-government to the Nation's Capital. I urge the Congress to move promptly in this direction and also to revise District revenue measures to provide needed public works improvements.

The people of Hawaii are ready for statehood. I renew my request for this legislation in order that Hawaii may elect its State officials and its representatives in Washington along with the rest of the country this fall.

For years our citizens between the ages of 18 and 21 have, in time of peril, been summoned to fight for America. They should participate in the political process that produces this fateful summons. I urge Congress to propose to the States a constitutional amendment permitting citizens to vote when they reach the age of 18.

No government can inoculate its people against the fatal materialism that plagues our age. Happily, our people, though blessed with more material goods than any people in history, have always reserved their first allegiance to the kingdom of the spirit, which is the true source of that freedom we value above all material things.

DWIGHT D. EISENHOWER
THIRD STATE-OF-THE-UNION MESSAGE
January 6, 1955

The massive military machines and ambitions of the Soviet-Communist bloc still create uneasiness in the world. All of us are aware of the continuing reliance of the Soviet Communists on military force, of the power of their weapons, of their present resistance to realistic armament limitation, and of their continuing effort to dominate or intimidate free nations on their periphery. Their steadily growing power includes an increasing strength in nuclear weapons. This power combined with the proclaimed intentions of the Communist leaders to communize the world, is the threat confronting us today.

To protect our nations and our peoples from the catastrophe of a nuclear holocaust, free nations must maintain countervailing military power to persuade the Communists of the futility of seeking to advance their ends through aggression. . . . Now this, of course, is a form of world stalemate. But in this stalemate each of us—every American—may and must exercise his high duty to strive in every honorable way for enduring peace.

🐘 🐘 🐘

Nineteen hundred and fifty-four was one of the most prosperous years in our history. Business activity surges with new strength. Production is rising. Employment is high. Toward the end of last year average weekly wages in manufacturing were higher than ever before. Personal income after taxes is at a record level. So is consumer spending. Construction activity is reaching new peaks. Export demand for our goods is strong. State and local government expenditures on public works are rising. Savings are high, and credit is readily available.

So, today, the transition to a peacetime economy is largely behind us. The economic outlook is good. . . .

DWIGHT D. EISENHOWER
FOURTH STATE-OF-THE-UNION MESSAGE
January 5, 1956

Our country is at peace. Our security posture commands respect. A spiritual vigor marks our national life. Our economy, approaching the $4 billion mark, is at an unparalleled level of prosperity. The national income is more widely and fairly distributed than ever before. . . .

Government spending has been cut by more than $10 billion.

Nearly 300,000 positions have been eliminated from the Federal payroll. Taxes have been substantially reduced. A balanced budget is in prospect. Social security has been extended to 10 million more Americans and unemployment insurance to 4 million more. Unprecedented advances in civil rights have been made. The long-standing and deep-seated problems of agriculture have been forthrightly attacked.

The July meeting of heads of government held out promise to the world of moderation in the bitterness, of word and action, which tends to generate conflict and war. All were in agreement that a nuclear war would be an intolerable disaster which must not be permitted to occur. But in October, when the foreign ministers met again, the results demonstrated conclusively that the Soviet leaders are not yet willing to create the indispensable conditions for a secure and lasting peace.

In the face of Communist military power, we must, of course, continue to maintain an effective system of collective security. This involves two things—a system which gives clear warning that armed aggression will be met by joint action of the free nations, and deterrent military power to make that warning effective. Moreover, the awesome power of the atom must be made to serve as a guardian of the free community and of the peace.

In all things, change is the inexorable law of life. In much of the world the ferment of change is working strongly; but grave injustices are still uncorrected. We must not, by any sanction of ours, help to perpetuate these wrongs. I have particularly in mind the oppressive division of the German people, the bondage of millions elsewhere, and the exclusion of Japan from United Nations membership.

The sum of our international effort should be this: the waging of peace, with as much resourcefulness, with as great a sense of dedication and urgency, as we have ever mustered in the defense of our country in time of war. . . .

🐘 🐘 🐘

To conclude: The vista before us is bright. The march of science, the expanding economy, the advance in collective security toward a just peace—in this threefold movement our people are creating new standards by which the future of the Republic may be judged.

DWIGHT D. EISENHOWER
FIFTH STATE-OF-THE-UNION MESSAGE
January 10, 1957

In the world today, the surging and understandable tide of nationalism is marked by widespread revulsion and revolt against tyranny, injustice, inequality, and poverty. As individuals, joined in the common hunger for freedom, men and women and even children pit their spirit against guns and tanks. On a larger scale, in an ever more persistent search for the self-respect of authentic sovereignty and the economic base on which national independence must rest, peoples sever old ties; seek new alliances; experiment— sometimes dangerously—in their struggle to satisfy these human aspirations. . . .

This Republic cannot be aloof to these events heralding a new effort in the affairs of mankind.

🐘 🐘 🐘

The state of the Union, at the opening of the 85th Congress, continues to vindicate the wisdom of the principles on which this Republic is founded. Proclaimed in the Constitution of the Nation and in many of our historic documents, and founded in devout religious convictions, these principles enunciate:

First, a vigilant regard for human liberty.

Second, a wise concern for human welfare.

Third, a ceaseless effort for human progress.

🐘 🐘 🐘

High priority should be given the school-construction bill. This will benefit children of all races throughout the country—and children of all races need schools now. . . .

🐘 🐘 🐘

The existence of a strongly armed imperialistic dictatorship poses a continuing threat to the free world's and thus to our own Nation's security and peace. . . .

National security requires far more than military power. Economic and moral factors play indispensable roles. . . .

A sound and safeguarded agreement for open skies, unarmed aerial sentinels, and reduced armament would provide a valuable contribution toward a durable peace in the years ahead. And we have been persistent in our effort to reach such an agreement.

🐘 🐘 🐘

The cost of peace is something we must face boldly, fearlessly. Beyond money, it involves changes in attitudes, the renunciation of old prejudices, even the sacrifice of some seeming self-interest. . . .

The world has so shrunk that all free nations are our neighbors. Without cooperative neighbors, the United States cannot maintain its own security and welfare. . . .

DWIGHT D. EISENHOWER
SIXTH STATE-OF-THE-UNION MESSAGE
January 9, 1958

There are two tasks confronting us that so far outweigh all others that I shall devote this year's message entirely to them.

The first is to insure our safety through strength.

As to our strength I have repeatedly voiced this conviction: We now have a broadly based and efficient defensive strength including a great deterrent power, which is, for the present, our best guaranty against war; but, unless we act wisely and promptly, we could lose that capacity to deter attack or defend ourselves.

. . . Our second task is to do the constructive work of building a genuine peace. We must never become so preoccupied with our desire for military strength that we neglect those areas of economic development, trade, diplomacy, education, ideas and principles where the foundations of real peace must be laid.

The threat to our safety, and to the hope of a peaceful world, can be simply stated. It is Communist imperialism.

This threat is not something imagined by critics of the Soviets. Soviet spokesmen, from the beginning, have publicly and frequently declared their aim to expand their power, one way or another, throughout the world. . . .

But what makes the Soviet threat unique in history is its all-inclusiveness. Every human activity is pressed into service as a weapon of expansion. Trade, economic development, military power, arts, science, education, the whole world of ideas—all are harnessed to this same chariot of expansion. . . .

The only answer to a regime that wages total cold war is to wage total peace.

Among our assets, let us first briefly glance at our military power. . . .

As of today, our defensive shield comprehends a vast complex of ground, sea, and air units, superbly equipped and strategically deployed around the world. The most powerful deterrent to war in the world today lies in the retaliatory power of our Strategic Air Command and the aircraft of our Navy. They present to any potential attacker who would unleash war upon the world the prospect of virtual annihilation of his own country.

We must have sure warning in case of any attack. The improvement of warning equipment is becoming increasingly important as we approach the period when long-range missiles will come into use.

We must protect and disperse our striking forces and increase their readiness for instant reaction. This means more base facilities and more standby crews.

We must maintain deterrent retaliatory power. This means, among other things, stepped-up, long-range missile programs; accelerated programs for other effective missile systems; and, for some years, more advanced aircraft.

We must maintain freedom of the seas. This means nuclear submarines and cruisers; improved antisubmarine weapons; missile ships; and the like.

With these and other improvements, we intend to assure that our vigilance, power, and technical excellence keep abreast of any realistic threat we face.

. . . We must continue to strengthen our mutual-security efforts.

Most people now realize that our programs of military aid and defense support are an integral part of our own defense effort. If the foundations of the free world structure were progressively allowed to crumble under the pressure of Communist imperialism, the entire house of freedom would be in danger of collapse.

This is the spirit of what we Americans would like to say:

"In the last analysis, there is only one solution to the grim problems that lie ahead. The world must stop the present plunge toward more and more destructive weapons of war, and turn the corner that will start our steps firmly on the path toward lasting peace.

"Our greatest hope for success lies in a universal fact: the people of the world, as people, have always wanted peace and want peace now.

"The problem, then, is to find a way of translating this universal desire into action.

"This will require more than words of peace. It requires works of peace.". . .

But of all the works of peace, none is more needed now than a real first step toward disarmament. . . .

DWIGHT D. EISENHOWER
SEVENTH STATE-OF-THE-UNION MESSAGE
January 9, 1959

As we meet today, in the 170th year of the Republic, our Nation must continue to provide—as, indeed, all other free governments have had to do throughout time—a satisfactory answer to a question as old as history. It is: Can government based upon liberty and the God-given rights of man, permanently endure when ceaselessly challenged by a dictatorship, hostile to our mode of life, and controlling an economic and military strength of great and growing power?

For us the answer has always been found, and is still found in the devotion, the vision, the courage, and the fortitude of our people.

🐘 🐘 🐘

To achieve this peace we seek to prevent war at any place and in any dimension. If, despite our best efforts, a local dispute should flare into armed hostilities, the next problem would be to keep the conflict from spreading, and so compromising freedom. In support of these objectives we maintain forces of great power and flexibility.

Our formidable air striking forces are a powerful deterrent to general war. Large, and growing portions of these units can depart from their bases in a matter of minutes. . . .

Ground and other tactical formations can move with swiftness and precision, when requested by friendly and responsible governments, to help curb threatened aggression. The stabilizing influence of this capacity has been dramatically demonstrated more than once over the past year.

Our military and related scientific progress has been highly gratifying.

Great strides have been made in the development of ballistic missiles. Intermediate-range missiles are now being deployed in operational units. The Atlas intercontinental ballistic missile program has been marked by rapid development as evidenced by recent successful tests. Missile training units have been established and launching sites are far along in construction.

New aircraft that fly at twice the speed of sound are entering our squadrons.

We have successfully placed five satellites in orbit, which have gathered information of scientific importance never before available. Our latest satellite illustrates our steady advance in rocketry and foreshadows new developments in world-wide communications.

Warning systems constantly improve.

Our atomic submarines have shattered endurance records and made historic voyages under the North Polar Sea.

Thrift is one of the characteristics that have made this Nation great; why should we ignore it now?

We must avoid any contribution to inflationary processes, which could disrupt sound growth in our economy.

Prices have displayed a welcome stability in recent months and, if we are wise and resolute, we will not tolerate inflation in the years to come. But history makes clear the risks inherent in any failure to deal firmly with the basic causes of inflation. Two of the most important of these causes are the wage-price spiral and continued deficit financing.

Inflation can be prevented. But this demands statesmanship on the part of business and labor leaders and of government at all levels.

Because we are human we err. But as free men we are also responsible for correcting the errors and imperfections of our ways.

The McClellan committee disclosures of corruption, racketeering, and abuse of trust and power in labor-management affairs have aroused America and amazed other peoples. . . . I shall recommend prompt enactment of legislation designed:

To safeguard workers' funds in union treasuries against misuses of any kind whatsoever.

To protect the rights and freedoms of individual union members, including the basic right to free and secret elections of officers.

To advance true and responsible collective bargaining.

To protect the public and innocent third parties from unfair and coercive practices such as boycotting and blackmail picketing.

The workers and the public must have these vital protections.

And lastly, let us remind ourselves that Marxist scripture is not new; it is not the gospel of the future. Its basic objective is dictatorship, old as history. What is new is the shining prospect that man can build a world where all can live in dignity.

We seek victory not over any nation or people but over the ancient enemies of us all; victory over ignorance, poverty, disease, and human degradation wherever they may be found.

DWIGHT D. EISENHOWER
EIGHTH STATE-OF-THE-UNION MESSAGE
January 7, 1960

My purpose today is to discuss some features of America's position, both at home and in her relations to others.

First, I point out that for us, annual self-examination is made a definite necessity by the fact that we now live in a divided world of uneasy equilibrium, with our side committed to its own protection and against aggression by the other.

With both sections of this divided world in possession of unbelievably destructive weapons, mankind approaches a state where mutual annihilation becomes a possibility. No other fact of today's world equals this in importance—it colors everything we say, plan, and do. . . .

Second, we note that recent Soviet deportment and pronouncements suggest the possible opening of a somewhat less strained period in the relationships between the Soviet Union and the rest of the world. If these pronouncements be genuine, there is brighter hope of diminishing the intensity of past rivalry and eventually of substituting persuasion for coercion. Whether this is to become an era of lasting promise remains to be tested by actions.

Third, we now stand in the vestibule of a vast new technological age—one that, despite its capacity for human destruction, has an equal capacity to make poverty and human misery obsolete. If our efforts are wisely directed—and if our unremitting efforts for dependable peace begin to attain some success—we can surely become participants in creating an age characterized by justice and rising levels of human well-being.

America possesses an enormous defense power. It is my studied conviction that no nation will ever risk general war against us unless we should be so foolish as to neglect the defense forces we now so powerfully support. It is world-wide knowledge that any nation which might be tempted today to attack the United States, even though our country might sustain great losses, would itself promptly suffer a terrible destruction. But I once again assure all peoples and all nations that the United States, except in defense, will never turn loose this destructive power.

We realize that however much we repudiate the tenets of imperialistic communism, it represents a gigantic enterprise. Its leaders compel its subjects to subordinate their freedom of action and spirit and personal desires for some hoped for advantage in the future.

The fissure that divides our political planet is deep and wide.

We live, moreover, in a storm of semantic disorder in which old labels no longer faithfully describe.

Police states are called "people's democracies."

Armed conquest of free people is called "liberation."

Such slippery slogans make difficult the problem of communicating true faith, facts, and beliefs.

On my recent visit to distant lands I found one statesman after another eager to tell me of the elements of their government that had been borrowed from our American Constitution, and from the indestructible ideals set forth in our Declaration of Independence. . . . By our every word and action we must strive to make ourselves worthy of this trust, ever mindful that an accumulation of seemingly minor encroachments upon freedom gradually could break down the entire fabric of a free society. . . .

DWIGHT D. EISENHOWER
NINTH STATE-OF-THE-UNION MESSAGE
January 13, 1961

Throughout the world the years since 1953 have been a period of profound change. The human problems in the world grow more acute hour by hour; yet new gains in science and technology continually extend the promise of a better life. People yearn to be free, to govern themselves; yet a third of the people of the world have no freedom, do not govern themselves. The world recognizes the catastrophic nature of nuclear war; yet it sees the wondrous potential of nuclear peace.

Yet while we have worked to advance national aspirations for freedom, a divisive force has been at work to divert that aspiration into dangerous channels. The Communist movement throughout the world exploits the natural striving of all to be free and attempts to subjugate men rather than free them. These activities have caused and are continuing to cause grave troubles in the world.

For the first time in our Nation's history we have consistently maintained in peacetime, military forces of a magnitude sufficient to deter and if need be to destroy predatory forces in the world. . . .

Today the United States has operational Atlas missiles which can strike a target five thousand miles away in a half hour. The Polaris weapons system became operational last fall and the Titan is scheduled to become so this year. Next year, more than a year ahead of schedule, a vastly improved ICBM, the solid propellant Minuteman, is expected to be ready.

Squadrons of accurate intermediate-range ballistic missiles are now operational. The Thor and Jupiter IRBM's based in forward areas can hit targets fifteen hundred miles away in eighteen minutes.

🐘 🐘 🐘

Eight years ago we had no nuclear-powered ships. Today forty-nine nuclear warships have been authorized. Of these fourteen have been commissioned, including three of the revolutionary Polaris submarines. Our nuclear submarines have cruised under the North Pole and circumnavigated the earth while submerged. Sea warfare has been revolutionized, and the United States is far and away the leader.

Our tactical air units overseas and our aircraft carriers are alert; Army units, guarding the frontiers of freedom in Europe and the Far East, are in the highest state of readiness in peacetime history; our marines, a third of whom are deployed in the Far East, are constantly prepared for action; our Reserve establishment has maintained high standards of proficiency, and the Ready Reserve now number over two and one-half million citizen-soldiers.

🐘 🐘 🐘

. . . We have honored our commitment to pursue and attain specific objectives. Among them, as stated eight years ago: Strengthening of the mutual security program; development of world trade and commerce; ending of hostilities in Korea; creation of a powerful deterrent force; practicing fiscal responsibility; checking the menace of inflation; reducing the tax burden; providing an effective internal security program; developing and conserving our natural resources; reducing governmental interference in the affairs of the

farmer; strengthening and improving services by the Department of
Labor, and the vigilant guarding of civil and social rights.

Our goal always has been to add to the spiritual, moral, and material strength of our Nation. I believe we have done this. But it is
a process that must never end. Let us pray that leaders of both
the near and distant future will be able to keep the Nation strong and
at peace, that they will advance the well-being of all our people,
that they will lead us on to still higher moral standards, and that, in
achieving these goals, they will maintain a reasonable balance between private and governmental responsibility.

JOHN F. KENNEDY
(1961–   )

*"A deadly threat
has been removed
from Cuba"*

Paced by television, radio, barnstorming, and the costliest political campaign in presidential history, *John F. Kennedy* of Massachusetts was, on January 20, 1961, inducted into office as the youngest man ever elected to the nation's highest station.

The highlight of President Kennedy's first two years in office was the Cuban Crisis of 1962, with its threat of devastation by Russian nuclear missiles fired from bases in Cuba. Yet in his Third State-of-the-Union Message, on January 14, 1963, the President said little about the confrontation with the Soviet Union over Cuba. He struck, perhaps, his most appealing note in this message with his words about the Peace Corps and what it had accomplished around the world.

JOHN F. KENNEDY
FIRST STATE-OF-THE-UNION MESSAGE
January 30, 1961

I speak today in an hour of national peril and national opportunity. Before my term has ended, we shall have to test anew whether a Nation organized and governed such as ours can endure. The outcome is by no means certain.

482

The present state of the economy is disturbing. We take office in the wake of seven months of recession, three and one half years of slack, seven years of diminished economic growth, and nine years of falling farm income. Business bankruptcies have reached their highest level since the Great Depression. Save for a brief period in 1958, insured employment is at the highest peak in our history. Nearly one eighth of those who are without jobs live almost without hope in nearly one hundred depressed and troubled areas. In short, the American economy is in trouble. The most resourceful, industrialized country on earth ranks among the last in the rate of economic growth. Since last spring our economic growth rate has actually receded. Business investment is in a decline. A million unsold automobiles are in inventory.

🐐 🐐 🐐

But all these problems pale when placed beside those which confront us around the world. Our greatest challenge is still the world that lies beyond the Cold War, but the first great obstacle is still our relations with the Soviet Union and Communist China. To meet this array of challenges, to fulfill the role we cannot avoid on the world scene, we must reexamine and revise our whole arsenal of tools: military, economic, and political.

We cannot escape our dangers; neither must we let them drive us into panic or narrow isolation. In many areas of the world where the balance of power already rests with our adversaries, the forces of freedom are sharply divided. It is one of the ironies of our times that the techniques of a harsh and repressive system should be able to instill discipline and ardor in its servants while the blessings of liberty have too often stood for privilege, materialism, and a life of ease.

But I have a different view of liberty.

Life in 1961 will not be easy. Wishing it, predicting it, even asking for it, will not make it so. There will be further setbacks before the tide is turned. But turn it we must. The hopes of all mankind rest upon us; not simply upon those of us in this Chamber, but upon the peasant in Laos, the fisherman in Nigeria, the exile in Cuba, the spirit that moves every man and nation who shares our hopes for freedom and the future. And in the final analysis they must rest most of all upon the pride and perseverance of our fellow citizens of the Great Republic.

In the words of a great President, whose birthday we honor today, closing his final State of the Union Message sixteen years ago, "We pray that we may be worthy of the unlimited opportunities that God has given us."

JOHN F. KENNEDY
SECOND STATE-OF-THE-UNION MESSAGE
January 11, 1962

Our overriding obligation in the months ahead is to fulfill the world's hopes by fulfilling our own faith. That task must begin at home. . . .

At home we began the year in the valley of recession—we completed it on the highroad of recovery and growth. With the help of the new congressionally approved or administratively increased stimulants to our economy, the number of major surplus labor areas has declined from 101 to 60; nonagricultural employment has increased by more than a million jobs; and the average factory work week has risen to well over forty hours. At year's end the economy which Mr. Krushchev once called a stumbling horse was racing to new records in consumer spending, labor income and industrial production.

☒   ☒   ☒

But recession is only one enemy of a free economy—inflation is another. Our first line of defense against inflation is the good sense and public spirit of business and labor—keeping their total increases in wages and profits in step with productivity. There is no single statistical test to guide each company and each union. But I strongly urge them—for their country's interests, and for their own—to apply the test of public interest to these transactions.

☒   ☒   ☒

But America stands for progress in human rights as well as economic affairs, and a strong America requires the assurance of full and equal rights to all its citizens of any race or of any color. In matters of health no piece of unfinished business is more important or more urgent than the enactment under the social security system of health insurance for the aged.

🐗 🐗 🐗

In the past twelve months our military posture has steadily improved. We intend to have at all times the capacity to resist nonnuclear or limited attacks—as a complement to our nuclear capacity, not as a substitute.

With the approval of Congress we have undertaken in the past year a great new effort in outer space. Our aim is not simply to be the first on the moon any more than Charles Lindbergh's real aim was to be the first in Paris. . . . This nation belongs among the first to explore it [the moon], and among the first, if not the first, we shall be.

🐗 🐗 🐗

A year ago in assuming the tasks of the Presidency I said that few generations in all history had been granted the role of being the great defender of freedom in its hour of maximum danger. This is our good fortune, and I welcome it now as I did a year ago. For it is the fate of this generation—of you in the Congress and of me as President—to live with a struggle we did not start, in a world we did not make. No nation has ever faced such a choice. No nation has ever been so ready to seize the burden and glory of freedom.

JOHN F. KENNEDY
THIRD STATE-OF-THE-UNION MESSAGE
January 14, 1963

. . . You and I are privileged to serve the Great Republic in what could be the most decisive decade of its life. The choices we make, for good or ill, may well shape the State of the Union for generations to come.

. . . Today, having witnessed in recent months a heightened respect for our national purpose and power—having seen the courageous calm of a united people in a perilous hour—and having observed a steady improvement in the opportunities and well-being of our citizens—I can report to you that the State of this old but youthful Union, in the 175th year of its life, is good.

In the world beyond our borders, steady progress has been made in building a world of order. The people of West Berlin remain both free and secure. . . . And, while danger continues, a deadly threat has been removed from Cuba.

At home the recession is behind us. Well over a million more men and women are working today than were working two years ago. America has enjoyed twenty-two months of uninterrupted economic recovery. . . . But recovery is not enough. If we are to prevail in the long run, we must expand the long-run strength of our economy. We must move along the path to a higher rate of growth and full employment.

For this would mean tens of billions of dollars more each year in production, profits, wages and public revenues. . . . To achieve these greater gains, one step, above all, is essential—the enactment this year of a substantial reduction and revision in Federal income taxes. . . . Now, when inflationary pressures of the war and postwar years no longer threaten, and the dollar commands new respect—now, when no military crisis strains our resources—now is the time to act. We cannot afford to be timid or slow. For this is the most urgent task confronting the Congress in 1963.

Tax reduction alone, however, is not enough to strengthen our society, to provide opportunities for the 4,000,000 new Americans who are born every year, to improve the lives of the 32,000,000 Americans who still live on the outskirts of poverty.

𝛖   𝛖   𝛖

First, we need to strengthen our Nation by investing in our youth. The future of any country which is dependent on the will and wisdom of its citizens is damaged, and irreparably damaged, whenever any of its children is not educated to the fullest extent of his capacity, from grade school through graduate school. . . .

Second, we need to strengthen our Nation by safeguarding its health. Our working men and women—instead of being forced to beg for help from public charity once they are old and ill—should start contributing now to their own retirement health program through the Social Security System. . . .

Third, we need to strengthen our Nation by protecting the basic rights of its citizens. . . . The most precious and powerful right in the world, the right to vote in a free American election, must not be denied to any citizen on grounds of his race or color. . . .

Fourth, we need to strengthen our Nation by making the best and most economical use of its resources and facilities. Our economic health depends on healthy transportation arteries; and I believe the way to a more modern, economical choice of national transportation service is through increased competition and decreased regulation. . . .

🐾 🐾 🐾

Neither money nor technical assistance . . . can be our only weapon against poverty. In the end the crucial effort is one of purpose—requiring not only the fuel of finance but the torch of idealism. And nothing carries the spirit of American idealism more effectively to the far corners of the earth than the Peace Corps.

A year ago, less than nine hundred Peace Corps volunteers were on the job. A year from now they will number more than nine thousand—men and women, aged eighteen to seventy-nine, willing to give two years of their lives to helping people in other lands.

🐾 🐾 🐾

What comfort can we take from the increasing strains and tensions within the Communist bloc? Here hope must be tempered with caution. For the Soviet-Chinese disagreement is over means, not ends. A dispute over how best to bury the Free World is no grounds for Western rejoicing.

🐾 🐾 🐾

I foresee no spectacular reversal in Communist methods or goals. But if all these trends and developments can persuade the Soviet Union to walk the path of peace, then let her know that all free nations will journey with her. But until that choice is made, and until the world can develop a reliable system of international security, the free peoples have no choice but to keep their arms nearby. . . . We seek not the world-wide victory of one nation or system but a world-wide victory of man. The modern globe is too small, its weapons too destructive, and its disorders too contagious to permit any other kind of victory.

I close on a note of hope. We are not lulled by the momentary calm of the sea, or the somewhat clearer skies above. We know the turbulence that lies below, the storms beyond the horizon. But now the winds of change appear to be blowing more strongly than ever, in the world of communism as well as our own. For 175 years we have sailed with those winds at our back, and with the tides of human freedom in our favor. We steer our ship with hope, as Thomas Jefferson said, "leaving Fear astern."

Today we still welcome those winds of change—and we have every reason to believe that our tide is running strong. With thanks to Almighty God for seeing us through a perilous passage, we ask His help anew in guiding the "Good Ship Union."

INDEX

INDEX

491